ARSENAL
THE FOOTBALL FACTS

ARSENAL
THE FOOTBALL FACTS

DEAN HAYES

JOHN BLAKE

Published by John Blake Publishing Ltd,
3 Bramber Court, 2 Bramber Road,
London W14 9PB, UK

www.blake.co.uk

First published in paperback in 2007

ISBN: 978-1-84454-433-2

British Library Cataloguing-in-Publication Data:
A catalogue record for this book is available from the British Library.

Design by www.envydesign.co.uk

Printed in the UK by CPI Bookmarque, Croydon, CR0 4TD

3 5 7 9 10 8 6 4 2

CONTENTS

THE ARSENAL STORY

THE ARSENAL STORY begins way back in 1886 when a group of men in a government-run munitions factory at Woolwich, south-east London, caught the national fervour for recreation. Long, hard shifts in the foundry encouraged the men to think that there was more to life than work. They wanted to play some sort of sport in their spare time. Cricket and rugby were big in Kent but the growing sport for working class lads in Victorian times was football.

A soccer-loving Scot named David Danskin decided to start a works football team and no sooner had he persuaded the players of the factory's Dial Square workshop to have a whip round to buy a football than two Nottingham Forest players, Morris Bates and Fred Beardsley, arrived to work at the factory. Beardsley was a football fanatic. He had been sacked from jobs for taking too much time off to play football but if he tended to upset shop floor foremen over his enthusiasm for the game, the new club was only too happy for his support.

The first game of the new club was against a team called Eastern Wanderers on 11 December 1886. The team crossed the River Thames to play the game on the Isle of Dogs but the pitch bore no resemblance to the handsome, manicured grass of the Emirates Stadium! There were no crossbars, hardly any pitch markings and the players spent most of the match trespassing in back gardens to retrieve the ball or risking their health – and lives – in fishing the ball from a stinking sewer that ran the length of one side of the pitch.

Still, history says that Dial Square won the game 6–0, but they were worth better than this first uncomfortable experience and, on Christmas Day that year, David Danskin called a meeting in the Royal Oak next to Woolwich Arsenal Station. Apparently no-one was happy with the name Dial Square and a combination of Royal Oak and Woolwich Arsenal resulted in the regal sounding name, Royal Arsenal which was met by approval from all.

Goalkeepers wore the same colour shirt as outfield players in those days and Fred Beardsley's red Forest shirt was so admired by Royal Arsenal that he wrote to his old club to see whether they could supply his new team with a set of their old kit. Forest generously sent Beardsley a complete set of red shirts and a ball!

Royal Arsenal used part of Plumstead Common as their home ground. Stones lying on the surface of the pitch could cut a player's legs to ribbons and deep ruts could rupture ankles. The common was used for exercising dogs and in midweek it echoed to the thud of horses' hooves carrying the Royal Horse Artillery through the morning mists of Victorian England.

The first official fixture that Royal Arsenal played at Plumstead Common was against Erith on 8 January 1887 – the year in which Queen Victoria enjoyed her Jubilee celebrations – and the final result was a 6–1 home victory. Their keenest local rivals were the Millwall Dockers, whom they beat 3–0 in their first meeting. Although the club were obliged to move pitches from time to time, the Woolwich Reds, as they were known, began to attract quite a reputation.

⚽ ARSENAL FACT ⚽

In Arsenal's first season in the FA Cup, 1889–90, they met Thorpe (Norfolk) in a second qualifying round tie away and drew 2–2 after extra-time. Thorpe players were unable to travel for the replay and Arsenal were given a walkover.

The club had started to win local trophies such as the Kent Senior Cup and the London Charity Cup in 1890 – the latter being concluded with a 3–1 win over Old Westminsters at the club's Manor Ground in front of a 10,000 crowd. After these successes, the club decided to move just across Plumstead High Street to a new ground which already had a stand, terraces and dressing-rooms – the Invicta.

Already proclaimed Football Champions of the South, they decided to turn professional and changed their name to Woolwich Arsenal. The year was 1891 and the decision was a bold step forward for a club which had been in existence for only five years. Although Arsenal had won all the London cup competitions and had overtaken clubs such as Millwall and Tottenham Hotspur, who had been formed before them, as amateurs they were unable to compete with the big clubs of the north. This was brought home to them by an FA Cup match in which they were beaten 5-1 by the Swifts. But there was a stigma attached to professionalism in the south and this was to threaten the very existence of the club over the following years.

The first result of turning professional was that the club was excommunicated by the London FA. Most southern clubs who were still amateur cancelled their fixtures with them. The Woolwichers tried to persuade southern clubs such as Queen's Park Rangers, Spurs, Fulham and Millwall to join them in a Southern League but when this idea was rejected, Arsenal took their next major step; they applied for membership of the expanding Football League.

In 1893, they were admitted to the Second Division and set out on a League career which was to lead them to unrivalled supremacy some forty years later. Playing back at the Manor Ground, which had been transformed for their debut by an army of enthusiastic supporters, they proved hard to beat. Arsenal's first League opponents were fellow newcomers Newcastle United. Their defence was cracked twice by Walter Shaw and Arthur Elliott but they popped in two goals to share the points on that memorable day in early September 1893. However, long journeys, made all the more tiring by poor transport, saw their away form suffer. Arsenal finished ninth in their first season and continued their mid-table position for the next few years.

⚽ **ARSENAL FACT** ⚽

John Heath scored a hat-trick in Arsenal's first League win, a 4-0 triumph over Walsall Town Swifts in September 1893.

Arsenal's first captain in the League was right-back Joe Powell, a powerfully built man whose play typified the rugged and physical style of the day. Like a number of other players during the Woolwich years, he'd been bought out of the army. Also sought for their skills were Scots; at one time they held eight of the available places!

Despite the club's entry into the Football League, it was still poorly supported and so couldn't keep its star players. Men like Caesar Llewellyn Jenkyns, a Welshman who was the club's first international and who skippered Arsenal in 1895–96, left for pastures new. Also around this time, the Manor Field Ground was closed for six weeks following an assault on a referee! On 12 December 1896, Arsenal suffered what remains their heaviest defeat in the Football League when they crashed 8-0 to Loughborough, but gained revenge four years later by thrashing Loughborough 12-0.

⚽ ARSENAL FACT ⚽

When Arsenal beat Loughborough Town 12-0 in 1900 they established their record victory as well as gained revenge for the 8-0 defeat they had suffered at the hands of Loughborough four years earlier.

The arrival of the club's first professional manager reversed the decline and by the turn of the century, the club's performances were showing a steady improvement. Harry Bradshaw brought in the two most notable players of the period – left-back Jimmy Jackson, who became club captain and a leader determined to control everything on the pitch, and a new goalkeeper from Sheppey United, Jimmy Ashcroft. When Ashcroft played in all three internationals in 1905–06, he became the first Arsenal player to be capped for England.

⚽ ARSENAL FACT ⚽

Former Arsenal chairman Samuel Hill-Wood played county cricket for Derbyshire against the MCC at Lords in 1900 and scored ten runs off one ball. It's still the highest-recorded score from a single delivery.

Under Bradshaw's guidance, Arsenal finished fourth in 1901–02, third in 1902–03 and the following season, 1903–04, won promotion as runners-up to Preston North End. This was almost entirely the result of an excellent home record, with an astonishing goal average of 67 to 5. Not a match was lost at home – all were won apart from the last two, and there were 8–0 wins over both Burton United and Leicester Fosse. Of the twenty players to appear in the promotion season, only two had been with the club before Bradshaw's arrival.

⚽ ARSENAL FACT ⚽

When Woolwich Arsenal defeated a Paris XI 26-1 at Plumstead on Christmas Day 1904, the visitor's goal was scored by an Englishman called Hodge. He was brought on as a substitute and the Arsenal defence stood aside to allow him to score!

Arsenal made their First Division debut under new management. Bradshaw was tempted by a big offer from Fulham and the new man at the helm was Phil Kelso, a tough Scot who twice guided them to the semi-finals of the FA Cup, in 1905–06 and 1906–07. League performances were average, but backed by some big crowds the club were able to buy some outstanding players – Bert Freeman, Bill Garbutt, Tim Coleman and Jimmy Sharp. But the club's support and finances were not strong enough to survive a decline in results and once things started to go wrong, they accelerated virtually out of control.

Phil Kelso resigned, initially to run a hotel in Scotland, but almost immediately joined Fulham, replacing Harry Bradshaw who had left to become secretary of the Southern League. The new Arsenal manager, George Morrell, found himself having to sell to survive and, within a year of his appointment, all the big names – Coleman, Freeman, Sharp, Ashcroft and Garbutt – had gone. But one of the greatest of the pre-war Gunners, Andy Ducat, who became a double international for England at cricket and football, scored a hat-trick in his first-ever game for Arsenal on Christmas Day 1905 against Newcastle United – though he eventually had to be transferred to Aston Villa.

> ### ⚽ ARSENAL FACT ⚽
>
> November 7th in 1907 was King Edward VII's birthday, celebrated with special enthusiasm by workers at the Royal Arsenal works at Woolwich, which closed for the day. It was also the date for the first all-London clash in the First Division, when Woolwich Arsenal met Chelsea at Stamford Bridge. Arsenal won 2-1 thanks to the huge Arsenal following that accounted for a large proportion of the 65,000 present to watch the game.

For the next decade or so, the major events in the Arsenal story happened off the field rather than on it. The club were rescued by one Henry Norris, the chairman of Fulham. He wanted to take over the club and move it to Craven Cottage! Norris, later to become an MP and receive a knighthood, was a ruthless and determined man. He was also rich and influential. Although his proposal to amalgamate the two clubs was rejected by the League, Norris set about restoring Arsenal's fortunes in a way that the League felt powerless to challenge.

After a couple more years of mid-table insignificance, 1912–13 was a disaster. Arsenal finished bottom of the First Division with only 18 points, 26 goals and three wins, only one at home. The points, goals and wins were all the lowest ever recorded in the top flight and remained records until the end of the two-point system, after which the Stoke City side of 1984–85 managed an even more disastrous campaign.

With Division Two football only a matter of months away, Norris decided that if the club was to have any chance of becoming the power in the land that he desired, it would have to move. New sites were sought but none south of the river materialised. Then came the possibility of leasing land used by St John's College of Divinity at Highbury. Norris negotiated a 21-year lease at a cost of £20,000, with the only proviso being that the club could not stage games on Good Friday and Christmas Day – although this restriction was lifted in 1925 when a further £64,000 was paid. The objection of Arsenal moving to Highbury came from other clubs, notably Tottenham Hotspur and Clapton Orient. Both were within four miles of Highbury but Arsenal would be closer to the city centre. Local residents also joined in the outcry – it was one thing to have a college of divinity on the doorstep but quite another to suddenly see it turn into a football ground! Both the club and the local residents appealed to the

League Management Committee and, though the debate was quite heated, Arsenal won the day.

Having played their last game at the Manor Ground against Middlesbrough in April 1913, Woolwich Arsenal said goodbye to their name, their home and the south-east of London. Woolwich was dropped from the name and, though the club apparently never officially called itself 'The Arsenal', that was the name it was publicly known as until Herbert Chapman insisted on the single word some twelve years later.

They began the new 1913–14 season at Highbury with a 2-1 win over Leicester Fosse. Scottish striker Andy Devine had the honour of scoring the first goal but his team-mate George Jobey was to go down in the history books for an episode that puts the players of those days in another world from the millionaire superstars of today's game. Jobey, injured in the game, was taken to his lodgings by milk cart during the match, as there were no dressing-rooms!

All in all, Arsenal did quite well in that Second Division season – finishing third and failing to go up only on goal average behind Bradford Park Avenue. Norris, though, desperately needed First Division football and seemed to have a team that might achieve it, but within a year of that first game at Highbury, Europe was at war. The result of war was a disaster for The Arsenal – the many players with Woolwich Arsenal connections went back to munitions work, others joined the forces, the crowds dwindled and the League – though it was contested in 1914–15 – was something of an irrelevance.

At the end of the 1914–15 season, George Morrell was sacked to save money, though after beating Nottingham Forest 7-0 on the final day of the season with Harry King scoring four goals, Arsenal squeezed into fifth place in Division Two. What no one knew at the time was that it was to be Arsenal's last game in the Second Division.

In 1919, Norris pulled his most audacious stroke. The war over, the League had decided to expand each division by an extra two clubs to a total of 22. Norris knew that for Arsenal to survive their deepening financial crisis, they had to get back into the top flight. By now Sir Henry Norris MP, he used his position and influence to the greatest degree in canvassing support for Arsenal's restoration. He drew attention to Arsenal's length of service and loyalty to the League and brilliantly outflanked neighbours and rivals Spurs, who were hoping for, and expecting, a reprieve, despite having finished bottom of the First Division in 1915. By managing to get their re-election discussed as a separate matter from that of Chelsea, who had finished second from bottom, Norris was able to divide and rule.

Derby County and Preston North End, the top two teams in Division Two in 1915, were elected along with Chelsea; then came the crucial vote on whether it should be Arsenal or Spurs who joined them. Norris had won the backing of the League president, John McKenna and it was McKenna's eloquent speech that carried the day at the AGM. Arsenal were voted in with 18 votes to Spurs' eight!

Norris had already appointed Leslie Knighton, formerly with Huddersfield Town and Manchester City as manager and so in every sense Arsenal were given a fresh start for the re-opening of League soccer, following the war, in the 1919–20 season. However, the new boss received the shock of his life when he studied Norris's instructions on how to run the playing side of the club. His commandments read: 'You must not sign players under the height of 5ft 8in; you must encourage local talent; you must not spend more than £1,000 on players; you must not run a scouting system.'

✪ ARSENAL FACT ✪

On 26 March 1921 in a Division One match between Arsenal and Sheffield United, there was a tussle close to the United goal-line between the Gunners' Dr Paterson and Willie Cook the Blades' full-back. The ball went over the line and the referee awarded a corner kick to Arsenal. However, Dr Paterson walked across to the referee and protested that he had been the last to play the ball so the official changed his decision and awarded a goal-kick!

In the next six years, Arsenal were to enjoy only one season when they won more games than they lost in a League campaign. Knighton tried his best in difficult circumstances and before one important FA Cup match against West Ham United in January 1925, the Arsenal boss was approached by a Harley Street doctor to administer a 'courage pill' to each of his players. 'They do no harm, but tone up the nerves to produce maximum effort,' claimed the doctor. Knighton, by now desperate for success, decided to pin his faith in the pills against a backcloth of scepticism within the team. Knighton himself swallowed the first tablet to reassure the players. At 2.30 pm on match day they had all taken their tablets. At 2.50 pm, the referee burst into the Arsenal dressing-room to make a dramatic announcement: 'Gentlemen, the match is off because of fog.'

By the end of that 1924–25 season, Arsenal had slipped perilously close to relegation, finishing in 20th place. Far from fulfilling Norris's objective of being the best club in the country, Arsenal were looked on as one of the poor relations of the First Division. Norris sacked Knighton and advertised for a replacement in the *Athletic News* on 11 May 1925. It read: 'Arsenal Football Club is open to receive applications for the position of Team Manager. He must be experienced and possess the highest qualifications for the post, both as to ability and personal character. Gentlemen whose sole ability to build up a good side depends on the payment of heavy and exorbitant transfer fees need not apply.'

But Sir Henry Norris already knew the manager he wanted. He looked no further than Huddersfield Town and their brilliant team boss Herbert Chapman.

Fortified by an FA Cup triumph and two straight League Championships at Leeds Road, Chapman transformed Arsenal over the next decade into a club whose very mention would gain instant recognition and approval across the great soccer-playing continents of the globe. Quite simply, Arsenal in those days were the greatest club in the world.

⚽ **ARSENAL FACT** ⚽

During the 20 seasons between the two world wars, the only Arsenal player ordered off in a Division One match was Welsh goalkeeper Dan Lewis in a game at Sunderland in April 1926.

However, initially, Chapman would make no promises of instant success – indeed, he predicted it would take five years for the club to win their first major honour. Norris had been impressed by Chapman's ability to manage on meagre resources at Huddersfield and because of Arsenal's financial situation, he made it clear that he expected Chapman to do the same at Highbury. However, a combination of Chapman's persuasiveness and Norris's need for a crowning glory to his distinguished career soon changed all that. Chapman convinced Norris that he had to spend to succeed and set about buying the best players that money could buy.

His first major purchase showed the new Arsenal management's flair for business and publicity. Charlie Buchan had once been an Arsenal player at Woolwich but had left in disgust when a former manager rejected an expenses claim. It was Arsenal's loss as Buchan went to Sunderland where he won a League Championship medal, appeared in an FA Cup Final and won international honours with England. Norris struck a deal that was to be the forerunner of many a future transfer. He agreed a fee of £2,000 plus £100 for every goal Buchan scored in his first season. With the offside law changed that year, reducing from three to two the number of players required to be between the goal and an opposing forward to keep him onside, Buchan's task was eased. He scored 19 times in the League and twice in the Cup. Arsenal finished a highest-ever second behind Huddersfield, who completed a record third consecutive success.

Chapman certainly benefited from Buchan's immense knowledge of the game. Indeed, it was Buchan who showed him the possibilities opened up by the new offside law and this laid the foundations for an Arsenal style which was to become known as the 'W' formation. The seeds were sown after a disastrous start to that first season in which the Gunners were thrashed 7-0 by Newcastle United. Buchan, who had been appointed Arsenal captain, persuaded Chapman that because teams were now able to push more players into attack, their opponents would need more cover at the back.

While 1926–27 was not a notable season in the League, it did end on a high note as Arsenal made their first appearance in an FA Cup Final. The run to the final was a tough one – Sheffield United were beaten 3-2 at Bramall Lane, then Port Vale 1-0 in a replay; Liverpool were beaten 2-0 at Highbury in the fifth round with both goals coming from headers at free-kicks. Wolves also came to Highbury for the quarter-final. Arsenal won 2-1 with the winning goal being a truly remarkable one – a Joe Hulme centre was headed straight into the net from around 25 yards by centre-half Jack Butler! Arsenal's opponents in the semi-final were Second Division Southampton – a match the Gunners were lucky to win 2-1 on a blustery, wet day at Stamford Bridge.

Their opponents at Wembley were Cardiff City, whose basic plan was to mark Buchan out of the game. It worked and with just a quarter-of-an-hour to go and the game goalless, Arsenal's Welsh international goalkeeper Dan Lewis made an error which haunted him for the rest of his life. Going down to cover an apparently harmless shot by Bluebirds' centre-forward Hugh Ferguson, Lewis fumbled the ball and watched in horror as it trickled over the line. Cardiff won 1-0 and the Cup left England for the first and only time in its history. Lewis was so upset that he tossed his loser's medal on to the Wembley turf and it was left to his team-mates to go and recover it.

⚽ ARSENAL FACT ⚽

The first radio football commentary was undertaken by George Allison on 23 April 1927. He was an Arsenal director at the time, but still covered the Arsenal v Cardiff City FA Cup Final. His assistant was Derek McCulloch, later to become famous as 'Uncle Mac' on Children's Hour.

Chapman was not discouraged – he had lost important matches before and continued to build his side, signing future captain Eddie Hapgood from Kettering Town. Arsenal finished the 1927–28 season in mid-table and reached the semi-finals of the FA Cup where they went out to the eventual winners Blackburn Rovers. At the end of the season, Charlie Buchan retired to go into journalism and, over the course of the next twelve months, Chapman signed the three players who were to complete the jigsaw.

⚽ ARSENAL FACT ⚽

Charlie Buchan started *Football Monthly* magazine – as well as The Football Writers' Association Player of the Year awards.

In October 1928 he set a British record transfer fee of £11,500 for Bolton Wanderers' inside-forward, David Jack, the man who scored the first-ever goal in a Wembley Cup final. Alex James followed from Preston North End for £9,000 and so too did Cliff Bastin, picked up for a snip from Exeter City.

Arsenal, meanwhile had an indifferent 1928–29 season and the early results in the following season showed no indication of the success that was about to mark the club over the next decade. As the chance of the League title slipped away, the Gunners channelled all their energy into the FA Cup. Herbert Chapman made the courageous decision to drop Alex James for the third round tie against Chelsea, which Arsenal won 2-0 in a rainstorm. In the fourth round, Birmingham came to Highbury and went away with a 2-2 draw but Alf Baker scored from the penalty-spot in the replay to see the Gunners through. The fifth and sixth rounds were no easier – a 2-0 win at Middlesbrough followed by a 3-0 defeat of West Ham United.

⚽ ARSENAL FACT ⚽

In a 1928 match at Sheffield Wednesday, Arsenal boss Herbert Chapman sent his team on to the field wearing numbers 12-22 with the Owls numbered 1-11.

The semi-final looked easy with Arsenal's opponents being Hull City who were firmly rooted to the bottom of Division Two and a month later were relegated to the Third Division. All the interest seemed to be in the other semi-final between Huddersfield Town and Sheffield Wednesday. Huddersfield were leading 2-1 when the Owls got the ball in the net just as the whistle blew for full-time. The referee disallowed the goal but there were many of the crowd who went home not knowing whether there would be a replay or not!

In the supposedly less-interesting semi-final, Arsenal went a goal down after quarter of an hour when Dan Lewis' clearance went straight to Hull's Hewison who lobbed it straight back into the net on the volley from 45 yards. By half-time the Gunners were 2-0 down when Eddie Hapgood sliced a David Duncan shot into his own net. Early in the second half, David Jack reduced the arrears before Cliff Bastin scored a splendid solo goal. The teams met again at Villa Park and with tackles flying in thick and fast, Hull's Arthur Childs became the first man to be sent-off in a semi-final. David Jack scored with a right foot volley midway through the second-half – Arsenal were at Wembley for the second time in four years; Huddersfield were there for the fourth time in a decade.

Two weeks before the cup final, the Gunners ran up their biggest top flight win to date when they beat Sheffield United 8-1. Five days before the final the club set another record when, having been 3-1 down at half-time, they eventually drew 6-6 at Leicester. It remains the highest-scoring draw in any English first-class game, having only been equalled by Charlton Athletic v Middlesbrough in 1960.

On the morning of the FA Cup Final, the papers had said King George V would not be well enough to attend, but he surprised everyone by arriving to a rousing reception for his first outdoor appearance since an illness some 18 months earlier. With the game 17 minutes old, Alex James was fouled 40 yards from goal. He sprang to his feet and looked at referee Tom Crew, who nodded to the Scotsman to take the kick without any ado. He slipped the ball to Cliff Bastin who, after drawing Goodall towards him, placed it into the path of James, following through to hit into the corner of the net. The goal was a complete surprise, partly because James rarely scored, but more so because of the speed of the free-kick! Some minutes later, the *Graf Zeppelin,* Germany's giant airship, and pride of a nation slowly rebuilding its self-confidence, suddenly loomed over the stadium like a massive cloud. Flying at 2,000 feet, well below the legal limit, it dipped its nose in salute of the King and flew on. The Arsenal goal led something of a charmed life but then with just seven minutes left, a long clearance from James found Jack Lambert. Slipping between Goodall and Spence, he raced nearly half the length of the pitch before shooting past Turner. He turned expecting to greet his onrushing team-mates but they were still all in their own half. So Lambert set off applauding himself as he went, to provide one of the game's most enduring memories.

It is probably no exaggeration to say that this game, which Arsenal won 2-0, was not only the moment when the greatness began, it was also the moment when everything could so easily have slipped away.

Success bred success and, in 1930–31, Arsenal won the League Championship for the first time with a record-breaking 66 points – a total not passed until 1969 when Leeds United (under the old two points for a win system) totalled 67. Also, Arsenal's remarkable total of 127 goals scored would have then been, and remained for all time, a First Division record had Aston Villa not scored an incredible 128 goals in the same year!

The season was a great success for the Gunners from start to finish. The club's first two games were both away at Blackpool and Bolton and both were won 4-1. In fact, Arsenal were not defeated until their 10th game when they lost to Derby County at the Baseball Ground. Despite some tremendous displays throughout the season, Arsenal were never really clear of challengers and only won the title a couple of weeks from the end of the campaign with a 3-1 defeat of Liverpool.

The Gunners' biggest threat came from Aston Villa who, having been beaten 5-2 at Highbury, exacted revenge with a 5-1 triumph at Villa Park. The Midlands club were also Arsenal's opponents in that season's FA Cup competition and went 2-0 up at Highbury before Lambert and Jack forced a replay. Arsenal won the replay 3-1 but then surprisingly lost 2-1 to Chelsea, a team they had beaten 5-1 at Stamford Bridge a few weeks earlier. Despite this disappointment, they had beaten Grimsby Town 9-1 – that remains their biggest First Division success. The Gunners lost only four games all season and had an identical home and away record of 14 wins, 5 draws and 2 defeats, whilst Jack Lambert set up an Arsenal record of 38 League goals in a season.

⚽ ARSENAL FACT ⚽

David Halliday scored four goals for Arsenal in a League game at Leicester on the Monday before the 1930 FA Cup Final as the Gunners drew 6-6 but was left out of the side for the Wembley win against Huddersfield! However, the game will probably be remembered more for the German airship, the Graf Zeppelin, dipping low over Wembley during the course of the match to give the passengers a bird's-eye view. And David Jack was the first man to appear in FA Cup Finals for different teams. He played in the 1930 final for Arsenal after scoring for Bolton in the 1923 White Horse Final.

Arsenal's success in the Cup and Championship in the two previous seasons generated the belief at Highbury that they could pull off the League and Cup Double in 1931-32. But after less than a month of the campaign, the talk was of what had happened to the League Champions. The Gunners lost their opening game of the season at home to West Bromwich Albion and didn't win a game until the fifth match. Sadly, they never made up the gap that had already opened up and although it was a good season, eventually finishing runners-up to Everton, it was something of an anti-climax.

The Gunners' run to that season's FA Cup Final was straightforward as they beat Lancashire Combination side Darwen 11-1 in the third round. Plymouth Argyle were then beaten 4-2 and a 2-0 success over Portsmouth saw Arsenal paired with old adversaries Huddersfield Town in the quarter-finals. A Herbie Roberts header separated the teams to take Arsenal into the semi-final at St Andrew's where their opponents were Manchester City. The game was goalless and had entered the 90th minute when Lambert, chasing what appeared to be a lost cause, hooked the ball back for Bastin to score with what proved to be the last kick of the game.

The final was against Newcastle United and although Bob John gave Arsenal the lead, they missed James' scheming and Bastin's raids, both out through injury. Five minutes from half-time came Newcastle's controversial equaliser. A long ball down the right appeared certain to go out of play, or so it seemed to Arsenal players as they pulled up expecting a goal-kick. But the Magpies' inside-right Jimmy Richardson continued his chase and crossed for Jack Allen to put the ball in the back of the net. Despite Arsenal's vigorous protests and to the disbelief of many fans, the referee allowed the goal to stand. Allen went on to score again for United to win 2-1. The Gunners had thus finished runners-up in both major competitions, only the second time this had ever happened, the first time being to Huddersfield Town in 1927–28.

☉ ARSENAL FACT ☉

Arsenal Tube Station on the Piccadilly Line is the only train station in Britain to be named after a football club. It used to be called Gillespie Road until renamed in October 1932, though the tiled walls along the platforms still bear the original name.

The 1932–33 season proved in many respects to be one of the most historic in the annals of Arsenal Football Club. It was the first leg of their Championship treble, the season in which a new 21,000 capacity West Stand at Highbury was opened, the season when Chapman brought in the new white-sleeved shirts and the season when the Arsenal manager changed the name of the old Gillespie Road Underground station to Arsenal.

The campaign did not start particularly well. In their first home match, Arsenal lost to West Bromwich Albion for the second season in succession. However, despite Villa beating the Gunners 5-3 in Birmingham, Arsenal dropped just four points from a possible 36, including a 9-2 Christmas Eve thrashing of Sheffield United.

> ### ☻ ARSENAL FACT ☻
>
> Jack Lambert scored five of Arsenal's goals in the 9-2 defeat of Sheffield United on Christmas Eve 1932.

Midway through the season, Arsenal lost to Walsall in an FA Cup third round tie in the mud of Fellows Park. The Saddlers scored twice in the second-half to send the Gunners to their most famous defeat. The club certainly didn't let it hinder their League progress where they clinched the title by four points from Aston Villa – whom they beat 5-0 at Highbury – and amassed 118 goals, including a 7-1 win at Wolves. Cliff Bastin set a record for a winger with a total of 33 goals – still a Football League record.

The 1933–34 season was marred by the death of Herbert Chapman. Arsenal were not the attacking side they had been the previous season – one major reason was Alex James' injury against Birmingham in the first match of the campaign. Even so, they quickly went to the head of the table, putting together a spell of 27 points out of a possible 32. The shock of Chapman's death in January 1934, showed itself in the games that followed – Arsenal lost three out of four games and were knocked off the top of the First Division with both Derby County and Huddersfield Town briefly taking the lead. The Gunners had to play both of these teams in Easter week and, after beating the Rams 4-2 at the Baseball Ground, followed it up with a 3-1 defeat of Huddersfield. In the end, only the Yorkshire club kept up the challenge, eventually finishing three points adrift of the Gunners.

Chapman was succeeded at Highbury by George Allison, who had been a director of the club and a well-known radio commentator on the game. The momentum established by Chapman was very much in evidence in the 1934–35 season and after some adjustments necessitated by retirement and a loss of form, Allison kept the honours rolling in to Highbury with a third consecutive League success.

The 1934–35 season had started with an 8-1 defeat of Liverpool and the first four games of the campaign produced 21 Arsenal goals. Among the new arrivals at Highbury was Ted Drake who was to score a record 42 goals for the Gunners in his first season. That total included four matches in which he scored four goals and three in which he notched mere hat-tricks! Arsenal headed the table until March when Sunderland, inspired by their manager Raich Carter, went a point ahead. Though the Wearsiders held Arsenal to a goalless draw at Highbury, the Gunners had games in hand and went on to take the Championship by four points from Sunderland.

Such was Arsenal's strength that season, that for England's international against Italy at Highbury, the North London club provided a record contingent of seven players – Frank Moss, George Male, Eddie Hapgood, Wilf Copping, Ray Bowden, Ted Drake and Cliff Bastin.

☉ ARSENAL FACT ☉

On 5 January 1935 Eddie Hapgood headed a goal from the rebound of his own penalty kick when it was fisted back to him by Liverpool keeper Riley.

The highlight of the 1935–36 season was without doubt the game against Aston Villa – a game the Gunners won 7-1 at Villa Park, with Ted Drake scoring all his side's goals! For the first quarter of an hour, the home side were the better team but at half-time they went in 3-0 down and Drake had a hat-trick. After an hour they were 6-0 down and Drake had a double hat-trick. Villa did score once but Drake had the last word in the final minute with yet another goal. It was a remarkable personal achievement because Drake spent much of the campaign on the treatment table. Manager George Allison needed to test Drake's fitness after a cartilage operation – the game in question was the return game with Villa. Drake scored the winning goal – a result that condemned them to relegation to Division Two. However, Drake's goals made little difference to the title race as Sunderland beat Arsenal 5-4 at Roker Park and went on to win the Championship. Arsenal ended the campaign in sixth place, their worst position since 1930.

However, the FA Cup was a different story. The Gunners beat Bristol Rovers 5-1 at Eastville, then Liverpool 2-0 at Anfield to set up another away tie, this time at Newcastle United. Arsenal did well to draw 3-3 before a couple of Cliff Bastin penalties helped them to a 3-0 win in the replay. The club were drawn at home in the quarter-final, beating Barnsley 4-1. The semi-final opposition were Grimsby Town, then a First Division club. In a hard game it was a Bastin goal that separated the sides. Arsenal were at Wembley for the fourth time in ten years – their opponents Second Division Sheffield United. The Blades were on top for most of the game and should have gone ahead in the opening minute when Alex Wilson dropped the ball. The Yorkshire side also hit the bar twice before Ted Drake scored what proved to be the winner.

⚽ ARSENAL FACT ⚽

The highest attendance for a game at Highbury is 73,295 against Sunderland on 9 March 1935.

Arsenal were now no longer the best side in the land, having fallen behind the likes of Sunderland and Manchester City, and the following season was to be the last for Alex James. In the circumstances, the Gunners did well to finish third and reach the FA Cup quarter-final. It is impossible to underestimate James' contribution to the successful Arsenal side of the 1930s. In the six years following his arrival, they won four League Championships and reached three FA Cup Finals.

⚽ ARSENAL FACT ⚽

The first televised broadcast of a football match featured Arsenal against the club's reserve side on 16 September 1937.

Therefore, it was most surprising that Arsenal won their fifth League title in the space of eight years in 1937–38. The Gunners side was not a settled one and the campaign was both tough and inconsistent. Midway through the season, Arsenal and Wolves were favourites for both major competitions and found themselves drawn together in the FA Cup, a week after they had met in the League. Wolves won the League encounter 3-1 to go ahead of the Gunners in the table but both clubs were well behind leaders Brentford. Arsenal won the cup game 2-1 but went out in the next round to eventual winners Preston North End.

Though Brentford were at one time seven points clear of Arsenal and beat the Gunners home and away over Easter, the Bees slipped out of the title race, leaving Arsenal and Wolves to contest the Championship. It went right down to the wire and on the very last day of the season, Wolves just had to beat Sunderland to take the title no matter what Arsenal did. The Gunners overran a poor Bolton side 5-0 and though the Wearsiders had nothing to play for and had a man sent-off, they beat Wolves 1-0. Arsenal were the champions.

⚽ **ARSENAL FACT** ⚽ ⚽

When Arsenal won the League Championship in 1937–38 they did so with 52 points, only 16 more than the bottom club.

The last full season before the Second World War saw Arsenal finish on a quiet note – fifth in the League and knocked out of the Cup in the third round by Chelsea. In fact, the campaign was perhaps most notable for the purchase of Bryn Jones, who joined the club from Wolves for a record fee of £14,500. Sadly, he was never given time to reproduce his best form at Highbury.

Rebuilding in every sense of the word was the main priority at Highbury after the hostilities. The stadium, which had been shut down and used as an Air Raid Precaution station, had been extensively damaged by incendiary bombs. On the field, virtually a new squad of players were about to experience their own baptism of fire as League football began again.

⚽ **ARSENAL FACT** ⚽

Arsenal lost nine players to the Second World War – more than any other club.

Arsenal lost their opening game of the 1946–47 season 6-1 to Wolves, and for the early part of the campaign hovered just above the relegation zone. It was then that Allison pinned his hopes on a couple of players, Joe Mercer and Ronnie Rooke. Inspired by Mercer, and with 21 goals in 24 games from Rooke and a season's total of 29 from Reg Lewis – having started the campaign with an 11-goal burst in 10 games – the Gunners finished in mid-table.

After four decades of total commitment to the Arsenal cause, George Allison decided the demands of post-war management were too great and retired. Arsenal looked no further than Tom Whittaker and Joe Shaw returned from Chelsea to become his right-hand man in June 1947. A 3-1 victory over Sunderland at Highbury gave Whittaker the perfect start to what became a remarkable first season in management. When Leslie Compton returned from summer service with Middlesex Cricket Club, the Gunners had won six games on the trot. Whittaker handed Compton the ball for the game at Preston but just when the team was leaving the dressing-room at Deepdale, Compton made a moving gesture. 'If you don't mind Mr Whittaker, I think Joe should have this', said Compton, handing the ball to Mercer, who had led the sides in the opening games. Joe Mercer led the team on to the pitch and retained the captaincy for a season that saw him raise the Championship trophy for the first time by an Arsenal captain since 1938. It was a magnificent achievement for Whittaker in his first campaign in charge.

The 1948–49 season saw the arrival from Walsall of Doug Lishman but on the field, the Gunners could manage no better than fifth behind champions Portsmouth. While the south coast club then carried off the League title for a second successive season, Arsenal made their mark on that campaign's FA Cup.

The Gunners were drawn at home in every round – indeed they never left London during the entire competition. Arsenal reached the semi-finals conceding just one goal. They beat Sheffield Wednesday 1-0, Swansea 2-1, Burnley 2-0 and Leeds United 1-0. Arsenal's opponents in the semi-final at White Hart Lane were Chelsea who had also been favourites to make it through to Wembley. Midway through the first-half, Chelsea were 2-0 ahead but just before the interval, Freddie Cox curled in a corner which was over the line before Harry Medhurst's vain attempt to keep it out. The Gunners drew level in the second-half after Leslie Compton headed home brother Denis' corner. In the replay, it was Cox who provided an extra-time breakthrough, scoring the only goal of the game to send Arsenal into their fifth FA Cup Final.

Tom Whittaker showed his flair in preparations for the final in which the Gunners faced Liverpool – by an odd coincidence, they reached Wembley without leaving Lancashire! Because the two sides traditionally played in red, they were both obliged to change colours for the Wembley meeting and it was Arsenal who had to choose a new colour scheme. The Arsenal manager came up with the most eye-catching combination he could think of – old gold, black and white for all the outfield players, while goalkeeper George Swindin was kitted out in a brilliant crimson jersey.

⚽ **ARSENAL FACT** ⚽

At the end of the 1949–50 season, Arsenal retained all of the 59 professional players on their staff. It is believed to have been the largest number recorded in Football League history.

Tom Whittaker's biggest problem was in choosing his centre-forward but after much deliberation, he kept faith with 30-year-old Reg Lewis, deciding his big match temperament would be best suited to Wembley. His judgement proved absolutely correct. Lewis scored twice and Joe Mercer was carried shoulder-high round Wembley parading the Cup.

⚽ **ARSENAL FACT** ⚽

Arsenal won the FA Cup in 1950 without once leaving London.

If good luck played a part in Arsenal's FA Cup success, bad luck deprived them of a seventh League Championship in 1950–51. Doug Lishman had forced his way into the Gunners' side on a regular basis and by Christmas had scored 16 goals including two hat-tricks, as Arsenal topped the table. Then, unfortunately, tragedy struck – in the Christmas Day fixture against Stoke, he broke a leg and was out for virtually the rest of the season. Arsenal's form suffered and they finished fifth, while the League title went to Spurs.

⚽ **ARSENAL FACT** ⚽

The oldest player to make his England debut was Arsenal's Leslie Compton. He was 38 years 64 days old when he played against Wales at Roker Park on 15 November 1950.

The 1951–52 season saw the Gunners again challenging for both major honours. They scored 15 goals with only two conceded in reaching the semi-finals of the FA Cup and 40 goals from Lishman (23) and Cliff Holton (17) powered them to joint-top of the First Division alongside Manchester United with only two matches remaining.

⚽ **ARSENAL FACT** ⚽

In the 1951–52 season, Doug Lishman netted a hat-trick of hat-tricks in home games against Fulham, West Bromwich Albion and Bolton Wanderers. It remained a unique achievement until emulated by Thierry Henry in 2002–03.

In the Cup they were again paired with Chelsea in the semi-final at White Hart Lane and again it was Freddie Cox who scored in a 1-1 draw which led to another replay. Cox, the scourge of the Blues, then scored twice in a 3-0 replay win to send Arsenal to their sixth FA Cup Final. Meanwhile in the race for the League title, injuries to Leslie Compton and Ray Daniel and a bout of food poisoning which laid low Lishman and Logie, dealt a most devastating blow to the Gunners' hopes. Tom Whittaker's men needed a 7-0 win in the final game of the season at Old Trafford to take the title. But by the time the two sides met, Whittaker had already conceded the Championship and United's 6-1 victory was emphatic confirmation.

⚽ **ARSENAL FACT** ⚽

Arsenal were the first team to play under floodlights. In 1951 a friendly against Israel's Hapoel Tel Aviv saw the controversial innovation, although Herbert Chapman had lights installed at the club's training ground as early as 1932.

Arsenal's opponents in the FA Cup Final, Newcastle United, were going for their second consecutive Wembley victory. Nineteen minutes into the game, disaster struck when Walley Barnes, the Gunners' full-back received a crippling knee injury and had to come off. Ten-men Arsenal battled on and the game remained goalless until late in the second-half. Then, after Lishman clipped the bar, George Robledo scored for Newcastle – Arsenal had lost. Whittaker told his men he was prouder of them in defeat than he had ever been in victory.

In 1952–53, the title came to Highbury for the seventh time, setting a new record, but it was to be mighty close. One of the best games of that season was against Bolton Wanderers at Burnden Park on Christmas Day. Arsenal won 6–4 with Jack Kelsey saving a last-minute penalty. The Gunners took their challenge for the League title to the very last game of the campaign. The forward pairing of Cliff Holton and Doug Lishman had already scored more than 40 goals between them when the Gunners stepped out against Burnley on a monsoon-like May day, needing victory to shade Preston North End for the title on goal average. More than 50,000 fans crammed into Highbury for a nail-biting encounter in which Burnley took an eighth minute lead. But by midway through the first-half, Arsenal had stormed back to go 3–1 ahead with goals by Alex Forbes, Jimmy Logie and Doug Lishman. A late rally by the Clarets brought the fans to the edge of their seats but the Gunners held on to triumph 3–2. The title was back at Highbury by virtue of goal difference. Both Arsenal and North End had 54 points, Arsenal had scored 97 for with 64 against while Preston's tally read 85-60. That's how close it was. Tom Whittaker had now emulated Chapman and Allison in terms of material success.

The 1953–54 season began sadly with the death of Alex James. Then in a game against Liverpool, Joe Mercer broke his leg and was out of football for good.

✪ ARSENAL FACT ✪

Arsenal beat Newcastle United 2-1 at Highbury in November 1953. In the dying seconds, the Arsenal keeper Jack Kelsey made a brilliant one-handed save from Bobby Mitchell. The following day, the Welsh international goalkeeper received an anonymous £5 note from a spectator for 'the greatest save I have ever seen'.

The years that followed were a bleak period for the club. In 1956 Whittaker died, like Chapman, in service with the club which had been his life. He was Arsenal's third manager in 30 years. In the course of the next ten, they were to have four as the search for old glories took a heavy toll on those entrusted with the task.

⚽ ARSENAL FACT ⚽

Hearing what he thought was the final whistle in the match against Blackpool in December 1956, Arsenal's Dennis Evans turned to celebrate the Gunners' 4-0 victory by smashing the ball into his own net. Unfortunately the whistle had come from the crowd!

Players like Danny Clapton, David Herd, Jimmy Bloomfield, Vic Groves and Geoff Strong made their individual marks but the side as a whole rarely clicked. In 1960 the arrival of George Eastham from Newcastle at last gave the Gunners an inside-forward with the skills and generalship of Logie. But even then the team's performances failed to push Arsenal higher than mid-table.

⚽ ARSENAL FACT ⚽

Jack Kelsey and Danny Clapton played for Arsenal against Juventus on the evening of 26 November 1958. But earlier that same day they had played against each other in a 2-2 draw between Wales and England.

In 1962 the club broke with tradition by appointing a man with no previous managerial experience. Former Wolves and England captain Billy Wright arrived amid a fanfare of publicity, but great players do not necessarily make great football managers.

In his four-year reign, Wright laid the foundations for the club's phenomenal Double triumph, which was to come at the turn of the decade. His development of the youth team saw the recruitment of players like Peter Simpson, Peter Storey, Pat Rice, Jon Sammels and Ray Kennedy, who were all to play a major part in the success of the seventies. Wright also brought the future Double-winning captain, Frank McLintock, from Leicester City in 1964.

Wright's management climaxed in the 1965–66 season when the Gunners were a club at war – both with themselves and the fans. Midway through the season as the team failed to make any impact, England internationals Joe Baker and George Eastham were granted transfers and, soon afterwards, Don Howe broke his leg in a goalless draw against Blackpool. Even that tragedy could not quell the demonstrations by angry fans during the game and afterwards outside the club's offices. At the home match with Leeds United, short-sightedly rearranged for the night of the European Cup Winners' Cup Final in which Liverpool were playing, one supporter brought a bugle to play the *Last Post*. But there were not too many with him to administer the last rites – just 4,554, the lowest First Division crowd since the First World War.

Just six weeks before England staged the World Cup, Wright was dismissed. With the country in the thrall of that competition, Arsenal's decision to promote their trainer of six years, Bertie Mee, to acting manager, passed by almost unnoticed. Mee had no background of managerial success, having joined the Gunners as a physiotherapist in 1960. His initial move to strengthen the staff that summer was not on the playing side but to bring in Dave Sexton from Fulham, one of the brightest young coaches in the game.

Mee inherited a team which featured six of the eventual Double-winning side – McLintock, George Armstrong, John Radford, Jon Sammels, Peter Simpson and Peter Storey, whilst keeper Bob Wilson and young full-backs Pat Rice and Sammy Nelson were also on the staff. Within a month of the start of the campaign, George Graham and Bob McNab had arrived at Highbury.

Mee's first two seasons saw the club finish seventh and ninth but in the second of those campaigns and in 1968–69, the team came within a whisker of their first major trophy since the 1953 Championship, only to suffer the disappointment of being Wembley losers in quick succession. But just as the club's first League Cup run was getting underway, the camp was rocked by the departure of the much respected Sexton who was tempted back to manage his first love, Chelsea.

The club made the decision to promote Don Howe and he soon earned the players' respect. Highbury again began to buzz as the cup run quickly gathered momentum. First Division newcomers Coventry City were beaten 2-1 at Highfield Road and there were wins over Reading, Blackpool and Burnley, which took the Gunners to a two-leg semi-final against Huddersfield Town. The Yorkshire club were struggling near the lower reaches of the Second Division and 3-1 wins home and away secured a place in the final against Leeds United. Unfortunately, the two sides cancelled each other out and provided one of Wembley's worst-ever games, which was decided by a controversial goal by Leeds' full-back Terry Cooper.

If that was a disappointment, being beaten as red-hot favourites the following year by Third Division Swindon Town was a disaster – especially as the Gunners were growing in stature and good enough to finish fourth in the League behind Leeds. The route to Wembley included a 6-1 win at Scunthorpe, a 2-1 defeat of Liverpool and a semi-final epic with Spurs. John Radford's only goal of the game in the first leg at Highbury proved decisive because the Gunners held their rivals to a 1-1 draw at White Hart Lane with Radford cancelling out a Jimmy Greaves goal. In the final, the Gunners, weakened by six first teamers suffering from flu, were well beaten by the Wiltshire side. Swindon Town rose to the occasion with a two-goal performance from Don Rogers plus some outstanding saves from keeper Peter Downsborough, in a 3-1 victory.

Despite their disappointment at Wembley, Arsenal made it into Europe for the first time because of their League position. The club's success in Europe was in direct contrast to a very disappointing domestic season in which the Gunners made early exits in the League and FA Cups and finished halfway down the table because they failed to turn superiority into goals, especially in 18 drawn games.

Arsenal's progress in the Fairs Cup was convincing against Glentoran, Sporting Lisbon, Rouen and Dinamo Bacau – whom they beat 7-1 at Highbury – to set up a semi-final showdown with Ajax. The Gunners outplayed their Dutch opponents with a 3-0 win at Highbury and then restricted them to 1-0 in Amsterdam.

Arsenal's opponents in the two-legged final were Anderlecht, who defeated Inter Milan 3-0 on aggregate in the semi-final including a 1-0 win in Italy. In the first leg in Brussels, two goals from Jan Mulders, plus a third from Johan Devrindt, gave the Belgian side what looked like an unassailable lead. But Bertie Mee threw on young Ray Kennedy and he headed home in the closing minutes to salvage hope for the return. At Highbury, Eddie Kelly made the breakthrough with a shot from the edge of the area and then midway through the second-half, John Radford nodded in a Bob McNab cross. Thanks to Kennedy's 'away' goal, Arsenal now led but Sammels made sure the Cup was not won on a technicality by converting George Graham's pass.

Sir Stanley Rous, then FIFA's President, presented the Fairs Cup to Frank McLintock – the trophy staying in England for the third successive year following the victories of Leeds United and Newcastle United.

Prior to the start of the 1970–71 season, Peter Simpson had collected a cartilage injury and an operation kept him out until November. Sammels cracked a bone in a warm-up match and Charlie George came back from the opening game at Everton with a cracked bone in an ankle.

Before the season opened there was good news for the club's European ambitions when UEFA decided that, as holders, Arsenal could defend the Fairs Cup, even though they had not finished high enough in the First Division to qualify. Their first opponents were Lazio.

John Radford had netted a hat-trick against Manchester United before the Gunners set off for the first leg in Rome. It was a very hostile atmosphere but two more Radford goals cancelled out two from Chinaglia. But as the players left the after-match dinner, they were attacked by their Lazio opponents who had been lying in wait! UEFA opted to side with Arsenal's version of events and fined the Italians before the Gunners won the second leg 2-0. The following Saturday, Arsenal crashed 5-0 at Stoke before bouncing back with a 4-0 League Cup replay win over Ipswich Town. The club then embarked on a League run that brought 25 out of a possible 28 points until January when they went down 2-1 at Huddersfield.

⚽ ARSENAL FACT ⚽

In November 1970, Arsenal carried out tests on their players to determine whether they were colour blind. They were not.

In the FA Cup, wins over Yeovil Town and Portsmouth took the Gunners into the fifth round and a tie with Manchester City at Maine Road. Two goals from Charlie George on a snow covered ground settled the issue.

All wasn't as well in Europe and after Sturm Graz beat them 1-0 in Austria, it needed Peter Storey's last-minute penalty to give Arsenal a 2-1 aggregate win. The Gunners then saw off Beveren 4-0 before beating

Cologne 2-1 at Highbury in the first leg of the quarter-finals. But the away goal was to prove fatal when the German side clung on to a controversial penalty goal at home. Just prior to this second leg, Arsenal had beaten Second Division champions Leicester City after a replay to win through to the FA Cup semi-finals.

The Gunners breathed a huge sigh of relief when Peter Storey grabbed the chance of a replay with another last-minute penalty. In the replay, first-half goals from Kennedy and Graham took Arsenal to Wembley.

Meanwhile, the title race was hotting up, although Leeds were eight points clear with eight games to play. However, come April, successive victories over Chelsea and Newcastle United sent the team top on goal average as Leeds lost at home to West Bromwich Albion. Although a dubious Jack Charlton goal gave the Yorkshire club the points when they entertained Arsenal at the end of the month, the Gunners were not to be denied. A week later came Arsenal's last game against Spurs. All results were possible. A win would give the title to Arsenal, a defeat would send the trophy to Elland Road; a goalless draw would mean success for the Gunners but, because of the peculiarities of the goal average system then in force, any scoring draw would conclude matters in Leeds' favour. With just a minute to go, Ray Kennedy headed home Armstrong's cross and the title belonged to Arsenal for a record eighth time. One of the game's most compelling seasons had been decided by a single point.

In the FA Cup Final against Liverpool, the game was goalless in normal time with both sides cautious in their attempts to seek an advantage. However, just three minutes into extra-time, Steve Heighway raced up the left-wing and his shot beat the embarrassed Bob Wilson on his near post. Arsenal's equaliser came out of the blue. Tommy Smith and Emlyn Hughes dithered in their penalty area and Eddie Kelly nipped in to sweep the ball past Ray Clemence. Graham followed the ball but the TV cameras suggested it was Kelly's goal. Then, a stunning climax as Charlie George moved forward. Radford laid the ball into his path some 20 yards out and his rising right foot shot whistled past a despairing Clemence. It was all over. George had written the last line in one of the most memorable pages of soccer history.

Frank McLintock had success at last, it was the first time he had been a Wembley winner in five cup final attempts. Arsenal captain, new Footballer of the Year and soon to become MBE, McLintock was a fine example of the type of player who brought Highbury such momentous days. Arsenal looked capable of dominating English football for a decade but amazingly within a matter of months, that dream was turning sour.

The euphoria of the Gunners' Double win had hardly subsided when Don Howe, the club's outstanding coach, left to become manager of his first club, West Bromwich Albion. To fill the coaching void, the club's reserve coach for the last four years, Steve Burtenshaw, was appointed.

Even so, there was no hint of a sudden decline when the new European Cup Winners' Cup holders Chelsea were beaten 3-0 on the opening day of the 1971–72 season. Yet, by the end of August, the club had suffered three successive defeats including one by Sheffield United that was their first at home for more than a year and a half. The club made progress in the European Cup beating Stromgodset of Norway and Grasshoppers of Switzerland to reach the quarter-finals.

But Arsenal's form in the League was approaching crisis point and Mee's remedies were drastic. Out went favourites, McNab, Nelson, Simpson and the recently restored Charlie George. Then, just before the turn of the year, the Arsenal manager paid £220,000 for Everton's inspirational midfielder, Alan Ball. He launched the club's FA Cup run to Wembley with his first goal in a 2-0 defeat of Swindon Town and, with George restored to the side and finding the net with great regularity, they embarked on a 12-game unbeaten run in the League. By mid-February, not only another Double but a unique Treble was in their sights. However, Ball had arrived too late to be eligible for the European Cup quarter-final and the Gunners lost 3-1 on aggregate to Ajax. This elimination came in the middle of three League defeats which effectively ended the club's title challenge, too. The FA Cup was the club's last hope of success but after making it to the Centenary Final, the game against Leeds was a physical battle littered with too many fouls. Allan Clarke's header made it a third Wembley defeat for the Gunners in four years and a fifth losing visit for skipper Frank McLintock.

☻ ARSENAL FACT ☻

In the 1971 and 1972 FA Cup semi-finals, Arsenal played Stoke. Both times the tie went to a replay, both times at Villa Park – and both times the Gunners were victorious.

After a disappointing start to the 1972–73 season, the team went 15 matches without defeat and with Radford and Kennedy having rediscovered their shooting boots, they were chasing Liverpool for the title and heading for Wembley again. But Second Division Sunderland, who went on to shock red-hot favourites Leeds at Wembley, disposed of the Gunners in the semi-final; and Liverpool pipped them to the Championship by three points.

Bertie Mee was obviously bent on rebuilding and let two key players depart – Frank McLintock left for Queen's Park Rangers and had four good years there, taking them to within a whisker of the title, and George Graham joined Manchester United. Importantly for the future, a young Irishman by the name of Liam Brady had forced his way into a struggling Arsenal team; but on a night Bob Wilson made his farewell appearance against Queen's Park Rangers, Alan Ball broke his leg.

⚽ ARSENAL FACT ⚽!

Alan Ball scored in the first minute in different Football League matches against the same team on the same ground. Playing for Arsenal against West Ham United at Highbury on 29 August 1972, he scored in 40 seconds and then again on 20 March 1976 after 55 seconds.

Arsenal's management team had a dramatic rethink on tactics in the close season and after deciding the long ball game with Kennedy as a target man hadn't been working, allowed him to join Liverpool. In came Brian Kidd and, although he became leading scorer with 19 goals in his first season, an unsettled team sank to the bottom of the League accompanied by Spurs after a run of ten games without a win. In the game at Derby, Ball and McNab were sent off. It was only the second occasion since the war that two players from the same side had been dismissed in the same match. The other time had involved Arsenal players, too – McLintock and Storey in 1967. The club's decision not to support the players at an appeal – both were banned for three games – caused a rift between the club and Alan Ball that was never healed. The club did reach the FA Cup quarter-final but were beaten by West Ham United. It was the first time they had ever been beaten at home in the FA Cup by another London side. There was still a chance that the Gunners could be relegated but the team battled hard and ended the season in 16th place.

The 1975–76 season marked the end of the Mee era but it proved a sad finale to one of the greatest periods in the club's history – the team finished 17th and failed at the first hurdle in both cup competitions. In the summer, two more of Arsenal's Double-winning side left. Charlie George, who almost joined Spurs, signed for Derby County whilst Bob McNab moved to Wolves. Though Alan Ball was still on the transfer list, Rice and Nelson had blossomed into a fine pair of full-backs, David O'Leary and Frank Stapleton looked top-class players and Brady was beginning to have a great influence on the team. But all this promise was not enough to prevent Bertie Mee bowing to the pressure after 10 years in charge.

Mee, who will always be remembered as Arsenal's Double-winning manager, restored the pride, passion and power to the Highbury club.

Speculation as to who would replace Mee was intense, with Jack Charlton, Brian Clough, Bolton's Ian Greaves and Wales' manager Mike Smith all apparently in the frame. In the end, Arsenal appointed their former centre-half, Terry Neill, who had just resigned from the Tottenham job after succeeding Bill Nicholson.

⚽ ARSENAL FACT ⚽

Terry Neill became Arsenal's youngest captain when he was handed the armband in the 1960s and then became the club's youngest manager in 1976.

Not a man to let the grass grow under his feet, Neill paid £333,333 for Newcastle's Malcolm Macdonald. He netted 29 goals in his first season including a hat-trick against his former club and began to have a vital influence on the young Frank Stapleton. The signing of Alan Hudson proved a disaster whilst John Radford moved to West Ham United and Peter Storey to Fulham. There seemed no end to the comings and goings. Following the arrival of big Willie Young from Spurs, the Gunners steadied themselves following six successive defeats to finish a creditable eighth behind champions, Liverpool.

Don Howe returned to Highbury and Neill made one of his most astute signings by bringing in Pat Jennings from Spurs for a fee of £40,000 in August 1977. With new striker Alan Sunderland recruited from Wolves, the Gunners featured strongly in the title race but were denied a place in the

League Cup Final by a Ray Kennedy goal for Liverpool. They did, however, make it to the FA Cup Final but with Brady not fully fit, they lost 1-0 to Ipswich Town.

☻ ARSENAL FACT ☻

In 1979 Arsenal played Sheffield Wednesday five times in 17 days in the FA Cup third round. It took an embarrassing 540 minutes for the Gunners to beat the Third Division team.

Brady, Stapleton and Sunderland were now at the peak of their careers with the Gunners and in 1979 they helped bring the FA Cup back to Highbury for the fifth time with a dramatic victory over Manchester United. Arsenal led 2-0 at half-time with goals from Brian Talbot and Stapleton but with the cup apparently won, Gordon McQueen reduced the arrears before Sammy McIlroy equalised. Liam Brady then set Graham Rix free down the left and his cross was met at the far post by the incoming Sunderland for one of Wembley's most memorable winning goals.

☻ ARSENAL FACT ☻

The first player to win the FA Cup in consecutive seasons with different clubs was Brian Talbot with Arsenal in 1979 after winning it the previous year with Ipswich, ironically against the Gunners.

The Arsenal side was now beginning to be compared with the Double-winning team and in 1979–80, they went one better by reaching two cup finals – a third successive FA Cup Final and the European Cup Winners' Cup Final. In the semi-final of the latter against Juventus an eventful first leg at Highbury saw the Italian side take the lead through a twice taken penalty before O'Leary was put out of the game by a Roberto Bettega tackle and Marco Tardelli was sent-off for a similar challenge on Brady. Justice was done though, when Bettega put through his own goal to give Arsenal a 1-1 draw. Three days later they played out a goalless draw with Liverpool in the FA Cup semi-final. A week later, the Gunners produced one of the outstanding results in European competition by winning in Turin.

Paul Vaessen scored the winner with two minutes left as Arsenal became the first British club to triumph there.

The Italian club had not lost at home in Europe for 10 years. Five days later in the replay with Liverpool, Alan Sunderland scored after just 20 seconds but Kenny Dalglish equalised to take the tie to a third meeting. Finally, Brian Talbot's goal killed off the Anfield club to set up a Wembley final with Second Division West Ham United. Unfortunately for the Gunners, Trevor Brooking deflected the ball past Jennings for an unusual winning goal.

In the European Cup Winners' Cup Final against Valencia, the scoresheet was still blank after extra-time and so the game had to be decided on penalties. Argentinian World Cup star Mario Kempes and Liam Brady missed the first attempts but everybody else scored to make it 4-4. Arias made it 5-4 for the Spanish club but Graham Rix's shot was saved to produce a shattering climax for the Gunners.

They came home completely drained but there was still a UEFA Cup place in the offing if they could take the maximum four points from their last two League games. Wolves were beaten 2-1 but in what was their 70th match of the season, the Gunners lost 5-0 at Middlesbrough.

Liam Brady then moved abroad, ironically to Juventus and, within a year, Frank Stapleton moved to Manchester United in acrimonious circumstances. Arsenal valued him at £2 million, United offered £750,000 and the independent tribunal settled on £900,000 – a figure that disgusted the Arsenal board. Then Arsenal were involved in the amazing Clive Allen transfer saga. The 19-year-old striker had scored 30 goals for Queen's Park Rangers and the Gunners paid £1 million for him in the summer of 1980. But, before the season got underway, he joined Crystal Palace in a deal that saw Kenny Sansom move to Highbury.

☉ ARSENAL FACT ☉

In reaching the European Cup Winners' Cup and FA Cup Finals in 1979–80, the Gunners played a remarkable 70 matches – still a record.

The Gunners then entered another barren period during which not only were they not serious title challengers but they could not rediscover their FA Cup form either. That is until 1982–83 when they reached the semi-finals of both cup competitions only to be knocked out of them both by Manchester United.

⚽ ARSENAL FACT ⚽

Highbury was the venue for the first streaker on a Football League pitch in April 1982.

Terry Neill was under great pressure – little was going right for him and one of his most recent acquisitions, the Scot Charlie Nicholas, had yet to show his true potential. Midway through the 1983–84 season following a shock League Cup exit at the hands of Walsall, Neill was sacked.

⚽ ARSENAL FACT ⚽

Tony Woodcock smashed five goals past a hapless Aston Villa side in the space of just 48 minutes in a 6-2 win at Villa Park in 1983–84.

His successor was long-time servant of the club, Don Howe, but his two-and-a-half years in charge were not to be happy ones. Attendances fell somewhat dramatically and after four successive victories, Howe resigned. The reason: he was hurt by constant speculation that the club were keen to bring Terry Venables back from Barcelona.

It was to the Double-winning side that the Arsenal board turned for Howe's replacement. George Graham was appointed manager in the summer of 1986. He had done a good job at Millwall. Initially he didn't bring any new players in, relying on what he had – Steve Williams, Niall Quinn and the emerging Tony Adams. Indeed, it wasn't until the end of the season that he signed Alan Smith from Leicester City.

The season itself was a revelation. After losing to the then League leaders Nottingham Forest at the end of September, the Gunners went 22 games without defeat – winning 17 and drawing five – and at Christmas they were top of the League. When they eventually did lose – to a struggling Manchester United at Old Trafford – they were still going well in both cup competitions. On 27 December 1986, the Gunners capped what has so far been a wonderful season with a 1-0 win over Southampton, a game that marked the club's centenary.

After wins over Huddersfield Town, Manchester City, Charlton Athletic and Nottingham Forest, Arsenal met Spurs in the League Cup semi-final. After going down 2-0 on aggregate in the second leg, Arsenal scored twice to force a replay. Spurs went 1-0 up but the Gunners came back to win 2-1 and so face Liverpool in the final. A quarter-final defeat at the hands of Watford ended their interest in the FA Cup and, with players who might have found themselves suspended for the League Cup Final rested, any hopes of winning the League also disappeared.

In the League Cup Final, Ian Rush gave Liverpool the lead midway through the first-half – the Anfield club had never lost any of the games in which Rush had scored but even the oldest of records have to go sometime! Charlie Nicholas equalised on the stroke of half-time and then hit the winner seven minutes from time.

⚽ ARSENAL FACT ⚽

In 1987 the Milk Cup became the Littlewoods Cup. The first winners' of the newly named trophy were Arsenal, beating Liverpool 2-1.

The 1987–88 season was a disappointing one in terms of the League but there was a pleasing conclusion to the end of the campaign with a second successive appearance in the League Cup Final. Arsenal's opponents at Wembley were Luton Town, who had never won a major trophy in their then 102-year history. However, the Gunners were in for a shock as Ray Harford almost put the Hatters ahead in the opening minute before Brian Stein gave Luton a 1-0 lead. Early in the second-half, John Lukic made a brilliant save to deny Stein a second before Martin Hayes equalised. Alan Smith then gave Arsenal the lead before, two minutes later, heading against the bar. Hayes hit the rebound against the post. Then Arsenal were awarded a penalty for a trip on David Rocastle. Nigel Winterburn took the kick but Andy Dibble turned the ball round the post. Arsenal were made to pay as Danny Wilson levelled the scores and then with the last move of the match, Ashley Grimes crossed for Brian Stein to make it 3-2 to Luton.

In George Graham's third season, 1988–89, the club won their first League title since 1971, in highly dramatic fashion. To a certain degree, Arsenal's League ambitions were helped by early exits in both cup competitions. The League campaign began brightly with Alan Smith netting a hat-trick in a 5-1 win at Wimbledon but this was followed by two reverses against Aston Villa and Sheffield Wednesday. After that, results were steady until a 4-1 win at Nottingham Forest made the Press take the Gunners' season seriously. By the turn of the year, Arsenal were five points clear at the top of the table and, after demolishing Everton 3-1 at Goodison Park, their great rivals Liverpool were 11 points behind. The gap at one time was as great as 19 points but the Anfield club clawed it back in remarkable fashion. The Gunners were overtaken by Liverpool in early May and, after losing to Derby County and only drawing at home to Wimbledon, they had seemingly thrown away the title.

Arsenal's final game of the season was against Liverpool at Anfield. All the Merseyside club had to do to complete the Double (they had already won the FA Cup, beating Everton 3-2 in the final) was to avoid defeat by two goals, whilst the Gunners had to win by two goals. Alan Smith scored early in the second-half to make it 1-0 but as time ticked by, Arsenal struggled to get a second. With 90 minutes gone, The Kop whistled frantically for the finish but with only seconds to go, a Smith flick-on found Michael Thomas who calmly lifted the ball over Bruce Grobbelaar and into the net. Arsenal were League Champions by the closest of margins. The most dramatic domestic season for many a year was at an end. The Kop applauded the Arsenal side as they were presented with the League Championship trophy; the dream for the Anfield club was over.

Winning the Championship and retaining it were different propositions. The Gunners finished fourth in the League in 1989–90 but were 17 points behind champions Liverpool and failed to make their mark in the cups.

Graham went out to improve his side and, in the close season, signed David Seaman and Swedish winger Anders Limpar. Their season started with 17 games undefeated – the run coming to an end in astonishing fashion as Manchester United won 6-2 at Highbury! There were a couple of other major setbacks this season. In October 1990, Arsenal players were involved in a brawl with Manchester United players in a match at Old Trafford. Both clubs were fined £50,000, the Gunners had two points deducted and United one. It was the first time the FA had deducted points for 'on the field' activities. Then, in the week before Christmas, skipper Tony Adams was sentenced to four months imprisonment after being convicted of drink driving. Thankfully, these setbacks did not hinder Arsenal's progress – their only league defeat of the season was a 2-1 reversal at Chelsea – and they went on to finish the season seven points clear of runners-up Liverpool.

The club also reached the FA Cup semi-finals where they faced Spurs at Wembley. Up to this point, the FA had never allowed a tie other than the final itself to be played at Wembley – but no other stadium in the country could have coped with the demand for tickets. Less than five minutes had been played when Paul Gascoigne netted with a venomous free-kick from 30 yards out. Gary Lineker made it 2-0 before Alan Smith's far post header reduced the arrears. However, Lineker netted a third to dash Arsenal's hopes of a second Double.

In 1991–92, Arsenal were finally in the European Cup. They had not entered after their last League Championship success because of the post-Heysel ban on English clubs. In the first round, Alan Smith scored four of his side's goals in a 6-1 rout of Austria Vienna. Before the second leg, Graham had left his domestic rivals behind with the record £2.5 million signing of Ian Wright from Crystal Palace. Back in Europe, the Gunners crashed out of the competition in the second round to Benfica, thus failing to make the lucrative group stage. The season then went from bad to worse as the club were knocked out of the FA Cup by Fourth Division Wrexham, but they did recover to finish fourth in the League.

✪ ARSENAL FACT ✪

In September 1991, Lee Dixon who had a habit of scoring spectacular own goals, lobbed his own keeper from outside the area after just 54 seconds of the match against Coventry City.

The next season was to bring a more dramatic change – the end of the old First Division and the start of the Premier League. Graham changed his tactics, becoming more defensive and turning out far less attack-minded sides. The Gunners relied too heavily for goals on Ian Wright and ended the inaugural Premiership campaign in 10th place, scoring fewer goals than any other team in the division.

> **☉ ARSENAL FACT ☉**
>
> Arsenal scored six goals in the space of 18 minutes in a 7-1 win over Sheffield Wednesday on 15 February 1992. The goals came between the 71st and 89th minute.

But if there was to be a saving grace about the season at Highbury, it was Arsenal's form in the cup competitions. Their momentous progress towards two Wembley Cup Finals began in earnest with a 3-1 victory over Yeovil Town. Further successes over Leeds United, Nottingham Forest and Ipswich set up the prospect of a mouth-watering semi-final against Spurs. Tottenham had of course disposed of the Gunners at the same stage in 1991 but on this occasion it was a Tony Adams header that avenged the disappointment of two seasons before.

Important goals by defenders were to become something of a fashion with Stephen Morrow popping up with his first goal for the club to help Arsenal to a 2-1 League Cup Final win over Sheffield Wednesday. Tragically, Morrow suffered a freak accident as he participated in the post-match celebrations and a badly broken elbow meant he would miss the FA Cup Final, also against the Owls. Arsenal struggled to a 1-1 draw after extra-time. In the replay, which also went to extra-time after goals by Wright and Chris Waddle, there were just seconds remaining when Andy Linighan headed home to complete an amazing season for Arsenal.

The double Cup winners got off to a bad start in 1993–94, losing the Charity Shield against Manchester United in a penalty shoot-out after Ian Wright had scored the first of his 35 League and Cup goals that season in a 1-1 draw. After Mick Quinn grabbed a hat-trick for Coventry City in a 3-0 opening day win at Highbury, Arsenal conceded just another 12 goals at home all season. The club's form in Europe was excellent and after beating Standard Liege 3-0 at Highbury, the Gunners won 7-0 in the return in Brussels – their best-ever victory in Europe. The defence of the League Cup ended with a 1-0 home defeat by Aston Villa whilst Bolton Wanderers went to Highbury for a fourth round FA Cup replay and won 3-1. League form was only moderate and they were never able to mount a serious challenge to Manchester United, which meant that the Cup Winners' Cup was now the prime target.

A quarter-final victory over Torino was followed by a 2-1 aggregate win over Paris St Germain in the semi-final to send Arsenal through to the European Cup Winners' Cup Final for the first time since 1980. But Arsenal's plans were hit by suspension and injury – Ian Wright, booked in the second leg of the semi-final was suspended and John Jensen injured whilst playing for Denmark. Despite their losses, Arsenal battled to a 1-0 win over holders Parma in the final. A great defensive performance ensured the victory and Graham's sixth major trophy in eight years in charge.

Rarely can a club have attracted such adverse publicity during a season as did Arsenal in 1994–95. George Graham had to contend with Paul Merson admitting to being a drug addict; but that was not the biggest cloud hanging over the Gunners' boss. He was accused of receiving illegal payments totalling £286,000 following the transfer of John Jensen. In February 1995, Arsenal sacked Graham when the FA found him guilty of the charge; Stewart Houston was put in charge until the end of the season.

Europe again looked to be Arsenal's only outlet as the defence of the Cup Winners' Cup kept their season alive. Ian Wright became the first player to score in every match up to the European final as Omonia Nicosia, Brondby, Auxerre and, more dramatically, Sampdoria, were removed from the competition. Against the Italians, Seaman saved three penalties to put Arsenal on the verge of being the first team to successfully defend the cup. But, with another penalty shoot-out less than ten seconds away at the end of extra-time in the final against Real Zaragoza, Seaman's semi-final heroics were forgotten. The former Spurs midfielder Nayim scored what was either the finest or flukiest cup-winning goal of all-time, looping the ball over the Arsenal keeper from fully fifty yards!

Bolton Wanderers boss Bruce Rioch was appointed Arsenal manager at the start of the 1995–96 season in June 1995 and he immediately smashed the club record transfer fee and much maligned Highbury wage structure when signing Dutch international Dennis Bergkamp from Internazionale for £7.5 million.

Rioch's re-structuring of the team didn't always go down well with all the players and for a while there was even serious talk of perennial top-scorer Ian Wright leaving the club following a transfer request.

It was the League Cup that kept the Gunners' season alive and their hopes of reaching their fifth cup final in four seasons looked bright as

Dennis Bergkamp scored twice to give them an early lead in the first leg of the semi-final against Aston Villa. But surprising defensive lapses allowed the Midlanders to draw level and they eventually went through on the away goal rule after a scoreless second leg. Although cup success proved to be beyond Rioch, the supporters relished the new style as Bergkamp and Wright formed a formidable partnership. Arsenal made a return to the higher echelons of the Premier League, although they were never serious title contenders. They reclaimed the mantle of London's top club with victory over Bolton Wanderers on the final day of the season – a win that clinched fifth position and a UEFA Cup place.

Despite lifting Arsenal's League standing during his first season in charge at Highbury, Bruce Rioch found himself out of the club just five days before the start of the 1996–97 season. Stewart Houston stepped in for his second spell as caretaker-manager but then surprised the club with a move across London to Queen's Park Rangers as respected French coach Arsène Wenger waited in the wings to take charge of the club after seeing out his contract abroad.

Wenger's pre-arrival influence was clear as French stars Patrick Vieira and Remi Garde crossed the water to join the Gunners. During the early part of the season, Ian Wright scored a hat-trick in a 4-1 defeat of Sheffield Wednesday which included his 100th League goal for the club. Arsenal continued to mount the only serious title challenge from the capital but ironically, it was ultimately a loss of form at Highbury which ensured that the title would not be going to North London for the first time in six years. Having gone unbeaten at home in the League for 13 months, Arsenal lost four of their last seven games at Highbury. They finished third and a Champions League place was missed on goal difference.

☻ ARSENAL FACT ☻

In 1997, Jason Crowe came on as a substitute in a League Cup game against Birmingham City. He was immediately adjudged to have committed a high tackle and shown a straight red card. He had been on the field of play for just 33 seconds!

Despite enjoying great cup success in the early part of the decade, the Gunners suffered a first round UEFA Cup defeat by Borussia Moenchengladbach while defeats by Liverpool and Leeds United ended their interest in the League and FA Cups respectively.

Wenger was the most active of the Premiership managers during the close season with a host of top signings bound for Highbury – Marc Overmars the most notable at £7 million, along with French pair Emmanuel Petit and Nicolas Anelka.

In Wenger's first full season in charge, Arsenal were quickly into their stride, finding the target nine times in their opening four games. Shortly afterwards, Dennis Bergkamp, the eventual PFA and Sports Writers' Player of the Year, hit five goals in two games including a hat-trick in a stormy 3-3 draw at Leicester City. Two games later, Ian Wright netted three times during a 4-1 destruction of Bolton at Highbury which took him past Cliff Bastin's club record of 178 goals. After a 12-match unbeaten run, Arsenal's bubble burst at Derby and then they lost at home to Blackburn. Their title hopes now looked shattered. But the Gunners had a magnificent defence and thereafter dropped very few points. They became an unstoppable force as a Premiership record of ten consecutive victories was achieved. Champions Manchester United were six points ahead of Arsenal but the Gunners had three games in hand. After four successive 1-0 wins and eight consecutive clean sheets, Arsenal went into overdrive as United's lead was wiped out. With an awesome performance, Arsenal destroyed Everton 4-0 at Highbury to clinch their third title in ten years.

☺ ARSENAL FACT ☺

The largest crowd to watch an Arsenal home game is 73,707 who packed into Wembley Stadium for the club's European encounter with Lens on 25 November 1998.

Despite an early exit in the UEFA Cup, there was no stopping the Gunners in the FA Cup, although they did need penalty shoot-outs to account for Port Vale and West Ham United. Two games were also required to repel Crystal Palace but Middlesbrough, and Wolves in the semi-final, were seen off at the first attempt. Goals by Overmars and Anelka in the final against Newcastle United ensured Wenger's place in folklore as the first overseas manager to win not only the League title but the historic Double.

The 1998–99 season was one in which the Gunners came agonisingly close to emulating the Double-winning feat of the previous campaign but ended it with nothing more than a Champions League place. An indifferent spell of form just before the turn of the year was followed by a 21-game unbeaten run which eventually ended with defeat in the epic FA Cup semi-final against Manchester United; Ryan Giggs scored the winner in extra-time after a mazy solo run through the Arsenal defence. Fifteen wins including victories over Wimbledon (5-1) and Middlesbrough (6-1) and just one defeat in the last 20 League games matched the form and points of the Double-winning season. But with Arsenal and Manchester United level on points with two games to play, the Gunners lost at Leeds. The following day, United drew with Blackburn. Arsenal fans were hoping Spurs could do them a favour at Old Trafford and actually cheered as Tottenham took the lead, but United came back to win and though Arsenal beat Aston Villa, the title went to Old Trafford.

⚽ ARSENAL FACT ⚽

In 1999, Arsenal received their largest ever transfer fee when Real Madrid splashed out £23 million for current Bolton player Nicolas Anelka.

The following season was one of disappointment, although the Gunners ended the campaign as runners-up in the Premiership again and were beaten finalists in the UEFA Cup. Results in the early stages of the Champions League were promising but it eventually turned sour following defeats at Wembley by Barcelona and Fiorentina that cost Arsenal the chance of qualifying for the second stage of the competition. Around this time, Arsenal lost a League match at West Ham 2-1 but, more importantly, Patrick Vieira was sent off for spitting in the direction of Neil Ruddock and suspended for seven games. In the game against Spurs, both Freddie Ljungberg and Martin Keown were shown red cards but the club started their UEFA Cup campaign with a 6-3 aggregate win over Nantes. It continued to gather momentum as Deportivo La Coruna were beaten 5-1 at Highbury.

The club then strung together eight consecutive League wins, which, though it was too late to catch Manchester United, ensured that the

Gunners clinched second spot and a place in the Champions League. In the UEFA Cup, both Werder Bremen and Lens were beaten leaving the Gunners to face Turkish side Galatasaray in the final in Copenhagen. The match was a tepid affair and goalless after ninety minutes. Arsenal then contrived to miss a number of chances in extra-time against ten men and eventually lost the game on penalties.

Despite reaching the FA Cup Final and the quarter-finals of the Champions League, Arsenal failed to make a serious challenge to Manchester United in the race for the Premiership title during the 1999-2000 season and this lack of silverware was a huge disappointment to the Arsenal fans.

In their 2000-01 campaign, the Gunners followed up a first day defeat at Sunderland with a 15-game unbeaten run. This included home victories over Manchester United, Liverpool and Lazio. Arsenal were top of the League and had reached the second stage of the Champions League. The results that followed were mixed - a 6-1 thrashing by Manchester United ended the club's hopes for Premiership success but a win at Lens saw the club qualify for the quarter-finals in Europe. An FA Cup semi-final win over rivals Spurs was followed by a 2-1 defeat of Valencia in the Champions League quarter-final first-leg. Unfortunately a 1-0 defeat in the return in Spain meant the Gunners went out on the 'away' goal rule. Arsenal lost the FA Cup Final to Liverpool as two Michael Owen goals in the last ten minutes at the Millennium Stadium saw the trophy go to Anfield. But a draw at Newcastle a few days later did secure runners-up place in the Premiership.

Arsenal's exciting style of free-scoring football in which Thierry Henry, signed in August 1999, excelled saw them go through the 2001-02 season unbeaten on their travels in the Premiership and FA Cup and become only the second English club to win the Double for a third time.

In the League, the Gunners had signalled their early intent with a 4-0 rout of Middlesbrough at the Riverside but then suffered a number of home defeats. Just a couple of days before Christmas, Arsenal beat League leaders Liverpool 2-1 at Anfield. This signalled the start of a quite remarkable run which saw them go undefeated for the rest of the campaign. Following an injury to Robert Pires, Freddie Ljungberg switched to the left-wing and scored seven goals in seven games - crucial strikes which ensured that the Premiership trophy returned to Highbury. The Gunners secured the title in the penultimate game of the season with a 1-

0 win over Manchester United at Old Trafford with Sylvain Wiltord the scorer. The Gunners then beat Everton in a seven-goal thriller to finish on 87 points, seven clear of runners-up Liverpool.

The FA Cup leg of the triumph was completed at the Millennium Stadium as Arsenal faced Chelsea in what was their second successive final. The game had added significance for Dennis Bergkamp who finally started an FA Cup Final after missing the 1998 final through injury and only making a brief appearance the previous season in the defeat by Liverpool. Arsenal beat Chelsea 2-0 with goals from Robert Pires and Ljungberg.

⚽ ARSENAL FACT ⚽

Arsenal hold the record for consecutive goalscoring. Between 19 May 2001 and 7 December 2002, the Gunners found the net in 55 unbroken games, amassing a total of 117 goals. In doing so, the club became the first team to score in every League match in a season, and set a record for the highest number of successive wins in the top flight – thirteen – in the 2001–02 season. Freddie Ljungberg scored in both the 2001 and 2002 FA Cup Finals, the first player to score in consecutive finals for 40 years.

In the 2002–03 season Arsenal were so far ahead in the Premiership at one stage that Irish bookmakers Paddy Power paid out to all punters who had bet on the Gunners retaining their title!

The title race was initially blown wide open when Arsenal were beaten by a fantastic goal at Everton by a youngster named Wayne Rooney. Later in the season, Arsenal drew 2-2 at Bolton, this after they had led the Wanderers 2-0, and then lost 3-2 at home to Leeds United a week or so later. With Manchester United, who at one stage trailed the Gunners by eight points, defeating Arsenal 2-0 in December and drawing 2-2 at Highbury in late April, Sir Alex Ferguson's side reeled Arsenal in to pick up the Premiership title on the penultimate game of the season.

⚽ ARSENAL FACT ⚽

Gilberto scored the fastest ever Champions League goal after just 20.07 seconds against PSV Eindhoven on 25 September 2002.

Though they had narrowly missed out on retaining the Premiership title, Arsenal became the first club to retain the FA Cup with Robert Pires scoring the goal that helped the Gunners defeat Southampton 1-0.

Little did they know at the time but the Gunners defeat to Leeds in May 2003 was their last in the Premiership for more than a year. Arsenal went through the entire 2003–04 season without a single loss and were crowned champions once more – this at the expense of Chelsea, who had spent heavily throughout the season. Arsenal's only signing was goalkeeper Jens Lehmann. Once again Thierry Henry was instrumental in the Gunners' success.

☻ ARSENAL FACT ☻

Francesc Fabregas is Arsenal's youngest-ever player, making his debut against Rotherham United in a Carling Cup third round tie on 28 October 2003, at the age of 16 years 17 days. The Spaniard is also the club's youngest scorer, netting against Wolves in the same competition aged 16 years 212 days.

Away from the Premiership, Arsène Wenger's team suffered disappointment in the cup competitions. They failed in their defence of the FA Cup, which they had held for the last two seasons, after losing to eventual winners Manchester United in the semi-final. Just prior to this, Arsenal were knocked out of the Champions League in the quarter-final by Chelsea. These two defeats came within a matter of days and it was feared that the Gunners might squander their lead in the Premiership for the second successive season. On 9 April 2004 they trailed Liverpool 2-1 but came from behind to win 4-2 with Thierry Henry netting a hat-trick. The Gunners then went on to win the title by drawing 2-2 in the derby match at White Hart Lane. Arsenal finished the season with the following record – the only time in the modern era a side has remained unbeaten for the duration of a League season:

P	W	D	L	F	A	Pts
38	26	12	0	73	26	90

Arsenal made an excellent start to the 2004–05 season, but they were unable to retain the title although the campaign had echoes of the club's Double triumph some two years earlier. The club's new signing from Seville, Jose Antonio Reyes, started off very brightly by tearing apart old adversaries Manchester United in the Community Shield and took that form into the Premiership by finding the net in each of Arsenal's first five games.

History was made when the club, who had of course gone through the previous season undefeated, equalled Brian Clough's Nottingham Forest side of the late 70s, with a 5-3 win over Middlesbrough – this after they had been 3-1 down. The Gunners went on to stretch their unbeaten run to 49 matches before losing 2-0 to Manchester United – a game that turned the whole season on its head. United's very physical approach saw Arsenal's other opponents follow suit and every so often, the tactic worked. Manchester United were not the only side to benefit from the Gunners' slight stutter and Chelsea, bankrolled by Roman Abramovich, took advantage. Arsenal lost at Bolton and Manchester United after the turn of the year and results in general left them with too much ground to make up. Even so, Wenger's young squad bounced back to finish runners-up, 12 points behind Chelsea but still ahead of Manchester United despite two defeats at the hands of the Old Trafford club. Without doubt the highlight of the run-in to the end of the season was the 7-0 rout of Everton, a match in which Dennis Bergkamp was magnificent.

Knocked out of the Champions League by Bayern Munich, the club concentrated on the FA Cup and reached a fourth final in five years. Their opponents at the Millennium Stadium were Manchester United and, though United dominated the game, a mixture of Jens Lehmann's brilliance and the woodwork kept them at bay. For the first time the FA Cup Final had to be decided by a penalty shoot-out – Lehmann saved Paul Scholes' kick and Patrick Vieira scored the winner at 5-4.

☻ ARSENAL FACT ☻

Arsenal have appeared in a record number of 25 FA Cup semi-finals.

During the course of this season, it was announced that Arsenal's new ground for the 2006–07 season was to be known as the Emirates Stadium, at least for the first 15 years, after the club agreed a £100 million sponsorship deal with the Emirates airline company. However, some supporters were adamant that they would continue to use the former road name of Ashburton Grove.

Arsenal began their last season at Highbury without the influential Vieira who had joined Juventus. With the captaincy handed to Thierry Henry, all Gunners' fans felt that he would once again be pivotal to the club's season. An injury suffered whilst on international duty with France ruled him out for a month. During this spell came the first sign that it was not going to be a successful season domestically, with defeats at Middlesbrough and West Bromwich Albion.

Following Henry's return, things began to pick up, but just before the turn of the year, Arsenal suffered three successive defeats at the hands of Bolton Wanderers, Newcastle United and Charlton – the Gunners being completely out-muscled in all of those games. Impressive home wins over Aston Villa (5-0) and Middlesbrough (7-0) failed to improve Arsenal's form for long because they then lost their next two games. The club's domestic form continued to be erratic, but a superb win against Real Madrid in the Bernabeu gave great confidence to a very young Arsenal side. As the season headed towards a close, the Gunners closed the gap between themselves and rivals Spurs and clinched Champions League football for 2006–07 by beating Wigan Athletic 4-2 in their final game.

Arsenal reached the Champions League final against Barcelona in Paris, being the first London club to do so. Finishing top of their group unbeaten above Ajax, FC Thun and Sparta Prague, they then beat Real Madrid, Juventus and Villareal. In the final itself, Arsenal were reduced to 10 men following the early sending-off of Jens Lehmann but nevertheless they took the lead through Sol Campbell. But there was heartbreak after two late goals by Samuel Eto'o and Juliano Belletti meant Barcelona ran out 2-1 winners.

Up to this point, Arsenal had always been also-rans in the Champions League but this season dispelled the myth that they couldn't translate their abilities into the European arena.

Moving into the Emirates Stadium, the Gunners' 2006-07 season has been hampered by injuries to a number of key players, notably Thierry Henry and Robin van Persie. This coincided, at the time of writing, with the club looking likely to win a Champions League place for next season but failing to win any silverware.

In April 2007, Arsenal vice-chairman David Dein walked out on the club, prompting speculation that the Gunners are about to be taken over. There have also been suggestions of mass discontent among the players and doubts over the future of manager Arsene Wenger. Though the Arsenal boss later promised he was staying with the North London club, he will undoubtedly be poorer for Dein's going but the club won't collapse. Most Arsenal fans and a number of former players don't think it matters who invests in the club as long as the integrity is protected and historical roots maintained.

⚽ ARSENAL FACT ⚽

Arsenal has the longest unbroken run in the English top division, having been there since 1919.

THE PLAYERS

Appearances (A)   Goals (G)

CHARLES ALBERT WILLIAMS
Goalkeeper
Born Welling, 19 November 1873
Died: South America, 1952
Clubs Phoenix; Clarence; Erith;
Woolwich Arsenal; Manchester
City; Tottenham Hotspur; Norwich
City; Brentford

		(A)	(G)
1893–94		19	0
	Total	19	0

JOSEPH POWELL
Right-back
Born Bristol, 1870
Died Plumstead, 29 November 1896
Clubs Walsall; 80th Staffordshire
Regiment; Woolwich Arsenal

		A	G
1893–94		26	0
1894–95		27	0
1895–96		25	1
1896–97		8	0
	Total	86	1

WILLAM WALLIS JEFFREY
Full-back
Born Dalderby, 1868
Clubs West Manchester;
Horncastle; Lincoln City; Boston
Town; Grimsby Town; Gainsborough
Trinity; Lincoln City; Burnley;
Woolwich Arsenal; Southampton
St Mary's

		A	G
1893–94		22	0
	Total	22	0

DANIEL DEVINE
Right-half
Born Dumbarton, 1870
Clubs Dumbarton; Renton;
Woolwich Arsenal; Partick Thistle

		A	G
1893–94		2	0
	Total	2	0

ROBERT BUIST
Centre-half/Full-back
Born Glasgow, 1870
Clubs Fairfield Rangers; Cowlairs;
Clyde; Woolwich Arsenal; Leith
Athletic; Royal Ordnance;
Gravesend United

		A	G
1893–94		17	1
	Total	17	1

DAVID HOWAT
Left-half
Born Preston, 1 October 1870
Clubs Fishwick Ramblers; Preston
North End; Woolwich Arsenal;
Third Lanark

		A	G
1893–94		27	1
1894–95		28	1
1895–96		1	0
	Total	56	2

DUNCAN GEMMELL
Outside-right
Born Glasgow, 1870
Clubs Elderslie Rangers Swifts; The
Wednesday; Woolwich Arsenal

		A	G
1893–94		5	0
	Total	5	0

JAMES HENDERSON
Inside-forward
Born Thornhill, Dumfries, 1867
Clubs 5th Kirkcudbright Rifle Vtrs;
Rangers; Woolwich Arsenal

		A	G
1893–94		23	12
1894–95		15	7
	Total	38	19

WALTER JAMES SHAW
Centre-forward/Inside-left
Born Small Heath, Birmingham, 1870
Clubs Singers; Unity Gas;
Birmingham St George's;
Woolwich Arsenal

		A	G
1893–94		17	11
1894–95		2	0
	Total	19	11

ARTHUR ELLIOTT
Inside-left
Born Nottingham, 1870
Clubs Notts Rangers; Gainsborough
Trinity; Accrington; Woolwich
Arsenal; Tottenham Hotspur

		A	G
1893–94		24	10
	Total	24	10

CHARLES BOOTH
Outside-left/Inside-right
Born Gainsborough, 1869
Died Wolverhampton,
17 September 1898

Clubs Gainsborough Trinity;
Wolverhampton Wanderers;
Woolwich Arsenal;
Loughborough Town

	A	G
1893–94	16	2
Total	16	2

FREDERICK WILLIAM DAVIS
Wing-half
Born Smethwick, 1871
Clubs Soho Villa; Birmingham
St George's; Woolwich Arsenal;
Nottingham Forest

	A	G
1893–94	26	1
1894–95	26	3
1895–96	24	0
1896–97	20	0
1897–98	23	4
1898–99	18	0
Total	137	8

JOSEPH FREDERICK HEATH
Centre-forward
Born Bristol, 1869
Clubs Walsall Town Swifts;
Wednesbury Old Athletic;
Wolverhampton Wanderers;
Woolwich Arsenal; Gravesend
United; Woolwich Arsenal

	A	G
1893–94	8	4
1894–95	2	1
Total	10	5

GAVIN CRAWFORD
Right-half/Outside-right
Born Kilmarnock, 1867
Died 2 March 1955
Clubs Fairfield Rangers; Sheffield
United; Woolwich Arsenal; Millwall
Athletic; Queen's Park Rangers

	A	G
1893–94	21	3
1894–95	29	7
1895–96	27	1
1896–97	26	2
1897–98	19	0
Total	122	13

JA STORRS
Left-back
Born Lincoln
Clubs Lincolnshire Regiment;
Woolwich Arsenal

	A	G
1893–94	12	0
Total	12	0

JOSEPH COOPER
Centre-forward
Born Wolverhampton
Clubs Wolverhampton Wanderers;
Woolwich Arsenal

	A	G
1893–94	6	0

STANLEY BRIGGS
Centre-half
Born Stamford Hill, 7 February 1872
Died 1935

Clubs Tottenham Hotspur; Woolwich
Arsenal; Tottenham Hotspur;
Clapton; Millwall Athletic;
Shepherds Bush

	A	G
1893–94	2	0

JAMES BOYLE
Wing-half
Born Glasgow
Clubs Celtic; Woolwich Arsenal;
Dartford

	A	G
1893–94	10	1
1894–95	28	3
1895–96	10	1
1896–97	13	2
Total	**61**	**7**

FRANK V KIRK
Outside-left
Born London
Clubs Woolwich Arsenal; Royal
Ordnance

	A	G
1893–94	1	0
Total	**1**	**0**

ARTHUR GEORGE WORRALL
Centre-forward/Inside-right
Born Wolverhampton,
8 September 1870
Clubs Goldthorne Villa;
Wolverhampton Wanderers; Burton
Swifts; Leicester Fosse; Woolwich
Arsenal; Nelson; Stockport County;

Crewe Alexandra; Barnsley; Belfast
Distillery; Kettering

	A	G
1893–94	4	1
Total	**4**	**1**

THOMAS BRYAN
Outside-left
Born London
Clubs Woolwich Ordnance Factory;
Woolwich Arsenal; Royal Ordnance;
New Brompton

	A	G
1893–94	9	1
Total	**9**	**1**

WALTER WILLIAMS
Inside-left
Born London
Clubs Bostall Rovers; Woolwich
Arsenal

	A	G
1893–94	1	0
Total	**1**	**0**

LYCURGUS BURROWS
Full-back
Born Ashton-under-Lyne,
26 June 1875
Died 1952
Clubs Woolwich Polytechnic;
Woolwich Arsenal; Tottenham
Hotspur; Woolwich Arsenal;
Tottenham Hotspur; Sheffield United

	A	G
1893–94	6	0
1894–95	3	0
1895–96	1	0
Total	10	0

WILLIAM McNAB
Centre-forward
Born Glasgow, 1870
Clubs Burnley; Woolwich Arsenal;
Royal Ordnance

	A	G
1893–94	2	1
Total	2	1

GH JACQUES
Outside-left
Born London, 1875
Clubs Rushden; Woolwich Arsenal

	A	G
1893–94	2	2
Total	2	2

HARRY STORER
Goalkeeper
Born Butterley, 24 July 1870
Died Derbyshire, 25 April 1908
Clubs Ripley Town; Derby Midland;
Derby County; Gainsborough Trinity;
Loughborough Town; Woolwich
Arsenal; Liverpool

	A	G
1894–95	28	0
1895–96	12	0
Total	40	0

JOHN CALDWELL
Left-back
Born Ayr, 28 November 1874
Clubs New Mills; Hibernian;
Woolwich Arsenal; Third Lanark;
Woolwich Arsenal; Brighton United;
Galston; Brighton & Hove Albion

	A	G
1894–95	30	1
1895–96	29	0
1896–97	15	1
1897–98	19	0
Total	93	2

ROBERT STEVENSON
Right-half
Born Barrhead, 1869
Clubs Third Lanark; Woolwich
Arsenal; Thames Ironworks

	A	G
1894–95	7	0
Total	7	0

PETER MORTIMER
Outside-left
Born Calton, 17 August 1875
Died 1951
Clubs Elm Park; Cowlairs; Elm Park;
Glasgow Northern; Leith Athletic;
Woolwich Arsenal; Chatham

	A	G
1894–95	22	14
1895–96	27	9
Total	49	23

WILLIAM HENRY SHARPE
Outside-left
Born Loughborough
Clubs Loughborough Town; Woolwich
Arsenal; Glossop North End

		A	G
1894–95		27	11
1895–96		10	2
1896–97		26	14
	Total	63	27

		A	G
1894–95		13	4
	Total	13	4

JAMES CROZIER
Goalkeeper
Born Glasgow
Clubs Partick Thistle; Woolwich
Arsenal; Partick Thistle

		A	G
1894–95		1	0
	Total	1	0

HENRY BOYD
Centre-forward
Born Pollokshaws, 1868
Clubs Sunderland Albion; Burnley;
West Bromwich Albion; Woolwich
Arsenal; Newton Heath

		A	G
1894–95		6	9
1895–96		22	13
1896–97		12	10
	Total	40	32

PATRICK O'BRIEN
Inside-left
Born 1875
Died 1951
Clubs Elm Park; Glasgow Northern;
Woolwich Arsenal; Bristol City;
Swindon Town

ROBERT BUCHANAN
Forward
Born Johnstone, 1868
Died 1907
Clubs Johnstone; Abercom;
Sunderland Albion; Burnley;
Woolwich Arsenal; Southampton St
Mary's; Sheppey United

		A	G
1894–95		25	9
1895–96		17	7
	Total	42	16

THOMAS GEORGE MEADE
Inside-right
Born Plumstead, 14 May 1877
Clubs Woolwich Arsenal; Tottenham
Hotspur; Fulham

		A	G
1894–95		3	1
1895–96		0	0
1896–97		8	4
	Total	11	5

GEORGE REECE
Centre-forward
Born Birmingham
Clubs Soho Villa; Woolwich
Arsenal

	A	G
1894–95	1	0
Total	1	0

CHARLES BOYD HARE
Forward
Born Birmingham,
20 June 1871
Died 1934
Clubs Warwick County; Birmingham United; Aston Villa; Woolwich Arsenal; Small Heath; Watford; Fulham; Plymouth Argyle

	A	G
1894–95	6	4
1895–96	13	3
Total	19	7

THOMAS HATFIELD
Goalkeeper
Born Woolwich 1874
Clubs Woolwich Arsenal; Tottenham Hotspur; Royal Engineers

	A	G
1894–95	1	0
1895–96	1	0
Total	2	0

CAESAR AUGUSTUS LLEWELLYN JENKYNS
Centre-half
Born Builth Wells, 24 August 1866
Died 1941
Clubs Builth; Small Heath St Andrew's; Walsall Swifts; Unity Gas; Small Heath; Woolwich Arsenal; Newton Heath; Walsall; Coventry City; Saltley Wednesday

	A	G
1895–96	27	6
Total	27	6

ALLEN WARD
Centre-half
Born Parkgate, Barnsley, 1872
Clubs Barnsley St Peter's; Sheffield Wednesday; Bolton Wanderers; Woolwich Arsenal

	A	G
1895–96	7	0
Total	7	0

ROBERT GORDON
Centre-forward
Born Leith, 1 July 1870
Died 1938
Clubs Edinburgh Thistle; Leith Rangers; Heart of Midlothian; Middlesbrough Ironopolis; Heart of Midlothian; Aston Villa; Leicester Fosse; Woolwich Arsenal; Reading

	A	G
1895–96	20	6
Total	20	6

SAMUEL MILLS
Outside-right
Born Derby 1871
Clubs Alvaston; Derby Midland; Derby County; Leicester Fosse;

Loughborough Town; Woolwich
Arsenal; Heanor Town

		A	G
1895–96		24	3
	Total	24	3

FRANCIS McAVOY
Left-half/Outside-left
Born Ayr, 16 November 1875
Clubs Ayr; Woolwich Arsenal;
Brighton United; Gravesend United;
Brighton & Hove Albion; Watford;
St Mirren; Ayr

		A	G
1895–96		11	1
1896–97		18	4
1897–98		15	3
	Total	44	8

CHARLES JAMES AMBLER
Goalkeeper
Born Alverstoke, 1868
Died 1952
Clubs Bostall Rovers; Royal Arsenal;
Clapton; Dartford; Luton Town;
Tottenham Hotspur; Woolwich
Arsenal; Tottenham Hotspur;
Gravesend United; New Brompton;
West Ham United; Millwall Athletic

		A	G
1895–96		1	0
	Total	1	0

WILLIAM GILMER
Goalkeeper

Born London
Clubs Royal Ordnance;
Woolwich Arsenal

		A	G
1895–96		3	0
	Total	3	0

WILLIAM OLIVER FAIRCLOUGH
Goalkeeper
Born London 1872
Died 1911
Clubs 1st Scots Guards; Woolwich
Arsenal; New Brompton

		A	G
1895–96		9	0
1896–97		17	0
	Total	26	0

ADAM HAYWOOD
Inside-forward
Born Hominglow, 23 March 1875
Died 1932
Clubs Burton Ivanhoe; Burton
Wanderers; Swadlincote; Woolwich
Arsenal; Queen's Park Rangers;
New Brompton; Wolverhampton
Wanderers; West Bromwich Albion;
Blackpool; Crystal Palace

		A	G
1895–96		9	4
1896–97		26	11
1897–98		26	4
1898–99		23	12
	Total	84	31

FINLAY SINCLAIR
Left-back
Born Glasgow, 18 June 1871
Clubs Clutha Swifts; Elderslie;
Linthouse; Rangers; Woolwich
Arsenal; Bristol City

	A	G
1896–97	26	0
Total	26	0

'PA' BOYLAN
Centre-half
Born Greenock 1876
Clubs Greenock Volunteers;
Woolwich Arsenal; Greenock Morton

	A	G
1896–97	11	0
Total	11	0

JAMES BROCK
Outside-right
Born Glasgow, 12 January 1878
Clubs East Stirlingshire, Woolwich
Arsenal; Cowes; Clyde; Paisley
Abercom

	A	G
1896–97	29	11
1897–98	25	9
1898–99	3	0
Total	57	20

GEORGE A FARMER
Inside-right
Born Derby, 25 November 1874
Clubs Derby Swifts; Derby Bedford

Rangers; Belper Town; Woolwich
Arsenal

	A	G
1896–97	1	0
Total	1	0

JOHN LEATHER
Goalkeeper
Born Macclesfield,1875
Clubs Macclesfield Swifts;
Macclesfield; Woolwich Arsenal;
Queen's Park Rangers

	A	G
1896–97	8	0
Total	8	0

THOMAS P SHREWSBURY
Right-half/Centre-half
Born Blackburn
Clubs Darwen; Woolwich Arsenal

	A	G
1896–97	2	0
1897–98	1	0
Total	3	0

JOHN (JOCK) RUSSELL
Outside-left
Born Carstairs, 29 December 1872
Died August 1905
Clubs Wishaw Thistle; Leith Athletic;
St Mirren; Woolwich Arsenal; Bristol
City; Blackburn Rovers; Brighton &
Hove Albion; Port Glasgow Athletic;
Motherwell; Doncaster Rovers

		A	G
1896–97		23	4
	Total	23	4

GEORGE BUIST
Right-back
Born Glasgow
Clubs Greenock Morton; Woolwich Arsenal

		A	G
1896–97		6	0
	Total	6	0

ALEXANDER McFARLANE
Outside-left
Born Airdrie, 1877
Clubs Airdrieonians; Woolwich Arsenal

		A	G
1896–97		5	0
	Total	5	0

ARTHUR TALBOT
Goalkeeper
Born Staffordshire
Clubs Hednesford Town; Woolwich Arsenal

		A	G
1896–97		5	0
	Total	5	0

GEORGE CARVER
Left-back
Born London
Clubs Woolwich Arsenal

		A	G
1896–97		1	0
	Total	1	0

JOB WHITFIELD
Right-back
Born 1875
Clubs Houghton-le-Ware; Woolwich Arsenal

		A	G
1896–97		2	0
	Total	2	0

JOHN WILLIAM ANDERSON
Left-half/Centre-half
Born 1878
Clubs Crook Town; Woolwich Arsenal; Portsmouth

		A	G
1896–97		12	0
1897–98		21	1
1898–99		21	2
1899–1900		22	3
1900–01		32	2
1901–02		28	2
1902–03		8	0
	Total	144	10

ALEXANDER S CAIE
Centre-forward
Born Aberdeen, 1878
Died December, 1914
Clubs Victoria United; Woolwich Arsenal; Bristol City; Millwall Athletic; Newcastle United;

Brentford; Motherwell; Westmount
(Canada); Sons of Scotland (Canada)

	A	G
1896–97	8	4
Total	8	4

HUGH CASSIDY
Right-back
Born 1877
Clubs Army; Woolwich
Arsenal

	A	G
1896–97	1	0
Total	1	0

EDWARD T KANE
Centre-half
Born Glasgow
Clubs Gordon Highlanders;
Woolwich Arsenal

	A	G
1896–97	1	0
Total	1	0

ROGER ORD
Goalkeeper
Born Northumberland, 1871
Clubs Hebburn Argyle;
Middlesbrough Ironopolis; Hebburn
Argyle; Woolwich Arsenal; Luton
Town; Wellingborough

	A	G
1897–98	30	0
1898–99	33	0

1899–1900	26	0
Total	89	0

JAMES McAULEY
Right-back
Born Glasgow
Clubs Greenock Morton; Woolwich
Arsenal

	A	G
1897–98	23	1
Total	23	1

PATRICK (PADDY) FARRELL
Centre-half
Born Belfast, 3 April 1872
Died 1950
Clubs Belfast Celtic; Distillery;
Celtic; Woolwich Arsenal; Brighton
United; Distillery; Brighton & Hove
Albion

	A	G
1897–98	19	2
Total	19	2

FERGUS HUNT
Forward
Born 1876
Clubs Mexborough; Middlesbrough
Ironopolis; Darwen; Woolwich
Arsenal; West Ham United;
Woolwich Arsenal; Fulham; Burton
United

	A	G
1897–98	22	12
1898–99	31	15

1899–1900	16	2
1902–03	3	1
Total	72	30

ANDREW STEVEN
Inside-right
Born Glasgow
Clubs Bathgate; Woolwich Arsenal; Dartford

	A	G
1897–98	5	1
Total	5	1

CRAIG ARCHIBALD McGEOCH
Centre-forward
Born Edinburgh
Clubs Dunblane; Woolwich Arsenal; Dundee

	A	G
1897–98	9	8
1898–99	26	5
Total	35	13

WILLIAM WHITE
Inside-right/Outside-right
Born Edinburgh, 1874
Clubs Heart of Midlothian; Woolwich Arsenal; New Brompton; Queen's Park Rangers; Liverpool

	A	G
1897–98	23	6
1898–99	16	10
Total	39	16

JAMES MONTIETH
Outside-left
Born Glasgow
Clubs Celtic; Woolwich Arsenal; Belfast Distillery

	A	G
1897–98	6	1
Total	6	1

JAMES STUART
Centre-forward
Born Coatbridge
Clubs Albion Rovers; Blackburn Rovers;Rossendale; Blackburn Rovers; Woolwich Arsenal; Northfleet; New Brompton

	A	G
1897–98	2	1
Total	2	1

DAVID HANNAH
Forward
Born Raffrey, 28 April 1867
Clubs Renton; Sunderland; Liverpool; Dundee; Woolwich Arsenal

	A	G
1897–98	20	12
1898–99	26	5
Total	46	17

ALEXANDER McCONNELL
Full-back
Born Glenbuck, 1875
Clubs Glenbuck Athletic; Everton; Woolwich Arsenal;

Queen's Park Rangers;
Grimsby Town

	A	G
1897–98	17	0
1898–99	20	1
Total	37	1

HUGH DUFF
Outside-left
Born London
Clubs Millwall Athletic; Woolwich
Arsenal; Millwall Athletic; Woolwich
Arsenal

	A	G
1897–98	1	1
Total	1	1

JAMES DEVLIN
Centre-forward
Born Bellshill, 10 January 1904
Clubs Dundee; Airdrieonians;
Hereford Thistle; Tottenham
Hotspur; Millwall Athletic;
Sunderland; Woolwich Arsenal;
Airdrieonians

	A	G
1897–98	1	1
Total	1	1

JAMES M CLARK
Centre-half/Left-half
Born 1876
Clubs Bostall Rovers; Woolwich
Arsenal

	A	G
1897–98	3	0
1898–99	1	0
Total	4	0

JAMES FYFE
Right-back
Born Scotland
Clubs Alloa Athletic; Woolwich
Arsenal

	A	G
1898–99	7	0
Total	7	0

JOHN DICK
Right-half/Centre-half
Born Eaglesham, 1876
Clubs Airdrieonians; Woolwich
Arsenal

	A	G
1898–99	30	0
1899–1900	33	6
1900–01	33	1
1901–02	28	3
1902–03	26	1
1903–04	33	1
1904–05	33	0
1905–06	16	0
1906–07	1	0
1907–08	17	0
1908–09	5	0
1909–10	7	0
Total	262	12

ANDREW MITCHELL
Outside-left

Born Scotland, 1879
Clubs Albion Rovers; Woolwich
Arsenal

	A	G
1898–99	10	2
Total	10	2

JAMES GLEGG MOIR
Right-half
Born Inverbervie, 7 January 1874
Died 1953
Clubs Gowan Athletic; Sunderland;
Woolwich Arsenal; Gravesend
United; Fulham

	A	G
1898–99	29	0
1899–1900	12	0
Total	41	0

HUGH (JOCK) DAILLY
Outside-left
Born Scotland, 1879
Clubs Dundee North End; Woolwich
Arsenal; Dundee Wanderers;
Wolverhampton Wanderers; Walsall

	A	G
1898–99	8	4
Total	8	4

JOHN McPHEE
Right-back
Born Glasgow, 1877
Clubs Glasgow; Perth; Woolwich
Arsenal

	A	G
1898–99	7	0
Total	7	0

ERNEST HERBERT COTTRELL
Inside-right
Born Nottingham, 31 January 1877
Died 12 January 1929
Clubs Nottingham Forest; Sheppey
United; Stockport County;
Woolwich Arsenal; Watford;
Fulham; Stockport County

	A	G
1898–99	18	9
1899–1900	1	2
1900–01	5	1
Total	24	12

JOHN S McAVOY
Full-back
Born Glasgow, 1878
Clubs Celtic; Airdrieonians;
Woolwich Arsenal;
Grimsby Town

	A	G
1898–99	25	0
Total	25	0

THOMAS S HAMILTON
Goalkeeper
Born 1877
Clubs Stockton; Woolwich Arsenal;
Gravesend United

	A	G
1898–99	1	0

| 1899–1900 | 6 | 0 |
| Total | 7 | 0 |

HERBERT SHAW
Outside-left
Born 1876
Clubs Haverton Hill; Woolwich
Arsenal

	A	G
1898–99	16	7
1899–1900	10	2
Total	26	9

JOHN GARTON
Right-back
Born Castle Donington, 1879
Clubs Woolwich Arsenal

	A	G
1898–99	5	0
Total	5	0

DUNCAN McNICHOL
Right-back
Born Alexandria 1876
Clubs St Bernard's; Woolwich
Arsenal; Aberdeen

	A	G
1899–1900	30	1
1900–01	30	0
1901–02	20	0
1902–03	21	0
Total	101	1

JAMES JACKSON
Left-back

Born Cambuslang, 15 September 1875
Clubs Hamilton Academical;
Elmstown Rosebuds; Newton
Thistle; Cambuslang; Rangers;
Newcastle United; Woolwich
Arsenal; Leyton; West Ham United;
Rangers; Greenock Morton

	A	G
1899–1900	28	0
1900–01	32	0
1901–02	33	0
1902–03	28	0
1903–04	33	0
1904–05	29	0
Total	183	0

JOSEPH 'JUDGE' MURPHY
Right-half
Born Stockton, 1873
Clubs Hibernian; Stoke; Woolwich
Arsenal; Raith Rovers

	A	G
1899–1900	27	0
Total	27	0

MOSES SANDERS
Centre-half/Left-half
Born Preston, 26 September 1873
Died 29 April 1941
Clubs Crewe Alexandra; Accrington;
Preston North End; Woolwich
Arsenal; Dartford

	A	G
1899–1900	4	1
Total	4	1

RICHARD HANNIGAN

Outside-right
Born Glasgow
Clubs Greenock Morton; Notts
County; Woolwich Arsenal; Burnley

	A	G
1899–1900	1	0
Total	1	0

ANDREW McCOWIE

Inside-forward/Outside-right
Born Glasgow
Clubs Liverpool; Woolwich Arsenal;
Middlesbrough; Chesterfield

	A	G
1899–1900	25	7
1900–01	3	0
Total	28	7

PETER LOGAN

Forward
Born Glasgow
Clubs Motherwell; Notts County;
Woolwich Arsenal; Reading;
Woolwich Arsenal; Brentford

	A	G
1899–1900	23	6
1900–01	0	0
1901–02	5	1
Total	28	7

JAMES ASTON

Inside-forward
Born Walsall, 1877
Died 1934

Clubs Walsall White Star; Fulbrook
Saints; Willenhall; Pickwick;
Bloxwich Strollers; Wednesfield;
Walsall; Woolwich Arsenal; Small
Heath; Doncaster Rovers; Walsall;
Bilston United; Walsall; Blakenhall
St Luke's; Walsall Wood

	A	G
1899–1900	11	3
Total	11	3

JAMES TENNANT

Outside-left
Born Parkhead, 1878
Clubs Linton Villa; Parkhead; St
Bernard's; Woolwich Arsenal;
Middlesbrough; Watford;
Stenhousemuir

	A	G
1899–1900	26	6
1900–01	25	2
Total	51	8

ABRAHAM HARTLEY

Centre-forward/Outside-left
Born Dumbarton, 8 February 1872
Died 9 October 1909
Clubs Artizan Thistle; Dumbarton;
Everton; Liverpool; Southampton;
Woolwich Arsenal; Burnley

	A	G
1899–1900	5	1
Total	5	1

JOHN GRAHAM
Right-back
Born Derby, 1873
Clubs Cray Wanderers; Millwall
Athletic; Woolwich Arsenal; Millwall
Athletic; Woolwich Arsenal;
Brentford; Fulham

	A	G
1899–1900	1	0
Total	1	0

RALPH GAUDIE
Centre-forward/Outside-right
Born Guisborough
Clubs South Bank; Sheffield
United; Woolwich Arsenal;
Manchester United

	A	G
1899–1900	25	15
1900–01	22	8
Total	47	23

CHARLES RICHARD DUNSBEE
Left-half
Born Worcester
Clubs Kidderminster Harriers;
Woolwich Arsenal

	A	G
1899–1900	8	0
Total	8	0

FRANK LLOYD
Outside-right
Born London, September 1876
Died 1945

Clubs Finsbury Park; Wednesbury
Old Athletic; Woolwich Arsenal;
Aston Villa; Dundee

	A	G
1899–1900	18	3
Total	18	3

ALEXANDER 'SANDY' MAIN
Inside-forward/Centre-half
Born Edinburgh
Clubs West Calder; Hibernian;
Woolwich Arsenal; Motherwell;
Watford

	A	G
1899–1900	8	3
1900–01	20	6
1901–02	28	5
1902–03	7	0
Total	63	14

HARRY ROBERT 'JOE' MURRELL
Left-back
Born Hounslow, 19 November 1879
Died 15 August 1952
Clubs Plumstead Albion; Middlesex
Regiment; Woolwich Arsenal;
Clapton Orient

	A	G
1899–1900	6	0
Total	6	0

THOMAS ASHLEY SPICER
Goalkeeper
Born 1877
Clubs Sheppey United; Brighton

United; Woolwich Arsenal; Leyton;
Brentford

	A	G
1899–1900	2	0
1900–01	2	0
Total	4	0

WALTER PLACE jnr
Outside-left/Left-half
Born Burnley
Clubs Blue Star; Union Stars;
Burnley; Woolwich Arsenal;
Padiham

	A	G
1900–01	25	5
1901–02	17	1
Total	42	6

THOMAS POLLOCK
Outside-right
Born Cambuslang, 3 October 1874
Clubs Celtic; Rangers; Dundee;
Woolwich Arsenal

	A	G
1900–01	24	1
Total	24	1

JOHN BLACKWOOD
Centre-forward
Born Glasgow, 1877
Clubs Partick Thistle; Celtic;
Woolwich Arsenal; Reading;
Queen's Park Rangers; West
Ham United

	A	G
1900–01	17	6
Total	17	6

PETER J TURNER
Inside-left
Born Glasgow
Clubs Parkhead; St Bernard's;
Woolwich Arsenal;
Middlesbrough; Luton Town;
Watford; Leyton

	A	G
1900–01	33	5
Total	33	5

JAMES ASHCROFT
Goalkeeper
Born Liverpool, 12 September 1878
Died 9 April 1943
Clubs Wilbyn's United; Anfield
Recreation Club; Gartson
Copperworks; Everton;
Gravesend United; Woolwich
Arsenal; Blackburn Rovers;
Tranmere Rovers

	A	G
1900–01	32	0
1901–02	34	0
1902–03	34	0
1903–04	34	0
1904–05	33	0
1905–06	35	0
1906–07	35	0
1907–08	36	0
Total	273	0

THOMAS GRIEVE
Outside-right
Born Gravesend
Clubs Northfleet; New Brompton;
Gravesend United; Woolwich
Arsenal; Brentford; Watford;
Brighton & Hove Albion

	A	G
1900–01	6	0
Total	6	0

FREDERICK GORDON COLES
Right-half/Centre-half
Born Nottingham, 1875
Died 22 April 1947
Clubs Nottingham Post Office;
Notts County; Nottingham
Forest; Woolwich Arsenal;
Grimsby Town

	A	G
1900–01	27	2
1901–02	32	0
1902–03	18	0
1903–04	1	0
Total	78	2

ARTHUR GEORGE CROSS
Full-back
Born Dartford, 1880
Clubs Dartford; New Brompton;
Woolwich Arsenal; Dartford

	A	G
1900–01	3	0
1901–02	15	0
1902–03	14	0

1903–04	25	0
1904–05	12	0
1905–06	15	0
1906–07	16	0
1907–08	11	0
1908–09	12	0
1909–10	9	0
Total	132	0

GEORGE WOLFE
Centre-half
Born East London
Clubs Northfleet; Folkestone;
Woolwich Arsenal; Swindon Town;
Nottingham Forest

	A	G
1900–01	3	0
1901–02	0	0
1902–03	2	0
Total	5	0

THOMAS BRIERCLIFFE
Outside-right
Born Chorley
Clubs St Luke's Wheelton; Clitheroe;
Blackburn Rovers; Stalybridge
Rovers; Woolwich Arsenal;
Plymouth Argyle; Brentford;
Darwen

	A	G
1901–02	34	11
1902–03	33	8
1903–04	27	10
1904–05	28	4
Total	12	33

ANDREW SWANN
Centre-forward
Born Dalbeattie, 1878
Clubs Dalbeattie; Lincoln City; New
Brompton; Barnsley; Woolwich
Arsenal; Gainsborough Trinity;
Stockport County; Mexborough
United; Tottenham Hotspur

	A	G
1901–02	7	2
Total	7	2

ABRAHAM FOXALL
Outside-left
Born Sheffield, 1874
Clubs Gainsborough Trinity;
Liverpool; Queen's Park Rangers;
Woolwich Arsenal; Gainsborough
Trinity

	A	G
1901–02	31	3
Total	31	3

JAMES A LAIDLAW
Outside-right/Inside-right
Born Glasgow, 1877
Clubs Burnley; Leith Athletic;
Newcastle United; Woolwich Arsenal

	A	G
1901–02	3	2
Total	3	2

JOHN EDGAR
Inside-right
Born Glasgow

Clubs Parkhead; Woolwich Arsenal;
Aberdeen

	A	G
1901–02	10	1
Total	10	1

ISAAC OWENS
Inside-left/Centre-forward
Born Darlington, 1881
Clubs Darlington; Bishop Auckland;
Crook Town; Woolwich Arsenal;
Plymouth Argyle; Bristol
Rovers; Crystal Palace; Grimsby
Town; Darlington

	A	G
1901–02	9	2
Total	9	2

WILLIAM HENRY GOOING
Centre-forward
Born Penistone, 1874
Died 1969
Clubs Wath; Sheffield Wednesday;
Wath; Chesterfield; Woolwich
Arsenal; Northampton Town

	A	G
1901–02	24	9
1902–03	25	16
1903–04	34	19
1904–05	11	1
Total	94	45

WALTER ANDERSON
Centre-forward/Inside-left
Born 1879

Died March 1904
Clubs Darlington; Thornaby United;
Sheffield United; Woolwich Arsenal;
Plymouth Argyle

		A	G
1901–02		13	5
1902–03		15	5
	Total	**28**	**10**

THOMAS TINDAL FITCHIE
Inside-forward
Born Edinburgh, 11 December 1881
Died 17 October 1947
Clubs West Norwood; Woolwich
Arsenal; Tottenham Hotspur;
Woolwich Arsenal; London
Caledonians; Woolwich Arsenal;
Queen's Park; Fulham; London
Caledonians; Woolwich Arsenal;
Queen's Park; Norwich City; Queen's
Park; Brighton & Hove Albion;
Woolwich Arsenal; Glossop; Fulham

		A	G
1901–02		3	3
1902–03		1	0
1903–04		0	0
1904–05		9	6
1905–06		22	9
1906–07		0	0
1907–08		0	0
1908–09		21	9
	Total	**56**	**27**

RODERICK JOHN McEACHRANE
Left-half
Born Inverness, 1878

Died 16 November 1952
Clubs Inverness Thistle; Thames
Ironworks; Woolwich Arsenal

		A	G
1902–03		28	0
1903–04		33	0
1904–05		24	0
1905–06		31	0
1906–07		34	0
1907–08		38	0
1908–09		36	0
1909–10		32	0
1910–11		30	0
1911–12		18	0
1912–13		7	0
1913–14		2	0
	Total	**313**	**0**

MAURICE JOSEPH CONNOR
Inside-right
Born Lochee, 14 July 1880
Died August 1934
Clubs Dundee Fereday; Glentoran;
Gordon Highlanders; West
Bromwich Albion; Walsall; Bristol
City; Woolwich Arsenal; Brentford;
New Brompton; Fulham; Blackpool;
Glentoran; Treharris

		A	G
1902–03		14	2
	Total	**14**	**2**

JOHN GEORGE 'TIM' COLEMAN
Inside-forward
Born Kettering, 26 October 1881
Died 20 November 1940

Clubs Kettering Town; Northampton Town; Woolwich Arsenal; Everton; Sunderland; Fulham; Nottingham Forest; Tunbridge Wells Rangers

		A	G
1902–03	30	17	
1903–04	28	23	
1904–05	26	5	
1905–06	28	12	
1906–07	34	14	
1907–08	26	8	
	Total	172	79

EVERARD THOMAS LAWRENCE
Outside-left
Born 1880
Clubs Wellingborough; Northampton Town; Kettering Town; Northampton Town; Woolwich Arsenal; Fulham; Glossop

		A	G
1902–03		20	3
	Total	20	3

WILLIAM BRADSHAW
Outside-right
Born Padiham, 1885
Clubs Woolwich Arsenal; Fulham; Burton United; Burnley; Fulham; Ton Pentre

		A	G
1902–03		1	1
1903–04		3	1
	Total	4	2

W STEPHEN THEOBALD
Centre-half
Born Plumstead
Clubs St Andrew's (Woolwich); Woolwich Polytechnic; Woolwich Arsenal

		A	G
1902–03		2	0
1903–04		0	0
1904–05		0	0
1905–06		14	0
1906–07		2	0
1907–08		3	0
1908–09		3	0
	Total	24	0

WILLIAM LINWARD
Outside-left
Born Hull, 1877
Clubs Grimsby Town; Doncaster Rovers; West Ham United; Woolwich Arsenal; Norwich City; Kilmarnock; Maidstone United

		A	G
1902–03		14	5
1903–04		27	5
1904–05		6	0
	Total	47	10

WILLIAM BANNISTER
Centre-half
Born Burnley, 1879
Died 26 March 1942
Clubs Earley; Burnley; Bolton Wanderers; Woolwich Arsenal;

Leicester Fosse; Burnley;
Leicester Imperial

	A	G
1902–03	16	0
1903–04	2	0
Total	**18**	**0**

THOMAS SHANKS
Inside-forward
Born Wexford, 1880
Clubs Wexford; Derby West
End; Derby County; Brentford;
Woolwich Arsenal; Brentford;
Leicester Fosse; Leyton; Clapton
Orient; York City

	A	G
1902–03	14	4
1903–04	30	24
Total	**44**	**28**

HAROLD CHEETHAM THORPE
Full-back
Born Barrow Hill, 1880
Died 9 September 1908
Clubs Poolsbrook United;
Chesterfield; Woolwich Arsenal;
Fulham; Leicester Fosse

	A	G
1903–04	10	0
Total	**10**	**0**

PERCY ROBERT SANDS
Centre-half
Born Norwood, 1881
Died December 1965

Clubs Cheltenham Town; Woolwich
Arsenal; Southend United

	A	G
1903–04	32	3
1904–05	31	0
1905–06	26	0
1906–07	24	3
1907–08	34	2
1908–09	32	1
1909–10	12	0
1910–11	31	0
1911–12	34	0
1912–13	28	1
1913–14	33	0
1914–15	10	0
Total	**327**	**10**

THOMAS PEET PRATT
Forward
Born Fleetwood, 28 August 1873
Died August 1935
Clubs Fleetwood Rangers; Grimsby
Town; Preston North End; Tottenham
Hotspur; Preston North End;
Fleetwood; Woolwich Arsenal;
Fulham; Blackpool

	A	G
1903–04	8	2
Total	**8**	**2**

WALTER BUSBY
Outside-left
Born Wellingborough, 1882
Clubs Wellingborough; Queen's
Park Rangers; Woolwich
Arsenal; Leyton

		A	G
1903–04		5	2
	Total	5	2

FRANK RANSOM
Left-half
Born Ireland
Clubs Woolwich Arsenal; Southern
United; Crystal Palace

		A	G
1903–04		1	0
	Total	1	0

EDWARD T ANDERSON
Outside-left/Centre-forward
Born Glasgow, 1881
Clubs St Mirren; Woolwich Arsenal;
Fulham; Willington; Sheffield United;
Queen's Park Rangers

		A	G
1903–04		2	0
	Total	2	0

ROBERT WATSON
Inside-right/Centre-forward
Born Middlesbrough, 1883
Clubs South Bank; Middlesbrough;
Woolwich Arsenal; Leeds
City; Rochdale; Exeter City;
Stalybridge Celtic

		A	G
1903–04		6	1
1904–05		3	0
	Total	9	1

ARCHIBALD GRAY
Full-back
Born Govan, 1883
Clubs Glasgow Ashfield; Hibernian;
Woolwich Arsenal; Fulham

		A	G
1904–05		26	0
1905–06		28	0
1906–07		23	0
1907–08		30	0
1908–09		33	0
1909–10		13	0
1910–11		26	0
1911–12		5	0
	Total	184	0

JAMES BUCHAN
Wing-half
Born Perth
Clubs Hibernian; Woolwich Arsenal;
Manchester City; Motherwell

		A	G
1904–05		8	0
	Total	8	0

JAMES HENRY BIGDEN
Wing-half
Born London, 1880
Clubs Gravesend United; West Ham
United; Woolwich Arsenal; Bury;
Southend United

	A	G
1904–05	7	0
1905–06	25	0
1906–07	37	1

1907–08	6	0
Total	75	1

JOHN 'SAILOR' HUNTER

Inside-left/Centre-forward
Born Johnstone, 6 April 1878
Died 12 January 1966
Clubs Westmarch; Abercom;
Liverpool; Heart of Midlothian;
Woolwich Arsenal; Portsmouth;
Dundee; Clyde; Motherwell

	A	G
1904–05	22	4
Total	22	4

CHARLES OLIVER SATTERTHWAITE

Inside-left/Outside-left
Born Cockermouth, 1877
Died 5 May 1948
Clubs Black Diamonds; Bury; Burton
Swifts; Liverpool; New Brompton;
West Ham United; Woolwich Arsenal

	A	G
1904–05	30	11
1905–06	18	10
1906–07	38	17
1907–08	21	3
1908–09	18	4
1909–10	4	0
Total	129	45

ALEXANDER DAVIDSON

Goalkeeper
Born Strathclyde
Clubs Woolwich Arsenal

	A	G
1904–05	1	0
Total	1	0

ALFRED 'HAPPY' CROWE

Centre-forward
Born London
Clubs North Woolwich Invicta;
Woolwich Arsenal

	A	G
1904–05	4	3
1905–06	2	1
Total	6	4

DAVID NEAVE

Outside-left
Born Arbroath, 1883
Clubs Forfar; Montrose; Arbroath;
Woolwich Arsenal; Leyton;
Woolwich Arsenal; Merthyr Town

	A	G
1904–05	3	0
1905–06	18	6
1906–07	33	4
1907–08	35	7
1908–09	25	5
1909–10	21	5
1910–11	15	3
1911–12	4	0
Total	154	30

ROBERT BRYSON TEMPLETON

Winger
Born Coylton, 22 June 1879
Died 2 November 1919
Clubs Neilston Victoria; Kilmarnock;

Hibernian; Aston Villa; Newcastle
United; Woolwich Arsenal; Celtic;
Kilmarnock; Fulham; Kilmarnock

	A	G
1904–05	16	1
1905–06	17	0
Total	33	1

FREDERICK DWIGHT
Left-back
Born London
Clubs Fulham; Woolwich Arsenal;
Nelson

	A	G
1904–05	1	0
Total	1	0

ANDREW DUCAT
Right-half/ Centre-forward
Born Brixton, 16 February 1886
Died 23 July 1942
Clubs Westcliff Athletic; Southend
Athletic; Woolwich Arsenal; Aston
Villa; Fulham; Casuals

	A	G
1904–05	10	1
1905–06	15	4
1906–07	4	1
1907–08	18	1
1908–09	33	1
1909–10	29	3
1910–11	33	3
1911–12	33	5
Total	175	19

JAMES T BELLAMY
Right-half/Outside-right
Born Barking, October 1881
Clubs Barking; Grays United;
Reading; Woolwich Arsenal;
Dundee; Portsmouth; Norwich City;
Dundee; Motherwell; Burnley;
Fulham; Southend United

	A	G
1904–05	1	0
1905–06	17	3
1906–07	11	1
Total	29	4

JAMES SHARP
Left-back
Born Jordanstone, 11 October 1880
Died 18 November 1949
Clubs East Craigs; Dundee; Fulham;
Woolwich Arsenal; Rangers;
Fulham; Chelsea; Fulham

	A	G
1905–06	35	2
1906–07	36	1
1907–08	32	1
Total	103	4

JAMES BLAIR
Left-half/Inside-left
Born Dumfries, 1885
Died March 1913
Clubs Dumfries Volunteer; 5th Kings
Own Highlanders; Kilmarnock;
Woolwich Arsenal; Manchester
City; Bradford City; Stockport County

		A	G
1905–06	12	3	
1906–07	1	0	
	Total	13	3

THOMAS ARNOLD
Outside-right
Born Coventry, 1879
Clubs Foleshill Great Heath;
Coventry City; Woolwich Arsenal;
Coventry City

		A	G
1905–06	2	0	
	Total	2	0

FREDERICK KEMP
Outside-left
Born Tottenham
Clubs Barking; Woolwich
Arsenal; West Ham United;
Bristol Rovers

		A	G
1905–06	2	0	
	Total	2	0

BERTRAM CLEWLEY 'BERTIE' FREEMAN
Centre-forward
Born Handsworth, 2 October 1885
Died 11 August 1955
Clubs Gower Street Old Boys;
Aston Manor; Aston Villa; Woolwich
Arsenal; Everton; Burnley; Wigan
Borough; Kettering Town;
Kidderminster Harriers

		A	G
1905–06		17	9
1906–07		12	8
1907–08		15	4
	Total	44	21

WILLIAM GARBUTT
Outside-right
Born Stockport
Clubs Royal Artillery; Reading;
Woolwich Arsenal; Blackburn
Rovers

		A	G
1905–06		19	3
1906–07		25	3
1907–08		8	2
	Total	52	8

HUGH LACHLAN McDONALD
Goalkeeper
Born Beith, 1884
Died 27 August 1920
Clubs Ayr Westerlea; Maybole; Ayr
Academical; Beith; Woolwich
Arsenal; Brighton & Hove Albion;
Oldham Athletic; Bradford Park
Avenue; Woolwich Arsenal; Fulham;
Bristol Rovers

		A	G
1905–06		2	0
1906–07		0	0
1907–08		0	0
1908–09		38	0
1909–10		36	0
	Total	76	0

EDWARD BATEUP

Goalkeeper
Born Hooley, 1886
Clubs Faversham; Woolwich
Arsenal; New Brompton; Woolwich
Arsenal; Port Vale

	A	G
1905–06	1	0
1906–07	3	0
1907–08	2	0
1908–09	0	0
1909–10	0	0
1910–11	28	0
Total	34	0

NEVILLE JOSEPH GRICE

Outside-right
Born London
Clubs Ealing; Woolwich
Arsenal

	A	G
1905–06	1	0
Total	1	0

PETER KYLE

Centre-forward/Inside-right
Born Rutherglen, September 1880
Died 1961
Clubs Glasgow Parkhead; Clyde;
West Ham United; Kettering Town;
Heart of Midlothian; Larkhall
Thistle; Tottenham Hotspur;
Woolwich Arsenal; Aston Villa;
Sheffield United; Royal Albert;
Watford

	A	G
1906–07	29	13
1907–08	23	8
Total	52	21

ARCHIBALD B LOW

Left-half
Born Glasgow
Clubs Glasgow Ashfield; Woolwich
Arsenal; Partick Thistle

	A	G
1906–07	3	0
Total	3	0

THOMAS HYNDS

Centre-half
Born Hurlford, 1880
Clubs Hurlford Thistle; Celtic; Bolton
Wanderers; Clyde; Manchester City;
Woolwich Arsenal; Leeds City;
Heart of Midlothian; Ladysmith
(Canada); Musselburgh

	A	G
1906–07	13	0
Total	13	0

JAMES FERGUSON

Outside-left
Born Glasgow
Clubs Cambuslang Hibernian;
Woolwich Arsenal

	A	G
1906–07	1	0
Total	1	0

JOHN 'JACKIE' MORDUE

Winger
Born Edmondsley, 13 December 1886
Died 1957
Clubs Sacriston; Spennymoor
United; Barnsley; Woolwich
Arsenal; Sunderland;
Middlesbrough; Durham
City; Pyhope

	A	G
1906–07	3	0
1907–08	23	1
Total	**26**	**1**

HAROLD GODFREY LEE

Forward
Born Erith, 1886
Clubs Erith Albion; Erith Town; Cray
Wanderers; Sittingbourne;
Woolwich Arsenal; Bury; Dartford

	A	G
1907–08	18	5
1908–09	17	8
1909–10	6	2
Total	**41**	**15**

JOSEPH EBENEZER SHAW

Full-back
Born Bury, 1882
Died September, 1963
Clubs Bury Athenaeum; Accrington
Stanley; Woolwich Arsenal

	A	G
1907–08	2	0
1908–09	28	0

	A	G
1909–10	29	0
1910–11	35	0
1911–12	36	0
1912–13	38	0
1913–14	36	0
1914–15	38	0
1919–20	33	0
1920–21	28	0
1921–22	6	0
Total	**309**	**0**

CHARLES HENRY LEWIS

Forward
Born Plumstead, 1886
Died 1967
Clubs East Wickham; Eltham;
Maidstone United; Woolwich
Arsenal; Margate

	A	G
1907–08	13	8
1908–09	23	6
1909–10	28	3
1910–11	34	2
1911–12	29	3
1912–13	24	3
1913–14	26	0
1914–15	24	4
1919–20	5	1
Total	**206**	**30**

JAMES RODGER

Outside-left
Born Glasgow
Clubs Paisley St Mirren; Renton;
Woolwich Arsenal

	A	G
1907–08	1	0
Total	1	0

JOSEPH NORMAN SATTERTHWAITE
Inside-left
Born Cockermouth, 1885
Clubs Workington; Woolwich Arsenal; Grimsby Town; New Brompton; Mexborough

	A	G
1907–08	5	1
Total	5	1

GORDON RAHERE HOARE
Forward
Born Blackheath, 19 April 1884
Died 27 October 1973
Clubs West Norwood; Woolwich Polytechnic; Burnley; Woolwich Arsenal; Glossop; Woolwich Arsenal; Glossop; West Norwood; Burnley; Queen's Park; Arsenal; Northfleet; Fulham

	A	G
1907–08	1	0
1908–09	11	5
1909–10	1	0
1910–11	14	6
1911–12	3	1
Total	30	12

JAMES M MAXWELL
Outside-right
Born New Cumnock, 1882

Clubs Kilmarnock Shawbank; Petershill Juniors; Kilmarnock; Sheffield Wednesday; Woolwich Arsenal; Hurlford; Galston; Carlisle United; Lanemark; Kilmarnock; Nithsdale Wanderers

	A	G
1908–09	2	0
Total	2	0

SAMUEL F RAYBOULD
Centre-forward/Outside-right
Born Chesterfield, 1875
Clubs Ilkeston Town; Chesterfield Town; Derby County; Ilkeston Town; Poolsbrook United; Ilkeston Town; Bolsover Colliery; New Brighton Tower; Liverpool; Sunderland; Woolwich Arsenal; Chesterfield

	A	G
1908–09	26	6
Total	26	6

DAVID GREENAWAY
Outside-right
Born Coatdyke, 1889
Clubs Shettleston; Woolwich Arsenal

	A	G
1908–09	36	3
1909–10	36	5
1910–11	22	2
1911–12	23	2
1912–13	27	1
1913–14	8	0

	1914–15	6	0
	1919–20	3	0
	Total	**161**	**13**

WILLIAM CURLE
Centre-forward
Born Glasgow, 1886
Clubs Rutherglen Glencairn;
Woolwich Arsenal

	A	G
1908–09	3	0
Total	**3**	**0**

NORMAN W CHISHOLM
Right-back
Born Arbroath
Clubs Woolwich Arsenal

	A	G
1908–09	3	0
Total	**3**	**0**

ANGUS McKINNON
Left-half
Born Paisley, 6 December 1885
Died 1968
Clubs Petershill; Heart of
Midlothian; Carlisle United;
Woolwich Arsenal; Charlton
Athletic; Wigan Borough

	A	G
1908–09	2	0
1909–10	8	0
1910–11	10	0
1911–12	22	0
1912–13	29	0

1913–14	24	0
1914–15	21	2
1919–20	41	0
1920–21	37	2
1921–22	17	0
Total	**211**	**4**

ALBERT BENEY
Forward
Born Hastings, 1887
Clubs Hastings & St Leonard's;
Woolwich Arsenal; Carlisle
United; Bury

	A	G
1908–09	8	3
1909–10	8	3
Total	**16**	**6**

MATTHEW THOMSON
Right-half; Centre-half
Born Maryhill, 1887
Clubs Maryhill; Woolwich Arsenal;
Swindon Town

	A	G
1908–09	3	0
1909–10	30	1
1910–11	17	0
1911–12	7	0
1912–13	25	0
1913–14	7	0
Total	**89**	**1**

THOMAS DRAIN
Forward
Born Pollokshaws, 1880
Clubs Drongan Juniors; Celtic; Ayr

United; Maybole; Bradford City;
Leeds City; Kilmarnock; Aberdeen;
Carlisle United; Exeter City;
Woolwich Arsenal; Nithsdale
Wanderers; Glaston

	A	G
1909–10	2	0
Total	2	0

FRANK HEPPINSTALL
Outside-left/Inside-left
Born South Hiendley, 1885
Clubs Denaby United;
Barnsley; Denaby United; Swindon
Town; Woolwich Arsenal;
Stalybridge Celtic; Hamilton
Academical

	A	G
1909–10	18	0
1910–11	5	0
Total	23	0

WALTER HENRY LAWRENCE
Inside-left
Born London
Clubs Summerstown; Crystal
Palace; Woolwich Arsenal; Crystal
Palace; Merthyr Town

	A	G
1909–10	25	5
Total	25	5

GEORGE FISHER
Goalkeeper
Born Lancashire

Clubs Woolwich Arsenal;
Manchester United

	A	G
1909–10	2	0
Total	2	0

SPENCER T BASSETT
Right-half
Born Blackheath
Died 9 April 1917
Clubs Maidstone United; Woolwich
Arsenal; Exeter City; Swansea Town

	A	G
1909–10	1	0
Total	1	0

HAROLD OLIVER
Centre-forward
Born Holloway
Clubs Great Eastern Rovers;
Woolwich Arsenal

	A	G
1909–10	1	0
Total	1	0

DUNCAN McDONALD
Right-back
Born Bo'ness
Clubs Bo'ness; Woolwich Arsenal;
West Hartlepool

	A	G
1909–10	25	0
1910–11	1	0
Total	26	0

ROBERT C STEVENS
Inside-right
Born Maryhill, 1886
Clubs Rangers; Woolwich Arsenal

	A	G
1909–10	7	1
Total	7	1

MATTHEW T McKELLAR
Centre-forward
Born Campsie, 1887
Clubs Campsie; Kirkintilloch Harp;
Woolwich Arsenal

	A	G
1909–10	3	1
Total	3	1

WILLIAM ELIJAH BUCKENHAM
Centre-forward
Born Woolwich, 1888
Died 1954
Clubs Plumstead Park Villa;
Plumstead Melrose; Farnham; 86th
Battallion Royal Artillery; Woolwich
Arsenal; Southampton; 12th Royal
Field Artillery

	A	G
1909–10	21	5
Total	21	5

CHARLES EDWARD McGIBBON
Centre-forward
Born Portsmouth, 1880
Died May 1954
Clubs Royal Artillery; Eltham;
Woolwich Arsenal; Leyton; New
Brompton; Crystal Palace;
Southampton; Woolwich Arsenal;
Leyton; Reading; Southampton

	A	G
1909–10	4	3
Total	4	3

ALFRED COMMON
Forward
Born Millfield, Co. Durham,
25 May 1880
Died 3 April 1946
Clubs South Hylton; Jarrow;
Sunderland; Sheffield United;
Sunderland; Middlesbrough;
Woolwich Arsenal; Preston
North End

	A	G
1910–11	29	6
1911–12	36	17
1912–13	12	0
Total	77	23

WILLIS RIPPON
Centre-forward
Born Beighton, 15 May 1886
Died 1956
Clubs Hackenthorpe; Rawmarsh
Albion; Sandhill Rovers; Kilnhurst
Town; Bristol City; Woolwich
Arsenal; Brentford; Hamilton
Academical; Grimsby Town;
Rotherham Town

	A	G
1910–11	9	2
Total	9	2

HENRY MORRISON LOGAN
Inside-right
Born Glasgow, 1888
Clubs Shettleston; Sunderland; Woolwich Arsenal

	A	G
1910–11	11	0
Total	11	0

JOHN 'JACKIE' CHALMERS
Centre-forward
Born Beith, 1886
Clubs Rutherglen Glencairn; Rangers; Stoke; Bristol Rovers; Clyde; Woolwich Arsenal; Greenock Morton

	A	G
1910–11	29	15
1911–12	19	6
Total	48	21

JAMES A QUAYLE
Left-back
Born Charlton, 1890
Clubs Fossdene Old Boys; Woolwich Arsenal; Northfleet; Woolwich Arsenal

	A	G
1910–11	1	0
Total	1	0

MATTHEW SHORTT
Inside-left
Born Dumfries, 15 February 1889
Died 1974
Clubs Dumfries; Dalbeattie Star; Woolwich Arsenal; Kilmarnock; Clydebank; Kilmarnock; Llanelly; Fall River Marksmen; Brooklyn Wanderers; Philadelphia Field Club; Boston Wonder Workers; Brooklyn Wanderers

	A	G
1910–11	4	0
Total	4	0

THOMAS 'WEE' WINSHIP
Outside-left
Born Byker, 14 July 1890
Clubs Wallsend Park Villa; Woolwich Arsenal; Fulham; Woolwich Arsenal; Darlington; Crewe Alexandra; Wallsend; Spen Black & White; Marley Hill UCG

	A	G
1910–11	6	0
1911–12	8	2
1912–13	14	1
1913–14	15	2
1914–15	12	2
Total	55	7

JOHN 'PAT' FLANAGAN
Inside-forward
Born Preston, 1891
Clubs Stourbridge; Norwich City; Fulham; Woolwich Arsenal

	A	G
1910–11	9	1
1911–12	33	7
1912–13	22	2
1913–14	24	12
1914–15	26	6
Total	114	28

GEORGE BURDETT
Goalkeeper
Born Tottenham
Clubs Fusiliers; Woolwich Arsenal

	A	G
1910–11	10	0
1911–12	18	0
Total	28	0

JOHN CHARLES PEART
Full-back
Born Tewkesbury, 1887
Clubs Woolwich Arsenal; Croydon Common; Arsenal; Margate

	A	G
1910–11	7	0
1911–12	34	0
1912–13	16	0
1919–20	5	0
1920–21	1	0
Total	63	0

LESLIE A CALDER
Centre-forward
Born Southampton
Clubs Woolwich Arsenal

	A	G
1910–11	1	0
Total	1	0

FREDERICK J CALVERT
Inside-right
Born Southend-on-Sea
Clubs Army; Woolwich Arsenal

	A	G
1910–11	1	0
1911–12	1	1
Total	2	1

GEORGE M GRANT
Right-half
Born Plumstead, 1891
Clubs Woolwich Wesley Guild; Northumberland Oddfellows; Dartford Invicta; Woolwich Arsenal; Millwall Athletic; Queen's Park Rangers; Northfleet

	A	G
1911–12	1	0
1912–13	13	2
1913–14	12	1
1914–15	28	1
Total	54	4

CHARLES EDWARD RANDALL
Inside-left
Born Burnopfield, 1882
Died 27 September 1916
Clubs Hobson Wanderers; Newcastle United; Huddersfield Town; Castleford Town; Woolwich Arsenal; North Shields

	A	G
1911–12	27	8
1912–13	15	4
1913–14	1	0
Total	43	12

LEIGH RICHMOND 'DICK' ROOSE
Goalkeeper
Born Holt, 27 November 1877
Died 1916
Clubs Druids; Aberystwyth; London Welsh; Stoke; Everton; Stoke; Sunderland; Huddersfield Town; Aston Villa; Fulham; Woolwich Arsenal; Aberystwyth Town; Llandudno Town

	A	G
1911–12	13	0
Total	13	0

JOSEPH JS McLAUGHLAN
Centre-forward
Born Edinburgh, 1891
Clubs Linlithgow; Bathgate; Woolwich Arsenal; Watford; Mansfield Town

	A	G
1911–12	3	0
1912–13	13	3
Total	16	3

HAROLD SIDNEY CRAWFORD
Goalkeeper
Born Dundee, 7 October 1887
Died 1979
Clubs Newcastle United; Hebburn

Argyle; Woolwich Arsenal; Reading; Millwall Athletic; Workington

	A	G
1911–12	7	0
1912–13	19	0
Total	26	0

JOHN W GRANT
Centre-forward
Born Southport
Clubs Southport Central; Woolwich Arsenal

	A	G
1911–12	4	3
Total	4	3

GEORGE CLARK PAYNE
Inside-left
Born Hitchin, 17 February 1887
Died 21 August 1932
Clubs Hitchin Union Jack; Hitchin Town; Barnet Alston; Tottenham Hotspur; Crystal Palace; Sunderland; Leyton; Woolwich Arsenal

	A	G
1912–13	3	0
Total	3	0

GEORGE BURRELL
Outside-left
Born Newcastle, 1892
Clubs Shildon Athletic; South Shields; Leyton; Woolwich Arsenal; South Shields

	A	G
1912–13	17	2
1913–14	6	1
Total	**23**	**3**

ERNEST HANKS
Centre-forward
Born London
Clubs Army Service Corps;
Woolwich Arsenal; Southend United

	A	G
1912–13	4	1
Total	**4**	**1**

WILLIAM ARTHUR SPITTLE
Inside-forward
Born Southfields, April 1893
Clubs Southfields Juniors;
Woolwich Arsenal; Leicester
City; Nuneaton Town; Tamworth
Castle

	A	G
1912–13	6	0
1913–14	1	0
Total	**7**	**0**

EDWARD KING
Right-half
Born Blyth, 1890
Clubs Leyton; Woolwich Arsenal;
Clapton Orient

	A	G
1912–13	11	0
Total	**11**	**0**

FREDERICK WILLIAM GROVES
Outside-right/Inside-right
Born Shadwell, 13 January 1891
Clubs Barnet Albion; Glossop;
Woolwich Arsenal; Brighton &
Hove Albion; Charlton Athletic;
Dartford

	A	G
1912–13	3	0
1913–14	3	0
1914–15	2	0
1919–20	29	5
1920–21	13	1
Total	**50**	**6**

DAVID DUNCAN
Outside-left/Centre-forward
Born County Antrim, 1891
Clubs Glasgow St Anthony's;
Bellshill Athletic; Albion Rovers;
Fulham; Woolwich Arsenal;
Albion Rovers

	A	G
1912–13	3	1
Total	**3**	**1**

JOHN ALEXANDER 'ALEX' GRAHAM
Centre-half/Wing-half
Born Hurlford, 11 July 1890
Died 1943
Clubs Hurlford; Hamilton
Academical; Larkhall United;
Woolwich Arsenal; Brentford;
Folkestone

	A	G
1912–13	12	2
1913–14	13	0
1914–15	26	0
1919–20	22	5
1920–21	30	5
1921–22	21	3
1922–23	17	1
1923–24	25	1
Total	166	17

GEORGE E FORD

Left-back
Born Woolwich, 1891
Clubs Gravesend United; Dartford;
Woolwich Arsenal

	A	G
1912–13	3	0
1913–14	0	0
1914–15	6	0
Total	9	0

ROBERT EVANS

Right-back
Born North London
Clubs Woolwich Arsenal; Clapton
Orient

	A	G
1912–13	1	0
Total	1	0

JOSEPH E FIDLER

Left-back
Born Sheffield, 1885
Clubs Sheffield United;
Fulham; Queen's Park

Rangers; Woolwich Arsenal;
Port Vale

	A	G
1912–13	13	0
1913–14	12	0
Total	25	0

STEPHEN J STONLEY

Centre-forward
Born Sunderland, 1891
Clubs Seaham; Northampton
Town; Newcastle City; Woolwich
Arsenal; Brentford

	A	G
1912–13	10	1
1913–14	28	13
Total	38	14

ARCHIBALD F DEVINE

Inside-left
Born Lochore, 2 April 1887
Died 30 September 1964
Clubs Minto Rovers; Lochgelly
Rangers; Lochgelly United;
Heart of Midlothian; Lochgelly
United; Raith Rovers; Heart of
Midlothian; Falkirk; Bradford
City; Woolwich Arsenal; Bradford
City; Dunfermline Athletic;
Lochgelly United

	A	G
1912–13	11	2
1913–14	13	3
Total	24	5

OLIVER WILSON
Goalkeeper
Born London
Clubs Leyton; Woolwich Arsenal

	A	G
1912–13	1	0
Total	**1**	**0**

JOSEPH LIEVESLEY
Goalkeeper
Born Staveley, 25 July 1883
Died 18 October 1941
Clubs Poolsbrook United; Sheffield United; Woolwich Arsenal

	A	G
1913–14	35	0
1914–15	38	0
Total	**73**	**0**

HAROLD THOMAS WILLIAM 'WALLY' HARDINGE
Inside-forward
Born Greenwich, 25 February 1886
Died 8 May 1965
Clubs Eltham; Tonbridge; Maidstone United; Newcastle United; Sheffield United; Woolwich Arsenal

	A	G
1913–14	29	4
1914–15	12	7
1919–20	13	3
Total	**54**	**14**

GEORGE JOBEY
Right-half/Centre-half
Born Heddon-on-the-Wall, July 1885
Died 9 March 1962
Clubs Morpeth Harriers; Newcastle United; Woolwich Arsenal; Bradford Park Avenue; Hamilton Academical; Leicester City; Northampton Town

	A	G
1913–14	28	3
Total	**28**	**3**

JAMES H CALDWELL
Goalkeeper
Born Carronshore, 1886
Clubs Dunipace; East Stirling; Tottenham Hotspur; Reading; Everton; Woolwich Arsenal; Reading

	A	G
1913–14	3	0
Total	**3**	**0**

JOHN 'JOCK' RUTHERFORD
Outside-right
Born Percy Main, 12 October 1884
Died 21 April 1963
Clubs Willington Athletic; Newcastle United; Woolwich Arsenal; Stoke; Arsenal; Clapton Orient; Tunbridge Wells Rangers

	A	G
1913–14	21	6
1914–15	26	3
1919–20	36	3

	A	G
1920–21	32	7
1921–22	36	1
1922–23	26	1
1923–24	22	2
1924–25	20	2
1925–26	3	0
Total	222	25

ROBERT WILLIAM BENSON
Full-back
Born Whitehaven, 9 February 1883
Died 19 February 1916
Clubs Shankhouse; Shalwell;
Newcastle United; Southampton;
Sheffield United; Woolwich Arsenal

	A	G
1913–14	25	2
1914–15	27	5
Total	52	7

DONALD SLADE
Centre-forward/Inside-right
Born Southampton,
26 November 1888
Died 1980
Clubs Southampton Ramblers;
Blackpool; Southampton; Lincoln
City; Woolwich Arsenal; Fulham;
Dundee; Ayr United

	A	G
1913–14	12	4
Total	12	4

CHARLES O BELL
Centre-forward
Born Dumfries, 1884

Clubs Carlisle United; Woolwich
Arsenal; Chesterfield; Barrow;
Queen's Park Rangers

	A	G
1913–14	1	2
Total	1	2

CHRISTOPHER SEBASTIAN BUCKLEY
Centre-half
Born Urmston, 9 September 1886
Died 1974
Clubs Victoria Park; Manchester
Ship Canal; Manchester City;
Xaverian Brothers College; West
Bromwich Albion; Brighton & Hove
Albion; Aston Villa; Arsenal

	A	G
1914–15	29	1
1919–20	23	1
1920–21	4	1
Total	56	3

HENRY EDWIN 'HARRY' KING
Centre-forward/Inside-right
Born Evesham, 1884
Clubs Evesham Star; Worcester
City; Birmingham; Crewe Alexandra;
Northampton Town; Arsenal;
Leicester City; Brentford

	A	G
1914–15	37	26
Total	37	26

FRANCIS 'FRANK' BRADSHAW
Inside-forward/Right-back
Born Sheffield, 31 May 1884
Clubs Oxford Street Sunday School;
Sheffield Wednesday; Northampton
Town; Everton; Arsenal

	A	G
1914–15	29	10
1919–20	33	2
1920–21	21	0
1921–22	32	2
1922–23	17	0
Total	132	14

JAMES NORMAN
Outside-left
Born Hackney Wick, 1893
Clubs Eton Mission; Walthamstow
Grange; Arsenal

	A	G
1914–15	4	0

WILLIAM NAISMITH 'BILLY' BLYTH
Inside-left/Left-half
Born Dalkeith, 17 June 1895
Died 1968
Clubs Wemyss Athletic; Manchester
City; Arsenal; Birmingham; Arsenal

	A	G
1914–15	12	2
1919–20	29	5
1920–21	40	7
1921–22	25	1
1922–23	31	9
1923–24	27	3
1924–25	17	1
1925–26	40	7
1926–27	33	2
1927–28	39	7
1928–29	21	1
Total	314	45

EDWARD 'NED' LIDDELL
Centre-half/Wing-half
Born Sunderland, 27 May 1878
Died November 1968
Clubs Seaham White Star;
Sunderland; Southampton;
Gainsborough Trinity; Clapton
Orient; Southend United; Arsenal;
Southend United

	A	G
1914–15	2	0
Total	2	0

ALFRED A FLETCHER
Centre-half/Right-half
Born Ripley, 6 September 1892
Died 1984
Clubs Ilkeston; Glossop; Arsenal;
Chesterfield Municipal; Heanor
Town; Chesterfield; Shirebrook;
Kettering Town

	A	G
1914–15	3	0
Total	3	0

ERNEST CLARK 'TIM' WILLIAMSON
Goalkeeper
Born Murton Colliery, 24 May 1890

Died 30 April 1964
Clubs Murton Red Star; Wingate
Albion; Croydon Common; Arsenal;
Norwich City

	A	G
1919–20	26	0
1920–21	33	0
1921–22	41	0
1922–23	5	0
Total	105	0

CLEMENT ROSS VOYSEY

Centre-half/Inside-right
Born New Cross,
January 1899
Died 1989
Clubs Royal naval Air Service;
Arsenal

	A	G
1919–20	5	0
1920–21	0	0
1921–22	1	0
1922–23	18	4
1923–24	10	2
1924–25	0	0
1925–26	1	0
Total	35	6

HENRY ALBERT 'BERT' WHITE

Inside-right/Centre-forward
Born Watford, 17 April 1892
Died 27 November 1972
Clubs Brentford; Arsenal;
Blackpool; Fulham; Walsall;
Nelson; Walsall; Stafford
Rangers; Thames

	A	G
1919–20	29	15
1920–21	26	10
1921–22	35	14
1922–23	11	1
Total	101	40

ALFRED BAKER

Right-half/Right-back
Born Ilkeston, 27 April 1898
Died 14 April 1955
Clubs Eastwood Rangers;
Arsenal

	A	G
1919–20	17	0
1920–21	37	2
1921–22	32	4
1922–23	29	6
1923–24	21	1
1924–25	32	2
1925–26	31	6
1926–27	23	0
1927–28	37	2
1928–29	31	0
1929–30	19	0
1930–31	1	0
Total	310	23

DANIEL 'DICK' BURGESS

Inside-forward
Born Goldenhill, 23 October 1896
Clubs Port Vale; Arsenal;
West Ham United; Aberdare
Athletic; Queen's Park
Rangers; Sittingbourne

	A	G
1919–20	7	1
1920–21	4	0
1921–22	2	0
Total	13	1

ARTHUR VICTOR HUTCHINS
Full-back
Born Bishop's Waltham,
15 September 1890
Clubs Croydon Common; Arsenal;
Charlton Athletic

	A	G
1919–20	18	0
1920–21	39	0
1921–22	37	0
1922–23	10	1
Total	104	1

STEPHEN DUNN
Goalkeeper
Born Darlaston
Clubs Army; Arsenal

	A	G
1919–20	16	0
1920–21	9	0
1921–22	1	0
1922–23	17	0
Total	43	0

JOSEPH TONER
Outside-left
Born Castlewellan, 30 March 1894
Died November 1954
Clubs Belfast United; Arsenal; St
Johnstone; Coleraine

	A	G
1919–20	15	1
1920–21	12	3
1921–22	24	1
1922–23	7	0
1923–24	3	0
1924–25	26	1
1925–26	2	0
Total	89	6

FREDERICK PAGNAM
Centre-forward/Outside-right
Born Poulton-le-Fylde,
4 September 1891
Died 7 March 1962
Clubs Lytham; Blackpool Wednesday;
Huddersfield Town; Doncaster
Rovers; Southport Central; Blackpool;
Gainsborough Trinity; Liverpool;
Arsenal; Cardiff City; Watford

	A	G
1919–20	25	12
1920–21	25	14
Total	50	26

JOHN DENNIS 'JACK' BUTLER
Centre-half
Born Colombo, Sri Lanka,
14 August 1894
Died 5 January 1961
Clubs Fulham Thursdays;
Fulham; Dartford; Arsenal; Torquay
United; Daring

	A	G
1919–20	21	1
1920–21	6	0

1921–22	25	2
1922–23	18	0
1923–24	24	0
1924–25	39	3
1925–26	41	0
1926–27	31	1
1927–28	38	0
1928–29	22	0
1929–30	2	0
Total	267	7

FRANCIS FREDERICK COWNLEY
Right-back
Born Swallownest
Clubs Scunthorpe & Lindsey United; Arsenal

	A	G
1919–20	4	0
1920–21	1	0
1921–22	10	0
Total	15	0

WALTER ERNEST COOPLAND
Right-half/Outside-left
Born Sheffield, 1900
Clubs Birley Carr; Arsenal; Exeter City; Aberdare Athletic

	A	G
1919–20	1	0
Total	1	0

ERNEST JOHN 'JOE' NORTH
Centre-forward/Inside-left
Born Burton-on-Trent, 23 September 1895
Died 24 August 1955

Clubs Sheffield Works; Sheffield United; Tank Corps; Arsenal; Reading; Gillingham; Norwich City; Watford; Northfleet

	A	G
1919–20	4	1
1920–21	8	2
1921–22	11	3
Total	23	6

THOMAS JAMES WHITTAKER
Left-half/Left-back
Born Aldershot, 21 July 1878
Died 24 October 1956
Clubs Newcastle Swifts; Arsenal

	A	G
1919–20	1	0
1920–21	5	0
1921–22	36	1
1922–23	13	1
1923–24	8	0
1924–25	1	0
Total	64	2

GEORGE CHARLTON PATTISON
Centre-half
Born North Shields, 20 February 1895
Died 1972
Clubs Wallsend; Arsenal; West Ham United

	A	G
1919–20	1	0
1920–21	6	0
1921–22	2	0
Total	9	0

JAMES SMITH

Outside-right
Born Preston, 27 March 1887
Clubs Stalybridge Celtic; Bury;
Stalybridge Rovers; Accrington
Stanley; Chorley; Fulham; Arsenal

	A	G
1920–21	10	1
Total	10	1

DR JAMES A 'JIMMY' PATERSON

Winger
Born London
Clubs Queen's Park Rangers;
Arsenal

	A	G
1920–21	20	0
1921–22	2	0
1922–23	26	0
1923–24	21	0
1924–25	0	0
1925–26	1	1
Total	70	1

HAROLD ADRIAN WALDEN

Centre-forward
Born Manchester 1887
Died 1955
Clubs Linfield; Army; Northern
Nomads; Halifax Town; Bradford
City; Arsenal; Bradford Park Avenue

	A	G
1920–21	2	1
Total	2	1

ALEXANDER McKENZIE

Inside-forward
Born Leith
Clubs Arniston Rangers; Arsenal;
Blackpool

	A	G
1920–21	5	1
1921–22	3	0
1922–23	7	1
Total	15	2

JAMES HOPKINS

Inside-left
Born Ballymoney, 12 July 1899
Died 1943
Clubs Willowfield United; Belfast
United; Arsenal; Brighton & Hove
Albion; Aldershot

	A	G
1920–21	8	2
1921–22	11	3
1922–23	2	2
Total	21	7

WILLIAM JAMES HENDERSON

Outside-right
Born Carlisle, 11 January 1899
Died 1934
Clubs Carlisle United; Arsenal; Luton
Town; Southampton; Coventry City;
Carlisle United

	A	G
1920–21	5	0
1921–22	2	0
Total	7	0

THOMAS MAXWELL
Inside-right
Born Dunfermline
Clubs Arsenal; St Mary's Barn

	A	G
1920–21	1	0
Total	1	0

ROBERT HAMILTON TURNBULL
Centre-forward
Born Dumbarton, 22 June 1894
Died 1946
Clubs Royal Engineers; Arsenal;
Charlton Athletic; Chelsea; Clapton
Orient; Southend United; Chatham;
Crystal Palace

	A	G
1921–22	5	0
1922–23	35	20
1923–24	18	6
1924–25	1	0
Total	59	26

WALTER WARDEN CREEGAN
Outside-right
Born Manchester, 4 June 1902
Died 1967
Clubs Arsenal

	A	G
1921–22	5	0
Total	5	0

WILLIAM MILNE
Right-half
Born Buckie, 24 November 1895

Died 27 July 1975
Clubs Buckie Thistle;
Seaforth Highlanders; Tottenham
Hotspur; Arsenal

	A	G
1921–22	4	0
1922–23	31	0
1923–24	36	1
1924–25	32	0
1925–26	5	0
1926–27	6	0
Total	114	1

STANLEY GEORGE JAMES EARLE
Inside-right
Born Stratford, 6 September 1897
Died 23 September 1971
Clubs Clapton; Arsenal; West Ham
United; Clapton Orient

	A	G
1921–22	1	0
1922–23	1	1
1923–24	2	2
Total	4	3

ANDREW YOUNG
Centre-forward/Wing-half
Born Darlington, 17 September 1896
Died 1964
Clubs Blyth Spartans; Aston Villa;
Arsenal; Bournemouth;
Kidderminster Harriers

	A	G
1921–22	9	2
1922–23	13	3

	A	G
1923–24	25	2
1924–25	8	2
1925–26	7	0
1926–27	6	0
Total	68	9

FRANCIS ALBERT 'FRANK' TOWNROW

Left-half/Inside-left
Born West Ham, 15 November 1902
Clubs Arsenal; Dundee; Bristol City;
Bristol Rovers; Taunton Town

	A	G
1922–23	1	0
1923–24	7	2
Total	8	2

ARCHIBALD ROE

Centre-forward
Born Hull, 9 December 1893
Died 1947
Clubs Sheffield Wednesday; South
Shields; Birmingham; Gillingham;
Castleford Town; Arsenal; Lincoln
City; Rotherham County

	A	G
1922–23	4	1
Total	4	1

ROBERT FREDERICK 'BOB' JOHN

Left-half/ Left-back
Born Barry Dock, 3 February 1900
Died 1982
Clubs Caerphilly; Barry Town;
Arsenal

	A	G
1922–23	24	0
1923–24	15	0
1924–25	39	1
1925–26	29	0
1926–27	41	3
1927–28	39	1
1928–29	34	1
1929–30	34	0
1930–31	40	2
1931–32	38	3
1932–33	37	0
1933–34	31	1
1934–35	9	0
1935–36	6	0
1936–37	5	0
Total	421	12

ANDREW LYND KENNEDY

Left-back/Centre-half
Born Belfast, 1 September 1895
Died 21 December 1963
Clubs Belfast Celtic;
Glentoran; Crystal Palace;
Arsenal; Everton;
Tranmere Rovers

	A	G
1922–23	24	0
1923–24	29	0
1924–25	40	0
1925–26	16	0
1926–27	11	0
1927–28	2	0
Total	122	0

JOHN ALEXANDER 'ALEX' MACKIE

Right-back
Born Belfast, 23 February 1903
Died 1984
Clubs Forth River; Arsenal; Portsmouth; Northampton Town

	A	G
1922–23	23	0
1923–24	31	0
1924–25	19	0
1925–26	35	0
Total	108	0

☻ ARSENAL FACT ☻

Brought over from Belfast, instead of asking for a signing-on fee new Arsenal defender Alec Mackie asked for – and got – a pet monkey!

JOHN HARDY 'JOCK' ROBSON

Goalkeeper
Born Innerleithen, 1898
Clubs Innerleithen; Arsenal; Bournemouth

	A	G
1922–23	20	0
1923–24	42	0
1924–25	26	0
1925–26	9	0
Total	97	0

JOHN CLARK

Winger
Born Bo'ness, 1900
Clubs Bo'ness; Arsenal; Luton Town; Bo'ness

	A	G
1922–23	2	0
1923–24	2	0
1924–25	2	0
Total	6	0

JOHN RICHARD ELVEY

Right-back
Born Luton
Clubs Luton Clarence; Luton Town; Bolton Wanderers; Arsenal

	A	G
1922–23	1	0
Total	1	0

HAROLD 'HARRY' WOODS

Centre-forward/Inside-forward
Born St Helens, 12 March 1890
Clubs St Helens Recreational; Ashton Town; St Helens Town; Norwich City; South Shields; Newcastle United; Arsenal; Luton Town; North Shields

	A	G
1923–24	36	9
1924–25	32	12
1925–26	2	0
Total	70	21

SAMSON HADEN
Outside-left/Inside-left
Born Royston, 17 January 1902
Clubs Castleford Town; Arsenal;
Notts County; Peterborough United

	A	G
1923–24	31	3
1924–25	15	1
1925–26	25	2
1926–27	17	4
Total	88	10

EDWARD ERNEST WALLINGTON
Outside-right
Born Rickmansworth, 8 July 1895
Died 15 February 1959
Clubs Rickmansworth Town;
Watford; Arsenal; Watford Old Boys

	A	G
1923–24	1	0
Total	1	0

JAMES HOWIE RAMSAY
Inside-left
Born Clydebank, 7 August 1898
Died 1969
Clubs Moor Park; Arthurlie; Renfrew
Victoria; Kilmarnock; Arsenal;
Kilmarnock; Galston

	A	G
1923–24	11	3
1924–25	30	6
1925–26	16	0
1926–27	12	2
Total	69	11

ANDREW NEIL
Inside-forward/Left-half
Born Kilmarnock, 18 November 1892
Died 1941
Clubs Kilmarnock; Galston;
Stevenston United; Brighton & Hove
Albion; Arsenal; Brighton & Hove
Albion; Queen's Park Rangers

	A	G
1923–24	11	2
1924–25	16	2
1925–26	27	6
Total	54	10

FREDERICK JOHN JONES
Inside-left/Outside-left
Born Greenwich, 11 February 1898
Died 1990
Clubs Royal Naval Depot (Chatham);
Arsenal; Aberdare Athletic; Charlton
Athletic; Blackpool

	A	G
1923–24	2	0
Total	2	0

JAMES 'JIMMY' BRAIN
Centre-forward/Inside-right
Born Bristol, 11 September 1900
Died 1971
Clubs Cardiff City; Ton Pentre;
Arsenal; Tottenham Hotspur;
King's Lynn

	A	G
1924–25	28	12
1925–26	41	34

1926–27	37	31
1927–28	39	25
1928–29	37	19
1929–30	6	0
1930–31	16	4
Total	204	125

DANIEL LEWIS

Goalkeeper
Born Mardy, 11 February 1902
Died 17 July 1967
Clubs Mardy; Clapton Orient;
Arsenal; Gillingham

	A	G
1924–25	16	0
1925–26	14	0
1926–27	17	0
1927–28	33	0
1928–29	32	0
1929–30	30	0
Total	142	0

SIDNEY WALTER HOAR

Winger
Born Leagrave, 28 November 1895
Died 1969
Clubs Luton Clarence; Luton Town;
Arsenal; Bedford Town; Clapton
Orient

	A	G
1924–25	19	1
1925–26	21	3
1926–27	16	2
1927–28	38	9
1928–29	6	1
Total	100	16

DONALD JAMES COCK

Centre-forward/Inside-left
Born Hayle, 8 July 1896
Died 31 August 1974
Clubs Brentford; Fulham; Notts
County; Arsenal; Clapton Orient;
Wolverhampton Wanderers

	A	G
1924–25	2	0
1925–26	1	0
Total	3	0

JOSEPH HUGHES

Centre-forward
Born Manchester, 4 June 1902
Clubs New Cross (Manchester);
Bolton Wanderers; Chelsea;
Guildford United; Arsenal

	A	G
1924–25	1	0
Total	1	0

ARTHUR ROE

Wing-half/Centre-half
Born South Normanton, 1892
Clubs South Normanton; Luton
Town; Arsenal; Bournemouth;
Mansfield Town

	A	G
1924–25	1	0
Total	1	0

CHARLES MURRAY BUCHAN

Inside-right
Born Plumstead, 22 September 1891

Died 25 June 1960
Clubs Woolwich Polytechnic;
Plumstead St Nicholas;
Plumstead; Woolwich Arsenal;
Northfleet; Leyton; Sunderland;
Arsenal

	A	G
1925–26	39	19
1926–27	33	14
1927–28	30	16
Total	102	49

JOHN JAMES RUTHERFORD
Outside-right
Born South Shields, 4 March 1907
Clubs Ilford; Arsenal; West
Ham United

	A	G
1925–26	1	0
Total	1	0

WILLIAM HARPER
Goalkeeper
Born Tarbrax, 19 January 1897
Died April 1989
Clubs Winchburgh Violet; Edinburgh
Emmett; Hibernian; Arsenal; Fall
River Marksmen; Boston Wonder
Workers; Boston Bears; Boston;
New Bedford Whalers; Arsenal;
Plymouth Argyle

	A	G
1925–26	19	0
1926–27	23	0
1930–31	19	2

1931–32	2	0
Total	63	2

HERBERT 'BERT' LAWSON
Outside-right/Right-half
Born Luton, 12 April 1905
Clubs Frickers Athletic; Luton
Clarence; Arsenal; Brentford; Luton
Town; Bedford Town;

	A	G
1925–26	13	2
Total	13	2

JOSEPH HAROLD ANTHONY HULME
Outside-right
Born Stafford, 26 August 1904
Died 26 September 1991
Clubs Stafford YMCA; York City;
Blackburn Rovers; Arsenal;
Huddersfield Town

	A	G
1925–26	15	2
1926–27	37	8
1927–28	36	8
1928–29	41	6
1929–30	37	14
1930–31	32	14
1931–32	40	14
1932–33	40	20
1933–34	8	5
1934–35	16	8
1935–36	21	6
1936–37	3	0
1937–38	7	2
Total	333	107

THOMAS ROBERT PARKER
Right-back
Born Woolston, 19 November 1897
Died 5 November 1987
Clubs Sholing Rangers; Sholing
Athletic; Woolston St Mark's;
Southampton; Arsenal

	A	G
1925–26	7	3
1926–27	42	4
1927–28	42	4
1928–29	42	3
1929–30	41	3
1930–31	41	0
1931–32	38	0
1932–33	5	0
Total	258	17

WILLIAM CHARLES SEDDON
Right-half/Centre-half
Born Clapton, 28 July 1901
Died 1993
Clubs Villa Athletic; Gillingham;
Aston Villa; Arsenal; Grimsby Town;
Luton Town

	A	G
1925–26	1	0
1926–27	17	0
1927–28	4	0
1928–29	0	0
1929–30	24	0
1930–31	18	0
1931–32	5	0
Total	69	0

JOHN 'JACK' LAMBERT
Centre-forward/Inside-forward
Born Greasborough, 22 May 1902
Died 7 December 1940
Clubs Army; Greasborough; Methley
Perseverance; Sheffield
Wednesday; Rotherham County;
Leeds United; Doncaster Rovers;
Arsenal; Fulham; Margate

	A	G
1926–27	16	1
1927–28	16	3
1928–29	6	1
1929–30	20	18
1930–31	34	38
1931–32	36	22
1932–33	12	14
1933–34	3	1
Total	143	98

JOHN WILLIAM 'JACK' LEE
Outside-left
Born Marylebone, 1 February 1902
Died 1944
Clubs Blackhall Wesleyans; Horden
Athletic; Hartlepool United; Luton
Town; Horden Athletic; Arsenal;
Chesterfield; Aldershot

	A	G
1926–27	7	0
Total	7	0

HORACE WALTER COPE
Left-back
Born Treeton, 24 May 1899
Died 1961

Clubs Treeton United; Notts County; Arsenal; Bristol Rovers

	A	G
1926–27	11	0
1927–28	24	0
1928–29	23	0
1929–30	1	0
1930–31	1	0
1931–32	1	0
1932–33	4	0
Total	**65**	**0**

HAROLD BURSTON PEEL

Inside-left/Outside-left
Born Bradford, 26 March 1900
Died 16 January 1976
Clubs Calverley; Bradford Park Avenue; Arsenal; Bradford City

	A	G
1926–27	9	0
1927–28	13	0
1928–29	24	5
1929–30	1	0
Total	**47**	**5**

JOHN CHARLES BARLEY

Left-half/Inside-left
Born Staveley, October 1904
Clubs Staveley Town; Arsenal; Reading; Maidenhead United

	A	G
1926–27	3	1
1927–28	2	0
1928–29	3	0
Total	**8**	**1**

JAMES SHAW

Inside-forward
Born Goldenhill, 8 August 1904
Clubs Goldenhill Wanderers; Bolton Wanderers; Frickley Colliery; Arsenal; Brentford; Gillingham

	A	G
1926–27	5	1
1927–28	6	3
Total	**11**	**4**

REGINALD WILLIAM TRICKER

Forward
Born Karachi, 5 October 1905
Clubs Beccles Town; Luton Town; Beccles Town; Charlton Athletic; Arsenal; Clapton Orient; Margate

	A	G
1926–27	4	3
1927–28	7	2
1928–29	1	0
Total	**12**	**5**

HERBERT ROBERTS

Centre-half
Born Oswestry, 19 February 1905
Died 19 June 1944
Clubs Oswestry Town; Arsenal

	A	G
1926–27	2	0
1927–28	3	0
1928–29	20	0
1929–30	26	0
1930–31	40	1
1931–32	35	0

1932–33	36	0
1933–34	30	1
1934–35	36	0
1935–36	26	1
1936–37	30	1
1937–38	13	0
Total	297	4

JOHN 'JACK' MOODY
Goalkeeper
Born Heeley, 10 November 1903
Clubs Hathersage; Sheffield United;
Arsenal; Bradford Park Avenue;
Doncaster Rovers; Manchester
United; Chesterfield

	A	G
1926–27	2	0
1927–28	4	0
Total	6	0

EDWARD C 'TED' BOWEN
Centre-forward
Born Goldthorpe, 1 July 1903
Clubs Wath Athletic; Arsenal;
Northampton Town; Bristol City

	A	G
1926–27	1	0
Total	1	0

ARCHIBALD W CLARK
Born Shoreham, 4 April 1902
Died 14 January 1967
Clubs Aylesford Paper Mills; Grays
Thurrock; Brentford; Arsenal; Luton
Town; Everton; Tranmere Rovers;
Gillingham

	A	G
1927–28	1	0
Total	1	0

EDRIS ALBERT 'EDDIE' HAPGOOD
Left-back
Born Bristol, 27 September 1908
Died 20 April 1973
Clubs Bristol Rovers; Kettering
Town; Arsenal; Shrewsbury Town

	A	G
1927–28	3	0
1928–29	17	0
1929–30	38	0
1930–31	38	0
1931–32	41	0
1932–33	38	0
1933–34	40	0
1934–35	34	1
1935–36	33	0
1936–37	32	1
1937–38	41	0
1938–39	38	0
Total	393	2

WILLIAM PATERSON
Goalkeeper
Born Dunfermline, 1902
Clubs Dunfermline Athletic; Boston
Wonder Workers; Dunfermline
Athletic; Dundee United; Arsenal;
Airdrieonians; Dundee United

	A	G
1927–28	5	0
1928–29	10	0
Total	15	0

LEONARD THOMPSON
Inside-left
Born Sheffield, 18 February 1901
Clubs Shiregreen Primitive
Methodists; Norfolk Amateurs;
Hallam; Barnsley; Hallam;
Birmingham; Swansea Town;
Arsenal; Crystal Palace; Islington
Corinthians

	A	G
1927–28	1	0
1928–29	17	5
1929–30	5	1
1930–31	2	0
1931–32	1	0
Total	26	6

CHARLES JONES
Outside-left/Right-half
Born Troedyrhiw, 12 December 1899
Died 1966
Clubs Cardiff City; Stockport County;
Oldham Athletic; Nottingham Forest;
Arsenal

	A	G
1928–29	39	6
1929–30	31	1
1930–31	24	1
1931–32	37	0
1932–33	16	0
1933–34	29	0
Total	176	8

DAVID BONE NIGHTINGALE JACK
Inside-right/Centre-forward
Born Bolton, 3 April 1898

Died 10 September 1958
Clubs Plymouth Presbyterians;
Plymouth Argyle; Bolton Wanderers;
Arsenal; Southend United

	A	G
1928–29	31	25
1929–30	33	13
1930–31	35	31
1931–32	34	21
1932–33	34	18
1933–34	14	5
Total	181	113

RAYMOND PARKIN
Inside-right/Right-half
Born Crook, 28 January 1911
Died 1971
Clubs Newcastle United; Esh
Winning; Arsenal; Middlesbrough;
Southampton

	A	G
1928–29	5	3
1929–30	0	0
1930–31	0	0
1931–32	9	7
1932–33	5	0
1933–34	5	0
1934–35	0	0
1935–36	1	1
Total	25	11

ALEXANDER WILSON 'ALEX' JAMES
Inside-left
Born Mossend, 14 September 1901
Died 1 June 1953

Clubs Brandon Amateurs; Orbiston Celtic; Glasgow Ashfield; Motherwell; Raith Rovers; Preston North End; Arsenal

	A	G
1929–30	7	3
1930–31	2	1
Total	**9**	**4**

	A	G
1929–30	31	6
1930–31	40	5
1931–32	32	2
1932–33	40	3
1933–34	22	3
1934–35	30	4
1935–36	17	2
1936–37	19	1
Total	**231**	**26**

CHARLES JAMES FANE PREEDY
Goalkeeper
Born Neemuch, India, 11 January 1900
Died 1978
Clubs Bostall Heath; Redhill; Charlton Athletic; Wigan Borough; Arsenal; Bristol Rovers; Luton Town; Margate

	A	G
1929–30	12	0
1930–31	11	0
1931–32	13	0
1932–33	1	0
Total	**37**	**0**

WILLIAM JOHNSTONE
Centre-forward/Inside-left
Born Fife, 18 May 1900
Clubs Rosyth Juniors; King's Park; Dundee United; Clyde; Reading; Arsenal; Oldham Athletic; Clyde

JOSEPH JOSHUA 'JOEY' WILLIAMS
Winger
Born Rotherham, 4 June 1902
Clubs Rotherham Town; Rotherham County; Huddersfield Town; Stoke City; Arsenal; Middlesbrough; Carlisle United

	A	G
1929–30	12	3
1930–31	9	2
1931–32	1	0
Total	**22**	**5**

CLIFFORD SYDNEY BASTIN
Winger
Born Exeter, 14 March 1912
Died 4 December 1991
Clubs Exeter City; Arsenal

	A	G
1929–30	21	7
1930–31	42	28
1931–32	40	15
1932–33	42	33
1933–34	38	13
1934–35	36	20
1935–36	31	11
1936–37	33	5
1937–38	38	15

1938–39	23	3
1946–47	6	0
Total	350	150

DAVID HALLIDAY
Centre-forward
Born Dumfries, 11 December 1897
Died 23 January 1970
Clubs Queen of the South
Wanderers; St Mirren; Dundee;
Sunderland; Arsenal; Manchester
City; Clapton Orient; Yeovil
& Petters United

	A	G
1929–30	15	8
Total	15	8

ALFRED EDWARD HAYNES
Right-half/Right-back
Born Oxford, 1910
Died January 1953
Clubs Oxford City; Arsenal; Crystal
Palace

	A	G
1929–30	13	0
1930–31	2	0
1931–32	7	0
1932–33	6	0
1933–34	1	0
Total	29	0

ALBERT EDWARD HUMPISH
Right-half/Inside-right
Born Bury, 3 April 1902
Died 1986
Clubs Halifax Town; Walker Celtic;

Bury; Wigan Borough; Arsenal;
Bristol City; Stockport County;
Rochdale; Ashton National

	A	G
1929–30	3	0
Total	3	0

GERALD PEITER KEYSER
Goalkeeper
Born Holland, 1910
Died 1980
Clubs Millwall; Margate; Arsenal;
Queen's Park Rangers

	A	G
1930–31	12	0
Total	12	0

CHARLES GEORGE MALE
Right-back
Born Plaistow, 8 May 1910
Died 19 February 1998
Clubs Clapton; Arsenal

	A	G
1930–31	3	0
1931–32	9	0
1932–33	35	0
1933–34	42	0
1934–35	39	0
1935–36	35	0
1936–37	37	0
1937–38	34	0
1938–39	28	0
1946–47	15	0
1947–48	8	0
Total	285	0

FRANK MOSS

Goalkeeper
Born Leyland, 5 November 1909
Died February 1970
Clubs Leyland Motors; Preston
North End; Oldham Athletic; Arsenal

	A	G
1931–32	27	0
1932–33	41	0
1933–34	37	0
1934–35	33	1
1935–36	5	0
Total	143	1

ERNEST 'TIM' COLEMAN

Forward
Born Blidworth, 4 January 1908
Died 20 January 1984
Clubs Hucknall Colliery; Nottingham
Forest; Halifax Town; Grimsby Town;
Arsenal; Middlesbrough; Norwich
City; Linby Colliery

	A	G
1931–32	6	1
1932–33	27	24
1933–34	12	1
Total	45	26

ALBERT EDWARD 'PAT' BEASLEY

Outside-left/Left-half
Born Stourbridge, 27 July 1913
Died 3 March 1986
Clubs Stourbridge; Arsenal;
Huddersfield Town; Fulham;
Bristol City

	A	G
1931–32	3	0
1932–33	0	0
1933–34	23	10
1934–35	20	6
1935–36	26	2
1936–37	7	1
Total	79	19

LESLIE HARRY COMPTON

Centre-half/Full-back
Born Woodford, 12 September 1912
Died 27 December 1984
Clubs Hampstead Town; Arsenal

	A	G
1931–32	4	0
1932–33	4	0
1933–34	0	0
1934–35	5	1
1935–36	12	1
1936–37	15	0
1937–38	9	1
1938–39	18	2
1946–47	36	0
1947–48	35	0
1948–49	40	0
1949–50	35	0
1950–51	26	0
1951–52	4	0
Total	253	5

REGINALD ROBERT STOCKHILL

Forward
Born York, 23 November 1913
Died 24 December 1995
Clubs York City; Scarborough;
Arsenal; Derby County; Luton Town

	A	G
1931–32	3	1
1932–33	4	3
Total	**7**	**4**

FRANK ROBERT HILL
Wing-half/Outside-left
Born Forfar, 21 May 1906
Died 1993
Clubs Forfar Athletic; Aberdeen;
Arsenal; Blackpool; Southampton;
Wrexham; Preston North End;
Crewe Alexandra

	A	G
1932–33	26	1
1933–34	25	0
1934–35	15	3
1935–36	10	0
Total	**76**	**4**

NORMAN WILLIAM SIDEY
Centre-half/Right-half
Born Nunhead
Clubs Nunhead; Arsenal

	A	G
1932–33	2	0
1933–34	12	0
1934–35	6	0
1935–36	11	0
1936–37	6	0
1937–38	3	0
Total	**40**	**0**

EDWIN RAYMOND 'RAY' BOWDEN
Forward
Born Looe, 13 September 1909

Died September 1998
Clubs Looe; Plymouth Argyle;
Arsenal; Newcastle United

	A	G
1932–33	7	2
1933–34	32	13
1934–35	24	14
1935–36	22	6
1936–37	28	6
1937–38	10	1
Total	**123**	**42**

RALPH JAMES EVANS BIRKETT
Outside-right
Born Newton Abbot, 9 January 1913
Clubs Dartmouth United; Torquay
United; Arsenal; Middlesbrough;
Newcastle United

	A	G
1933–34	15	5
1934–35	4	2
Total	**19**	**7**

JAMES DUNNE
Centre-forward
Born Ringsend, 3 September 1905
Died December 1949
Clubs Shamrock Rovers; New
Brighton; Sheffield United; Arsenal;
Southampton; Shamrock Rovers

	A	G
1933–34	21	9
1934–35	1	0
1935–36	6	1
Total	**28**	**10**

PETER G DOUGALL
Inside-left
Born Denny, 21 March 1909
Died 1974
Clubs Denny Pace; Burnley; Clyde;
Southampton; Arsenal; Everton;
Bury

	A	G
1933–34	5	0
1934–35	8	1
1935–36	8	3
Total	21	4

GEORGE R COX
Centre-forward
Born Warnham, 23 August 1911
Died 30 March 1985
Clubs Horsham; Arsenal; Fulham;
Luton Town

	A	G
1933–34	2	0
1934–35	0	0
1935–36	5	1
Total	7	1

ALEXANDER A WILSON
Goalkeeper
Born Wishaw, 29 October 1908
Died 25 April 1971
Clubs Overtown Athletic; Morton;
Arsenal; St Mirren; Brighton
& Hove Albion

	A	G
1933–34	5	0
1934–35	9	0
1935–36	37	0
1936–37	2	0
1937–38	10	0
1938–39	19	0
Total	82	0

EDWARD JOSEPH 'TED' DRAKE
Centre-forward
Born Southampton, 16 August 1912
Died 31 May 1995
Clubs Winchester City;
Southampton; Arsenal

	A	G
1933–34	10	7
1934–35	41	42
1935–36	26	24
1936–37	26	20
1937–38	27	17
1938–39	38	14
Total	168	124

WILFRED 'WILF' COPPING
Left-half
Born Middlecliffe, 17 August 1909
Died 16 June 1980
Clubs Dearne Valley Old Boys;
Middlecliffe & Darfield Rovers;
Barnsley; Leeds United; Arsenal;
Leeds United

	A	G
1934–35	31	0
1935–36	33	0
1936–37	38	0
1937–38	38	0
1938–39	26	0
Total	166	0

WILLIAM JOHN 'JACK' CRAYSTON

Right-half/Centre-half
Born Grange-over-Sands, 9 October 1910
Died December 1992
Clubs Ulverston Town; Barrow; Bradford Park Avenue; Arsenal

	A	G
1934–35	37	3
1935–36	36	5
1936–37	30	1
1937–38	31	4
1938–39	34	3
Total	168	16

DR JAMES MARSHALL

Inside-right
Born Avonbridge, 3 January 1908
Died 27 December 1977
Clubs Shettleston Juniors; Rangers; Arsenal; West Ham United; Ashford Town

	A	G
1934–35	4	0
Total	4	0

ROBERT TRIMMING DAVIDSON

Inside-forward
Born Lochgelly, 27 April 1913
Died 1988
Clubs Bowhill Juniors; St Bernard's; St Johnstone; Arsenal; Coventry City; Hinckley Athletic; Redditch Town

	A	G
1934–35	11	2
1935–36	13	0
1936–37	28	9
1937–38	5	2
Total	57	13

ALFRED JOHN KIRCHEN

Outside-right
Born Shouldham, 26 April 1913
Died 1999
Clubs Shouldham; Norwich City; Arsenal

	A	G
1934–35	7	2
1935–36	6	3
1936–37	33	18
1937–38	19	6
1938–39	27	9
Total	92	38

EHUD 'TIM' ROGERS

Outside-right
Born Chirk, 15 October 1909
Died 25 January 1996
Clubs Oswestry Town; Wrexham; Arsenal; Newcastle United; Swansea Town; Wrexham

	A	G
1934–35	5	2
1935–36	11	3
Total	16	5

REGINALD FREDERICK TRIM

Full-back
Born Portsmouth, 10 October 1913

Clubs Bournemouth Postal; Winton
& Moordown; Bournemouth;
Arsenal; Nottingham Forest; Derby
County; Swindon Town

	A	G
1934–35	1	0
Total	1	0

JOHN VANCE 'JACKIE' MILNE
Winger
Born Stirling, 25 March 1911
Clubs Glasgow Ashfield; Blackburn
Rovers; Arsenal; Middlesbrough;
Dumbarton

	A	G
1935–36	14	6
1936–37	19	9
1937–38	16	4
Total	49	19

SIDNEY CARTWRIGHT
Wing-half
Born Kiveton Park, 16 July 1910
Died 16 December 1988
Clubs High Moor; Kiveton Park;
Arsenal

	A	G
1935–36	5	0
1936–37	2	0
1937–38	6	2
1938–39	3	0
Total	16	2

ERNEST WILLIAM TUCKETT
Inside-right/Centre-half

Born Lingdale, 1 January 1914
Died 1943
Clubs Scarborough; Arsenal;
Margate; Arsenal; Bradford City;
Fulham

	A	G
1935–36	2	0
Total	2	0

RONALD WESTCOTT
Centre-forward
Born Wallasey, 19 September 1910
Clubs Banbury Spencer; Arsenal

	A	G
1935–36	2	1
Total	2	1

BERNARD JOY
Centre-half/Left-back
Born Fulham, 29 October 1911
Clubs London University;
Corinthians; Casuals; Southend
United; Fulham; Arsenal; Corinthian
Casuals

	A	G
1935–36	2	0
1936–37	6	0
1937–38	26	0
1938–39	39	0
1946–47	13	0
Total	86	0

GEORGE HEDLEY SWINDIN
Goalkeeper
Born Campsall, 4 December 1914

Died 26 October 2005
Clubs Rotherham YMCA; New
Stubbin Colliery; Rotherham United;
Bradford City; Arsenal;
Peterborough United

	A	G
1936–37	19	0
1937–38	17	0
1938–39	21	0
1946–47	38	0
1947–48	42	0
1948–49	32	0
1949–50	23	0
1950–51	21	0
1951–52	42	0
1952–53	14	0
1953–54	2	0
Total	271	0

DENIS CHARLES SCOTT COMPTON

Outside-left
Born Hendon, 23 May 1918
Died 23 April 1997
Clubs Hampstead Town; Nunhead;
Arsenal

	A	G
1936–37	14	4
1937–38	7	1
1938–39	1	0
1946–47	1	1
1947–48	14	6
1948–49	6	2
1949–50	11	1
Total	54	15

FRANK PREECE BOULTON

Goalkeeper
Born Chipping Sodbury, 12 August 1917
Died 20 June 1987
Clubs Bristol City; Bath City;
Arsenal; Derby County; Swindon
Town; Crystal Palace; Bedford Town

	A	G
1936–37	21	0
1937–38	15	0
Total	36	0

DAVID NELSON

Right-half/Inside-right
Born Douglas Water, 3 February 1918
Died 23 September 1988
Clubs Douglas Water Thistle; St
Bernard's; Arsenal; Fulham;
Brentford; Queen's Park Rangers;
Crystal Palace; Ashford Town

	A	G
1936–37	8	3
1937–38	0	0
1938–39	9	1
1946–47	10	0
Total	27	4

ARTHUR GILBERT BIGGS

Inside-right/Centre-forward
Born Wootton
Clubs Arsenal; Heart of Midlothian

	A	G
1936–37	1	0
1937–38	2	0
Total	3	0

GEORGE SAMUEL HUNT
Centre-forward/Inside-right
Born Barnsley, 22 February 1910
Died 19 September 1996
Clubs Barnsley; Sheffield United;
Port Vale; Regent Street
Congregationals; Chesterfield;
Tottenham Hotspur; Arsenal;
Bolton Wanderers; Sheffield
Wednesday; Bolton Wanderers

	A	G
1937–38	18	3
Total	**18**	**3**

ERNEST COLLETT
Left-half
Born Sheffield, 17 November 1914
Died 25 April 1980
Clubs Oughtibridge WMC;
Arsenal

	A	G
1937–38	5	0
1938–39	9	0
1946–47	6	0
Total	**20**	**0**

LESLIE JENKIN JONES
Inside-forward
Born Aberdare, 1 July 1911
Died 1981
Clubs Aberdare Athletic; Cardiff
City; Coventry City; Arsenal;
Swansea Town; Barry Town;
Brighton & Hove Albion

	A	G
1937–38	28	3
1938–39	18	0
Total	**46**	**3**

REGINALD J LEWIS
Centre-forward/Inside-forward
Born Bilston, 7 March 1920
Clubs Nunhead; Dulwich Hamlet;
Arsenal; Margate; Arsenal

	A	G
1937–38	4	2
1938–39	15	7
1946–47	28	29
1947–48	28	14
1948–49	25	16
1949–50	31	19
1950–51	14	8
1951–52	9	8
Total	**154**	**103**

WILLIAM MALWYN 'MAL' GRIFFITHS
Outside-right
Born Merthyr Tydfil, 8 March 1919
Died 5 April 1969
Clubs Merthyr Thursday; Arsenal;
Margate; Arsenal; Leicester City;
Burton Albion

	A	G
1937–38	9	5
Total	**9**	**5**

EDWARD MILLER CARR
Inside-left/Centre-forward
Born Wheatley Hill, 3 October 1917

Died 1998
Clubs Wheatley Hill Colliery;
Arsenal; Margate; Arsenal;
Huddersfield Town; Newport
County; Bradford City; Darlington

	A	G
1937–38	11	7
1938–39	1	0
Total	12	7

GEORGE BENJAMIN DRURY

Inside-left/Outside-right
Born Hucknall, 22 January 1914
Died 19 June 1972
Clubs Loughborough Town; Heanor
Town; Sheffield Wednesday;
Arsenal; West Bromwich Albion;
Watford; Darlaston

	A	G
1937–38	11	0
1938–39	23	3
1946–47	4	0
Total	38	3

GORDON HUTTON BREMNER

Inside-right/Outside-right
Born Glasgow
Clubs Cartha Athletic; Arsenal;
Motherwell

	A	G
1937–38	2	1
1938–39	13	3
Total	15	4

BRYNMOR 'BRYN' JONES

Inside-left
Born Penyard, 14 December 1912
Died 18 October 1985
Clubs Merthyr Amateurs; Plymouth
United; Southend United; Swansea
Town; Glenavon; Aberaman Athletic;
Wolverhampton Wanderers;
Arsenal; Norwich City

	A	G
1938–39	30	4
1946–47	26	1
1947–48	7	1
1948–49	8	1
Total	71	7

REGINALD HORACE CUMNER

Outside-left/Inside-left
Born Cwmaman, 31 March 1918
Died January 1999
Clubs Arsenal; Margate; Hull City;
Arsenal; Notts County; Watford;
Scunthorpe United; Bradford City;
Poole Town; Bridport

	A	G
1938–39	12	2
Total	12	2

WILFRED WALSH

Inside-right/Outside-right
Born Pentelottyn, 29 July 1917
Died 23 December 1977
Clubs Arsenal; Margate; Arsenal;
Derby County; Walsall; Huddersfield
Town; Redditch Town

		A	G
1938–39		3	0
	Total	3	0

DAVID PRYDE
Wing-half
Born Newtongrange,
10 November 1913
Died 1987
Clubs Arsenal; Margate; Arsenal;
Torquay United

		A	G
1938–39		4	0
	Total	4	0

ALFRED GEORGE FIELDS
Centre-half
Born Canning Town, 15 November 1918
Clubs West Ham Youth Club;
Margate; Arsenal

		A	G
1938–39		3	0
1946–47		8	0
1947–48		6	0
1948–49		1	0
	Total	18	0

SIDNEY JOHN PUGH
Left-half
Born Dartford
Died March 1944
Clubs Nunhead; Margate; Arsenal

		A	G
1938–39		2	0
	Total	2	0

GEORGE FREDERICK CURTIS
Inside-right/Right-half
Born West Thurrock,
3 December 1919
Clubs Anglo (Purfleet);
Arsenal; Margate; Arsenal;
Southampton; Valenciennes;
Chelmsford City

		A	G
1938–39		2	0
1946–47		11	0
	Total	13	0

WILLIAM GEORGE MARKS
Goalkeeper
Born Amesbury, 9 April 1915
Died 1 February 1998
Clubs Salisbury Corinthians;
Arsenal; Margate; Arsenal;
Blackburn Rovers; Bristol City;
Reading; Bulford United

		A	G
1938–39		2	0
	Total	2	0

ANDREW MARTIN FARR
Inside-right
Born Larkhall
Clubs Yoker Athletic; Margate;
Arsenal; Airdrieonians; Heart of
Midlothian

		A	G
1938–39		2	1
	Total	2	1

LAWRENCE SCOTT
Full-back
Born Sheffield, 23 April 1917
Clubs Bradford City; Arsenal;
Crystal Palace

	A	G
1946–47	28	0
1947–48	39	0
1948–49	12	0
1949–50	15	0
1950–51	17	0
1951–52	4	0
Total	115	0

IAN BUCHANAN McPHERSON
Winger
Born Glasgow, 26 July 1920
Died 4 March 1983
Clubs Glasgow Rangers; Notts
County; Arsenal; Notts County;
Brentford

	A	G
1946–47	37	6
1947–48	29	5
1948–49	33	5
1949–50	27	3
1950–51	26	0
Total	152	19

WALTER JOSEPH 'PADDY' SLOAN
Wing-half
Born Lurgan, 30 April 1921
Died 1993
Clubs Glenavon; Manchester
United; Tranmere Rovers; Arsenal;
Sheffield United; Brescia (Italy);
Norwich City

	A	G
1946–47	30	1
1947–48	3	0
Total	33	1

JAMES TULLIS LOGIE
Inside-forward
Born Edinburgh, 23 November 1919
Died 30 April 1984
Clubs Lochore Welfare; Arsenal

	A	G
1946–47	35	8
1947–48	39	8
1948–49	35	11
1949–50	34	7
1950–51	39	9
1951–52	34	4
1952–53	32	10
1953–54	35	8
1954–55	13	3
Total	296	68

HENRY WALLER
Wing-half
Born Ashington, 20 August 1917
Died 1984
Clubs Ashington; Arsenal; Leyton
Orient

	A	G
1946–47	8	0
Total	8	0

DR KEVIN PATRICK O'FLANAGAN

Winger
Born Dublin, 10 June 1919
Died 26 May 2006
Clubs Bohemians; Arsenal; Barnet;
Brentford

	A	G
1946–47	14	3
Total	14	3

CYRIL LESLIE HODGES

Forward
Born Hackney, 18 September 1919
Died 1979
Clubs Eton Manor; Arsenal;
Brighton & Hove Albion

	A	G
1946–47	2	0
Total	2	0

ALAN SMITH

Outside-left
Born Newcastle, 15 October 1921
Clubs Arsenal; Brentford; Leyton
Orient

	A	G
1946–47	3	0
Total	3	0

ALBERT GUDMUNDSSON

Inside-forward
Born Iceland, 5 October 1923
Died 1994
Clubs Glasgow Rangers; Arsenal

	A	G
1946–47	2	0
Total	2	0

WALLEY BARNES

Full-back
Born Brecknock, 16 January 1920
Died 4 September 1975
Clubs Southampton; Arsenal

	A	G
1946–47	26	0
1947–48	35	0
1948–49	40	0
1949–50	38	5
1950–51	35	3
1951–52	41	2
1952–53	0	0
1953–54	19	1
1954–55	25	0
1955–56	8	0
Total	267	11

CYRIL GRANT

Centre-forward
Born Wath, 10 July 1920
Clubs Mexborough; Lincoln City;
Arsenal; Fulham; Southend United

	A	G
1946–47	2	0
Total	2	0

EDWARD HEWITT 'TED' PLATT

Goalkeeper
Born Newcastle-under-Lyme,
26 March 1921
Died 1996

Clubs Colchester United; Arsenal; Portsmouth; Aldershot

	A	G
1946–47	4	0
1947–48	0	0
1948–49	10	0
1949–50	19	0
1950–51	17	0
1951–52	0	0
1952–53	3	0
Total	**53**	**0**

SAMUEL JOSEPH WADE
Full-back
Born Shoreditch, 7 July 1921
Clubs Hoxton BC; Arsenal

	A	G
1946–47	2	0
1947–48	3	0
1948–49	0	0
1949–50	1	0
1950–51	0	0
1951–52	8	0
1952–53	40	0
1953–54	18	0
1954–55	14	0
Total	**86**	**0**

JOSEPH MERCER
Wing-half
Born Ellesmere Port, 9 August 1914
Died 9 August 1990
Clubs Ellesemere Port; Everton; Arsenal

	A	G
1946–47	25	0
1947–48	40	0
1948–49	33	0
1949–50	35	0
1950–51	31	0
1951–52	36	0
1952–53	28	2
1953–54	19	0
Total	**247**	**2**

RONALD LESLIE ROOKE
Centre-forward
Born Guildford, 7 December 1911
Died July 1985
Clubs Guildford City; Crystal Palace; Fulham; Arsenal; Crystal Palace

	A	G
1946–47	24	21
1947–48	42	23
1948–49	22	14
Total	**88**	**58**

ALFRED STANLEY MORGAN
Inside-forward
Born Abergwynfl, 10 October 1920
Clubs Gwynfl Welfare; Arsenal; Walsall; Millwall; Leyton Orient

	A	G
1946–47	2	0
Total	**2**	**0**

THOMAS WILLIAM RUDKIN
Outside-left
Born Peterborough, 17 June 1919

Clubs Creswell; Wolverhampton Wanderers; Lincoln City; Peterborough United; Arsenal

	A	G
1946–47	5	2
Total	5	2

ALFRED CALVERLEY
Winger
Born Huddersfield, 24 November 1917
Died 1991
Clubs Huddersfield Town; Mansfield Town; Arsenal; Preston North End; Doncaster Rovers

	A	G
1946–47	11	0
Total	11	0

ARCHIBALD RENWICK MACAULAY
Inside-forward/Wing-half
Born Falkirk, 30 July 1915
Died June 1993
Clubs Glasgow Rangers; West Ham United; Brentford; Arsenal; Fulham

	A	G
1947–48	40	0
1948–49	39	1
1949–50	24	0
Total	103	1

DONALD GEORGE BEAUMONT ROPER
Winger
Born Botley, 14 December 1922

Clubs Bitterne Nomads; Southampton; Arsenal; Southampton

	A	G
1947–48	40	10
1948–49	31	5
1949–50	27	7
1950–51	34	7
1951–52	30	9
1952–53	41	14
1953–54	39	12
1954–55	35	17
1955–56	16	4
1956–57	4	3
Total	297	88

ALEXANDER ROONEY FORBES
Wing-half
Born Dundee, 21 January 1925
Clubs Dundee North End; Sheffield United; Arsenal; Leyton Orient; Fulham

	A	G
1947–48	11	2
1948–49	25	4
1949–50	23	2
1950–51	32	4
1951–52	38	2
1952–53	33	1
1953–54	30	4
1954–55	20	1
1955–56	5	0
Total	217	20

LIONEL SMITH
Full-back
Born Doncaster, 23 August 1920
Died 8 November 1980
Clubs Denaby United; Arsenal;
Watford

	A	G
1947–48	1	0
1948–49	32	0
1949–50	31	0
1950–51	32	0
1951–52	28	0
1952–53	31	0
1953–54	7	0
Total	162	0

DOUGLAS JOHN LISHMAN
Inside-forward
Born Birmingham,
14 September 1923
Died December 1994
Clubs Paget Rovers; Walsall;
Arsenal; Nottingham Forest

	A	G
1948–49	23	12
1949–50	14	9
1950–51	26	17
1951–52	38	23
1952–53	39	22
1953–54	39	18
1954–55	32	19
1955–56	15	5
Total	226	125

THOMAS HENSHALL WILSON VALLENCE
Outside-left
Born Stoke, 28 March 1924
Died 1980
Clubs Torquay United; Arsenal

	A	G
1948–49	14	2
1949–50	1	0
Total	15	2

WILLIAM RAYMOND DANIEL
Centre-half
Born Swansea, 2 November 1928
Died 7 November 1997
Clubs Swansea City; Arsenal;
Sunderland; Cardiff City; Swansea
City

	A	G
1948–49	1	0
1949-50	6	0
1950–51	5	0
1951–52	34	0
1952–53	41	5
Total	87	5

HARRY 'PETER' GORING
Centre-forward/Wing-half
Born Bishops Cleeve, 2 January 1927
Died 1994
Clubs Cheltenham Town; Arsenal

	A	G
1949–50	29	21
1950–51	34	15
1951–52	16	4

		A	G
1952–53		29	10
1953–54		9	0
1954–55		41	1
1955–56		37	0
1956–57		13	0
1957–58		10	0
1958–59		2	0
	Total	220	51

ARTHUR SHAW
Wing-half
Born Limehouse, 9 April 1924
Clubs Hayes; Brentford; Arsenal;
Watford

		A	G
1949–50		5	0
1950–51		16	0
1951–52		8	0
1952–53		25	0
1953–54		2	0
1954–55		1	0
	Total	57	0

FREDERICK JAMES ARTHUR COX
Outside-right
Born Reading, 1 November 1920
Died 7 August 1973
Clubs Tottenham Hotspur; Arsenal;
West Bromwich Albion

		A	G
1949–50		32	3
1950–51		13	2
1951–52		25	3
1952–53		9	1
	Total	79	9

NOEL KELLY
Inside-forward
Born Dublin, 28 December 1921
Died 1991
Clubs Glentoran; Arsenal; Crystal
Palace; Nottingham Forest;
Tranmere Rovers

		A	G
1949–50		1	0
	Total	1	0

CLIFFORD CHARLES HOLTON
Centre-forward
Born Oxford, 29 April 1929
Died 30 May 1996
Clubs Oxford City; Arsenal; Watford;
Northampton Town; Crystal Palace;
Watford; Charlton Athletic; Leyton
Orient

		A	G
1950–51		10	5
1951–52		28	17
1952–53		21	19
1953–54		32	17
1954–55		8	0
1955–56		31	8
1956–57		39	10
1957–58		26	4
1958–59		3	3
	Total	198	83

ALFRED JOHN 'JACK' KELSEY
Goalkeeper
Born Llansamlet, 19 November 1929
Died 19 March 1992
Clubs Winch Wen; Arsenal

	A	G
1950–51	4	0
1951–52	0	0
1952–53	25	0
1953–54	39	0
1954–55	38	0
1955–56	32	0
1956–57	30	0
1957–58	38	0
1958–59	27	0
1959–60	22	0
1960–61	37	0
1961–62	35	0
Total	**327**	**0**

REUBEN JOHN 'BEN' MARDEN
Outside-left
Born Fulham, 10 February 1927
Clubs Chelmsford City; Arsenal; Watford

	A	G
1950–51	11	2
1951–52	7	2
1952–53	8	4
1953–54	9	3
1954–55	7	0
Total	**42**	**11**

CLEMENT ARTHUR MILTON
Outside-right
Born Bristol, 10 March 1928
Clubs Arsenal; Bristol City

	A	G
1950–51	1	0
1951–52	20	5
1952–53	25	7

1953–54	21	3
1954–55	8	3
Total	**75**	**18**

DAVID LLOYD BOWEN
Wing-half
Born Maesteg, 7 June 1928
Died 25 September 1995
Clubs Northampton Town; Arsenal; Northampton Town

	A	G
1950–51	7	0
1951–52	8	0
1952–53	2	0
1953–54	10	0
1954–55	21	0
1955–56	22	0
1956–57	30	2
1957–58	30	0
1958–59	16	0
Total	**146**	**2**

JOHN COLIN CHENHALL
Full-back
Born Bristol, 23 July 1927
Clubs Maidenhead United; Arsenal; Fulham

	A	G
1951–52	3	0
1952–53	13	0
Total	**16**	**0**

JAMES WRIGHT ROBERTSON
Winger
Born Falkirk, 20 February 1929

Clubs Dunipace Thistle; Arsenal; Brentford

	A	G
1951–52	1	0
Total	1	0

DONALD JOSEPH OAKES
Wing-half
Born St Asaph, 8 October 1928
Died 1977
Clubs Downend; Arsenal

	A	G
1952–53	2	1
1953–54	0	0
1954–55	9	0
Total	11	1

WILLIAM DODGIN
Centre-half
Born Gateshead, 4 November 1931
Died June 2000
Clubs Southampton; Fulham; Arsenal; Fulham

	A	G
1952–53	1	0
1953–54	39	0
1954–55	3	0
1955–56	15	0
1956–57	41	0
1957–58	23	0
1958–59	39	0
1959–60	30	0
Total	191	0

DENNIS JOSEPH EVANS
Full-back
Born Ellesmere Port, 18 May 1930
Died 23 February 2000
Clubs Ellesmere Port; Arsenal

	A	G
1953–54	10	0
1954–55	21	0
1955–56	42	0
1956–57	40	4
1957–58	32	0
1958–59	37	5
1959–60	7	1
Total	189	10

GERALD WARD
Wing-half
Born Stepney, 5 October 1936
Died January 1994
Clubs Arsenal; Leyton Orient; Cambridge City; Barnet

	A	G
1953–54	3	0
1954–55	0	0
1955–56	0	0
1956–57	0	0
1957–58	10	0
1958–59	31	4
1959–60	15	1
1960–61	9	1
1961–62	11	4
1962–63	2	0
Total	81	10

PETER TILLEY
Wing-half
Born Lurgan, 13 January 1930
Clubs Witton Albion; Arsenal; Bury;
Halifax Town

	A	G
1953–54	1	0
Total	**1**	**0**

JOHN BRIAN WALSH
Winger
Born Aldershot, 26 March 1932
Clubs Arsenal; Cardiff City;
Newport County

	A	G
1953–54	10	0
1954–55	6	0
1955–56	1	0
Total	**17**	**0**

WILLIAM DICKSON
Wing-half
Born Lurgan, 15 April 1923
Clubs Glenavon; Notts
County; Chelsea; Arsenal;
Mansfield Town

	A	G
1953–54	24	1
1954–55	4	0
1955–56	1	0
Total	**29**	**1**

LEONARD EDWARD WILLS
Full-back
Born Hackney, 18 October 1912

Died 1993
Clubs Eton Manor; Arsenal

	A	G
1953–54	30	0
1954–55	24	1
1955–56	15	0
1956–57	18	0
1957–58	18	1
1958–59	33	1
1959–60	33	1
1960–61	24	0
Total	**195**	**4**

THOMAS LAWTON
Centre-forward
Born Bolton, 6 October 1919
Died 6 November 1996
Clubs Burnley; Everton;
Chelsea; Notts County;
Brentford; Arsenal

	A	G
1953–54	9	1
1954–55	18	6
1955–56	8	6
Total	**35**	**13**

DEREK ROBERT TAPSCOTT
Centre-forward
Born Barry, 30 June 1932
Clubs Barry Town; Arsenal; Cardiff
City; Newport County

	A	G
1953–54	5	5
1954–55	37	13
1955–56	31	17

1956–57	38	25
1957–58	8	2
Total	**119**	**62**

CORNELIUS HENRY 'CON' SULLIVAN
Goalkeeper
Born Bristol, 22 August 1928
Clubs Horfield OB; Bristol City; Arsenal

	A	G
1953–54	1	0
1954–55	2	0
1955–56	10	0
1956–57	12	0
1957–58	3	0
Total	**28**	**0**

JAMES HENRY BLOOMFIELD
Inside-forward
Born Kensington, 15 February 1934
Died 3 April 1983
Clubs Walthamstow Avenue; Brentford; Arsenal; Birmingham City; Brentford; West Ham United; Plymouth Argyle; Leyton Orient

	A	G
1954–55	19	4
1955–56	32	3
1956–57	42	10
1957–58	40	16
1958–59	29	10
1959–60	36	10
1960–61	12	1
Total	**210**	**54**

OSEPH HAVERTY
Outside-left
Born Dublin, 17 February 1936
Clubs St Patricks Athletic; Arsenal; Blackburn Rovers; Millwall; Glasgow Celtic; Bristol Rovers

	A	G
1954–55	6	0
1955–56	8	2
1956–57	28	8
1957–58	15	0
1958–59	10	3
1959–60	35	8
1960–61	12	4
Total	**114**	**25**

RALPH GUTHRIE
Goalkeeper
Born Hartlepool, 13 September 1932
Died 996
Clubs Tow Law Town; Arsenal; Hartlepool United

	A	G
1954–55	2	0
Total	**2**	**0**

JAMES GIBB FOTHERINGHAM
Centre-half
Born Hamilton, 19 December 1933
Died 23 September 1977
Clubs Arsenal; Heart of Midlothian; Northampton Town

	A	G
1954–55	27	0
1955–56	25	0

J

		A	G
1956–57		0	0
1957–58		19	0
1958–59		1	0
	Total	72	0

DANIEL ROBERT CLAPTON
Outside-right
Born Stepney, 22 July 1934
Died June 1986
Clubs Leytonstone; Arsenal; Luton Town

		A	G
1954–55		16	0
1955–56		39	2
1956–57		39	2
1957–58		28	5
1958–59		39	6
1959–60		23	7
1960–61		18	2
1961–62		5	1
	Total	207	25

DAVID GEORGE HERD
Centre-forward
Born Hamilton, 15 April 1934
Clubs Stockport County; Arsenal; Manchester United; Stoke City

		A	G
1954–55		3	1
1955–56		5	2
1956–57		22	12
1957–58		39	24
1958–59		26	15
1959–60		31	14
1960–61		40	29
	Total	166	97

JACK WILKINSON
Centre-forward
Born Middlewich, 17 September 1931
Died 10 April 1996
Clubs Witton Albion; Arsenal; Sheffield United; Port Vale; Poole Town; Exeter City; Wellington Town

		A	G
1954–55		1	0
	Total	1	0

RAYMOND SWALLOW
Winger
Born Southwark, 15 June 1935
Clubs Tooting & Mitcham; Arsenal; Derby County; Poole Town

		A	G
1954–55		1	0
1955–56		1	1
1956–57		4	0
1957–58		7	3
	Total	13	4

MICHAEL DOUGLAS TIDDY
Outside-right
Born Helston, 4 April 1929
Clubs Torquay United; Cardiff City; Arsenal; Brighton & Hove Albion

		A	G
1955–56		21	0
1956–57		15	6
1957–58		12	2
	Total	48	8

GORDON EDWARD NUTT

Winger
Born Birmingham, 8 November 1932
Clubs Coventry City; Cardiff City;
Arsenal; Southend United

		A	G
1955–56	8	1	
1956–57	1	0	
1957–58	21	3	
1958–59	16	6	
1959–60	3	0	
	Total	49	10

VICTOR GEORGE GROVES

Inside-forward/Wing-half
Born Stepney, 5 November 1932
Clubs Leytonstone; Tottenham
Hotspur; Walthamstow Avenue;
Leyton Orient; Arsenal

		A	G
1955–56		15	8
1956–57		5	2
1957–58		30	10
1958–59		33	10
1959–60		30	1
1960–61		32	0
1961–62		16	0
1962–63		9	0
1963–64		15	0
	Total	185	31

STANLEY CHARLTON

Full-back
Born Exeter, 28 June 1929
Clubs Bromley; Leyton Orient;
Arsenal; Leyton Orient

		A	G
1955–56		19	0
1956–57		40	0
1957–58		36	0
1958–59		4	0
	Total	99	0

JOHN BARNWELL

Wing-half
Born Newcastle, 24 December 1938
Clubs Bishop Auckland; Arsenal;
Nottingham Forest; Sheffield United

		A	G
1956–57		1	0
1957–58		0	0
1958–59		16	3
1959–60		28	7
1960–61		26	6
1961–62		14	3
1962–63		34	2
1963–64		19	2
	Total	138	23

DANIEL LEOW LE ROUX

Outside-right
Born South Africa, 25 November
1933
Clubs Queen's Park (South Africa);
Arsenal

		A	G
1957–58		5	0
	Total	5	0

JAMES ALFRED STANDEN

Goalkeeper
Born Edmonton, 30 May 1935

Clubs Rickmansworth Town;
Arsenal; Luton Town; West Ham
United; Detroit (USA); Millwall;
Portsmouth

	A	G
1957–58	1	0
1958–59	13	0
1959–60	20	0
1960–61	1	0
Total	35	0

JOHN WILLIAM FREDERICK JAMES PETTS

Wing-half

Born Edmonton, 2 October 1938

Clubs Arsenal; Reading; Bristol
Rovers

	A	G
1957–58	9	0
1958–59	3	0
1959–60	7	0
1960–61	1	0
1961–62	12	0
Total	32	0

ANTHONY BIGGS

Centre-forward

Born Greenford, 17 April 1936

Clubs Hounslow Town; Arsenal;
Leyton Orient

	A	G
1957–58	2	0
1958–59	2	1
Total	4	1

THOMAS HENDERSON DOCHERTY

Wing-half

Born Glasgow, 24 August 1928

Clubs Glasgow Celtic; Preston North
End; Arsenal; Chelsea

	A	G
1958–59	38	1
1959–60	24	0
1960–61	21	0
Total	83	1

JOHN GILLESPIE 'JACKIE' HENDERSON

Centre-forward

Born Glasgow, 17 January 1932

Died 26 January 2005

Clubs Portsmouth;
Wolverhampton Wanderers;
Arsenal; Fulham

	A	G
1958–59	21	12
1959–60	31	7
1960–61	39	10
1961–62	12	0
Total	103	29

LEONARD BRUCE JULIANS

Centre-forward

Born Tottenham, 19 June 1933

Died 17 December 1993

Clubs Walthamstow Avenue;
Leyton Orient; Arsenal; Nottingham
Forest; Millwall

	A	G
1958–59	10	5
1959–60	8	2
Total	18	7

WILLIAM JAMES McCULLOUGH

Left-back
Born Larne, 27 July 1935
Clubs Portadown; Arsenal;
Millwall

	A	G
1958–59	10	0
1959–60	33	0
1960–61	41	0
1961–62	40	0
1962–63	42	3
1963–64	40	1
1964–65	30	0
1965–66	17	0
Total	253	4

PETER JOHN GOY

Goalkeeper
Born Beverley, 8 June 1938
Clubs Arsenal; Southend United;
Watford; Huddersfield Town

	A	G
1958–59	2	0
Total	2	0

ROY LEONARD GOULDEN

Inside-forward
Born Ilford, 22 September 1937
Clubs Arsenal; Southend United;
Ipswich Town

	A	G
1958–59	1	0
Total	1	0

MELVYN CHARLES

Centre-forward
Born Swansea, 14 May 1935
Clubs Leeds United; Swansea City;
Arsenal; Cardiff City; Port Vale;
Oswestry Town; Haverfordwest

	A	G
1959–60	20	8
1960–61	19	3
1961–62	21	15
Total	60	26

EDWARD JAMES MAGILL

Full-back
Born Lurgan, 17 May 1939
Clubs Portadown; Arsenal; Brighton
& Hove Albion

	A	G
1959–60	17	0
1960–61	6	0
1961–62	21	0
1962–63	36	0
1963–64	35	0
1964–65	1	0
Total	116	0

JOHN DUNCAN SNEDDEN

Centre-half
Born Bonnybridge, 3 February 1942
Clubs Arsenal; Charlton Athletic;
Leyton Orient; Halifax Town

	A	G
1959–60	1	0
1960–61	23	0
1961–62	15	0
1962–63	27	0
1963–64	14	0
1964–65	3	0
Total	83	0

DENNIS PATRICK CLAPTON

Centre-forward
Born Hackney, 12 October 1939
Clubs Arsenal; Northampton Town

	A	G
1959–60	3	0
1960–61	1	0
Total	4	0

MICHAEL DENNIS EVERITT

Left-back
Born Clacton, 16 January 1941
Clubs Arsenal; Northampton Town;
Plymouth Argyle; Brighton & Hove
Albion

	A	G
1959–60	5	0
1960–61	4	1
Total	9	1

ALAN FREDERICK GRAHAM SKIRTON

Winger
Born Bath, 23 January 1939
Clubs Bath City; Arsenal; Blackpool;
Bristol City; Torquay United

	A	G
1960–61	16	3
1961–62	38	19
1962–63	28	10
1963–64	15	7
1964–65	22	3
1965–66	23/1	9
1966–67	2	2
Total	144/1	53

PETER KANE

Inside-forward
Born Petershill, 4 April 1939
Clubs Queen's Park; Northampton
Town; Arsenal; Northampton Town;
Crewe Alexandra

	A	G
1960–61	4	1
Total	4	1

GEOFFREY HUGH STRONG

Inside-forward
Born Kirkheaton, 19 September 1937
Clubs Stanley United; Arsenal;
Liverpool; Coventry City

	A	G
1960–61	19	10
1961–62	20	12
1962–63	36	18
1963–64	38	26
1964–65	12	3
Total	125	69

GEORGE EDWARD EASTHAM

Inside-forward
Born Blackpool, 23 September 1936

Clubs Ards; Newcastle United; Arsenal; Stoke City

	A	G
1960–61	19	5
1961–62	38	6
1962–63	33	4
1963–64	38	10
1964–65	42	10
1965–66	37	6
Total	207	41

WILLIAM JOHN TERENCE NEILL

Centre-half
Born Belfast, 8 May 1942
Clubs Bangor; Arsenal; Hull City

	A	G
1960–61	14	1
1961–62	20	0
1962–63	17	0
1963–64	11	1
1964–65	29	1
1965–66	39	0
1966–67	34	0
1967–68	38	2
1968–69	21/1	2
1969–70	17	1
Total	240/1	8

ALLAN ROBERT YOUNG

Centre-half
Born Edmonton, 20 January 1941
Clubs Arsenal

	A	G
1960–61	4	0
Total	4	0

FRANK SIMON O'NEILL

Outside-right
Born Dublin, 13 April 1940
Clubs Home Farm; Arsenal

	A	G
1960–61	2	0
Total	2	0

JOHN 'JACK' McCLELLAND

Goalkeeper
Born Lurgan, 19 May 1940
Died 15 March 1976
Clubs Glenavon; Arsenal; Fulham; Lincoln City

	A	G
1960–61	4	0
1961–62	4	0
1962–63	33	0
1963–64	5	0
Total	46	0

RENO DAVID BACUZZI

Full-back
Born Islington, 12 October 1940
Clubs Eastbourne; Arsenal; Manchester City; Reading

	A	G
1960–61	13	0
1961–62	22	0
1962–63	6	0
1963–64	5	0
Total	46	0

ARFON TREVOR GRIFFITHS
Midfield
Born Wrexham, 23 August 1941
Clubs Wrexham; Arsenal; Wrexham

	A	G
1960–61	1	0
1961–62	14	2
Total	15	2

LAURENCE BROWN
Centre-half
Born Shildon, 22 August 1937
Died 30 September 1998
Clubs Bishop Auckland; Darlington;
Bishop Auckland; Northampton
Town; Arsenal; Tottenham Hotspur;
Norwich City; Bradford Park Avenue

	A	G
1961–62	41	0
1962–63	38	1
1963–64	22	1
Total	101	2

JOHN MURDOCH MACLEOD
Outside-right
Born Edinburgh, 23 November 1938
Clubs Hibernian; Arsenal;
Aston Villa

	A	G
1961–62	37	6
1962–63	33	9
1963–64	30	7
1964–65	1	1
Total	101	23

IAIN HECTOR McKECHNIE
Goalkeeper
Born Bellshill, 4 October 1941
Clubs Arsenal; Southend United;
Hull City

	A	G
1961–62	3	0
1962–63	9	0
1963–64	11	0
Total	23	0

HAROLD EDWIN CLAMP
Wing-half
Born Coalville, 14 September 1934
Died 11 December 1995
Clubs Wolverhampton Wanderers;
Arsenal; Stoke City; Peterborough
United

	A	G
1961–62	18	0
1962–63	4	1
Total	22	1

GEORGE ARMSTRONG
Winger
Born Felling, 9 August 1944
Died 31 October 2000
Clubs Arsenal; Leicester City;
Stockport County

	A	G
1961–62	4	1
1962–63	16	2
1963–64	28	3
1964–65	40	4
1965–66	39	6

1966–67	40	7
1967–68	42	5
1968–69	26/3	5
1969–70	17	3
1970–71	42	7
1971–72	41/1	2
1972–73	29/1	2
1973–74	40/1	0
1974–75	21/3	0
1975–76	28/1	4
1976–77	37	2
Total	490/10	53

FREDERICK ROBERT GEORGE CLARKE
Full-back
Born Banbridge, 4 November 1941
Clubs Glenavon; Arsenal

	A	G
1961–62	1	0
1962–63	5	0
1963–64	5	0
1964–65	15	0
Total	26	0

JOSEPH HENRY BAKER
Centre-forward
Born Liverpool, 17 July 1940
Died 6 October 2003
Clubs Hibernian; AC Torino (Italy); Arsenal; Nottingham Forest; Sunderland

	A	G
1962–63	39	29
1963–64	39	26

1964–65	42	25
1965–66	24	13
Total	144	93

DAVID JOHN COURT
Midfield
Born Mitcham, 1 March 1944
Clubs Arsenal; Luton Town; Brentford

	A	G
1962–63	6	3
1963–64	8	1
1964–65	33	3
1965–66	38	1
1966–67	10/3	0
1967–68	15/1	3
1968–69	40	6
1969–70	18/3	0
Total	168/7	17

RODNEY GEORGE SMITHSON
Central defender
Born Leicester, 9 October 1943
Clubs Arsenal; Oxford United

	A	G
1962–63	2	0
Total	2	0

TERENCE KEITH ANDERSON
Winger
Born Woking, 11 March 1940
Died January 1980
Clubs Arsenal; Norwich City; Colchester United; Baltimore (USA); Scunthorpe United; Crewe Alexandra; Baltimore (USA); Colchester United

	A	G
1962–63	5	1
1963–64	10	3
1964–65	10	2
Total	**25**	**6**

JONATHAN CHARLES SAMMELS

Midfield
Born Ipswich, 23 July 1945
Clubs Arsenal; Leicester City

	A	G
1962–63	2	1
1963–64	0	0
1964–65	17	5
1965–66	32	6
1966–67	42	10
1967–68	34/1	4
1968–69	36	4
1969–70	36	8
1970–71	13/2	1
Total	**212/3**	**39**

JOHN FRANCOMBE 'IAN' URE

Centre-half
Born Ayr, 7 December 1939
Clubs Dundee; Arsenal; Manchester United

	A	G
1963–64	41	1
1964–65	22	1
1965–66	21	0
1966–67	37	0
1967–68	21	0
1968–69	23	0
1969–70	3	0
Total	**168**	**2**

ROBERT PRIMROSE WILSON

Goalkeeper
Born Chesterfield, 30 October 1941
Clubs Wolverhampton Wanderers; Arsenal

	A	G
1963–64	5	0
1964–65	0	0
1965–66	4	0
1966–67	0	0
1967–68	13	0
1968–69	42	0
1969–70	28	0
1970–71	42	0
1971–72	37	0
1972–73	22	0
1973–74	41	0
Total	**234**	**0**

JAMES FURNELL

Goalkeeper
Born Manchester, 23 November 1937
Clubs Burnley; Liverpool; Arsenal; Rotherham United; Plymouth Argyle

	A	G
1963–64	21	0
1964–65	18	0
1965–66	31	0
1966–67	42	0
1967–68	29	0
Total	**141**	**0**

PETER FREDERICK SIMPSON
Central defender
Born Great Yarmouth, 13 January 1945
Clubs Arsenal

	A	G
1963–64	6	0
1964–65	6	2
1965–66	5/3	0
1966–67	34/2	1
1967–68	40	0
1968–69	34	0
1969–70	39	0
1970–71	25	0
1971–72	32/2	4
1972–73	27	1
1973–74	34/4	2
1974–75	39/1	0
1975–76	7/2	0
1976–77	19	0
1977–78	6/3	0
Total	353/17	10

JOHN RADFORD
Forward
Born Hemsworth, 22 February 1947
Clubs Arsenal; West Ham United; Blackburn Rovers

	A	G
1963–64	1	0
1964–65	13	7
1965–66	32	8
1966–67	30	4
1967–68	39	10
1968–69	31/3	15
1969–70	39	12
1970–71	41	15
1971–72	34	8
1972–73	38	15
1973–74	32	7
1974–75	29	7
1975–76	15	3
1976–77	1/1	0
Total	375/4	111

DONALD HOWE
Full-back
Born Wolverhampton, 12 October 1935
Clubs West Bromwich Albion; Arsenal

	A	G
1964–65	40	0
1965–66	29	1
1966–67	1	0
Total	70	1

GORDON FERRY
Centre-half
Born Sunderland, 22 December 1943
Clubs Arsenal; Leyton Orient

	A	G
1964–65	11	0
Total	11	0

FRANCIS McLINTOCK
Central defender
Born Glasgow, 28 December 1939
Clubs Shawfield Juniors; Leicester City; Arsenal; Queen's Park Rangers

	A	G
1964–65	25	2
1965–66	36	2
1966–67	40	9
1967–68	38	4
1968–69	37	1
1969–70	30	0
1970–71	42	5
1971–72	37	3
1972–73	27/2	0
Total	312/2	26

ANTHONY JOHN BURNS
Goalkeeper
Born Edenbridge, 27 March 1944
Clubs Tonbridge; Arsenal; Brighton
& Hove Albion; Charlton Athletic;
Durban United (South Africa);
Crystal Palace; Brentford;
Memphis (USA); Plymouth
Argyle

	A	G
1964–65	24	0
1965–66	7	0
Total	31	0

BRIAN TAWSE
Winger
Born Ellon, 30 July 1945
Clubs King Street 'A'; Arsenal;
Brighton & Hove Albion;
Brentford

	A	G
1964–65	5	0
Total	5	0

THOMAS BALDWIN
Forward
Born Gateshead, 10 June 1945
Clubs Wrekenton Juniors; Arsenal;
Chelsea; Millwall; Manchester
United; Gravesend & Northfleet;
Brentford

	A	G
1964–65	1	0
1965–66	8	5
1966–67	8	2
Total	17	7

PETER EDWIN STOREY
Defender
Born Farnham,
7 September 1945
Clubs Arsenal; Fulham

	A	G
1965–66	28	0
1966–67	34	1
1967–68	39	0
1968–69	42	0
1969–70	39	1
1970–71	40	2
1971–72	29	1
1972–73	40	4
1973–74	41	0
1974–75	37	0
1975–76	11	0
1976–77	7/4	0
Total	387/4	9

JOHN THOMAS WALLEY
Midfield
Born Caernarfon, 27 February 1945

Clubs Caernarfon; Arsenal; Watford; Leyton Orient; Watford

	A	G
1965–66	7/3	1
1966–67	3/1	0
Total	10/4	1

GORDON NEILSON
Winger
Born Glasgow, 28 May 1947
Clubs Glasgow United; Arsenal; Brentford

	A	G
1965–66	2	0
1966–67	12	2
Total	14	2

ROY JAMES PACK
Full-back
Born Stoke Newington, 20 September 1946
Clubs Arsenal; Portsmouth

	A	G
1965–66	1	0
Total	1	0

JAMES MORRISON McGILL
Midfield
Born Glasgow, 27 November 1946
Clubs Possilpark Juniors; Arsenal; Huddersfield Town; Hull City; Halifax Town

	A	G
1965–66	2	0
1966–67	4/4	0
Total	6/4	0

THOMAS COAKLEY
Outside-right
Born Bellshill, 21 May 1947
Clubs Bellshill Athletic; Motherwell; Arsenal; Detroit (USA); Morton

	A	G
1966–67	9	1
Total	9	1

COLIN ADDISON
Inside-forward
Born Taunton, 18 May 1940
Clubs York City; Nottingham Forest; Arsenal; Sheffield United; Hereford United

	A	G
1966–67	17	4
1967–68	10/1	5
Total	27/1	9

GEORGE GRAHAM
Forward/Midfield
Born Coatbridge, 30 November 1944
Clubs Aston Villa; Chelsea; Arsenal; Manchester United; Portsmouth; Crystal Palace

	A	G
1966–67	33	11
1967–68	38	16
1968–69	23/3	4

1969–70	36	7
1970–71	36/2	11
1971–72	39/1	8
1972–73	14/2	2
Total	**219/8**	**59**

MICHAEL COLIN BOOT
Forward
Born Leicester, 17 December 1947
Clubs Enderby Town; Arsenal; Port
Elizabeth (South Africa)

	A	**G**
1966–67	3/1	2
Total	**3/1**	**2**

JOHN WOODWARD
Central defender/Midfield
Born Glasgow, 10 January 1949
Clubs Possilpark Juniors; Arsenal;
York City

	A	**G**
1966–67	2/1	0
Total	**2/1**	**0**

ROBERT McNAB
Left-back
Born Huddersfield, 20 July 1943
Clubs Moldgreen YC; Huddersfield
Town; Arsenal; Wolverhampton
Wanderers

	A	**G**
1966–67	25/1	0
1967–68	30	0
1968–69	42	0
1969–70	37	0

1970–71	40	0
1971–72	20	0
1972–73	42	1
1973–74	23	1
1974–75	18	0
Total	**277/1**	**2**

GEORGE JOHNSTON
Forward
Born Glasgow, 21 March 1947
Clubs Cardiff City; Arsenal;
Birmingham City; Walsall;
Fulham; Hereford United;
Newport County

	A	**G**
1967–68	17/1	3
1968–69	0/3	0
Total	**17/4**	**3**

PATRICK JAMES RICE
Right-back
Born Belfast, 17 March 1949
Clubs Arsenal; Watford

	A	**G**
1967–68	2/4	0
1968–69	0	0
1969–70	7	1
1970–71	41	0
1971–72	42	1
1972–73	39	2
1973–74	41	1
1974–75	32	0
1975–76	42	1
1976–77	42	3
1977–78	38	2
1978–79	39	1

		A	G
1979–80		26	0
1980–81		0/2	0
	Total	**391/6**	**12**

		A	G
1967–68		0/1	0
	Total	**0/1**	**0**

DAVID JOHN JENKINS
Forward
Born Bristol, 2 September 1946
Clubs Arsenal; Tottenham Hotspur;
Brentford; Hereford United;
Newport County; Shrewsbury Town;
Workington

		A	G
1967–68		2/1	0
1968–69		14	3
	Total	**16/1**	**3**

ROBERT ALFRED GOULD
Forward
Born Coventry, 12 June 1946
Clubs Coventry City; Arsenal;
Wolverhampton Wanderers; West
Bromwich Albion; Bristol City; West
Ham United; Wolverhampton
Wanderers; Bristol Rovers; Hereford
United

		A	G
1967–68		15/1	6
1968–69		33/5	10
1969–70		9/2	0
	Total	**57/8**	**16**

ROGER DAVIDSON
Midfield
Born Islington, 27 October 1948
Clubs Arsenal; Portsmouth; Fulham;
Lincoln City; Aldershot

JAMES GILLEN ROBERTSON
Winger
Born Glasgow, 17 December 1944
Clubs St Mirren; Tottenham Hotspur;
Arsenal; Ipswich Town; Stoke City;
Walsall; Crewe Alexandra

		A	G
1968–69		18/1	3
1969–70		27	4
	Total	**45/1**	**7**

CHARLES FREDFERICK GEORGE
Forward
Born Islington, 10 October 1950
Clubs Arsenal; Derby County;
Southampton; Nottingham Forest;
Bulova (Hong Kong); Bournemouth;
Derby County

		A	G
1969–70		21/7	6
1970–71		17	5
1971–72		20/3	7
1972–73		18/9	6
1973–74		28	5
1974–75		9/1	2
	Total	**113/20**	**31**

EDWARD PATRICK KELLY
Midfield
Born Glasgow, 7 February 1951
Clubs Arsenal; Queen's Park
Rangers; Leicester City; Notts

County; Bournemouth; Leicester
City; Melton Town; Torquay United

	A	G
1969–70	14/2	2
1970–71	21/2	4
1971–72	22/1	2
1972–73	27	1
1973–74	35/2	1
1974–75	32	1
1975–76	17	2
Total	168/7	13

MALCOLM WALTER WEBSTER
Goalkeeper
Born Doncaster, 12 November 1950
Clubs Arsenal; Fulham; Southend
United; Cambridge United

	A	G
1969–70	3	0
Total	3	0

GEOFFREY COLIN BARNETT
Goalkeeper
Born Northwich, 16 October 1946
Clubs Everton; Arsenal

	A	G
1969–70	11	0
1970–71	0	0
1971–72	5	0
1972–73	20	0
1973–74	0	0
1974–75	2	0
1975–76	1	0
Total	39	0

JOHN GRIFFITH ROBERTS
Central defender/Forward
Born Abercynon, 11 September 1946
Clubs Abercynon Athletic; Swansea
City; Northampton Town; Arsenal;
Birmingham City; Wrexham; Hull City

	A	G
1969–70	11	1
1970–71	18	0
1971–72	21/2	3
1972–73	6/1	0
Total	56/3	4

RAYMOND KENNEDY
Midfield/Forward
Born Seaton Delaval, 28 July 1951
Clubs Arsenal; Liverpool; Swansea
City; Hartlepool United

	A	G
1969–70	2/2	1
1970–71	41	19
1971–72	37	12
1972–73	34	9
1973–74	42	12
Total	156/2	53

SAMUEL NELSON
Left-back
Born Belfast, 1 April 1949
Clubs Arsenal; Brighton & Hove Albion

	A	G
1969–70	4	0
1970–71	2/2	0
1971–72	24	1
1972–73	2/4	0

	A	G
1973–74	18/1	1
1974–75	19/1	0
1975–76	36	0
1976–77	31/1	3
1977–78	41	1
1978–79	33	2
1979–80	35	2
1980–81	0/1	0
Total	**245/10**	**10**

PETER MARINELLO

Winger
Born Edinburgh, 20 February 1950
Clubs Hibernian; Arsenal; Portsmouth; Motherwell; Fulham

	A	G
1969–70	14	1
1970–71	1/2	0
1971–72	4/4	1
1972–73	13	1
Total	**32/6**	**3**

PAUL DAVIES

Centre-forward
Born St Asaph, 10 October 1952
Clubs Arsenal; Charlton Athletic

	A	G
1971–72	0/1	0
Total	**0/1**	**0**

ALAN JAMES BALL

Midfield
Born Farnworth, 12 May 1945
Died 25 April 2007
Clubs Blackpool; Everton; Arsenal; Southampton; Vancouver Whitecaps (Canada); Blackpool; Southampton; Eastern (Hong Kong); Bristol Rovers

	A	G
1971–72	18	3
1972–73	40	10
1973–74	36	13
1974–75	30	9
1975–76	39	9
1976–77	14	1
Total	**177**	**45**

BRENDON MARTIN BATSON

Right-back
Born Grenada, West Indies, 6 February 1953
Clubs Arsenal; Cambridge United; West Bromwich Albion

	A	G
1971–72	0/2	0
1972–73	3	0
1973–74	3/2	0
Total	**6/4**	**0**

JEFFREY PAUL BLOCKLEY

Central defender
Born Leicester, 12 September 1949
Clubs Coventry City; Arsenal; Leicester City; Notts County

	A	G
1972–73	20	0
1973–74	26	1
1974–75	6	0
Total	**52**	**1**

BRIAN GEOFFREY HORNSBY
Midfield
Born Great Shelford, 10 September 1954
Clubs Arsenal; Shrewsbury Town; Sheffield Wednesday; Chester City; Edmonton (Canada); Carlisle United; Chesterfield

	A	G
1972–73	1	0
1973–74	6/3	3
1974–75	12	3
1975–76	4	0
Total	23/3	6

DAVID JAMES PRICE
Midfield
Born Caterham, 23 June 1955
Clubs Arsenal; Peterborough United; Crystal Palace; Leyton Orient

	A	G
1972–73	0/1	0
1973–74	3/1	0
1974–75	0/1	0
1975–76	0	0
1976–77	6/2	1
1977–78	38/1	5
1978–79	39	8
1979–80	21/1	1
1980–81	9/3	1
Total	116/10	16

BRIAN MARK CHAMBERS
Midfield
Born Newcastle, 31 October 1949
Clubs Sunderland; Arsenal; Luton Town; Millwall; Bournemouth; Halifax Town

	A	G
1973–74	1	0
Total	1	0

WILLIAM 'LIAM' BRADY
Midfield
Born Dublin, 13 February 1956
Clubs Arsenal; Juventus; Sampdoria; Inter Milan; Ascoli (Italy); West Ham United

	A	G
1973–74	9/4	1
1974–75	30/2	3
1975–76	41/1	5
1976–77	37/1	5
1977–78	39	9
1978–79	37	13
1979–80	34	7
Total	227/8	43

RICHARD FREDERICK POWLING
Defender
Born Barking, 21 May 1956
Clubs Arsenal; Barnet

	A	G
1973–74	2	0
1974–75	5/3	0
1975–76	28/1	1
1976–77	11/1	0
1977–78	4	2
Total	50/5	3

JOHN JAMES RIMMER
Goalkeeper
Born Southport, 10 February 1948
Clubs Manchester United; Swansea
City; Arsenal; Aston Villa; Swansea City

	A	G
1973–74	1	0
1974–75	40	0
1975–76	41	0
1976–77	42	0
Total	124	0

JOHN MELVIN MATTHEWS
Midfield
Born Camden, 1 November 1955
Clubs Arsenal; Sheffield United;
Mansfield Town; Chesterfield;
Plymouth Argyle; Torquay United

	A	G
1974–75	20	0
1975–76	0/1	0
1976–77	14/3	2
1977–78	4/3	0
Total	38/7	2

BRIAN KIDD
Forward
Born Manchester, 29 May 1949
Clubs Manchester United; Arsenal;
Manchester City; Everton; Bolton
Wanderers

	A	G
1974–75	40	19
1975–76	37	11
Total	77	30

TERENCE JOHN MANCINI
Central defender
Born Camden Town, 4 October 1942
Clubs Watford; Port Elizabeth (South
Africa); Leyton Orient; Queen's Park
Rangers; Arsenal; Aldershot

	A	G
1974–75	26	0
1975–76	26	1
Total	52	1

ALEXANDER JAMES CROPLEY
Midfield
Born Aldershot, 16 January 1951
Clubs Edina Hearts; Hibernian;
Arsenal; Aston Villa; Newcastle
United; Toronto Blizzards (Canada);
Portsmouth; Hibernian

	A	G
1974–75	7	1
1975–76	20	4
1976–77	2/1	0
Total	29/1	5

TREVOR WILLIAM ROSS
Midfield
Born Ashton-under-Lyne, 16
January 1957
Clubs Arsenal; Everton; Portsmouth;
AEK Athens (Greece); Sheffield
United; Bury

	A	G
1974–75	1/1	0
1975–76	17	1
1976–77	29	4

| 1977–78 | 10 | 0 |
| Total | 57/1 | 5 |

JOHN WILFRED ROSTRON
Left-back
Born Sunderland,
29 September 1956
Clubs Arsenal; Sunderland; Watford;
Sheffield Wednesday; Sheffield
United; Brentford

	A	G
1974–75	6	2
1975–76	2/3	0
1976–77	4/2	0
Total	12/5	2

FRANCIS ANTHONY STAPLETON
Forward
Born Dublin, 10 July 1956
Clubs Arsenal; Manchester United;
Ajax (Holland); Derby County; Le
Havre (France); Blackburn Rovers;
Aldershot; Huddersfield Town;
Bradford City; Brighton & Hove
Albion

	A	G
1974–75	1	0
1975–76	23/2	4
1976–77	40	13
1977–78	39	13
1978–79	41	17
1979–80	39	14
1980–81	40	14
Total	223/2	75

DAVID ANTHONY O'LEARY
Central defender
Born Stoke Newington, 2 May 1958
Clubs Arsenal; Leeds United

	A	G
1975–76	27	0
1976–77	33	2
1977–78	41	1
1978–79	37	2
1979–80	34	1
1980–81	24	1
1981–82	40	1
1982–83	36	1
1983–84	36	0
1984–85	36	0
1985–86	35	0
1986–87	39	0
1987–88	23	0
1988–89	26	0
1989–90	28/6	1
1990–91	11/10	1
1991–92	11/14	0
1992–93	6/5	0
Total	523/35	11

MALCOLM IAN MacDONALD
Forward
Born Fulham, 7 January 1950
Clubs Tonbridge; Fulham; Luton
Town; Newcastle United; Arsenal

	A	G
1976–77	41	25
1977–78	39	15
1978–79	4	2
Total	84	42

PATRICK HOWARD
Central defender
Born Dodworth, 7 October 1947
Clubs Barnsley; Newcastle United;
Arsenal; Birmingham City; Bury

		A	G
1976–77		15/1	0
	Total	15/1	0

ALAN ANTHONY HUDSON
Midfield
Born Chelsea, 21 June 1951
Clubs Chelsea; Stoke City; Arsenal;
Seattle (USA); Chelsea; Stoke City

		A	G
1976–77		19	0
1977–78		17	0
	Total	36	0

WILLIAM DAVID YOUNG
Central defender
Born Edinburgh, 25 November 1951
Clubs Aberdeen; Tottenham
Hotspur; Arsenal; Nottingham
Forest; Norwich City; Brighton &
Hove Albion; Darlington

		A	G
1976–77		14	1
1977–78		35	3
1978–79		33	0
1979–80		38	3
1980–81		40	4
1981–82		10	0
	Total	170	11

GRAHAM RIX
Midfield
Born Askern, 23 October 1957
Clubs Arsenal; Brentford; Dundee;
Chelsea

		A	G
1976–77		4/3	1
1977–78		37/2	2
1978–79		39	3
1979–80		38	4
1980–81		35	5
1981–82		39	9
1982–83		36	6
1983–84		34	4
1984–85		18	2
1985–86		38	3
1986–87		13/5	2
1987–88		7/3	0
	Total	338/13	41

PATRICK ANTHONY JENNINGS
Goalkeeper
Born Newry, 12 June 1945
Clubs Newry Town; Watford;
Tottenham Hotspur; Arsenal

		A	G
1977–78		42	0
1978–79		39	0
1979–80		37	0
1980–81		31	0
1981–82		16	0
1982–83		19	0
1983–84		38	0
1984–85		15	0
	Total	237	0

STEPHEN JAMES WALFORD

Defender
Born Islington, 5 January 1958
Clubs Tottenham Hotspur; Arsenal;
Norwich City; West Ham United;
Huddersfield Town; Gillingham;
West Bromwich Albion

	A	G
1977–78	2/3	0
1978–79	26/7	2
1979–80	16/3	1
1980–81	20	0
Total	**64/13**	**3**

DAVID MARK HEELEY

Winger
Born Peterborough, 8 September
1959
Clubs Peterborough United;
Arsenal; Northampton Town

	A	G
1977–78	3/2	0
1978–79	6/4	1
Total	**9/6**	**1**

ALAN SUNDERLAND

Forward/Midfield
Born Mexborough, 1 July 1953
Clubs Wolverhampton Wanderers;
Arsenal; Ipswich Town

	A	G
1977–78	23	4
1978–79	37	9
1979–80	36/1	14
1980–81	34	7
1981–82	38	11
1982–83	25	6
1983–84	11/1	4
Total	**204/2**	**55**

JOHN ANTHONY DEVINE

Midfield
Born Dublin, 11 November 1958
Clubs Arsenal; Norwich City;
Stoke City

	A	G
1977–78	3	0
1978–79	7	0
1979–80	20	0
1980–81	38/1	0
1981-82	10/1	0
1982–83	8/1	0
Total	**86/3**	**0**

JAMES HARVEY

Midfield
Born Lurgan, 2 May 1958
Clubs Glenavon; Arsenal; Hereford
United; Bristol City; Wrexham;
Tranmere Rovers; Crewe
Alexandra

	A	G
1977–78	1	0
1978–79	1/1	0
Total	**2/1**	**0**

ALEXANDER JOHN KOSMINA

Forward
Born Australia, 17 August 1956
Clubs Polonia (Australia); Arsenal

	A	G
1978–79	0/1	0
Total	0/1	0

PAUL GEORGE BARRON

Goalkeeper

Born Woolwich, 16 September 1953

Clubs Slough Town; Plymouth Argyle; Arsenal; Crystal Palace; West Bromwich Albion; Stoke City; Queen's Park Rangers; Reading

	A	G
1979–80	3	0
1980–81	5	0
Total	8	0

KEVIN STEAD

Defender

Born West Ham, 2 October 1958

Clubs Tottenham Hotspur; Arsenal

	A	G
1979–80	1/1	0
Total	1/1	0

STEPHEN PAUL GATTING

Central defender

Born Willesden, 29 May 1959

Clubs Arsenal; Brighton & Hove Albion; Charlton Athletic

	A	G
1979–80	19/2	1
1980–81	9/5	1
1981–82	22/1	3
Total	50/8	5

BRIAN ERNEST TALBOT

Midfield

Born Ipswich, 21 July 1953

Clubs Ipswich Town; Arsenal; Watford; Stoke City; West Bromwich Albion; Fulham; Aldershot

	A	G
1978–79	20	0
1979–80	42	1
1980–81	40	7
1981–82	42	7
1982–83	38/4	9
1983–84	26/1	6
1984–85	37/4	10
Total	245/9	40

BRIAN JAMES McDERMOTT

Winger

Born Slough, 8 April 1961

Clubs Arsenal; Fulham; Oxford United; Huddersfield Town; Cardiff City; Exeter City

	A	G
1978–79	0/2	0
1979–80	0/1	0
1980–81	16/7	5
1981–82	9/4	1
1982–83	7/2	4
1983–84	6/7	2
Total	38/23	12

STEPHEN JAMES CHARLES BRIGNALL

Defender

Born Tenterden, 12 June 1960

Clubs Arsenal; Hastings United

	A	G
1978–79	0/1	0
Total	**0/1**	**0**

PAUL LEON VAESSEN
Forward
Born Gillingham, 16 October 1961
Died 8 August 2001
Clubs Arsenal

	A	G
1978–79	1	0
1979–80	8/6	2
1980–81	5/2	2
1981–82	9/1	2
Total	**23/9**	**6**

JOHN WILLIAM HOLLINS
Midfield
Born Guildford, 16 July 1946
Clubs Chelsea; Queen's Park
Rangers; Arsenal; Chelsea

	A	G
1979–80	23/3	1
1980–81	38	5
1981–82	40	1
1982–83	22/1	2
Total	**123/4**	**9**

PAUL VINCENT DAVIS
Midfield
Born Dulwich, 9 December 1961
Clubs Arsenal; Brentford

	A	G
1979–80	1/1	0
1980–81	9/1	1

		A
1981–82	37/1	4
1982–83	40/1	4
1983–84	31/4	1
1984–85	21/3	1
1985–86	28/1	4
1986–87	39	4
1987–88	28/1	5
1988–89	11/1	1
1989–90	8/3	1
1990–91	36/1	3
1991–92	12	0
1992–93	6	0
1993–94	21/1	0
1994–95	3/1	1
Total	**331/20**	**30**

KENNETH GRAHAM SANSOM
Left-back
Born Camberwell, 26 September 1958
Clubs Crystal Palace; Arsenal;
Newcastle United; Queen's Park
Rangers; Coventry City; Everton;
Brentford; Chertsey Town; Watford

	A	G
1980–81	42	3
1981–82	42	0
1982–83	40	0
1983–84	40	1
1984–85	39	1
1985–86	42	0
1986–87	35	0
1987–88	34	1
Total	**314**	**6**

GEORGE WOOD
Goalkeeper
Born Douglas, 26 September 1952

Clubs East Stirling; Blackpool; Everton; Arsenal; Crystal Palace; Cardiff City; Blackpool; Hereford United

	A	G
1980–81	11	0
1981–82	26	0
1982–83	23	0
Total	60	0

PETER NICHOLAS
Midfield
Born Newport, 10 November 1959
Clubs Crystal Palace; Arsenal; Crystal Palace; Luton Town; Chelsea; Watford

	A	G
1980–81	8	1
1981–82	28/3	0
1982–83	21	0
Total	57/3	1

JOHN EAST HAWLEY
Forward
Born Withernsea, 8 May 1954
Clubs Hull City; Leeds United; Sunderland; Arsenal; Leyton Orient; Hull City; Happy Valley (Hong Kong); Bradford City; Scunthorpe United

	A	G
1981–82	12/2	3
1982–83	2/4	0
Total	14/6	3

CHRISTOPHER ANDERSON WHYTE
Central defender
Born Islington, 2 September 1961
Clubs Arsenal; Crystal Palace; Los Angeles (USA); West Bromwich Albion; Leeds United; Birmingham City; Coventry City; Charlton Athletic; Detroit Neon (USA); Leyton Orient; Oxford United

	A	G
1981–82	32	2
1982–83	36	3
1983–84	14/1	2
1984–85	0	0
1985–86	4/3	1
Total	86/4	8

RAPHAEL JOSEPH MEADE
Forward
Born Islington, 22 November 1962
Clubs Arsenal; Dundee United; Luton Town; BK Odense (Denmark); Ipswich Town; BK Odense (Denmark); Plymouth Argyle; Brighton & Hove Albion; Hong Kong; Brighton & Hove Albion

	A	G
1981–82	8/8	4
1982–83	2/2	2
1983–84	9/4	5
1984–85	6/2	3
Total	25/16	14

STEWART IAN ROBSON
Midfield
Born Billericay, 6 November 1964
Clubs Arsenal; West Ham United;
Coventry City

		A	G
1982–83		12/7	3
1983–84		3/1	1
	Total	15/8	4

		A	G
1981–82		20	2
1982–83		31	2
1983–84		28	6
1984–85		40	2
1985–86		26/1	4
1986–87		5	0
	Total	150/1	16

ANTHONY STEWART WOODCOCK
Forward
Born Eastwood, 6 December 1955
Clubs Nottingham Forest; Lincoln
City; Doncaster Rovers; Cologne
(Germany); Arsenal; Cologne
(Germany); Fortuna

		A	G
1982–83		24	14
1983–84		37	21
1984–85		27	10
1985–86		31/2	11
	Total	129/2	56

PAUL ANTHONY GORMAN
Midfield/Full-back
Born Dublin, 6 August 1963
Clubs Arsenal; Birmingham City;
Carlisle United; Shrewsbury Town;
Carlisle United

		A	G
1981–82		4	0
1982–83		0	0
1983–84		1/1	0
	Total	5/1	0

DANIEL EDWARD O'SHEA
Defender/Midfield
Born Newington, 26 March 1963
Clubs Arsenal; Charlton Athletic;
Exeter City; Southend United;
Cambridge United; Northampton
Town

		A	G
1982–83		6	0
	Total	6	0

LEE ROY CHAPMAN
Forward
Born Lincoln, 5 December 1959
Clubs Stoke City; Plymouth Argyle;
Arsenal; Sunderland; Sheffield
Wednesday; Niort (France);
Nottingham Forest; Leeds United;
Portsmouth; West Ham United;
Southend United; Ipswich Town;
Leeds United; Swansea City

VLADIMIR PETROVIC
Midfield
Born Yugoslavia, 1 July 1955
Clubs Red Star Belgrade
(Yugoslavia); Arsenal; Antwerp
(Belgium)

		A	G
1982–83		10/3	2
	Total	10/3	2

JOHN KAY
Right-back
Born Great Lumley, 29 January 1964
Clubs Arsenal; Wimbledon;
Middlesbrough; Sunderland;
Shrewsbury Town; Preston North
End; Scarborough; Workington

		A	G
1982–83		7	0
1983–84		6/1	0
	Total	13/1	0

COLIN FREDERICK HILL
Central defender
Born Uxbridge, 12 November 1963
Clubs Arsenal; Maritimo (Portugal);
Colchester United; Sheffield United;
Leicester City; Trelleborg (Sweden);
Northampton Town

		A	G
1982–83		7	0
1983–84		37	1
1984–85		2	0
	Total	46	1

CHARLES NICHOLAS
Forward
Born Glasgow, 30 December 1961
Clubs Glasgow Celtic; Arsenal;
Aberdeen; Glasgow Celtic

		A	G
1983–84		41	11
1984–85		35/3	9
1985–86		41	10
1986–87		25/3	4
1987–88		3	0
	Total	145/6	34

TONY ALEXANDER ADAMS
Central defender
Born Romford, 10 October 1966
Clubs Arsenal

		A	G
1983–84		3	0
1984–85		15/1	0
1985–86		10	0
1986–87		42	6
1987–88		39	2
1988–89		36	4
1989–90		38	5
1990–91		30	0
1991–92		35	2
1992–93		33/2	0
1993–94		35	1
1994–95		27	3
1995–96		21	1
1996–97		27/1	3
1997–98		26	3
1998–99		26	1
1999–2000		21	0
2000–01		26	1
2001–02		10	0
	Total	500/4	32

THOMAS STEPHEN CATON
Central defender
Born 6 October 1962

Died April 1993
Clubs Manchester City; Arsenal;
Oxford United; Charlton Athletic

	A	G
1983–84	26	0
1984–85	35	1
1985–86	20	1
Total	**81**	**2**

DAVID JOHN MADDEN
Midfield
Born Stepney, 6 January 1963
Clubs Southampton; Bournemouth;
Arsenal; Charlton Athletic; Los
Angeles (USA); Reading; Crystal
Palace; Birmingham City; Maidstone
United

	A	G
1983–84	2	0
Total	**2**	**0**

IAN JAMES ROBERT ALLINSON
Winger
Born Hitchin, 1 October 1957
Clubs Colchester United; Arsenal;
Stoke City; Luton Town; Colchester
United

	A	G
1983–84	7/2	0
1984–85	20/7	10
1985–86	28/5	6
1986–87	5/9	0
Total	**60/23**	**16**

DAVID CORK
Forward
Born Doncaster, 28 October 1962
Clubs Arsenal; Huddersfield Town;
West Bromwich Albion; Scunthorpe
United; Darlington;

	A	G
1983–84	5/2	1
Total	5/2	1

PAUL MARINER
Forward
Born Bolton, 22 May 1953
Clubs Chorley; Plymouth Argyle;
Ipswich Town; Arsenal; Portsmouth

	A	G
1983–84	15	7
1984–85	34/2	7
1985–86	3/6	0
Total	**52/8**	**14**

BRIAN EDWARD SPARROW
Left-back
Born Bethnal Green, 24 June 1962
Clubs Arsenal; Wimbledon; Millwall;
Gillingham; Crystal Palace

	A	G
1983–84	2	0
Total	**2**	**0**

JOVAN 'JOHN' LUKIC
Chesterfield, 11 December 1960
Clubs Leeds United; Arsenal; Leeds
United; Arsenal

	A	G
1983–84	4	0
1984–85	27	0
1985–86	40	0
1986–87	36	0
1987–88	40	0
1988–89	38	0
1989–90	38	0
1996–97	15	0
2000–01	3	0
Total	241	0

VIVIAN ALEXANDER ANDERSON
Right-back
Born Nottingham, 29 July 1956
Clubs Nottingham Forest; Arsenal; Manchester United; Sheffield Wednesday; Barnsley; Middlesbrough

	A	G
1984–85	41	3
1985–86	39	2
1986–87	40	4
Total	120	9

STEVEN CHARLES WILLIAMS
Midfield
Born Hammersmith, 12 July 1958
Clubs Southampton; Arsenal; Luton Town; Exeter City

	A	G
1984–85	14/1	1
1985–86	17	0
1986–87	33/1	2
1987–88	29	1
Total	93/2	4

DAVID CARLYLE ROCASTLE
Midfield
Born Lewisham, 2 May 1967
Died 31 March 2001
Clubs Arsenal; Leeds United; Manchester City; Chelsea; Norwich City; Hull City

	A	G
1985–86	13/3	1
1986–87	36	2
1987–88	40	7
1988–89	38	6
1989–90	28/5	2
1990–91	13/3	2
1991–92	36/3	4
Total	204/14	24

MARTIN HAYES
Winger
Born Walthamstow, 21 March 1966
Clubs Arsenal; Glasgow Celtic; Wimbledon; Swansea City

	A	G
1985–86	11	2
1986–87	31/4	19
1987–88	17/10	1
1988–89	3/14	1
1989–90	8/4	3
Total	70/32	26

MARTIN RAYMOND KEOWN
Central defender
Born Oxford, 24 July 1966
Clubs Arsenal; Brighton & Hove Albion; Aston Villa; Everton; Arsenal; Leicester City; Reading

	A	G
1985–86	22	0
1992–93	15/1	0
1993–94	23/10	0
1994–95	24/7	1
1995–96	34	0
1996–97	33	1
1997–98	18	0
1998–99	34	1
1999–2000	27	1
2000–01	28	0
2001–02	21/1	0
2002–03	22/2	0
2003–04	3/7	0
Total	**304/28**	**4**

NIALL JOHN QUINN

Forward
Born Dublin, 6 October 1966
Clubs Arsenal; Manchester City;
Sunderland

	A	G
1985–86	10/2	1
1986–87	35	8
1987–88	6/5	2
1988–89	2/1	1
1989–90	6	2
Total	**59/8**	**14**

GUS CASSIUS CAESAR

Central defender
Born Tottenham, 5 March 1966
Clubs Arsenal; Queen's Park
Rangers; Cambridge United;
Bristol City; Airdrieonians;
Colchester United

	A	G
1985–86	2	0
1986–87	6/9	0
1987–88	17/5	0
1988–89	2	0
1989–90	0/3	0
Total	**27/17**	**0**

RHYS JAMES WILMOT

Goalkeeper
Born Newport, 21 February 1962
Clubs Arsenal; Hereford United;
Leyton Orient; Swansea City;
Plymouth Argyle; Grimsby Town;
Crystal Palace; Torquay United

	A	G
1985–86	2	0
1986–87	6	0
Total	**8**	**0**

PERRY GROVES

Forward
Born Bow,
19 April 1965
Clubs Colchester United; Arsenal;
Southampton

	A	G
1986–87	19/6	3
1987–88	28/6	6
1988–89	6/15	4
1989–90	20/10	4
1990–91	13/19	3
1991–92	5/8	1
1992–93	0/1	0
Total	**91/65**	**21**

PAUL CHARLES MERSON
Forward
Born Harlesden, 20 March 1968
Clubs Arsenal; Brentford;
Middlesbrough; Aston Villa;
Portsmouth; Walsall

	A	G
1986–87	5/2	3
1987–88	7/8	5
1988–89	29/8	10
1989–90	21/8	7
1990–91	36/1	13
1991–92	41/1	12
1992–93	32/1	6
1993–94	24/9	7
1994–95	24	4
1995–96	38	5
1996–97	32	6
Total	289/38	78

MICHAEL LAURISTON THOMAS
Midfield
Born Lambeth, 24 August 1967
Clubs Arsenal; Portsmouth;
Liverpool; Middlesbrough; Benfica
(Portugal)

	A	G
1986–87	12	0
1987–88	36/1	9
1988–89	33/4	7
1989–90	35/1	5
1990–91	27/4	2
1991–92	6/4	1
Total	149/14	24

ALAN MARTIN SMITH
Forward
Born Bromsgrove,
21 November 1962
Clubs Alvechurch Town; Leicester
City; Arsenal

	A	G
1987–88	36/3	11
1988–89	36	23
1989–90	37/1	10
1990–91	35/2	22
1991–92	33/6	12
1992–93	27/4	3
1993–94	21/4	3
1994–95	17/2	2
Total	242/22	86

KEVIN RICHARDSON
Midfield
Born Newcastle, 4 December 1962
Clubs Everton; Watford; Arsenal;
Real Sociedad (Spain); Aston Villa;
Coventry City; Southampton;
Barnsley; Blackpool

	A	G
1987–88	24/5	4
1988–89	32/2	1
1989–90	32/1	0
Total	88/8	5

NIGEL WINTERBURN
Left-back
Born Nuneaton, 11 December 1963
Clubs Birmingham City; Wimbledon;
Arsenal; West Ham United

	A	G
1987–88	16/1	0
1988–89	38	3
1989–90	36	0
1990–91	38	0
1991–92	41	1
1992–93	29	1
1993–94	34	0
1994–95	39	0
1995–96	36	2
1996–97	38	0
1997–98	35/1	1
1998–99	30	0
1999–2000	19	0
Total	428/2	8

LEE MICHAEL DIXON
Right-back
Born Manchester,
17 March 1964
Clubs Burnley;
Chester City; Bury; Stoke City;
Arsenal

	A	G
1987–88	6	0
1988–89	31/2	1
1989–90	38	5
1990–91	38	5
1991–92	38	4
1992–93	29	0
1993–94	32/1	0
1994–95	39	1
1995–96	38	2
1996–97	31/1	2
1997–98	26/2	0
1998–99	36	0
1999–2000	28	4

2000–01		26/3	1
2001–02		3/10	0
	Total	439/19	25

BRIAN MARWOOD
Winger
Born Seaham,
5 February 1960
Clubs Hull City; Sheffield
Wednesday; Arsenal; Sheffield
United; Middlesbrough; Swindon
Town; Barnet

	A	G
1987–88	4	1
1988–89	31	9
1989–90	17	6
Total	52	16

KEVIN JOSEPH CAMPBELL
Forward
Born Lambeth,
4 February 1970
Clubs Arsenal; Leyton Orient;
Leicester City; Nottingham
Forest; Everton; West
Bromwich Albion;

	A	G
1987–88	0/1	0
1988–89	0	0
1989–90	8/7	2
1990–91	15/7	9
1991–92	22/9	13
1992–93	32/5	4
1993–94	28/9	14
1994–95	19/4	4
Total	124/42	46

STEPHEN ANDREW BOULD
Central defender
Born Stoke, 16 November 1962
Clubs Stoke City; Torquay United;
Arsenal; Sunderland

	A	G
1988–89	26/4	2
1989–90	19	0
1990–91	38	0
1991–92	24/1	1
1992–93	24	1
1993–94	23/2	1
1994–95	30/1	0
1995–96	19	0
1996–97	33	0
1997–98	21/3	0
1998–99	14/5	0
Total	**271/16**	**5**

SIGURDUR 'SIGGI' JONSSON
Midfield
Born Iceland, 27 September 1966
Clubs Akranes (Iceland); Sheffield
Wednesday; Barnsley; Arsenal;

	A	G
1989–90	0/6	1
1990–91	2	0
Total	**2/6**	**1**

COLIN GEORGE PATES
Central defender
Born Carshalton, 10 August 1961
Clubs Chelsea; Charlton Athletic;
Arsenal; Brighton & Hove Albion

	A	G
1989–90	1/1	0
1990–91	0/1	0
1991–92	9/2	0
1992–93	2/5	0
Total	**12/9**	**0**

PATRICK KWAME AMPADU
Midfield
Born Bradford, 20 December 1970
Clubs Arsenal; Plymouth Argyle;
West Bromwich Albion; Swansea
City; Leyton Orient; Exeter City

	A	G
1989–90	0/2	0
Total	**0/2**	**0**

DAVID ANDREW SEAMAN
Goalkeeper
Born Rotherham, 19 September 1963
Clubs Leeds United; Peterborough
United; Birmingham City;
Queen's Park Rangers; Arsenal;
Manchester City

	A	G
1990–91	38	0
1991–92	42	0
1992–93	39	0
1993–94	39	0
1994–95	31	0
1995–96	38	0
1996–97	22	0
1997–98	31	0
1998–99	32	0
1999–2000	24	0
2000–01	24	0

2001–02	17	0
2002–03	28	0
Total	405	0

ANDERS ERIK LIMPAR
Left-winger
Born Sweden, 24 August 1965
Clubs Young Boys of Berne
(Switzerland); Cremonese
(Italy); Arsenal; Everton;
Birmingham City;

	A	G
1990–91	32/2	11
1991–92	23/6	4
1992–93	12/11	2
1993–94	9/1	0
Total	76/20	17

ANDREW LINIGHAN
Central defender
Born Hartlepool, 18 June 1962
Clubs Henry Smiths BC; Hartlepool
United; Leeds United; Oldham
Athletic; Norwich City; Arsenal;
Crystal Palace; Queen's Park
Rangers; Oxford United

	A	G
1990–91	7/3	0
1991–92	15/2	0
1992–93	19/2	2
1993–94	20/1	0
1994–95	13/7	2
1995–96	17/1	0
1996–97	10/1	1
Total	101/17	5

DAVID HILLIER
Midfield
Born Blackheath, 19 December 1969
Clubs Arsenal; Portsmouth; Bristol
Rovers; Barnet

	A	G
1990–91	9/7	0
1991–92	27	1
1992–93	27/3	1
1993–94	11/4	0
1994–95	5/4	0
1995–96	3/2	0
1996–97	0/2	0
Total	82/22	2

ANDREW ALEXANDER COLE
Forward
Born Nottingham, 15 October 1971
Clubs Arsenal; Fulham;
Bristol City; Newcastle United;
Manchester United; Blackburn
Rovers; Fulham; Manchester City;
Portsmouth

	A	G
1990–91	0/1	0
Total	0/1	0

IAN EDWARD WRIGHT
Forward
Born Woolwich, 3 November 1963
Clubs Greenwich Borough; Crystal
Palace; Arsenal; West Ham United;
Nottingham Forest; Glasgow Celtic;
Burnley

	A	G
1991–92	30	24
1992–93	30/1	15
1993–94	39	23
1994–95	30/1	18
1995–96	31	15
1996–97	30/5	23
1997–98	22/2	10
Total	212/9	128

JAMES WILLIAM CHARLES CARTER

Right-winger
Born Hammersmith, 9 November 1965
Clubs Crystal Palace; Queen's Park Rangers; Millwall; Liverpool; Arsenal; Oxford United; Portsmouth; Millwall

	A	G
1991–92	5/1	0
1992–93	11/5	2
1993–94	0	0
1994–95	2/1	0
Total	18/7	2

RAYMOND PARLOUR

Midfield
Born Romford, 7 March 1973
Clubs Arsenal; Middlesbrough

	A	G
1991–92	2/4	1
1992–93	16/5	1
1993–94	24/3	2
1994–95	22/8	0
1995–96	20/2	0

1996–97	17/13	2
1997–98	34	5
1998–99	35	6
1999–2000	29/1	1
2000–01	28/5	4
2001–02	25/2	0
2002–03	14/5	0
2003–04	16/9	0
Total	282/57	22

PAL LYDERSEN

Full-back
Born Norway, 10 September 1965
Clubs FK Start (Norway); Arsenal

	A	G
1991–92	5/2	0
1992–93	7/1	0
Total	12/3	0

STEPHEN JOSEPH MORROW

Midfield/Defender
Born Bangor, 2 July 1970
Clubs Arsenal; Reading; Watford; Reading; Barnet; Queen's Park Rangers

	A	G
1991–92	0/2	0
1992–93	13/3	0
1993–94	7/4	0
1994–95	11/4	1
1995–96	3/1	0
1996–97	5/9	0
Total	39/23	1

NEIL ANDREW HEANEY

Winger
Born Middlesbrough, 3 November 1971
Clubs Arsenal; Hartlepool United; Cambridge United; Southampton; Manchester City; Charlton Athletic; Bristol City; Darlington; Dundee United; Plymouth Argyle

		A	G
1991–92		0/1	0
1992–93		3/2	0
1993–94		1	0
	Total	4/3	0

JOHN FAXE JENSEN

Midfield
Born Denmark, 3 May 1965
Clubs Brondby (Denmark); Hamburg SV (Germany); Brondby (Denmark); Arsenal; Brondby (Denmark)

		A	G
1992–93		29/3	0
1993–94		27	0
1994–95		24	1
1995–96		13/2	0
	Total	93/5	1

ALAN JOHN MILLER

Goalkeeper
Born Epping, 29 March 1970
Clubs Arsenal; Plymouth Argyle; West Bromwich Albion; Birmingham City; Middlesbrough; Grimsby Town; West Bromwich Albion; Blackburn Rovers; Bristol City; Coventry City

		A	G
1992–93		3/1	0
1993–94		3/1	0
	Total	6/2	0

IAN SELLEY

Midfield
Born Chertsey, 14 June 1974
Clubs Arsenal; Southend United; Fulham; Wimbledon; Southend United; Woking

		A	G
1992–93		9	0
1993–94		16/2	0
1994–95		10/3	0
1995–96		0	0
1996–97		0/1	0
	Total	35/6	0

MARK MICHAEL FLATTS

Winger
Born Islington, 14 October 1972
Clubs Arsenal; Cambridge United; Brighton & Hove Albion; Bristol City; Grimsby Town

		A	G
1992–93		6/4	0
1993–94		2/1	0
1994–95		1/2	0
	Total	9/7	0

PAUL DICKOV

Forward
Born Livingston, 1 November 1972
Clubs Arsenal; Luton Town; Brighton & Hove Albion;

Manchester City; Leicester City;
Blackburn Rovers

	A	G
1992–93	2/1	2
1993–94	0/1	0
1994–95	4/5	0
1995–96	1/6	1
1996–97	0/1	0
Total	7/14	3

SCOTT RODERICK MARSHALL
Central defender
Born Edinburgh, 1 May 1973
Clubs Arsenal; Rotherham United;
Sheffield United; Southampton;
Glasgow Celtic

	A	G
1992–93	1	0
1993–94	1	0
1994–95	0	0
1995–96	10/1	1
1996–97	6/2	0
1997–98	1/2	0
Total	19/5	1

GAVIN GREGORY McGOWAN
Full-back
Born Blackheath, 16 January 1976
Clubs Arsenal; Luton Town;
Bromley

	A	G
1992–93	0/2	0
1993–94	0	0
1994–95	1	0
1995–96	1	0

1996–97	1	0
1997–98	0/1	0
Total	3/3	0

EDWARD JOHN PAUL McGOLDRICK
Midfield
Born Islington, 30 April 1965
Clubs Nuneaton Borough;
Northampton Town; Crystal Palace;
Arsenal; Manchester City; Stockport
County

	A	G
1993–94	23/3	0
1994–95	9/2	0
1995–96	0/1	0
Total	32/6	0

STEPHAN HANS SCHWARZ
Midfield
Born Sweden, 18 April 1969
Clubs Kulldall; Malmo (Sweden);
Bayer Leverkusen (Germany);
Benfica (Portugal); Arsenal;
Fiorentina (Italy)

	A	G
1994–95	34	2
Total	34	2

VINCENT LEE BARTRAM
Goalkeeper
Born Birmingham, 7 August 1968
Clubs Wolverhampton Wanderers;
Blackpool; Bournemouth; Arsenal;
Huddersfield Town; Gillingham

	A	G
1994–95	11	0
Total	**11**	**0**

PAUL SHAW
Forward
Born Burnham,
4 September 1973
Clubs Arsenal; Burnley; Cardiff City;
Peterborough United; Millwall;
Gillingham; Sheffield United

	A	G
1994–95	0/1	0
1995–96	0/3	0
1996–97	1/7	2
Total	**1/11**	**2**

STEPHEN JOHN HUGHES
Midfield
Born Reading, 18 September 1976
Clubs Arsenal; Fulham; Everton;
Watford; Charlton Athletic;
Coventry City

	A	G
1994–95	1	0
1995–96	0/1	0
1996–97	9/5	1
1997–98	7/10	2
1998–99	4/10	1
1999–2000	1/1	0
Total	**22/27**	**4**

ADRIAN JAMES CLARKE
Midfield
Born Cambridge, 28 September 1974
Clubs Arsenal; Rotherham United;
Southend United; Stevenage
Borough

	A	G
1994–95	0/1	0
1995–96	4/2	0
Total	**4/3**	**0**

JOHN HARTSON
Forward
Born Swansea, 5 April 1975
Clubs Luton Town; Arsenal; West
Ham United; Wimbledon; Coventry
City; Glasgow Celtic

	A	G
1994–95	14/1	7
1995–96	15/4	4
1996–97	14/5	3
Total	**43/10**	**14**

CHRISTOPHER MARK KIWOMYA
Forward
Born Huddersfield, 2 December 1969
Clubs Ipswich Town; Arsenal; Le
Havre (France); Queen's Park
Rangers

	A	G
1994–95	5/9	3
Total	**5/9**	**3**

GLENN HELDER
Forward
Born Holland,
28 October 1968
Clubs Sparta Rotterdam; Vitesse
Arnhem (Holland); Arsenal

	A	G
1994–95	12/1	0
1995–96	15/9	1
1996–97	0/2	0
Total	**27/12**	**1**

DENNIS NICOLAAS BERGKAMP
Forward
Born Amsterdam, Holland,
18 May 1969
Clubs Ajax (Holland); Inter Milan
(Italy); Arsenal

	A	G
1995–96	33	11
1996–97	28/1	12
1997–98	28	16
1998–99	28/1	12
1999–2000	23/5	6
2000–01	19/6	3
2001–02	22/11	9
2002–03	23/6	4
2003–04	21/7	4
2004–05	20/9	8
2005–06	8/16	2
Total	**253/62**	**87**

MATTHEW ROSE
Central defender
Born Dartford, 24 September 1975
Clubs Arsenal; Queen's Park
Rangers

	A	G
1995–96	1/3	0
1996–97	1	0
Total	**2/3**	**0**

DAVID ANDREW PLATT
Midfield/Forward
Born Oldham, 10 June 1966
Clubs Chadderton; Manchester
United; Crewe Alexandra; Aston
Villa; Bari; Sampdoria (Italy);
Arsenal

	A	G
1995–96	27/2	6
1996–97	27/1	4
1997–98	11/20	3
Total	**65/23**	**13**

PATRICK VIEIRA
Midfield
Born Dakar, Senegal, 23 June 1976
Clubs Cannes (France); AC Milan
(Italy); Arsenal; Juventus (Italy)

	A	G
1996–97	30/1	2
1997–98	31/2	2
1998–99	34	3
1999–2000	29/1	2
2000–01	28/2	5
2001–02	35/1	2
2002–03	24	3
2003–04	29	3
2004–05	32	6
Total	**272/7**	**28**

REMI GARDE
Defender/Midfield
Born France, 3 April 1966
Clubs Strasbourg (France);
Arsenal

	A	G
1996–97	7/4	0
1997–98	6/4	0
1998–99	6/4	0
Total	19/12	0

LEE CHARLES PHILLIP HARPER
Goalkeeper
Born Chelsea, 30 October 1971
Clubs Sittingbourne; Arsenal;
Queen's Park Rangers; Walsall;
Northampton Town

	A	G
1996–97	1	0

NICOLAS ANELKA
Forward
Born Versailles, France,
24 March 1979
Clubs Paris St Germain (France);
Arsenal; Real Madrid (Spain); Paris
St Germain; Liverpool; Manchester
City; Fenerbahce (Turkey); Bolton
Wanderers

	A	G
1996–97	0/4	0
1997–98	16/10	6
1998–99	34/1	17
Total	50/15	23

GILLES GRIMANDI
Defender
Born Gap, France,
11 November 1970
Clubs AS Monaco (France); Arsenal;
Colorado Rapids (USA)

	A	G
1997–98	16/6	1
1998–99	3/5	0
1999–2000	27/1	2
2000–01	28/2	1
2001–02	11/15	0
Total	85/29	4

EMMANUEL PETIT
Midfield
Born Dieppe, France, 22 September
1970
Clubs AS Monaco (France); Arsenal;
Barcelona (Spain); Chelsea

	A	G
1997–98	32	2
1998–99	26/1	4
1999–2000	24/2	3
Total	82/3	9

MARC OVERMARS
Winger
Born Ernst, Holland, 29 March 1973
Clubs Willem II; Ajax (Holland);
Arsenal; Barcelona (Spain)

	A	G
1997–98	32	12
1998–99	37	6
1999–2000	22/9	7
Total	91/9	25

LUIS BOA MORTE
Forward
Born Lisbon, Portugal, 4 August 1977
Clubs Sporting Lisbon (Portugal);
Arsenal; Southampton; Fulham

	A	G
1997–98	4/11	0
1998–99	2/6	0
1999–2000	0/2	0
Total	6/19	0

ALBERTO RODRIGUEZ MENDEZ
Forward
Born Germany, 24 October 1974
Clubs FC Feucht (Germany); France;
Arsenal; Sp Vgg Unterhaching
(Germany)

	A	G
1997–98	1/2	0
1998–99	0/1	0
Total	1/3	0

CHRISTOPHER WREH
Forward
Born Liberia, 14 May 1975
Clubs Young Kotoko; La Modelle
International; Invincible Eleven
(Liberia); AS Monaco; Guingamp
(France); Arsenal; Birmingham City;
AEK Athens (Greece); Al Hilal (Saudi
Arabia); St Mirren

	A	G
1997–98	7/9	3
1998–99	3/9	0
Total	10/18	3

ISAIAH RANKIN
Forward
Born Edmonton, 22 May 1978
Clubs Arsenal; Colchester United;
Bradford City; Birmingham City;
Bolton Wanderers; Barnsley;
Grimsby Town; Brentford

	A	G
1997–98	0/1	0
Total	0/1	0

MATTHEW JAMES UPSON
Central defender
Born Diss, 18 April 1979
Clubs Luton Town; Arsenal;
Nottingham Forest; Crystal Palace;
Reading; Birmingham City; West
Ham United

	A	G
1997–98	5	0
1998–99	0/5	0
1999–2000	5/3	0
2000–01	0/2	0
2001–02	10/4	0
Total	20/14	0

ALEXANDER MANNINGER
Goalkeeper
Born Austria, 4 June 1977
Clubs Vorwaerts Steyr; Graz
(Austria); Arsenal; Fiorentina; (Italy);
RCD Espanyol (Spain); Torino;
Brescia; Siena (Italy); Red Bull
Salzburg (Austria); Siena

	A	G
1997–98	7	0
1998–99	6	0
1999–2000	14/1	0
2000–01	11	0
Total	38/1	0

PAOLO ANDREA VERNAZZA

Midfield
Born Islington, 1 November 1979
Clubs Arsenal; Ipswich Town;
Portsmouth; Watford; Rotherham
United; Barnet

	A	G
1997–98	1	0
1999–2000	1/1	0
2000–01	0/2	1
Total	2/3	1

NELSON DAVID VIVAS

Defender/Midfield
Born Buenos Aires, Argentina, 18
October 1969
Clubs Quilmes; Boca Juniors
(Argentina); Lugano (Switzerland);
Arsenal; Inter Milan (Italy)

	A	G
1998–99	10/13	0
1999–2000	1/4	0
2000–01	3/9	0
Total	14/26	0

KARL FREDRIK 'FREDDIE' LJUNGBERG

Midfield
Born Sweden, 16 April 1977
Clubs BK Halmstad (Sweden);
Arsenal

	A	G
1998–99	10/6	1
1999–2000	22/4	6
2000–01	25/5	6

2001–02	24/1	12
2002–03	19/1	6
2003–04	27/3	4
2004–05	24/2	10
2005–06	21/4	1
2006–07	12/3	0
Total	184/29	46

FABIAN CABALLERO

Forward
Born Argentina, 31 October 1978
Clubs Serro Portino (Argentina);
Arsenal; Atletico Tembet (Argentina)

	A	G
1998–99	0/1	0
Total	0/1	0

DAVID GRONDIN

Defender
Born Paris, France, 8 May 1980
Clubs St Etienne (France); Arsenal;
St Etienne; AS Cannes (France);
KSK Beveren (Belgium); Arsenal;
Dunfermline Athletic; Stade Brestois
(France); Excelsior de Mouscrou
(Belgium)

	A	G
1998–99	1	0
Total	1	0

KABA DIAWARA

Forward
Born Toulon, France,
16 December 1975
Clubs Toulon; Bordeaux; Rennes;
Bordeaux; Marseille (France);

Arsenal; Paris St Germain; Blackburn Rovers; West Ham United; Ferrol (Spain); Nice; Paris St Germain; Al-Ittihad Doha (Qatar); Ajaccio (France); Gazianteprepor (Turkey)

	A	G
1998–99	2/10	0
Total	2/10	0

NWANKWO KANU
Forward
Born Owerri, Nigeria, 1 August 1976
Clubs Fed Works; Iwuanyanwu National (Nigeria); Ajax (Holland); Inter Milan (Italy); Arsenal; West Bromwich Albion, Portsmouth

	A	G
1998–99	5/7	6
1999–2000	24/7	12
2000–01	13/14	3
2001–02	9/14	3
2002–03	9/7	5
2003–04	3/7	1
Total	63/56	30

SILVIO DE CAMPOS Junior 'SILVINHO'
Defender
Born Sao Paolo, Brazil, 30 June 1974
Clubs Corinthians (Brazil); Arsenal; Celta de Vigo; Barcelona (Spain)

	A	G
1999–2000	23/8	1
2000–01	23/1	2
Total	46/9	3

THIERRY HENRY
Forward
Born Paris, France, 17 August 1977
Clubs AS Monaco (France); Juventus (Italy); Arsenal, Barcelona

	A	G
1999–2000	26/5	17
2000–01	27/8	17
2001–02	31/2	24
2002–03	37	24
2003–04	37	30
2004–05	31/1	25
2005–06	30/2	27
2006–07	16/1	10
Total	235/19	174

OLEG LUZHNY
Defender
Born Ukraine, 5 August 1968
Clubs Dinamo Kiev (Ukraine); Arsenal; Wolverhampton Wanderers

	A	G
1999–2000	16/5	0
2000–01	16/3	0
2001–02	15/3	0
2002–03	11/6	0
Total	58/17	0

DAVOR SUKER
Forward
Born Osijek, Croatia, 1 January 1968
Clubs Osijek; Dinamo Zagreb; Sevilla; Real Madrid (Spain); Arsenal; West Ham United; TSV 1860 Munich

	A	G
1999–2000	8/14	8
Total	**8/14**	**8**

STEFAN MALZ
Midfield
Born Ludwigshafen, Germany, 15
June 1972
Clubs SV Pfingstweide; BW Oppau;
SW Ludwigshafen; Vfr Mannheim;
TSV 1860 Munich (Germany);
Arsenal; Kaiserslautern (Germany)

	A	G
1999–2000	2/3	1
2000–01	0/1	0
Total	**2/4**	**1**

GRAHAM BARRETT
Midfield
Born Dublin, 6 October 1981
Clubs Arsenal; Bristol Rovers;
Crewe Alexandra; Colchester
United; Brighton & Hove Albion;
Coventry City; Sheffield Wednesday;
Livingston

	A	G
1999–2000	0/2	0
Total	**0/2**	**0**

THOMAS ROBERT BLACK
Forward
Born Chigwell, 26 November 1979
Clubs Arsenal; Carlisle United;
Bristol City; Crystal Palace; Sheffield
United; Gillingham

	A	G
1999–2000	0/1	0
Total	**0/1**	**0**

RHYS DAVID WESTON
Right-back
Born Kingston, 27 October 1980
Clubs Arsenal; Cardiff City

	A	G
1999–2000	1	0
Total	**1**	**0**

ASHLEY COLE
Left-back
Born Stepney, 20 December 1980
Clubs Arsenal; Crystal Palace;
Chelsea

	A	G
1999–2000	1	0
2000–01	15/2	3
2001–02	29	2
2002–03	30/1	1
2003–04	32	0
2004–05	35	2
2005–06	9/2	0
Total	**151/5**	**8**

BRIAN McGOVERN
Defender
Born Dublin, 28 April 1980
Clubs Cherry Orchard; Arsenal;
Queen's Park Rangers; Norwich
City; Peterborough United; St
Patrick's Athletic

	A	G
1999–2000	0/1	0
Total	0/1	0

JULIAN RAYMOND GRAY
Midfield
Born Lewisham, 21 September 1979
Clubs Arsenal; Crystal Palace;
Cardiff City; Birmingham City

	A	G
1999–2000	0/1	0
Total	0/1	0

BISAN-ETAME MAYER
LAUREANO 'LAUREN'
Defender
Born Lodhji Kribi, Cameroon, 19
January 1977
Clubs Cant Sevilla; Utrera; Seville;
Levante; Real Mallorca (Spain);
Arsenal

	A	G
2000–01	15/3	2
2001–02	27	2
2002–03	26/1	1
2003–04	30/2	0
2004–05	32/1	1
2005–06	22	0
Total	152/7	6

ROBERT PIRES
Midfield/Forward
Born Rheims, France,
29 October 1973
Clubs Metz; Olympique Marseille
(France); Arsenal; Villareal (Spain)

	A	G
2000–01	29/4	4
2001–02	27/1	9
2002–03	21/5	14
2003–04	33/3	14
2004–05	26/7	14
2005–06	23/10	7
Total	159/30	62

SYLVAIN WILTORD
Forward
Born Paris, France, 10 May 1974
Clubs Rennes; Girondins; Bordeaux
(France); Arsenal; Lyon (France)

	A	G
2000–01	20/7	8
2001–02	23/10	10
2002–03	27/7	10
2003–04	8/4	3
Total	78/28	31

IGORS STEPANOVS
Central defender
Born Ogre, Latvia, 21 January 1976
Clubs FK Ventspils; Skonto Riga
(Latvia); Arsenal; SK Beveren
(Belgium)

	A	G
2000–01	9	0
2001–02	6	0
2002–03	2	0
Total	17	0

TOMAS DANILEVICIUS
Forward
Born Lithuania, 18 July 1978

Clubs FK Baltai; FK Atlantas; Beveren; Brugges (Belgium); FC Lausanne (Switzerland); Arsenal; Dunfermline Athletic; Livourne; Avellino; Livourne (Italy)

	A	G
2000–01	0/2	0
Total	0/2	0

EDUARDO CESAR DAUD 'EDU' GASPAR

Midfield
Born Sao Paulo, Brazil,
15 May 1978
Clubs Corinthians (Brazil); Arsenal; Valencia (Spain)

	A	G
2000–01	2/3	0
2001–02	8/6	1
2002–03	12/6	2
2003–04	13/17	2
2004–05	6/6	2
Total	41/38	7

SULZEER 'SOL' JEREMIAH CAMPBELL

Central defender
Born Newham,
18 September 1974
Clubs Tottenham Hotspur; Arsenal; Portsmouth

	A	G
2001–02	29/2	2
2002–03	33	2
2003–04	35	1

2004–05		16	1
2005–06		20	2
	Total	133/2	8

GIOVANNI 'GIO' CHRISTIAN VAN BRONCKHORST

Midfield
Born Rotterdam, Holland,
5 February 1975
Clubs Feyenoord (Holland); Glasgow Rangers; Arsenal; Barcelona (Spain)

	A	G
2001–02	13/8	1
2002–03	9/11	1
Total	22/19	2

FRANCIS JEFFERS

Forward
Born Liverpool, 25 January 1981
Clubs Everton; Arsenal; Everton; Charlton Athletic; Glasgow Rangers

	A	G
2001–02	2/4	2
2002–03	2/14	2
Total	4/18	4

RICHARD IAN WRIGHT

Goalkeeper
Born Ipswich, 5 November 1977
Clubs Ipswich Town; Arsenal; Everton

	A	G
2001–02	12	0
Total	12	0

STUART JAMES TAYLOR
Goalkeeper
Born Romford, 28 November 1980
Clubs Arsenal; Bristol Rovers;
Crystal Palace; Peterborough
United; Leicester City;
Aston Villa

	A	G
2001–02	9/1	0
2002–03	7/1	0
Total	16/2	0

JEREMIE ALIADIERE
Forward
Born Rambouillet, France,
30 March 1983
Clubs Arsenal; Glasgow Celtic;
West Ham United; Wolverhampton
Wanderers

	A	G
2001–02	0/1	0
2002–03	0/3	1
2003–04	3/7	0
2004–05	0/4	0
Total	3/15	1

KOLO ABIB TOURE
Defender
Born Ivory Coast, 19 March 1981
Clubs ASEC Mimosa (Ivory Coast);
Arsenal

	A	G
2002–03	9/17	0
2003–04	36/1	1
2004–05	35	0

	A	G
2005–06	33	0
2006–07	27	2
Total	140/18	3

GILBERTO SILVA
Midfield
Born Lagoa de Prate, Brazil, 7
October 1976
Clubs America-MG; Atletico Mineiro
(Brazil); Arsenal

	A	G
2002–03	32/3	0
2003–04	29/3	4
2004–05	13	0
2005–06	33	2
2006–07	27	8
Total	134/6	14

JERMAINE LLOYD PENNANT
Midfield
Born Nottingham, 15 January 1983
Clubs Notts County; Arsenal;
Watford; Leeds United; Birmingham
City; Liverpool

	A	G
2002–03	1/4	3
2003–04	0	0
2004–05	1/6	0
Total	2/10	3

PASCAL CYGAN
Central defender
Born Lens, France, 19 April 1974
Clubs Valenciennes; Wasquehal;
Lille (France); Arsenal

	A	G
2002–03	16/2	1
2003–04	10/8	0
2004–05	15	0
2005–06	1/1	2
Total	52/11	3

RAMI SHAABAN
Goalkeeper
Clubs Saltsjobadens; Zamalek;
Thadodosman; Nacka FF;
Djurgaarden (Sweden); Arsenal;
Brighton & Hove Albion; Fredrikstad
(Norway)

	A	G
2002–03	3	0
Total	3	0

RYAN FELIX MAYNE GARRY
Defender
Born Hornchurch, 29 September 1983
Clubs Arsenal

	A	G
2002–03	1	0
Total	1	0

EFSTATHIOS 'STATHIS' TAVLARIDIS
Central defender
Born Greece, 25 January 1980
Clubs Iraklis (Greece); Arsenal;
Portsmouth; Lille (France)

	A	G
2002–03	0/1	0
Total	0/1	0

JUSTIN RAYMOND HOYTE
Defender
Born Waltham Forest,
20 November 1984
Clubs Arsenal; Sunderland

	A	G
2002–03	0/1	0
2003–04	0/1	0
2004–05	4/1	0
2006–07	17/3	0
Total	21/6	0

JENS LEHMANN
Goalkeeper
Born Germany, 10 November 1969
Clubs SW Essen; Schalke 04
(Germany); AC Milan (Italy); Borussia
Dortmund (Germany); Arsenal

	A	G
2003–04	38	0
2004–05	28	0
2005–06	38	0
2006–07	28	0
Total	132	0

GAEL CLICHY
Defender
Born Paris, France, 26 February 1985
Clubs Cannes (France); Arsenal

	A	G
2003–04	7/5	0
2004–05	7/8	0
2005–06	5/2	0
2006–07	18/1	0
Total	37/16	0

JOSE ANTONIO REYES
Forward
Born Utrera, Spain,
1 September 1983
Clubs Sevilla (Spain); Arsenal; Real
Madrid (Spain)

	A	G
2003–04	7/6	2
2004–05	25/5	9
2005–06	22/4	5
Total	54/15	16

DAVID MICHAEL BENTLEY
Midfield/Forward
Born Peterborough, 27 August 1984
Clubs Arsenal; Norwich City;
Blackburn Rovers

	A	G
2003–04	1	0
Total	1	0

FRANCESC 'CESC' FABREGAS
Midfield
Born Barcelona, Spain, 4 May 1987
Clubs Arsenal

	A	G
2004–05	24/9	2
2005–06	30/5	3
2006–07	27/3	0
Total	81/17	5

MATHIEU FLAMINI
Midfield
Born Marseille, France, 7 March 1984
Clubs Marseille (France); Arsenal

	A	G
2004–05	9/12	1
2005–06	19/12	0
2006–07	9/11	3
Total	37/35	4

ROBIN VAN PERSIE
Forward
Born Rotterdam, Holland, 6 August 1983
Clubs Feyenoord (Holland); Arsenal

	A	G
2004–05	12/14	5
2005–06	13/11	5
2006–07	17/5	11
Total	42/30	21

MANUEL ALMUNIA
Goalkeeper
Born Pamplona, Spain, 19 May 1977
Clubs Celta Vigo (Spain); Arsenal

	A	G
2004–05	10	0
2006-07	1	0
Total	11	0

PHILIPPE SENDEROS
Central defender
Born Geneva, Switzerland,
14 February 1985
Clubs Servette (Switzerland); Arsenal

	A	G
2004–05	12/1	0
2005–06	19/1	2
2006–07	8/3	0
Total	39/5	2

EMMANUEL 'MANU' EBOUE
Right-back
Born Abidjan, Ivory Coast, 4 June 1983
Clubs ASEC Mimosas Abidjan (Ivory Coast); SK Beveren (Belgium); Arsenal

		A	G
2004–05		0/1	0
2005–06		11/7	0
2006–07		15/1	1
	Total	26/9	1

QUINCY JAMIE OWUSU-ABEYIE
Forward
Born Amsterdam, Holland, 15 April 1986
Clubs Arsenal; Spartak Moscow (Russia)

		A	G
2004–05		1	0
2005–06		0/4	0
	Total	1/4	0

ALEXANDER HLEB
Midfield
Born Minsk, Belarus, 1 May 1981
Clubs VfB Stuttgart (Germany); Arsenal

		A	G
2005–06		17/8	3
2006–07		20/5	2
	Total	37/13	5

ALEXANDRE DIMI SONG BILLONG
Midfield
Born Douala, Cameroon, 9 April 1987

Clubs Bastia (France); Arsenal

		A	G
2005–06		3/2	0
2006–07		1/1	0
	Total	4/3	0

JOHAN DANON DJOUROU-GBADJERE
Defender
Born Switzerland, 18 January 1987
Clubs Arsenal

		A	G
2005–06		6/1	0
2006–07		17/3	0
	Total	23/4	0

KERREA KUCHE GILBERT
Defender
Born Willesden, 28 February 1987
Clubs Arsenal

		A	G
2005–06		2	0
	Total	2	0

VASSIKIRI ABOU DIABY
Midfield
Born Paris, France, 11 May 1986
Clubs Auxerre (France); Arsenal

		A	G
2005–06		9/3	1
2006–07		3/1	1
	Total	12/4	2

SEBASTIAN BENET LARSSON
Central defender
Born Eskilstuna, Sweden, 6 June 1985
Clubs Arsenal

	A	G
2005–06	2/1	0
Total	2/1	0

SHEYI EMMANUEL ADEBAYOR
Forward
Born Lome, Togo, 26 February 1984
Clubs AS Monaco (France); Arsenal

	A	G
2005–06	12/1	4
2006–07	14/8	6
Total	26/9	10

ARTURO LUPOLI
Forward
Born Brescia, Italy, 24 June 1987
Clubs Parma (Italy), Arsenal; Derby County

	A	G
2005–06	0/1	0
Total	0/1	0

THEO WALCOTT
Forward
Born Newbury, 16 March 1989

	A	G
2006–07	5/10	0
Total	5/10	0

TOMAS ROSICKY
Midfield
Born Prague, Czech Republic, 4 October 1980
Clubs Sparta Prague; Borussia Dortmund;

	A	G
2006–07	18/4	1
Total	18/4	1

WILLIAM GALLAS
Defender
Born Asnieres-sur-Seine, France, 1 7 August 1977
Clubs Marseille; Chelsea;

	A	G
2006–07	14	3
Total	14	3

JULIO BAPTISTA
Forward
Born Sao Paulo, Brazil, 10 January 1981
Clubs Seville; Real Madrid;

	A	G
2006–07	8/8	1
Total	8/8	1

PEREIRA NEVES DENILSON
Midfield
Born Sao Paulo, Brazil, 16 February 1988

	A	G
2006–07	3/4	0
Total	3/4	0

TOP 50 PLAYERS' PROFILES

By popular reckoning:

Tony Adams
George Armstrong
Joe Baker
Alan Ball
Cliff Bastin
Dennis Bergkamp
Liam Brady
Charlie Buchan
Leslie Compton
Wilf Copping
Paul Davis
Lee Dixon
Ted Drake
George Eastham
Charlie George
George Graham
Eddie Hapgood
Thierry Henry
David Herd
Cliff Holton
Joe Hulme
David Jack

Alex James
Pat Jennings
Bob John
Jack Kelsey
Ray Kennedy
Reg Lewis
Jimmy Logie
Malcolm Macdonald
Frank McLintock
Bob McNab
Joe Mercer
Paul Merson
Terry Neill
David O'Leary
John Radford
Pat Rice
Graham Rix
Kenny Sansom
David Seaman
Peter Simpson
Alan Smith
Frank Stapleton

Peter Storey
Alan Sunderland
George Swindin
Patrick Vieira
Bob Wilson
Ian Wright

☉ TONY ADAMS

An inspirational leader for both Arsenal and England, Tony Adams was an integral part of both teams' defences for over a decade, going on to win 66 caps for England. An imposing central defender, strong in the tackle and hugely effective in the air, he became the second youngest player in Arsenal's history when, in November 1983, at the age of 17 years 26 days, he played against Sunderland.

During the next couple of seasons he admirably covered for the likes of David O'Leary and Tommy Caton before, in 1986–87, forming a formidable partnership at the heart of the Gunners' defence with O'Leary. Then aged 20, he made his full England debut against Spain, as well as helping Arsenal beat Liverpool in the League Cup Final. That day he was also named as the PFA Young Player of the Year.

In March 1988, George Graham handed Adams the Arsenal captaincy. The following season he led from the front as the Gunners won the League title. Despite his heroic performances for Arsenal, he was omitted from England's 1990 World Cup squad and six months later he was given a three-month prison sentence for a well-publicised drink-drive offence.

However, on his return to the side, he guided Arsenal to their second League Championship in three seasons. During the course of that 1992–93 season, he became the first captain to lift both the FA Cup and the League Cup trophies in the same season. The following campaign saw him lead the Gunners to success in the European Cup Winners' Cup and, though injuries often restricted his appearances over the following seasons, he continued to represent both Arsenal and England, captaining Arsenal to the 'Double' in 2001–02 and providing great inspiration to the side.

☉ ARSENAL FACT ☉

Tony Adams lifted more trophies than any other Arsenal captain – nine (four League Championships, three FA Cups, one League Cup and the European Cup Winners' Cup).

Arsène Wenger's plans to reduce the average age of the Gunners' back line led to Adams finally deciding to hang up his boots at the end of that memorable season, having appeared in 672 games in all competitions for the North London club. Adams, who later went on to manage Wycombe

Wanderers, is currently Harry Redknapp's right-hand man at Premiership club Portsmouth.

☉ GEORGE ARMSTRONG

George 'Geordie' Armstrong was one of Arsenal's greatest-ever servants. In a playing career that spanned 16 seasons, he appeared in 621 League and Cup games, having made his debut against Blackpool in February 1962, just six months after joining the club.

Little did the popular winger know, that he would keep his place in the Arsenal side virtually unchallenged until 1977, despite opposition from the likes of Alan Skirton, Johnny MacLeod, Jimmy Robertson and Peter Marinello. Capped by England at Under-23 level, perhaps the biggest surprise of his career was that he was never picked at senior level by Sir Alf Ramsey or Don Revie, although this of course was an era when wingers went out of fashion.

A specialist corner taker, he had boundless energy and was a constant thorn in the side of any defence – except his own, where he was always helping out if needed.

Missing very few games, he was not only ever-present in 1967–68 but helped the Gunners to their first major cup final for 15 years against Leeds in the League Cup. At the start of the following season, he was in disagreement with the club but eventually came back into the side to help them back to Wembley for the disastrous League Cup Final against Swindon Town. Injuries restricted his appearances in 1969–70 but he was in the side that defeated Anderlecht over two legs to lift the Inter Cities Fairs Cup.

There is little doubt that Armstrong's greatest success came in the Double-winning season of 1970–71, not only playing in all 62 games but being voted Arsenal's Player of the Season. The following season he was ever-present again, helping the club to the FA Cup Final against Leeds United. Over the next five seasons, he was still a regular in the Arsenal side but after a disagreement with the manager Terry Neill – a former playing colleague of his for eight seasons – he left Highbury to join Leicester City.

Armstrong later finished his playing career with Stockport County before coaching at a number of clubs in this country and in Kuwait. During the summer of 1990 he returned to Highbury as the club's reserve team coach. A sincere and generous man, universally liked and respected, Geordie Armstrong sadly collapsed and died during a Gunners' training session.

☺ JOE BAKER

Joe Baker's scoring record of 100 goals in 156 games for the Gunners stands comparison with the best strikers. Though he was at Highbury during the one decade since the 1920s when the club failed to win a major honour, England international Baker was one of the few Arsenal success stories of the time.

He began his career with Hibernian and in four seasons at Easter Road he scored 102 goals in 117 League games. This form won him the first of eight England caps when he played against Northern Ireland in November 1959. In doing so, he became the first Englishman to play for his country while with a Scottish club. His new England team-mates found his broad Scottish accent rather amusing!

In the summer of 1961 he decided to join Jimmy Greaves and his good friend Denis Law in Italy. Unfortunately, his spell at Torino was short-lived and in July 1962 he became Billy Wright's first signing for a new record Arsenal transfer fee of £70,000.

In his first season with the club, he topped the scoring charts with 29 League goals including hat-tricks in the games against Wolves and Fulham. The following season he was joint leading scorer with Geoff Strong with 26 League goals. In 1964–65, Baker was ever-present and again led the way in the scoring stakes with 25 League goals and, after a five-year break, returned to international action with England. The following season he was again the club's leading scorer but, with the Gunners having a disappointing season, he opted for a move to Nottingham Forest.

While with Forest he was picked but not selected in the original 40 for the England 1966 World Cup squad. He later had a spell with Sunderland before returning north of the border to play for both Hibernian and Raith Rovers.

Though he was often accused of unpredictability, for sheer excitement, Arsenal fans didn't see his like again until the arrival of Thierry Henry.

☺ ALAN BALL

The flame-haired little midfield terrier already had a glittering career behind him when Bertie Mee bought him for £220,000 from Everton to hold the side together in the disappointing aftermath of the Double-winning season.

After unsuccessful trials with Wolves and Bolton, it was only the persistence of his footballing father Alan Ball Snr that persuaded Blackpool to sign him. He made his first team debut for the Seasiders against Liverpool at Anfield in 1962 at 17 years of age. Within 12 months he had become a regular in the Bloomfield Road club's side and had played in 126 games for them before joining Everton just after the World Cup for £110,000.

Without doubt, Ball's best match for England – for whom he won 72 caps – was the final itself. His tirelessness, especially during extra-time, has become legendary and he set up the third and decisive goal for Geoff Hurst. The sight of him running with his socks down round his ankles during the World Cup Final endeared him to the public.

In his first two seasons with Everton, Ball was the club's leading scorer and in 1967–68 – when he scored 20 League goals – he netted four in a 6-2 win at West Bromwich Albion. Playing alongside Colin Harvey and Howard Kendall in the Everton midfield, he was instrumental in the Blues winning the League Championship in 1969–70.

For no apparent reason, the side broke up and in December 1971 Ball was transferred to Arsenal. In his first season at Highbury, he guided the Gunners to the 1972 FA Cup Final against Leeds and helped to arrest an alarming slide. He helped Arsenal to runners-up in the First Division in 1972–73, chipping in with 10 goals from midfield, whilst the following season he was leading scorer with 13 goals. After taking on the Arsenal captaincy, Ball broke a leg and, though he made a lightning-fast recovery, he fractured his ankle three months later!

Results were poor and, in Ball's absence, tensions began to mount, culminating in a row between the midfielder and the club's management who refused to back his appeal against a sending-off. Following the appointment of Terry Neill as manager, Ball was transferred to Southampton, later being appointed manager of his first club Blackpool.

After a year he resigned and returned to The Dell, playing his last game in the top flight in October 1982. He then had a spell in Hong Kong before resuming his playing career with Bristol Rovers. He was then made manager of Portsmouth, taking the south coast club into the First Division before having spells in charge at Stoke, Exeter, Southampton and Manchester City before returning to Fratton Park for a second spell as Pompey boss.

⚽ CLIFF BASTIN

Cliff Bastin was still only 17 when Herbert Chapman made a trip to Exeter to sign him for Arsenal. The young Bastin was unimpressed by Chapman's overtures – soccer's maximum wage meant that he could earn no more in

London than he could playing for Exeter – and he agreed only reluctantly!

Bastin made his League debut for Arsenal at inside-right – before later converting to his famous left-wing position – against Everton in October 1929. In his first full season with the club, Bastin was at the time, at the age of 18 years 43 days, the youngest player ever to appear in an FA Cup Final when helping Arsenal to victory over Huddersfield Town. In the Gunners' first League Championship winning season of 1930–31, his legendary partnership with Alex James began to flourish. Not only was he ever-present – the youngest to be so for the club – but he contributed 28 League goals including a hat-trick against Derby County. The following season he won the first of his 21 caps for England, against Wales, aged just 19 years 249 days. He became, and still is, the youngest player to win an England cap, League Championship and FA Cup Winners' Medal and therefore became known as 'Boy Bastin'.

In 1932–33, Bastin set a record that will undoubtedly stand for all time, when from the outside-left position he scored a staggering 33 League goals – this total included just one hat-trick, in the 9-2 home defeat of Sheffield United. The following season he secured his third League Championship medal but, midway through the campaign, no other player was more distressed than Bastin when he heard of the death of Herbert Chapman, his mentor and the man he absolutely idolised. The hat-trick of Championships was duly completed in 1934–35 when Bastin scored 20 goals in 36 appearances. The following season his contribution to Arsenal's winning of the FA Cup was immense as he scored six times in seven ties.

The new manager George Allison was in a quandary as to who was to replace Alex James and opted to switch Bastin to inside-forward. During the early part of the 1937–38 League Championship-winning season, Bastin even played a number of games at right-half before reverting back to the wing and scoring 15 goals.

Bastin, who had problems with his hearing throughout his playing days, was virtually deaf. This meant that he was exempt from active service and so during the war years, he appeared in 244 games, scoring 71 goals. He continued to turn out for the Gunners on the resumption of League football but a leg injury which had hindered him prior to, and during, the hostilities, forced his retirement.

Bastin, who set a club scoring record of 150 goals in 350 League appearances is not only a legend in the Gunners' history but is also one of football's true immortals.

☉ DENNIS BERGKAMP

One of the world's finest footballers, the multi-talented Dutchman joined Arsenal from Inter Milan for a fee of £7.5 million in the summer of 1995. He soon proved the classiest player to have graced Highbury since Liam Brady, with a superb first touch and powerful shooting ability.

He had started out in his native Holland with Ajax and in seven years he scored just over 100 goals in 185 League appearances. He helped his side to the Championship in 1989–90 and the Cup in 1992–93. In European football he won a European Cup Winners' Cup medal in 1986–87 and a runners-up medal the following season as well as a UEFA Cup winners' medal in 1991–92.

Earlier in his career he had set up a Dutch League record when scoring in ten consecutive League games. Leading scorer in Dutch football for three seasons, he was voted Dutch Footballer of the Year in both 1992 and 1993. Capped 79 times by Holland, he left Ajax to join Inter Milan and, in his first season, his 11 goals in 11 European ties helped Inter win the 1993–94 UEFA Cup. Injuries and a loss of form unsettled Bergkamp and he joined the Gunners.

He soon came to terms with the English game, his partnership with the mercurial Ian Wright developing with each game. In 1997–98 Bergkamp received both the PFA and Football Writers' Player of the Year awards. He was also elected by his fellow professionals to the Premiership XI. The scorer of 22 goals including a hat-trick against Leicester City, he collected a Championship medal but unfortunately broke down in training and was forced to miss the FA Cup Final as Arsenal completed the Double for the second time. He recovered to help Holland reach the World Cup semi-finals where they were unlucky to lose on penalties to Brazil.

Still suffering from the demands of the World Cup, he was forced to sit out a number of games the following season before returning to action and forming an effective partnership with Thierry Henry.

Despite his fear of flying and his non-appearance in the Champions League away games, many of his best displays for the club have occurred in this competition. In spite of Arsène Wenger's policy of rotating the club's strikers, Dennis Bergkamp continued to appear on a regular basis – except for suspensions and a number of minor injuries – and during his time with the club, helped the Gunners win three Premiership titles and three FA Cup Finals.

The magnificent Dutch master finally decided to bring down the curtain on 12 glorious years with the club at the end of the 2005–06 season, having scored 120 goals in 422 games. As part of the club's 'Farewell to Highbury' celebrations, the club honoured him with 'Dennis Bergkamp Day' against West Bromwich Albion and also awarded him a testimonial against his former club Ajax as the opening game at the new Emirates Stadium.

☺ LIAM BRADY

One of the greatest players ever to pull on an Arsenal shirt, Liam Brady's influence in his seven years at Highbury has only been matched by a handful of players – Alex James, Joe Mercer, Frank McLintock, Tony Adams and, of course, Thierry Henry.

The seventh son of a Dublin docker, Brady made his Arsenal debut against Birmingham City in October 1973, becoming a regular in the side in 1974–75, a season in which he won the first of his 72 caps for the Republic of Ireland. Ever-present in seasons 1975–76 and 1976–77, the latter of which saw him create most of the goals scored by Malcolm Macdonald and Frank Stapleton. In 1977–78 he was a regular in the Arsenal side which reached the League Cup semi-final and the FA Cup Final.

His golden display in the 1979 FA Cup Final earned Brady the only winners' medal of his Arsenal career. He was the general who plotted Manchester United's downfall in that final, dancing a merry Irish jig on the famous sward in the most exciting climax to a Cup Final. Arsenal somehow managed to lose a two-goal cushion in the dying minutes of the game, only to snatch victory with a Brady-inspired winner in the last seconds to run out 3-2 winners. He also played in the 1980 FA Cup Final which Arsenal lost 1-0 to West Ham United.

The newly crowned PFA Footballer of the Year was also a member of Arsenal's European Cup Winners' Cup side which lost on penalties to Valencia.

During the close season he turned down Manchester United's bid of £1.5 million – which would have smashed the British transfer record – and opted for a £600,000 move to Italian giants Juventus. Few foreign players can have settled so quickly into Italian football. He won the Italian League Championship in each of his two seasons with the club before being surprisingly replaced by Michel Platini. He moved to newly promoted Sampdoria before, two seasons later, signing for Inter Milan. Lastly, he played for Ascoli before returning to these shores to sign for West Ham United. After more than 100 games for the Hammers, he announced his retirement in the summer of 1990.

Brady later had spells as manager of both Celtic and Brighton and Hove Albion but neither were successful. In 1996 he rejoined Arsenal as Head of Youth Development and Academy Director. Overseeing the club's two FA Youth Cup wins in 2000 and 2001, Liam Brady remains at the club where he proved he was the most outstanding player of his generation.

⊕ CHARLIE BUCHAN

Charlie Buchan was the son of an Aberdonian blacksmith and was born in London after his father came to work at the old Woolwich Arsenal. In November 1909, Buchan, a 17-year-old still attending the Woolwich Polytechnic and playing for Woolwich Arsenal reserves put in an expense account for 11 shillings. George Morrell, the club manager, high-handedly refused to pay it. Buchan left, and after a spell with amateurs Northfleet, turned professional with Leyton in the Southern League before joining Sunderland.

Buchan, a true Londoner, did not even know where Sunderland was when they signed him in 1911. His early performances led to Scotland, no doubt going by his name, asking Sunderland if they would release him to play against England in the 1912 international. The answer of course, was that he was English-born – parentage not counting in those days. His first England cap came in February 1913, against Ireland in Belfast, when he headed England's goal in a 2-1 defeat.

The three Sunderland players in the England team were dropped for the next international but the Wearsiders almost did the Double, winning the League Championship by finishing four points ahead of Aston Villa but losing the Cup Final to their nearest rivals, 1-0.

With the outbreak of war, Buchan went into the Grenadier Guards. He was an NCO in the trenches and brought back in 1918 to take a commission. At the end of the fighting, he went into teaching for a time, found it a strain and opened a sports outfitters – all the while still playing for Sunderland.

In 1925, Arsenal's new manager Herbert Chapman wanted Buchan as his lieutenant, even though he was now 33. Buchan did not want to leave Sunderland but Chapman was as persuasive as ever. The end result was that Arsenal agreed to pay an initial £2,000 for Buchan plus £100 for every goal he scored during his first season. Sunderland reckoned he would maintain his pre-war average of 20 per season. Their calculation was surprisingly close, for Buchan scored 19 goals in the League and another two in the Cup. More important, however, was his alleged pioneering of the 'third-back game' with Herbert Chapman.

The offside law had just been changed to restrict the number of defenders needed to keep a player onside from three to two. Buchan is said to have suggested a stopper, centre-half and an inside-forward playing deep in midfield during a tactical discussion after a 7-0 defeat at Newcastle. Buchan expected to play this inside-forward role himself but Chapman kept him upfield and used a third team player called Andy Neil in this position.

The first game with the new formation was at Upton Park and the result was a 4-0 win for the Gunners with Buchan scoring two of the goals. Arsenal continued to flourish and had an excellent season, and the following year reached the FA Cup Final under Buchan's captaincy.

☻ LESLIE COMPTON

Big Leslie Compton stands high in the Arsenal roll of honour, a giant of a man whose 20 years at Highbury spanned two of the greatest periods in the club's history. His first team appearances were limited to just 67 in the eight seasons before the Second World War but the versatile Compton, who filled just about every position on the field during his career, returned afterwards to claim his first team place at centre-half and reap the rewards of his effort.

During those seasons before the hostilities, Compton won five Football Combination Championship medals, whilst during the war after being converted to centre-forward, scored 93 goals in 130 games. He won five wartime caps for England and, in February 1941 in a game against Leyton Orient, scored ten times – six with his head!

When League football returned in 1946–47, Compton was at centre-half and often captained the side. The following season, he missed the opening six fixtures owing to his cricket commitments with Middlesex but still played in 35 games as the club won the League Championship. By this time he was affectionately known as 'Big Leslie' or 'Big 'ead'. He missed very few games after this and in 1949-50 was unflappable after scoring one of Arsenal's most important goals – in the 1950 FA Cup semi-final, he headed the equalising goal from brother Denis' corner after his captain Joe Mercer had instructed him to remain in defence.

He was outstanding in the FA Cup Final of 1950 as the Gunners beat Liverpool and then in November 1950 he won the first of his two England caps. He was, at 38 years and two months old, the oldest ever debutant for England in a full international.

After playing in only four games in 1951–52, he decided to retire at the end of the season, though he continued to play county cricket until 1956. He later became Arsenal's coach and scout. He had a foot amputated in 1982 and died two years later at the age of 72.

⚽ WILF COPPING

'Iron Man' Wilf Copping could put opponents off even before the kick-off. He rarely shaved before a game and his stubble chin added to the menace of a man renowned for bone-jarring tackles. The destructive side of his game brought him fame but he was scrupulously fair, made excellent use of the ball and was a long-throw expert.

Starting his career with Leeds United, he was ever-present in his first full season at Elland Road. Appearing in the famous United half-back line of Edwards-Hart-Copping, he won the first of 20 England caps in May 1933, but a little over a year later he was transferred to Arsenal for £8,000.

During his first season in the Arsenal side, when the Gunners won the League Championship, he was virtually ever-present up until March when he received a terrible knee injury.

He was a superstitious player, who always put his left boot on first and insisted being sixth out of the dressing-room. In 1935–36 he again played in the majority of games, helping the club to the FA Cup Final where they beat Sheffield United. He continued to be a regular in the Arsenal side over the next couple of seasons, helping the Gunners win yet another League Championship title in 1937–38. He was still an England regular the following season and played for an FA Charity Shield team against Preston North End.

Having played in 179 League and Cup games for Arsenal he rejoined Leeds United in March 1939, fearing that war would soon break out and he wanted to get his family back up north before he enlisted.

During the hostilities he was a Company Sergeant Major Instructor in the army in North Africa. After coaching in Belgium with Royal Beerschot, he later coached the Belgian national team before returning to these shores to coach at Southend United, Bristol City and Coventry City.

⚽ PAUL DAVIS

A cultured midfielder with a magical left foot, Paul Davis always seemed to have time – the sign of a top player.

Joining Arsenal straight from school, he made great progress after turning professional and made his Football League debut in a 2-1 win over local rivals Spurs at White Hart Lane in April 1980.

Over the next couple of seasons he battled to establish himself in a talented Arsenal midfield and gained representative honours when doing so. Although winning a League Cup winners medal in 1987 and a runners-up medal the following year, a lengthy suspension imposed during the early part of the 1988–89 season meant he was unable to regain his place and was forced to spend most of the club's League Championship-winning season in the reserves. This suspension for a well publicised off-the-ball incident probably cost him an international career and subsequent injury problems left him out in the cold for almost two years.

Davis made up for that with a League Championship medal in 1990–91, only missing one match in the campaign. However, in 1991–92 he fell out of favour with Arsenal boss George Graham following the Gunners' surprise elimination from the European Cup and lost his place to David Hillier. After 18 months in the wilderness, he returned to first team action and picked up two cup winners medals following Arsenal's victories over Sheffield Wednesday in both the FA and League Cups. Davis had a superb game in the League Cup Final and was the architect of Paul Merson's opening goal.

After that, Graham chose to use him only fitfully, although he was recalled for the entire European Cup Winners' Cup campaign of 1993–94. Here he excelled underlining his sheer class once more.

The extremely talented midfielder, who had made 459 League and Cup appearances, was later left hurt and bemused when the club he loved so much allowed him to join Brentford on a free transfer.

☺ LEE DIXON

One of the game's best attacking full-backs, Lee Dixon broke into League football with Burnley after coming through the club's junior ranks and played in a handful of games before moving on to Chester City. He spent the best part of two seasons at Sealand Road until signing for Bury, but a season later he was on the move again, this time to Stoke City. He proved to be a most reliable defender at the Victoria Ground and, in January 1988, Arsenal manager George Graham paid £400,000 for his services.

However, it wasn't until the beginning of the 1988–89 season that he won a regular place in the Gunners' defence at right-back. He made the position his own and was rewarded for his consistency with a League Championship medal that season. In April 1990, Dixon realised another ambition when he won the first of 22 England caps against Czechoslovakia. He was ever-present for Arsenal in 1990–91, scoring five penalties as the Gunners stormed to their second League Championship in three seasons. His form dipped the following season but he recovered his poise and helped the Gunners to a superb end-of-season run, following their mid-season slump.

The 1992–93 season saw Dixon regain his England place having lost it first to Rob Jones and then Gary Stevens, and though he was outstanding throughout the campaign, it wasn't without its disappointments. After being sent-off in the FA Cup semi-final against Spurs, his subsequent suspension meant that he missed playing in the League Cup Final.

He later added to his Arsenal honours list when appearing in both the 1994 and 1995 European Cup Winners' Cup Finals prior to enjoying a new lease of life under new manager Arsène Wenger. Dixon's attacking instincts were given more freedom within a three-man defensive system and he scored a number of vital goals from open play.

Despite being one of the older members of the Arsenal team, he lost none of his verve or enthusiasm. Indeed such was his consistency in the club's Double-winning season of 1997–98 that manager Wenger extended his contract.

His service to the club was rewarded with a testimonial game against Real Madrid in November 1999 – the fact that 22,000 fans turned out on a bitterly cold evening is confirmation of the esteem in which Lee Dixon is held.

Eventually finding himself a victim of Arsène Wenger's attempts to reduce the average age of the Gunners' defence, Dixon, who appeared in 621 League and Cup games for the Gunners, announced his retirement.

☺ TED DRAKE

Ted Drake was unquestionably Arsenal's greatest centre-forward. He cost just £6,000 from Southampton in March 1934, a few months after Herbert Chapman's death, and immediately confirmed his worth with his lion-hearted courage and a glut of goals. His 42 in 1934–35 is still a club record – it included three hat-tricks and four, four-goal hauls – and the following season he equalled the First Division individual record with all seven in the 7-1 win over Aston Villa.

His goals in 1934–35 helped Arsenal to the League Championship and gained him international recognition when he won the first of five England caps as one of seven Arsenal players to play against the Italians in the 'Battle of Highbury' in November 1934.

At this stage of his career, Drake was one of the most feared centre-forwards in English football. His main attributes were his powerful runs and great strength combined with tremendous speed and a powerful shot. A fearless player, often too brave for his own good, he missed a number of games due to injury. It was one of these injuries that put him out of action for ten weeks and nearly prevented him from playing in the 1936 FA Cup Final.

Having scored the seven goals against Villa, the Midlands club must have been sick of the sight of him for, later that season in his comeback match to try and prove his fitness, he scored the only goal against them at Highbury – the result sending Villa down to the Second Division for the first time in their history. Although he wasn't fully match-fit, he played in the 1936 FA Cup Final and scored the game's only goal.

Ted Drake was the leading goalscorer in each of his five seasons at the club. In 1936–37 he scored 20 goals in just 26 games including four in a 5-0 defeat of Bolton at Burnden Park. He won a further League Championship medal in 1937–38, netting 17 times in 28 games, including his only hat-trick against Everton on the opening day of the season.

During the war he was still seen in Arsenal colours, scoring 86 goals in 128 games as well as being a flight-lieutenant in the RAF. Sadly, his career was brought to a premature end when he received a serious spinal injury in a game at Reading in 1945.

After a spell managing Reading he took charge at Chelsea and led them to the League Championship in 1954–55 – thus becoming the first man in Football League history to play for and manage a Division One League Championship-winning combination.

☺ GEORGE EASTHAM

George Eastham was more than a marvellously gifted footballer. He was a freedom fighter who changed the face of soccer in the 1960s.

Eastham came from footballing stock; his father George appeared for Bolton and England and elder brother Harry, for Liverpool and Newcastle during wartime football. He played alongside his father in Ireland before being spotted by Newcastle United scouts who quickly brought the 19-

year-old to Tyneside. He quickly flourished playing alongside the Welsh maestro Ivor Allchurch, soon becoming a regular for the young England side and almost a certainty for a full England cap.

Eastham became embroiled in a major dispute with the Magpies; an unsavoury affair over firstly money and a club house, then eventually the basic right of a footballer to ply his trade wheresoever he chose. He stood up for his principles and, backed by the Players' Union, took football's antiquated authorities as well as Newcastle United to the High Court and won a historic litigation battle.

By the time the legal battle had been resolved, Eastham had joined the Gunners for a club record fee of £47,500 and became the second most expensive man in British football.

He made his Arsenal debut against Bolton in December 1960, scoring twice in a 5-1 win. He won the first of his 19 England caps during the 1962–63 season and was a member of England's World Cup squads in both 1962 and 1966.

During his time at Highbury, Eastham was a great inspiration to the club and captained them for three seasons. However, after Arsenal's worst season for many a year – 1965–66 – he could not agree new terms and, after appearing in 223 games, he was transferred to Stoke City for £30,000.

He spent eight seasons with the Potters, helping them win their first major trophy – the League Cup in 1971–72. He later coached and managed Stoke and then, having been awarded the OBE for his services to the game, emigrated to Johannesburg where he operated a sportswear company.

☺ CHARLIE GEORGE

Charlie George, born just around the corner from Highbury, was the player who fulfilled every young fan's dream by coming off the terraces to become a star in the team at the age of 19. George appeared to have everything – pace, unbelievable natural skill, a devastating shot, and a masterly long pass. His Highbury team-mates were often left speechless in training by his sheer virtuosity.

He will of course always be remembered as the long-haired 20-year-old who scored Arsenal's winning goal in the 1971 FA Cup Final against Liverpool, taking the Double to Highbury.

George made his League debut for Arsenal against West Bromwich Albion in August 1969 and, in his first season in the side, helped the club win their first major honour for 17 years when they won the Inter Cities Fairs Cup.

However, in the opening game of the following season, George sustained a broken ankle resulting in him missing the first five months of the campaign. On recovery, he returned as an attacking midfield player, a role in which he gave a telling boost to Arsenal's Double triumph. He was especially lethal in the FA Cup, scoring in the fourth, fifth and sixth rounds, before topping the lot with the winner in the final.

During the next few seasons, George missed almost half of Arsenal's matches due to injuries, loss of form and for disciplinary reasons. By now he had surprisingly become disillusioned with the team he had supported as a boy and, after another disagreement with manager Bertie Mee, was placed on the transfer list at the bargain price of just £100,000.
He came close to joining Spurs, a move which of course would have caused an uproar on the North Bank, but in July 1975 he joined Derby County.

He spent three-and-a-half seasons at the Baseball Ground, winning an England cap, before being transferred to Southampton in December 1978. After spells in the United States and Hong Kong, he returned home to complete his career with a succession of short stints elsewhere.

A thrilling talent that was allowed to slip away, Charlie George later became curator of the Arsenal Museum at Highbury.

☻ GEORGE GRAHAM

George Graham arrived at Highbury in the early weeks of the 1966–67 season as one of Bertie Mee's first signings in exchange for Tommy Baldwin and £50,000. He quickly made his mark up front alongside John Radford, becoming a consistent scorer and finished his first season as top scorer with 12 goals. Next season it was up to 20 but he and Radford were not proving a perfect match of personalities and he dropped back into midfield.

This turned out to be a master-stroke, for not only did the Gunners win the Inter Cities Fairs Cup in 1969–70 but also the Double the following season, when he was the popular choice as man of the match in the final against Liverpool. In 1971–72, Graham won the first of his 12 full caps for Scotland, as well as helping Arsenal reach Wembley again. The fans were delighted with the conversion to midfield, for not only was he scheming openings for others, but he was also finding extra time and space for his own attempts on goal.

Unfortunately, after the arrival of Alan Ball, Graham's position in the Arsenal side was not automatic and, in December 1972, after scoring 77 goals in 308 first team games, he was transferred to Manchester United for £120,000. Whether Graham's touches might have helped the Gunners to avoid the anti-climax that gripped Highbury in the mid 1970s, we shall never know.

He spent two years at Old Trafford before finishing his playing career with Portsmouth and Crystal Palace.

After managing Millwall, Graham was appointed Arsenal boss, creating a Highbury dynasty that had not been seen at the club since the days of Herbert Chapman. Though it was a shame that his time at the club had to end in the circumstances that it did, it does mean that, among Arsenal fans, George Graham will be remembered with ambivalence.

⊙ EDDIE HAPGOOD

The former Bristol milkman brought grace, elegance and some say, arrogance to the position of left-back he filled with such distinction throughout the Chapman era. Those that knew him insist it was confidence rather than arrogance but no matter, Hapgood was the greatest of his day.

His career did not get off to the best of starts for he was turned down by his home-town club Bristol Rovers after a trial and was playing for Kettering Town when Herbert Chapman signed him in October 1927.

At this time, Hapgood was so frail that he almost got knocked out every time he headed the ball. It was discovered that he was a vegetarian but, even so, Arsenal trainer Tom Whittaker put him on a diet that consisted almost entirely of steak. Having made his debut against Birmingham in November 1927, Hapgood developed into a tough-tackling full-back, winning 30 caps for England and captaining his country on many occasions.

Eddie Hapgood was a most courageous player and this was exemplified than when he broke his nose against Italy in the 'Battle of Highbury' in November 1934.

He went on to appear in 440 League and Cup games for Arsenal, missing very few games during his time at Highbury. This consistency was rewarded, for he won five League Championship medals, played in three FA Cup Finals, as well as playing in six FA Charity Shield matches. He was justly proud on his ability to blot out the finest outside-right of his time, Stanley Matthews.

Unfortunately, like so many other players of the time, he was at the peak of his career – being only 30 – when the Second World War broke out. During the hostilities he served as a flying officer in the RAF, though he did find time to play in 102 wartime games for the club.

When Hapgood retired in December 1945, it was to become manager of Blackburn Rovers and, after a short spell at Ewood Park, he took over the managership of Watford, then in the Third Division (South). At neither club was his record a poor one but his impulsive honesty was perhaps a handicap in dealing with directors.

He then had six good years in his native West Country as manager of Southern League Bath City and won that League's 'Manager of the Year' award in 1952–53. However, here too it ended badly with Hapgood being forced out.

☉ THIERRY HENRY

A £10.5 million signing from Juventus during the summer of 1999, Thierry Henry has developed into the most exciting player in the Premiership. A French international World Cup star, he was his nation's leading goalscorer in the 1998 World Cup Finals and had previously played under Arsène Wenger at Monaco when he was just 17 years old.

A player with devastating speed and an eye for goal, he opened his Arsenal account with a wonderful strike at Southampton, just eight minutes after coming off the bench to secure a 1-0 victory. After that he went from strength to strength to end his first season as the club's leading goalscorer – 15 goals in 15 games leading up to the UEFA Cup Final.

He topped the club's scoring charts again in 2000–01 with 22 goals, was voted the French Player of the Year and was honoured by his fellow professionals who voted him into the PFA Premiership team.

He continued to find the net with great regularity in the club's Double-winning season of 2001–02 with a total of 32 first team goals including 24 from 31 Premiership starts and was again selected for the PFA Premiership team of the season.

Able to operate down either flank or as a lethal hit man as a central striker, he scored his 100th goal for the club in the away game at Birmingham in the 2002–03 season. An automatic choice for the French national side, he scored the deciding goal in the Confederations Cup final victory over Cameroon in the summer of 2003 and, after continuing to be voted into the PFA Premiership team, was named as the PFA Player of the Year.

He enjoyed another magnificent season in 2003–04 and became only the fourth player in Premiership history to score 30 goals in a season. Tying just about every Premiership defence in knots, he netted a brilliant hat-trick against Liverpool and in the aftermath of the exits from the FA Cup and Champions League, he registered four more against Leeds United to turn the title race decisively in the Gunners' favour. Runner-up in both the European and World Player of the Year awards, he became the first player to win the PFA and Football Writers' Association Player of the Year awards in successive seasons.

Ending the 2004–05 season as the top flight's leading scorer for the third time in four seasons, he also became the first player ever to win the European Golden Boot two seasons running as his 25 League goals saw him tie with Diego Forlan. He helped Arsenal finish runners-up in the Premiership and win the FA Cup on a penalty shoot-out and, not surprisingly, was once again selected for the PFA Premiership team of the season.

During the 2005 close season, Henry was made Arsenal captain before playing out the season against a backdrop of intense media speculation that he might leave the club at the end of the campaign. He went on to score 27 League goals including hat-tricks against Middlesbrough and Wigan.

He broke the club's all-time scoring record when he netted the second of two goals away to Sparta Prague in October, thereby surpassing Ian Wright's figure of 185 and he also broke Cliff Bastin's club League scoring record by netting against West Ham in February. Three days later he reached 200 goals for the club when he netted at Birmingham. He was named the Football Writers' Association Player of the Year for an unprecedented third time and was also voted into the Premiership team of the year as well as being runner-up in the FIFA World Player of the Year poll. In the wake of the club's Champions League Final defeat against Barcelona, Thierry lifted the spirits of all Arsenal fans by signing a new deal to keep him at the club.

☉ DAVID HERD

David Herd signed for Stockport County just after his 17th birthday and played in the same forward line as his father. During his four years at Edgeley Park, his appearances were limited due to being called up for two years national service.

Arsenal showed an interest in him after he was demobbed in 1954 and eventually signed him for £10,000. He then spent two seasons on the fringe of the Gunners' first team before claiming a regular place when Cliff Holton was switched to wing-half midway through the 1956–57 campaign, when he scored 10 goals in 22 games. Over the next couple of seasons he continued to find the back of the net, scoring 24 goals in 1957–58 and 15 in 1958–59. During the course of this latter season, Herd won the first of five Scottish caps when he played against Wales at Ninian Park.

He had an outstanding 1960–61 season, scoring 29 League goals including four hat-tricks – the largest number by an Arsenal player since Ronnie Rooke's 33 in 1947–48. Eventually, though, he became disillusioned by Arsenal's poor form and, having scored 107 goals in 180 games, headed for Old Trafford – though he would have been happy to stay had he felt wanted.

David Herd spent seven seasons with Manchester United, helping the Red Devils win two League Championships and the FA Cup. Maintaining his strike-rate with 114 goals in 202 league games, Herd broke his leg and this signalled the end of his top-level exploits.

After a short spell with Stoke City, he tried his hand at management with Lincoln City before becoming a garage proprietor in Manchester.

United fans still talk about his achievements. Meanwhile older Arsenal supporters are left to rue the premature departure of a forward who undoubtedly would have left them with a host of golden memories.

☺ CLIFF HOLTON

Hot-shot Holton was a typical example of Tom Whitttaker's ability to spot and develop raw talent. Holton was playing for Isthmian League club Oxford City as a full-back when Whittaker signed him in 1947. It took Holton three years to break into the Gunners' first team but, when he did so, it was as a centre-forward.

Having signed for Arsenal, he then spent two years on national service before in 1950–51, scoring 27 goals in 30 games for the club's reserve team. This form prompted Whittaker to hand him his League debut against Stoke on Boxing Day 1950, after which he was soon finding the net with great regularity.

Holton's tall, powerful build and lethal shot with either foot made him ideally suited for the centre-forward position. Over the next three seasons, Holton scored 53 goals in 81 League games and though his form deserted him in the 1952 FA Cup Final, won by a Jackie Milburn-inspired Newcastle, he was outstanding the following season as Arsenal won the League Championship. That season, Holton scored 19 goals in 21 matches including a hat-trick against Liverpool at Anfield and a spectacular four-goal display against Sheffield Wednesday at Hillsborough.

However, then Arsenal began to struggle and Holton's progress was not helped by the signing of former England star Tommy Lawton, a Whittaker gamble that failed. Other strikers appeared and Holton became a wing-half, a role in which his passing skills improved and his tackling and aerial ability served him well.

He was appointed Arsenal skipper for a brief spell under new manager George Swindin but, in October 1958, having scored 88 goals in 217 games, he was transferred to Watford. Although his subsequent feats were achieved in the lower divisions with Northampton, Crystal Palace, Charlton and Orient, there were many who believed that Cliff Holton would have been prolific at whatever level he played.

⦾ JOE HULME

Joe Hulme was reputed to be the fastest footballer in the game. He was one of Herbert Chapman's first signings, joining from Blackburn Rovers in 1926 and eventually becoming the first of the famous five – Hulme, Jack, Drake, James and Bastin.

In his first season at Highbury, Hulme won the first of many honours when he was chosen to represent the Football League XI. He was an all-round sportsman, playing cricket for Middlesex from 1929 to 1939. He also played golf, snooker, table tennis and billiards to a very high standard. He was later to put that down to not drinking or smoking!

During 1926–27, his first full season with the club, he won the first of his nine full caps for England when he played against Scotland and helped the Gunners reach that season's FA Cup Final. Over the course of the next two seasons, he was a permanent fixture on the club's right-wing but it was 1929–30 when he really came to the fore. With superb service from Alex James, he doubled his goal tally, netting 14 in 37 appearances. At the end of that season, he won an FA Cup winners' medal as Arsenal beat Huddersfield Town.

In the Gunners' record-breaking League Championship season of 1930–31, Hulme and his fellow forwards scored a remarkable 116 goals with Hulme scoring 14 and responsible for providing the pin-point crosses that gave Jack Lambert many of his goals. In 1931–32, Hulme netted 14 goals for the third successive season and played in his third FA Cup Final.

The following season, Hulme scored 20 goals including hat-tricks in the wins over Sunderland and Middlesbrough as the Gunners won the first of three Championships. He was plagued by injuries in 1933–34 but was back to his best the following season when the club again won the League title. His appearances in the League side dwindled in 1935–36 but he played in all the FA Cup matches and won a second winners' medal as Sheffield United were beaten 1–0.

He went on to score 115 goals in 374 games before being transferred to Huddersfield Town in January 1938. His last senior appearance was for the Yorkshire club against Preston North End in the 1938 FA Cup Final, thus becoming the first player ever to appear in five Wembley FA Cup Finals.

During the Second World War he was a reserve policeman and, after a spell as secretary of Tottenham Hotspur, he later managed the club.

☉ DAVID JACK

When Charlie Buchan retired in 1928, Arsenal's manager Herbert Chapman sent out the word to his scouts to comb the country for a suitable replacement – an inside-right with a proven goalscoring record at the highest level.

David Jack is perhaps most famous for scoring the first goal in a Wembley Cup Final but he contributed far more to the game than that. The son of former Bolton player Bob Jack, he started out with Plymouth Argyle where his father was manager and, though he was wanted by both Arsenal and Chelsea, he opted to join his home-town club, Bolton Wanderers.

After making his debut at Oldham in January 1921, he became a first team regular and over the next seven seasons, shared the goalscoring responsibilities with Joe Smith. In five of those seasons, he was the club's leading scorer, netting 27 in seasons 1923–24 and 1924–25. When the Wanderers won the FA Cup in 1923, Jack scored in six of the seven ties on the way to Wembley. A year later he won his first full cap for England but in October 1928, after scoring 161 goals in 324 games, he was transferred to Arsenal in a record £10,340 deal.

After making his Gunners' debut against Newcastle United, he went on to finish his first season with the club as their leading scorer with 25 goals from 31 appearances. This total included four in the match against Bolton's neighbours, Bury. Although not as prolific in 1929–30, it was Jack's goal in the FA Cup semi-final replay against Hull City which sent Arsenal through to the final at Wembley where they beat Huddersfield.

In the League Championship-winning season of 1930–31, David Jack scored 31 goals in 35 League outings including hat-tricks against Chelsea and Blackpool and four goals in the win over Grimsby Town. He was almost as prolific the following season with 21 goals in 34 League appearances and he returned to Wembley for his fourth FA Cup Final against Newcastle United.

A second League Championship medal came his way in 1932–33 and the following season, even though in the twilight of his career, he played in enough games to qualify for a third League Championship medal. On retirement, after scoring 124 goals in 208 games, he was appointed manager of Southend United, later taking over the reins of Middlesbrough and Shelbourne. He also worked for the Inland Revenue and as a sports writer before his death at the age of 59.

☻ ALEX JAMES

Alex James is probably the greatest player ever to have worn the red and white shirt, having avoided learning a trade, preferring to dedicate himself to football.

Having started out with Raith Rovers, he and his team-mate David Morris joined Preston North End as the Deepdale club tried to win back their place in the top flight. Following the signing of the little Scot, North End were fined 10 guineas for an irregularity in relation to the transfer form. After making his debut in a 5-1 defeat of Middlesbrough, James scored in each of his next four games and this led to him winning the first of eight full caps for Scotland.

Often the scorer of spectacular goals, he hit two specials in the 5-1 demolition of England at Wembley on a rain-soaked afternoon in April 1928 and this immortalised him in the eyes of Scottish supporters.

After topping North End's scoring charts for three successive seasons, he became frustrated by Preston's continued failure to gain promotion during his four-year spell at Deepdale and, early in 1929, he was transfer-listed. When the Arsenal manager Herbert Chapman approached him to sign for the Gunners, James was quick to point out that it was not to his advantage to uproot his family to move south where the cost of living was so much higher.

Chapman found a loophole in the League regulations which entitled a player to both work and play. He fixed James up as a football demonstrator with Selfridges while an evening paper agreed to take a weekly 'ghosted' article from the tiny Scot and pay him a salary for the privilege of using his, by now famous, name.

Although turned into a schemer at Highbury, he typically reserved his first goal for his new club for a very special event – the 1930 FA Cup Final against Huddersfield Town. Arsenal's success heralded the start of one of the most amazing runs of trophies any English League club has ever known – four League titles and two FA Cup wins in only six seasons. James also captained the Gunners to success in the 1936 FA Cup Final win over Sheffield United.

After playing the last of his 261 games for the Gunners in 1937, James worked for a pools promoter and as a reporter on a Sunday newspaper before returning to Highbury after the war to coach the club's youngsters.

In 1953 he fell gravely ill with cancer and his death at the age of 51 shocked the whole of the football world.

☺ PAT JENNINGS

At his peak, Pat Jennings was the best goalkeeper in the world and certainly a candidate for the best of all time.

Having played Gaelic football he turned to association football with Newry Town before, in the summer of 1963, signing for Watford. A year later he was on his way to White Hart Lane as Spurs manager Bill Nicholson paid £27,000 for his services.

In a 13-year spell at Tottenham, Jennings won an FA Cup winners' medal, two League Cup winners' medals and a UEFA Cup winners' medal. He was also the PFA Player of the Year in 1976 and went on to set a record number of appearances for Spurs, a figure bettered only by Steve Perryman.

He was awarded the MBE for his services to the game in the 1976 Queen's Birthday Honours list. He was tough and rarely injured but he did succumb to a serious ankle injury in 1976–77 and, during his enforced absence, Spurs were relegated! Even worse, manager Keith Burkinshaw allowed Jennings to join rivals Arsenal, then managed by his former Spurs boss and international colleague, Terry Neill.

Jennings remained the Gunners' first-choice keeper for the next eight seasons, playing a major role in enabling Arsenal to appear in three successive FA Cup Finals in the years 1978–1980. Jennings won an FA Cup winners' medal in 1979 as Arsenal beat Manchester United and then the following year won a runners-up medal in the European Cup Winners' Cup.

Jennings' proudest moment at international level came when Northern Ireland reached the second round phase of the 1982 World Cup Finals in Spain.

In May 1985, Jennings was granted a second testimonial – having had one when Spurs played Arsenal in November 1976 – this time against Spurs. On the verge of retiring after appearing in 327 games for Arsenal, he returned to White Hart Lane as goalkeeping cover for Ray Clemence and also to keep fit for Northern Ireland.

He eventually went on to win a world record total of 119 caps before the end of the World Cup saw his retirement. Since then, the popular keeper has shared his time between coaching the goalkeepers at White Hart Lane and making personal appearances.

☺ BOB JOHN

Bob John was the greatest discovery of Leslie Knighton, the Arsenal manager sacked to make way for Herbert Chapman. The hard-tackling wing-half was playing for his local club Caerphilly and was expected to join Cardiff City when Arsenal swooped in 1922 for one of their most famous transfer coups. John was actually signed in a hotel owned by the Cardiff chairman, who was in an adjacent room discussing his own club's interest in the player as Knighton was secretly concluding the transfer. The Cardiff chairman was dumbfounded when he discovered what had happened.

On his arrival at Highbury, John spent a couple of seasons playing reserve team football and it was whilst playing for the reserves that he won the first of his 15 full international caps for Wales.

Eventually he won a regular place in the Gunners' League side and, in 1927, played in the FA Cup Final defeat by Cardiff City. Playing at both left-back and left-half, Bob John was the club's first-choice No.3 for much of the next three seasons following the Cup Final defeat. However, he only won a place in the Arsenal side for the 1930 FA Cup Final against Huddersfield Town due to an injury to Charlie Jones.

In 1930–31 he helped the club win their first League Championship and, the following season, broke Percy Sands' 327 League appearances record – going on to play in a record 421 League games, a record he held for 42 years until surpassed by George Armstrong in November 1974.

In that 1931–32 season, John scored Arsenal's only goal in the famous 'over the line' Cup Final against Newcastle United. John won a further League Championship medal in 1932–33 when missing only five League games and his third medal in 1933–34 when he appeared in 31 games.

Following the signing of Wilf Copping from Leeds United, Bob John's appearances for the Arsenal side became fewer, though he still turned out for the Welsh national side. Retiring in the summer of 1938 after playing in 470 League and Cup games, he coached at West Ham United before, following the war, managing Torquay United and coaching both Crystal Palace and Cardiff City.

⊙ JACK KELSEY

Jack Kelsey was rightly regarded as the finest goalkeeper of his day but was unlucky to be at Highbury at a time when the club's fortunes were really at a low ebb. Although one of a long line of custodians who have graced the Arsenal side over the years, he won just one club honour, a League Championship medal in his first full season. His distinguished career was ended prematurely by injury at the age of 32.

Kelsey's early football career was spent with Swansea League club Winch Wen and after a trial with Llanelli, he was given a trial with Arsenal in the summer of 1949. Still only a teenager, he signed professional forms later that year and began an association with the North London club that was to last virtually up to his death in March 1992.

His early days were spent under the tuition of coach George Male at Hendon as he worked his way up through the ranks. He had to wait quite a while for his first team break. George Swindin was the club's first-choice keeper and Ted Platt his natural deputy. In February 1951, Kelsey was given his chance against Charlton Athletic but unfortunately a 5–2 defeat represented the club's heaviest home defeat for 22 years! He was given another chance the following week but after conceding three against Manchester United it was back to the reserves until he returned to play in 29 matches during the 1952–53 League Championship-winning season.

The following season Kelsey became the club's first-choice keeper, his displays winning him the first of 41 full caps for Wales. He missed just four of his country's games between his debut and his last appearance in 1962. The highlight of Jack Kelsey's international career was helping Wales reach the quarter-finals of the 1958 World Cup in Sweden where they lost 1–0 to the eventual winners Brazil. It was while playing against Brazil in 1962 that he collided heavily with Vava, damaging his spine. At a subsequent medical examination it was discovered that he had a deformity of the spine which, had it been noticed earlier, would have prevented him from playing League football. After a six month fight to regain his fitness, he was forced to retire after 352 League and Cup games for the Gunners.

Sufficiently well regarded at Highbury to be retained as one of the staff, he worked in the club's commercial department for over 25 years, an accessible and popular figure right up to his death.

⊙ RAY KENNEDY

Ray Kennedy was spotted by Arsenal's north-east scout and it led to a glittering career studded with five League Championship medals, one FA Cup winners' medal, one League Cup winners' medal, two European Cup winners' medals, one UEFA Cup winners' medal and one Fairs Cup winners' medal.

He joined the Gunners as an apprentice in April 1968 after having been rejected by Port Vale and gone to work in a sweet factory. After a couple of seasons in Arsenal's reserve side, he made his League debut against Sunderland in February 1970. He shot to fame after scoring one of Arsenal's goals in that season's two-legged Inter Cities Fairs Cup Final as the Gunners beat Anderlecht 4–3 on aggregate.

He became a regular in the Arsenal side the following season, ending the campaign in which the club did the Double with 26 goals, including the one at White Hart Lane that made certain of the title. He was also selected for the England Under-23 side and won the Rothman's Young Player of the Year award.

He spent a further three seasons at Highbury, winning another FA Cup winners' medal in 1971–72 and a further six caps for the England Under-23 side.

Kennedy joined Liverpool as Bill Shankly's last signing although injury kept him out of the opening four games of the 1974–75 season. Towards the end of that campaign new boss Bob Paisley began to experiment with playing Kennedy in a deep-lying position behind the strike force of Kevin Keegan and John Toshack and over the next six years or so, he helped Liverpool to win ten major honours.

Though short of pace, he read the game well and had the ability to make a late run into the box to finish off a move at the far post. He scored some vital goals for the Anfield club – including a late strike in the 1981 European Cup semi-final against Bayern Munich – but eventually he was squeezed out of the Liverpool side by Ronnie Whelan.

Capped 17 times by England, Kennedy joined Swansea City and the Welsh club were unbeaten in his first nine outings for them, but the following season he returned to his native north-east to see out his career with Hartlepool United.

It was later revealed that he had Parkinson's Disease. Since then he has spent his time raising public awareness of the illness and dealing with his own health and personal problems. In 1991, a special match was staged between Arsenal and Liverpool to finance Ray Kennedy's medical treatment.

☻ REG LEWIS

Reg Lewis holds the Arsenal record of scoring most goals for the club in all competitions – 392 goals in just 451 games. During the Second World War he alone netted 143 goals in 130 games and if it hadn't been for the hostilities, he would have headed the list of the all-time Arsenal greats.

He had played his early football for Nunhead and Dulwich Hamlet before arriving at Highbury as a 15-year-old from the club's nursery side, Margate. He made his debut against Everton on New Year's Day 1938, scoring his side's first goal in a 2-1 win. The following season he created a new club record when playing for the Gunners' reserve side, netting 43 times in just 31 appearances including six in a game against Reading.

During the war he played for Arsenal in the 1943 Wartime Cup Final, scoring four of his side's goals in a 7-1 defeat of Charlton Athletic.

In the first season of peacetime League football, 1946–47, Reg Lewis got off to a flying start by scoring six goals in Arsenal's trial match and played for England against Scotland in the 'Bolton Disaster Match'. In the opening six League games, Arsenal registered 10 goals – Lewis scored nine of them! He finished the campaign with 29 League goals in only 28 games including a well-taken hat-trick against Preston North End and four in the match against Grimsby Town. Despite this prolific marksmanship, he found himself playing second fiddle to Ronnie Rooke in the 1947–48 League Championship-winning season, though he still contributed 14 goals in 28 games – this included another four-goal haul against Charlton Athletic.

Despite injuries limiting his appearances the following season, he still managed to score 16 goals in 25 games to head the club's scoring charts, but 1949–50 was without doubt his best season. He played twice for the England 'B' team, scored 19 goals in 31 League games and netted both his side's goals in the 2-0 FA Cup Final victory over Liverpool. Injuries continued to affect his appearances, though, when he did play, he still managed to maintain his prowess in front of goal.

☻ JIMMY LOGIE

Jimmy Logie was hailed as Arsenal's post-war Alex James, a diminutive Scot with teasing ball skills, who inspired the triumphs of Tom Whittaker's teams. Logie in fact, signed for Arsenal just before the war from Lochore Welfare near Edinburgh. He was a bricklayer by trade though his 5ft 4in, 9 stone frame hardly fitted the image.

He made his first team debut for the Gunners on the opening day of the 1946–47 season in the match against Wolves at Molineux. Over the next nine seasons, Logie constantly masterminded the Arsenal attack, helping the likes of Lewis, Lishman, Rooke and Holton to find the net with great regularity.

He kept himself very fit and, out of a possible 336 League matches between 1946 and 1954, Logie played in 283 of them. During his time at Highbury, Logie, who was a brilliant dribbler of the ball, guided the Gunners to two League Championship successes and to victory in the 1950 FA Cup Final against Liverpool. During the latter years of his time with the club, he replaced Joe Mercer as captain.

Because Jimmy Logie won only one full international cap for Scotland against Northern Ireland in October 1952, many observers will read about him and think he was only an average player. That could not be further from the truth, for he was a great favourite at Highbury and one of the club's best players in the immediate post-war years.

In February 1955 he left Highbury after scoring 76 goals in 328 League and Cup games to joined Gravesend as player-manager before settling down in business as a newsagent.

☉ MALCOLM MACDONALD

Supermac's transfer fee was probably Arsenal's most publicised since Charlie Buchan's £100-a-goal deal in the 1920s. Arsenal paid £333,333 to Newcastle United for the bustling England centre-forward and goalscoring idol of Tyneside.

He began his career as a full-back with Tonbridge before joining Fulham in August 1968. Manager Bobby Robson switched him to centre-forward but when Robson left, Macdonald fell out of favour and moved to Luton Town. In two seasons with the Hatters, he averaged well over a goal every other game, scoring 49 goals in 88 League outings.

Eventually Newcastle United signed him for £180,000 in May 1971. On Tyneside he became the greatest idol since the days of Jackie Milburn. In one of his first matches for the Magpies he scored a hat-trick against Liverpool and he finished each of his five seasons at St James Park as the club's leading scorer. He also scored in every round of the FA Cup when Newcastle reached the final in 1974.

For England, Macdonald scored five goals in one match against Cyprus, thus equalling the national team's individual scoring record.

After joining Arsenal, Macdonald endeared himself to the Gunners' fans when, in his first season, he topped the club's scoring charts with 29 goals and also headed the First Division goalscoring charts with 25 strikes in the League. In 1977–78 he netted another 26 goals for Arsenal and helped the club to the FA Cup Final against Ipswich Town. The following season was only four games old when the popular striker suffered a serious leg injury in a League Cup tie at Rotherham United. He tried, unfortunately without success, to regain full fitness by playing in two games towards the end of the campaign but finally had to announce his premature retirement.

In just over two seasons with the North London club, Malcolm Macdonald scored 57 goals in 107 first team games and will always be remembered as one of the most prolific goalscorers of his era.

He later had spells managing Fulham and Huddersfield Town.

☺ FRANK McLINTOCK

Frank McLintock was one of Arsenal's best-ever captains. Successfully converted by Don Howe from a shrewd attacking wing-half to central defender in the season Arsenal won the Fairs Cup, the Scotland international became the inspirational skipper of the 1970–71 Double-winning side. The honours didn't end there because he was also named Footballer of the Year and made an MBE.

McLintock made his name with Leicester City in the 1960s and appeared in two FA Cup Finals for the Foxes. He had made 200 League and Cup appearances for the then Filbert Street club and made his full international debut when Arsenal paid City a then record outgoing transfer fee of £80,000 for his services.

McLintock guided Arsenal to the League Cup Final in 1968 against Leeds United. The following season, Arsenal finished fourth in the First Division – their highest position for 15 seasons and played in the League Cup Final against Swindon Town. In 1969–70, McLintock led Arsenal to their first major honour for 17 years, Arsenal winning the Inter Cities Fairs Cup. In 1970–71 he became only the second player that century to captain a Double-winning side. The following season he captained Arsenal to the FA Cup Final against Leeds, returning to Wembley for his sixth major final.

After nine years service and 403 League and Cup appearances for the Gunners he was surprisingly allowed to join Queen's Park Rangers for £30,000.

Few expected McLintock to make an impression but he stayed with Rangers for four seasons, helping them to finish runners-up in the First Division in 1975–76. During that season, Rangers were undefeated at home and only conceded 33 goals all season with McLintock at centre-half. On hanging up his boots, he managed Leicester City – it has to be said without much success. He was appointed manager of Brentford in 1984 and later became assistant-manager at Millwall. He is now a regular commentator on Capital Gold Radio.

☺ BOB McNAB

Bertie Mee put one over on the great Bill Shankly to secure the services of one of the most talented left-backs in the country; a man who became one of the key members of the club's Double-winning side. Arsenal stepped into the transfer negotiations at Liverpool in September 1966 to persuade McNab to move south from his home-town club Huddersfield for £65,000, then a record fee for a British full-back.

He immediately won a regular place in the Arsenal side and over the next nine seasons, was the club's first-choice left-back. During the 1967–68 and 1968–69 seasons, McNab played a major part in helping the Gunners reach two League Cup Finals. In 1969–70 he helped Arsenal beat Anderlecht in the final of the Inter Cities Fairs Cup and won the first of his four full international caps for England. His performances for the Gunners led to him being named in the England World Cup squad for the 1970 finals.

When Arsenal won the Double in 1970–71, McNab appeared in all but two of the 64 games they played, winning League and FA Cup winners' medals. Injury forced him to miss half of the following season when he was replaced by Sammy Nelson, though he had returned to the side in time for the FA Cup Final defeat by Leeds. Missing very few games in 1972–73 when Arsenal finished runners-up in Division One, McNab then suffered a spate of injuries and this, coupled with a loss of form, saw his first team appearances restricted.

With Irishman Nelson showing plenty of promise, McNab, who had played in 365 games for the Gunners was allowed to leave Highbury and join Wolves. After a season at Molineux he left to play in the United States before returning to end his playing career with Barnet.

McNab later coached Vancouver Whitecaps but is now living in California where he ran his own executive recruitment agency.

☺ JOE MERCER

One of the game's all-time greats, wing-half Joe Mercer was one of the most influential players that Arsenal have ever had.

He started his career with Everton and in 1938–39 helped them win the League Championship. Sadly, he lost seven seasons of top-class soccer but played regularly in wartime football, being part of a famous England half-back line with Stan Cullis and Cliff Britton.

Finding himself out of favour with Everton, Mercer, then aged 32, moved south to Arsenal where his career was rejuvenated. With the Gunners suffering at the foot of the First Division, he and Ronnie Rooke were instrumental in helping the side out of trouble. Mercer captained the Gunners to the League Championship in 1947–48 and played in his first FA Cup Final for the club when they beat Liverpool 2–0. Mercer, who continued to train at Anfield following his transfer, joining up with his team-mates on match days, had to train on his own in the weeks leading up to the final!

At the end of that season, Mercer was named Footballer of the Year and, after leading the club to another FA Cup Final in 1952 – Arsenal losing 1–0 to Newcastle – he gained another League Championship medal in 1952–53. He then announced his retirement but his love of the game was too great and he was back in the side for the start of the following season. His illustrious playing career came to an end when he broke his leg in April 1954 against Blackpool at Highbury, just before his 40th birthday.

Mercer went into management, first with Sheffield United and then with Aston Villa. At Villa Park he saw the club reach two FA Cup semi-finals and win the League Cup. However, in 1964 Mercer suffered a stroke due to over-work. The Villa directors waited until he was over the worst and then sacked him.

In 1965 he made a comeback with Manchester City. He revitalised the club, winning the Second Division Championship in 1965–66 and then the League Championship two years later. More trophies followed as City beat Leicester to win the 1969 FA Cup and the European Cup Winners' Cup the following year. After a spell as Coventry City's general manager, he took charge of the England team and was later awarded the OBE for his services to football.

⚽ PAUL MERSON

Paul Merson came back from his well-publicised personal problems and continued to prove himself an exciting player with an explosive finish.

Following a brief loan spell with Brentford during his early days with the club, Merson served notice that it would not be long before he challenged for a regular place in the Arsenal side. Getting his chance in 1988–89 he took it excellently, scoring 10 goals in 37 games and linking up well with Alan Smith as Arsenal pipped Liverpool in the last game of the season to become League Champions. His progress was acknowledged by his peers when he was voted the PFA Young Player of the Year in 1989.

In 1990–91 he missed only two games when winning his second League Championship medal in three years. The following season saw the emergence of Kevin Campbell and Ian Wright and manager George Graham switched him to a wide role on either flank. It was not only successful as he scored 12 goals – including his first hat-trick against Crystal Palace – but he provided numerous goalscoring chances for his fellow strikers. His form led to him winning full international honours for England and a place in the 1992 European Championship Finals squad.

In 1992–93 he collected League Cup and FA Cup winners' medals and played a vital role in the club reaching successive European Cup Winners' Cup Finals in 1994 and 1995. The following season of 1995–96 was Merson's testimonial year so it was very fitting that he was ever-present.

He continued to flourish under new manager Arsène Wenger, scoring in both legs of the UEFA Cup against Borussia Moenchengladbach and his traditional strike against boyhood idols, Chelsea. Having scored 98 goals in 427 games, Merson was surprisingly sold to Middlesbrough for a fee of £4.5 million.

In his first season on Teeside, he helped Boro win promotion to the Premiership and was voted by his fellow professionals into the PFA First Division select side. He also captained the England 'B' team and won inclusion for the 1998 World Cup Finals where he came off the bench and scored in the penalty shoot-out against Argentina, which England lost 4-3.

After just three games of the 1998–99 season, Merson left Boro, committing himself to his new club, Aston Villa. Injuries hampered his first season in the Midlands, but in 1999–2000 he led Villa to the FA Cup Final and was voted the club's Player of the Year, a feat he achieved again in each of the following two seasons.

He then played for Portsmouth, being voted into the PFA First Division

side before joining Walsall, later becoming the club's player-manager. He
had two seasons at the Bescot Stadium before a parting of the ways.

☉ TERRY NEILL

Terry Neill's long association with Arsenal began in 1959 when he joined
them as a 17-year-old after being spotted playing for Bangor City. There
was no doubting his dedication and there followed two-and-a-half years
of steady but unspectacular progress in and out of the League side until
his career gathered momentum with the appointment of Billy Wright.

At the age of 18, Neill won the first of his 59 caps for Northern Ireland
in the match against Italy and a year later at 19, he became Arsenal's
youngest-ever captain.

Over the next three seasons, although a regular in the Northern Ireland
side, he could not claim a regular place in the Gunners' League side. In
1964–65 he recaptured his form and for the next three seasons he missed
very few games including playing against Leeds United in the 1968 League
Cup Final. Around this time, Terry Neill was appointed captain of Northern
Ireland as well as becoming the PFA secretary. In 1968–69 a series of
injuries, including contracting jaundice, forced him to miss half a season
including the League Cup Final against Swindon Town.

One of the most memorable moments of Terry Neill's career came in his
50th international appearance – he scored the winning goal at Wembley
in a rare Irish victory over England. Neill, who went on to become, at the
time, the most capped Arsenal player, later broke Danny Blanchflower's
record of Irish caps; this in turn was to be broken by Pat Jennings.

Neill, who had played in 275 games for the Gunners, later left
Highbury to become player-manager of Hull City. At 29 he was the
youngest boss in the League, going on to assume the same dual role for
Northern Ireland.

His management career was to lead him to Tottenham in 1974, then to
Highbury in 1976 to succeed Bertie Mee. In partnership with Don Howe,
he guided the Gunners to three successive FA Cup Finals and to a near miss
in the 1980 European Cup Winners' Cup Final. Even this favourite son of
Highbury could not escape the usual fate of managers when things begin
to go wrong and he was sacked after eight seasons in charge. It was the
first real setback in a 25-year career in football for the serious-minded,
self-confident Ulsterman.

☺ DAVID O'LEARY

Though he was born in Stoke Newington, David O'Leary returned to Dublin with his family as a youngster and began his career as a junior with Shelbourne. By the time he was 15, the captain of the Republic of Ireland's schoolboy team was on his way back to London to start an apprenticeship with Arsenal.

He wasted little time in settling in at Highbury and Bertie Mee, the Gunners' manager, gave him his League debut as a 17-year-old against Burnley in August 1975. O'Leary was to hold down a regular place in the heart of the Arsenal defence for 17 seasons.

Having won the first of 68 caps for the Republic of Ireland as an 18-year-old, he helped Arsenal to the FA Cup Final of 1978 against Ipswich Town before winning an FA Cup winners' medal against Manchester United the following season. It was around this time that David O'Leary was considered not only the best centre-back in England but also in Europe. Throughout his career, it was his ability to read the game so well that made his job look so easy. He was unruffled, calm and used the ball as well as any in his position. Allied to these attributes was his speed of thought as well as great positional sense.

After a disagreement with Republic of Ireland manager Jack Charlton, O'Leary found himself out of the national side for over two years but returned to the international scene for Italia '90 when his spot-kick in the penalty shoot-out against Romania earned his side a place in the quarter-finals.

The only blot on David O'Leary's Highbury career was his demotion to the reserves after turning up late for pre-season training following his exploits in Italia '90. Several top clubs began hovering around Highbury waiting for an announcement of his release but he was labelled as 'not for sale' by Arsenal.

For Arsenal, O'Leary went on to make a record 558 League appearances, breaking the previous record held by George Armstrong. Towards the end of his playing days at Highbury, he became a utility player and injuries and suspensions meant that he could bring the curtain down on his Arsenal career with two Wembley appearances as the Gunners beat Sheffield Wednesday in the League Cup and FA Cup Finals of 1993.

He then joined Leeds United and, after hanging up his boots, remained at Elland Road, first as assistant-manager to George Graham and later as the man in charge. O'Leary later managed Aston Villa but at the time of writing is still looking to return to top-class management.

☉ JOHN RADFORD

John Radford, a likeable down-to-earth Yorkshireman, became the experienced half of one of the best scoring double acts of post-war football. He was also one of the best investments Arsenal ever made – all he cost manager Billy Wright was a £10 signing-on fee and the train fare down from his home in the mining community of Hemsworth.

After a couple of seasons of prolific goalscoring in Arsenal's youth side, Radford was given his League debut against West Ham United in March 1964. After scoring seven goals in 13 games in 1964–65, Radford won a regular place in the Gunners' side, playing at both inside- and centre-forward. However, during the 1968–69 season, he was switched to the right-wing with great success, scoring 19 goals and winning four caps for England at Under-23 level. After playing in the 1969 League Cup Final defeat by Swindon, Radford won full international honours for England and helped Arsenal win the Inter Cities Fairs Cup. He again netted 19 goals and was the club's leading scorer.

In the Double-winning season of 1970–71, Radford reverted to centre-forward and enjoyed great success alongside Ray Kennedy. He netted 21 goals as the two of them terrorised First Division defences. It was a pairing that the Arsenal boss thought would never work because they were both big, brave strikers in the typical English mould. But somehow they gelled instinctively, taking pressure off each other at vital moments and for a couple of seasons were the most effective pair in the country.

Radford continued to play on a regular basis until losing his place to Frank Stapleton. Having scored 149 goals in 481 games, he was transferred to West Ham United for £80,000 in December 1976. Radford later played for Blackburn Rovers before having more success with non-League Bishop's Stortford both as a player and as manager.

☉ PAT RICE

Everyone remembers Charlie George as the Arsenal fan who grew up to play for the team. But so was Pat Rice, and whereas George never really fulfilled his enormous potential, Rice, a determined, quick and agile full-back, exceeded even his own expectations in a fabulous career at Highbury.

One of the most loyal players the club has ever had, Rice played in no fewer than five Wembley FA Cup Finals – a record he shares with Joe Hulme, Frank Stapleton and Johnny Giles. He also won 49 caps for

Northern Ireland and played in 527 League and Cup games for the Gunners, a total only bettered by six other players.

Despite this, Pat Rice's career had a very unimpressive start. He appeared in just a handful of first team matches in his first five years at Highbury. However, when Peter Storey switched from right-back to midfield, Rice was drafted into the right-back position for the beginning of the 1970–71 season.

In his first full season, he helped Arsenal to the League and FA Cup Double and over the next 10 seasons, Pat Rice was undoubtedly Arsenal's most consistent player. Appearing in every League match during 1971–72, 1975–76 and 1976–77, Rice became one of the few Arsenal players to be an ever-present in three different seasons. Rice was made Arsenal captain in 1977 and skippered them to three consecutive FA Cup Finals between 1978 and 1980 and the European Cup Winners' Cup Final of 1980. By this time he was also leading his country and won the last of his caps against England in October 1979.

The following month Rice was transferred to Watford, helping the Hornets gain promotion to the First Division in 1981–82 and then finish the next season as runners-up to Liverpool.

In 1984 Rice returned to Highbury as youth team coach and over the next 10 years he helped the Gunners to success in two FA Youth Cup Finals. Now the club's assistant-manager having helped the Gunners to the Double in 1997–98 and the Premier League title in seasons 2001–02 and 2003–04, Pat Rice will forever be remembered for his dedication to the club he loves and supports.

☉ GRAHAM RIX

Graham Rix was not only plagued by injuries during his Highbury career but had the unenviable task of trying to replace Liam Brady on the left-side of midfield when the mercurial Irishman went to play in Italy.

After working his way through the ranks, Doncaster-born Rix made his League debut against Leicester City in April 1977, scoring the first goal in a 3-0 win. His performance that day helped him appear in seven of the club's last ten games of the campaign. In 1977–78 he took over from George Armstrong, playing in 39 League games and coming off the bench in the FA Cup Final defeat by Ipswich Town. He missed the first three games of the following campaign, but thereafter was a first team regular and was the player who provided the far post cross for Alan

Sunderland to net the winner in the 1979 FA Cup Final defeat of Manchester United.

In 1979–80, Rix appeared in his third consecutive FA Cup Final as Arsenal lost to West ham and then unfortunately was the player who missed the final spot-kick in the penalty shoot-out against Valencia in the final of the European Cup Winners' Cup.

In 1980–81, Graham Rix made history when he became the first Arsenal player to win caps at four different international levels, when he won the first of his 17 full caps against Norway.

The greater responsibility he had following Brady's departure seemed to rejuvenate Rix. In 1982 he was a member of England's World Cup squad and the following season he was a leading figure as the Gunners reached both major cup semi-finals. The following season he was appointed club captain, although he was later troubled by an Achilles tendon injury which continued to flare up again.

He had a spell on loan with Brentford before playing for French sides Caen and Le Havre. There followed a few games for Dundee before he became player-coach of Chelsea. His career was long and successful but could have been even more notable had he not been compared to Liam Brady quite so often.

☻ KENNY SANSOM

The most-capped full-back in England's history, Kenny Sansom began his long and illustrious career with Crystal Palace. After signing professional forms in December 1975, Sansom went on over the next five years to play in nearly 200 first team games for the club, helping them win the Second Division Championship in 1978–79.

The following season he started a remarkable record, when he was voted for the first of his eight consecutive left-back Division One PFA awards, a sequence that no other top-flight outfield player has come remotely close to emulating.

He was quite rightly regarded as the best left-back in the country when Arsenal paid £1.25 million for his services in August 1980 and, in his eight seasons at Highbury, he received 77 international caps.

Voted Arsenal's Player of the Year in 1981, he was remarkably consistent, being ever-present in his first two seasons with the club. He captained Arsenal in their League Cup Final against Liverpool in 1987 and was a member of the Arsenal side when they reached the final again the following season. At the start of the club's 1988–89 League Championship-winning campaign, Sansom had lost his place to Nigel Winterburn and rather than waste away in the club's Combination side, Sansom, who had made 394 appearances, opted for a move to Newcastle United.

However, his stay on Tyneside was brief and in June 1989 he returned to London to play for Queen's Park Rangers. He later played for Coventry City before joining Watford as player-coach. After short spells in similar capacities, he returned to Vicarage Road as the club's assistant-manager.

⊙ DAVID SEAMAN

One of the game's greatest goalkeepers, David Seaman was unable to break into the Leeds United side because of the consistency of John Lukic. He joined Peterborough United in the summer of 1982 and his brilliant form for The Posh was noted by Birmingham City manager Jim Smith who paid £100,000 for him in October 1984.

Having helped the Blues win promotion to the First Division with a series of outstanding displays, he could not save the club from relegation after just one season in the top flight. In order to remain playing at the highest level he joined Queen's Park Rangers in August 1986 and in four seasons at Loftus Road he was a first team fixture and won the first of his 75 caps for England.

In May 1990, after he had appeared in 175 games for Rangers, Arsenal paid out a record British fee for a goalkeeper of £1.3 million to obtain Seaman's services.

He proved superb value for money, making a solid Arsenal defence even more watertight and won his first League Championship medal as the Gunners celebrated their second title win in three years. His League statistics as an ever-present in 1990–91 include 24 clean sheets, 540 minutes without a goal being scored against him and just 18 goals conceded.

Very relaxed and composed both on and off the field of play, in 1992–93 he helped the club to the FA Cup and League Cup Double, while the following season he was a member of the Arsenal side that beat Parma to win the European Cup Winners' Cup. He enhanced his reputation even more in Euro '96 with two superb penalty saves, including one against Spain that was instrumental in England reaching the semi-final stage.

In 1997–98, after a series of niggling injuries, he helped Arsenal complete the League and Cup Double and then appeared in all four of England's World Cup games in France '98. He was again an integral member of the Arsenal side that completed another League and Cup Double in 2001–02 and was England's first-choice keeper for the 2002 World Cup Finals in Japan and Korea. Though he was at fault for Ronaldinho's winner in the quarter-final against Brazil, he remained a model of consistency behind Arsenal's back four, maintaining a high percentage of clean sheets in his 564 first team appearances.

In 2003, recognising that his days as first-choice keeper at Arsenal were over, Seaman joined Manchester City before retiring midway through the 2003–04 season.

⚽ PETER SIMPSON

Peter Simpson set himself such high standards that he was never satisfied with his play but his team-mates recognised him as the great unflappable sweeper, always neat and tidy in his play, a hard tackler and the master of playing football out of tight situations with that lovely touch in his left foot.

After working his way up through the ranks, Peter Simpson made his Arsenal debut against Chelsea in March 1964 but over the next couple of seasons, found himself in and out of the Gunners' side. His fortunes changed during the 1966–67 season, when playing in almost every outfield position, he appeared in 36 League games. He kept his place in the side over the next two seasons, settling down at left-half in 1968–69. He appeared in the League Cup Final defeats of those two seasons before, in 1969–70, playing his part in the club winning the Inter Cities Fairs Cup Final.

During the course of that season, Simpson was often called into the full England squad but he never won a full cap – along with George Armstrong, he must be one of the club's best outfield players never to have done so.

He played a leading role in the Arsenal side when the club did the Double in 1970–71. If Radford and Kennedy were the battering rams, Simpson and McLintock were the twin padlocks on the Gunners' mean defence which conceded only 29 goals in the Double year. He then appeared for the Gunners in the FA Cup Final of 1972 against Leeds United. For the next three seasons, Simpson missed very few games but then from 1975–76 onwards he found himself left out of the side more than he was selected.

Having appeared in 477 first team games he left Highbury to finish his career playing for New England Teamen in the United States.

⊙ ALAN SMITH

An unselfish striker and a wonderful team player, Alan Smith started out with Southern League Alvechurch before signing for Leicester City. In 1982–83, his first season at Filbert Street, he helped the club win promotion to the First Division – scoring 13 goals in 39 games – a remarkable achievement for a first year professional.

Partnering the up and coming Gary Lineker, he was the perfect foil but after the latter's transfer to Everton in the summer of 1985, he assumed the mantle of the club's leading scorer for the next two seasons. However, his 17 League goals in 1986–87 were not enough to save Leicester from relegation back to the Second Division and in the close season he joined Arsenal.

In his first term at Highbury, he topped the scoring charts with 11 goals including a hat-trick in his fourth game, a 6-0 defeat of Portsmouth. He also scored in the League Cup Final but couldn't prevent the Gunners losing 3-2 to Luton Town.

The following season he won a League Championship winners' medal, striking 23 times in 36 games and opened the scoring in the final game as Arsenal beat Liverpool 2-0 at Anfield to clinch the title. Bobby Robson recognised his form and selected him to win his first England cap against Saudi Arabia.

Though the goals dried up in 1989–90 he was back to his best the following season, netting 22 times as Arsenal won the League title. He started the 1991–92 season in sparkling form with seven goals in the first nine league games and netted four goals in the space of 16 minutes in the European Cup tie against Austria Vienna.

After losing his place to Kevin Campbell, he bounced back and, in 1992–93, scored twice in the first leg of the League Cup semi-final against Crystal Palace. Though he didn't appear in the League Cup Final defeat of Sheffield Wednesday, he collected an FA Cup winners' medal over the same opposition – and received his first ever recorded booking during this game.

After this he became more of a provider than a goalscorer, though he did go on to score more than 100 goals for the club until injury forced his premature retirement from the game at the age of only 32.

⊙ FRANK STAPLETON

Stapleton, a shy man off the field, did all his talking on it in terms of world-class performances and memorable goals. In his early years at

Highbury he showed great natural heading ability and a brave attitude which denied the existence of lost causes.

Bertie Mee had doubts about his pace and control but Stapleton was willing to work hard and in partnership, first with Malcolm Macdonald and then the skilful Alan Sunderland, he matured into a great centre-forward, a permanent fixture for Arsenal and the Republic of Ireland, for whom he won 71 full international caps.

Frank Stapleton helped the Gunners to three consecutive FA Cup Finals, 1978–1980, scoring one of the goals that helped beat Manchester United 3-2 in 1979. Many of Stapleton's goals for both club and country were set up by Liam Brady and Stapleton, like Brady, wanted to leave Highbury after the expiry of his contract. He had scored 108 goals in 300 games for Arsenal when, in August 1981, he joined Manchester United for a tribunal-set fee of £900,000. United had got one of the best all-round centre-forwards in the country.

He continued at Old Trafford where he'd left off at Highbury and was United's leading scorer in his first three seasons with the club. He was in the United side that lost the 1983 League Cup Final to Liverpool and which faced Brighton in that year's FA Cup Final. When Stapleton scored his side's first goal in the 2-2 draw, he wrote himself into the history books by becoming the first player to score in the final for two different FA Cup-winning teams.

In the summer of 1987 he was given a free transfer by United and he spent an unhappy eight months in Holland with Ajax. After a back operation for the removal of a disc, he joined Le Havre, but failed to settle in France. He returned to the north-west and spent two seasons with Blackburn Rovers. After a brief spell with Huddersfield, he was appointed player-manager of Bradford City but was sacked after failing to steer the club into the Second Division play-offs.

Since then he has worked in various coaching roles including one as manager of New England Revolution in the new American Soccer League.

☉ PETER STOREY

There have been few hard men in post-war football to compare with Peter Storey, whose gifts as a footballer for Arsenal were so often clouded by the controversies which marred his career on and off the field. What cannot be denied is that Peter Storey, when he moved into midfield from his usual right-back spot in the injury crisis that launched the Double-winning year, became the vital ball winner that the Gunners needed.

Storey lived more than died by the sword and his fearless approach in a tough and uncompromising era of football was to win him 19 full international caps for England under manager Sir Alf Ramsey.

He made his Arsenal debut in October 1965 as a replacement for Billy McCullough in the game against Leicester City at Filbert Street. Thereafter, he was a virtual constant in the Arsenal side for the next 12 seasons, appearing in League Cup Finals against Leeds United and Swindon Town and also being a member of the club's Inter Cities Fairs Cup winning team.

During the club's Double-winning season of 1970–71, Storey equalled Bobby Smith's record of winning League Championship and FA Cup winners' medals and England caps in the same season. He also played for Arsenal in the 1972 FA Cup Final against Leeds, by which time he had made the switch to midfield.

His short-fused temper let him down on many occasions and led to a series of sendings-off during his 16 years and 501 first team appearances at Arsenal. His final brush with authority came in 1977 when this son of an exiled Geordie miner walked out on the club when, after being at the top for so long, he found that he couldn't face another game in the reserves. Manager Terry Neill put him on the transfer list and, a month later, he moved into the Second Division with Fulham, where he played only 17 games before drifting sadly out of the game.

Since retiring he has led a colourful life and after managing a number of public houses, ran a market stall in London's West End.

☺ ALAN SUNDERLAND

Arsenal fans will have one vivid memory of Alan Sunderland as he wheeled away in triumph after scoring the last-minute winner against Manchester United in the 1979 FA Cup Final at Wembley. After Gordon McQueen and Sammy McIlroy had pulled United level after Arsenal led 2-0, extra-time looked certain. But Liam Brady found Graham Rix and his cross eluded everybody except hit-man Sunderland who slid in the winner at the far post.

He began his career with Wolverhampton Wanderers and during his seven seasons at Molineux, he appeared in a number of different positions. By the end of 1971–72, his first season with the club, he had helped them reach the UEFA Cup Final where they lost to Spurs. A member of the Wolves side that won the 1974 League Cup Final, he top-scored for the Midlands club during their 1976–77 Second Division Championship-winning season with 16 goals in 41 games. Then having scored 35 goals in 198 games for Wolves, he joined Arsenal for £220,000 in November 1977.

At the end of his first season with the Gunners, Sunderland played in the FA Cup Final against Ipswich and, in 1978–79, he scored six goals in the club's victorious FA Cup campaign including that Wembley winner. Also collecting a UEFA Cup winners' medal that season, Sunderland was plagued by a series of niggling injuries and, after losing his place in the side following the arrival of Charlie Nicholas and Paul Mariner, he decided to part company with the club. He had scored 92 goals in 281 first team outings for the Gunners when, after a loan spell with Ipswich Town, he joined them on a permanent basis.

After helping the Suffolk club regain their top flight status in 1983–84, he played in Ireland for Derry City.

☉ GEORGE SWINDIN

Tom Whittaker rated George Swindin as the finest goalkeeper Arsenal ever had. He was signed from Bradford City just a couple of weeks before the 1935 FA Cup Final and made his debut at the start of the following season, replacing Alec Wilson. During his early days with the club, Swindin lacked confidence and his kicking was very poor. However, the club stood by him and in 1937–38 he won the first of his three League Championship winners' medals.

During the war, George Swindin was a PT instructor in the army and on the resumption of League football in 1946–47 he found himself Arsenal's first-choice keeper. In the club's League Championship-winning season of 1947–48, Swindin was ever-present and conceded only 32 League goals – at the time a new First Division defensive record.

He would have undoubtedly been capped by England had it not been for the fine form of Frank Swift and later Wolves' Bert Williams. Due to the aerial command of centre-half Leslie Compton, Swindin's confidence of cutting out high balls grew and over the coming seasons, he missed very few matches. In 1950 he was between the posts when his scarlet top and marvellous saves helped Arsenal beat Liverpool 2-0 to win the FA Cup but then injuries forced him to share the goalkeeping duties with Ted Platt in 1950–51.

He was back to his best the following season when he helped the Gunners to the FA Cup Final when the 10 men of Arsenal lost 1-0 to Newcastle United. He played in just enough games in 1952–53 to qualify

Above left: Herbert Chapman in 1925. One of the most successful and influential managers, not only did he build a great side but converted Highbury into one of the best grounds in Britain.

Above right: Arsenal broke the British transfer record when they paid Bolton Wanderers £10,890 for David Jack.

Below left: Charles Buchan, a footballing immortal who led the club to their first-ever FA Cup Final.

Below right: Alex James was one of the greatest players ever to wear the famous red and white jersey.

 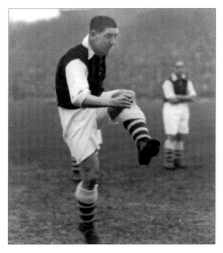

Above left: Arsenal legend Cliff Bastin, who in 1932-33 set a record from the outside-left position when he scored a staggering 33 league goals.

Above right: Ted Drake warms up before a game in 1934. A brave centre-forward, he scored the only goal of the 1936 FA Cup Final against Sheffield United.

Below left: Joe Mercer's career was rejuvenated at Highbury as he led the Gunners to the 1947-48 and 1952-53 League titles and FA Cup success in 1950.

Below right: An acrobatic Jack Kelsey in 1949. A Welsh international keeper, his career ended after he sustained a serious injury against Brazil in the 1962 World Cup.

Above left: George Armstrong, one of Arsenal's greatest-ever servants, who played in exactly 500 league games for the club.

Above right: Bob Wilson leads the team out in 1963. He figured prominently in the club's League and FA Cup double winning side of 1970-71.

Below left: Ray Kennedy was a striker who shot to fame when he scored one of Arsenal's goals in the two-legged 1969-70 Fairs Cup Final.

Below right: Frank McLintock in 1968. The Scottish international captained Arsenal to the double in 1970-71.

Above left: Charlie George, the long-haired 20-year-old who scored Arsenal's winning goal in the 1971 FA Cup Final, taking the double to Highbury.

Above right: Peter Simpson – one of Arsenal's best players never to have won an international cap.

Below: FA Cup winners – captain Frank McLintock held aloft by Charlie George and Pat Rice.

Above left: Bertie Mee on the Highbury terraces in 1973. As manager he guided Arsenal to the double in 1971 – not surprisingly he was voted Manager of the Year.

Above right: Kenny Sansom, a remarkably consistent defender who was ever-present in his first two seasons with the club.

Below left: David O'Leary in the away strip of 1984-85. He was the first player in the club's history to play in 1,000 competitive games for the Gunners.

Below right: David Seaman in 1990. One of the club's greatest-ever goalkeepers, he cost a British record fee of £1.3 million when signed from QPR.

Above: Tony Adams and George Graham celebrate the Double in 1991.

Below left: Ian Wright was a goalscoring legend who could turn a game with one dazzling moment of brilliance. Here he scores in the 1993 FA Cup final vs Sheffield Wednesday.

Below right: Paul Merson was a popular Arsenal forward – one of the few players in the top flight capable of the unexpected.

Above left: Arsène Wenger, the club's most successful manager in terms of trophies and the longest-serving in terms of matches.

Above right: The 'Flying Dutchman' Dennis Bergkamp, the magnificent Dutch international who was a huge influence at Arsenal.

Below left: Patrick Vieira, an inspirational Arsenal captain who blossomed under the managerial reins of Arsène Wenger.

Below right: Thierry Henry, prolific striker and one of the best footballers in the world.

Above: Highbury as it was...

Below: The new Emirates Stadium, 2006-07.

for a third League Championship medal. Swindin was now approaching his 40th year and Jack Kelsey had taken over the No.1 jersey. Having appeared in 297 games either side of the hostilities, he left to become player-manager of Peterborough United.

He later returned to Highbury and succeeded Jack Crayston as manager but in his four years in charge, he tended to make too many changes too quickly and the Gunners never seemed to have a settled side. After four years, he parted company with the club, later managing both Norwich City and Cardiff City.

☻ PATRICK VIEIRA

Patrick Vieira was manager Arsène Wenger's first signing when he paid AC Milan £3.5 million for the French international's signature. A tall and elegant midfielder, he quickly settled into the English game and in particular relished the physical side. But it was his visionary passing that excited the Arsenal fans, bringing back happy memories of former Gunners' legend, Liam Brady.

One of the club's most consistent players during the Double-winning campaign of 1997–98, he rounded off his season by coming off the bench for France in the 1998 World Cup Final as the hosts beat Brazil 3–0. He continued his tremendous form the following season, continuing to benefit from playing alongside his fellow French international Emmanuel Petit and was one of three Arsenal players elected by his fellow professionals for the PFA award-winning Premiership side.

Possessing good attacking and defending skills, he began to mature with each performance and having been selected for the PFA-select side again, helped France beat Italy in the final of Euro 2000.

The start of Vieira's 2000–01 season was soured by two red cards in the opening two games, but he quickly put his disciplinary problems behind him and ended the season – in which he scored a number of spectacular goals – by again being honoured by his fellow professionals with a place in the PFA Premiership team. Another effective season followed as he played an integral part in the club winning the League and FA Cup Double – not surprisingly he maintained his place in the PFA Premiership team for the season.

Taking over the captaincy in commanding fashion from Tony Adams, this world-class player dominated most games from start to finish and again was one of five Arsenal players selected for the PFA team.

Continuing to flourish under the managerial reins of Arsène Wenger, Vieira proudly lifted the Premiership trophy in May 2004. Named in the Premiership team of the season for the sixth season running, it is a feat no other player had previously achieved.

Having just led the Gunners to a historic unbeaten triumph, it seemed that he would be leaving Arsenal to join Real Madrid but he decided against a move and remained at Highbury. In what turned out to be his last season for the club, Vieira, who left to join Juventus, finished his Arsenal career on a high by lifting the FA Cup in 2005 following a penalty shoot-out win over Manchester United.

☺ BOB WILSON

Bob Wilson, as brave a goalkeeper as any to have played for Arsenal, was a most unlikely star and his story is one of the most unusual to come out of the Gunners' Double-winning side. A son of Chesterfield – a town which has produced many famous goalkeepers – Bob Wilson originally planned to be a teacher and played for Wolves as an amateur. He even refused to turn professional because he dreamt that one day he would play for the British Olympic team.

Wilson drifted away from Molineux and joined the Gunners, still as an amateur, in 1963, and made five appearances in the top flight before turning professional a year later. There was a major row when Wolves heard of it and the League had to step in to decide that the Midlands club should receive a £5,500 transfer fee.

Following the signing of Jim Furnell, Wilson found that the majority of his first three seasons with the club were spent playing reserve team football. However, after Furnell made a costly error in the FA Cup fifth round game against Birmingham City in March 1968, he was replaced by Wilson, who never looked back.

He played regularly in 1968–69 and was instrumental in the club's defensive record, conceding just 27 goals in 40 games. Despite suffering a broken arm in 1969–70, he still managed to appear in 28 games and helped Arsenal win the Inter Cities Fairs Cup. He played in all of the club's 64 games during the Double-winning season of 1970–71 and the following season, when he missed just a handful of games, he won full international honours for Scotland.

After a season in which he was plagued by a series of niggling injuries, he missed just one game in 1973–74 before he surprisingly announced his retirement from the game at the age of only 32.

Wilson, who had appeared in 308 League and Cup games for the Gunners, became a leading sports broadcaster and returned to Highbury as the club's goalkeeping coach.

⚽ IAN WRIGHT

One of the game's natural goalscorers, Ian Wright began his League career with Crystal Palace after being spotted by Eagles' manager Steve Coppell playing for Greenwich Borough. In his six seasons at Selhurst Park, he formed a prolific goalscoring partnership with Mark Bright but in 1989–90 he broke his leg twice. He recovered in time to be selected as a substitute for the 1990 FA Cup Final against Manchester United and when he came off the bench, he scored two stunning goals to take the game to a replay. Then in September 1991, after scoring 118 goals in 277 first team games for Palace, he joined Arsenal for £2.5 million.

Wright scored a hat-trick on his League debut for the Gunners at Southampton and ended the season as the First Division's leading scorer with 29 goals. He also won the Golden Boot as Europe's top scorer. In 1992–93 he was instrumental in helping the Highbury club win the FA and League Cups.

In 1994–95 he broke all club European goalscoring records when he scored in every match right up to the final of the European Cup Winners' Cup.

When the Gunners played Bolton Wanderers at the start of the 1997–98 season, he hit a hat-trick in a 4-1 win to make him Arsenal's greatest goalscorer of all-time, overtaking Cliff Bastin's record of 178 League and Cup goals. Wright also won FA Cup and League Championship winners' medals that season but was kept out of the World Cup by a hamstring injury. He had scored 185 goals in 288 games for Arsenal when, in July 1998, he was transferred to West Ham United for £750,000.

Midway through his first season at Upton Park, Wright went to Nottingham Forest on loan but he was soon on his way to Glasgow Celtic on a permanent basis. His stay north of the border was brief, however, and he returned to Football League action with Burnley.

Capped 33 times by England and once scoring four goals in a 7-1 defeat of San Marino, Wright retired from the game in the summer of 2000 and is now a hugely popular TV celebrity.

THE MANAGERS

⚽ SAM HOLLIS
1894 – 1897
Born in Nottingham, Sam Hollis worked in his early years in a Probate Office and the Post Office. There are conflicting arguments about whether Hollis was manager or trainer at Woolwich Arsenal but, whatever the truth, he had three rather mediocre seasons at the club, with a best finish of seventh in 1895–96.

On leaving the Gunners, Hollis became Bristol City's first manager. They had just been voted into the Southern League and he bought eight new players for just £40. Hollis resigned in March 1899 after increasing interference from the club's directors and moved to local rivals Bedminster, who later amalgamated with City, leading to Hollis losing his job. He returned as the Robins' manager in the summer of 1901 after the shock departure of Bob Campbell and remained in charge until March 1905. He then ran the Southville Hotel for six years before, in January 1911, returning for a third spell in charge of the club.

In April 1913 he left to manage Newport County, being at the helm for four years. He subsequently became chairman of Bristol City's shareholders association. Hollis remained in Bristol and was a local publican until his death in April 1942.

🏆 **Arsenal's record under Sam Hollis**

P	W	D	L	F	A	Success Rate
95	43	14	38	213	181	52%

☻ TOM MITCHELL
April 1897 – March 1898

Tom Mitchell was the secretary of Blackburn Rovers for 12 years before he was appointed Arsenal's first professional manager in 1897. During that time Rovers won the FA Cup five times but he cannot be directly credited with this, as he was not in charge of the playing side, only the administration.

Mitchell was only in charge at Plumstead for less than one season as the Gunners finished fifth in Division Two in 1897–98 and reached the first round of the FA Cup proper where they were knocked out by Burnley. Mitchell signed a number of new players during his short stay at the club but many of them, like Mitchell, lasted less than a year in their new surroundings.

Despite improved performances, support for the club fell away and the financial position of Woolwich Arsenal became acute. There is little doubt that it was because of these circumstances that Mitchell resigned his post in March 1898.

♆ Arsenal's record under Tom Mitchell

P	W	D	L	F	A	Success Rate
26	14	4	8	66	46	61%

☻ GEORGE ELCOAT
May 1898 – May 1899

George Elcoat succeeded Tom Mitchell as manager of Woolwich Arsenal but, like his predecessor, he too remained at the club for only one season. A native of Stockton-on-Tees, he showed a preference for Scottish footballing talent and during his season in charge, no less than eight of the first team squad were from north of the border! Elcoat's best capture was John Dick, who went on to give the club 12 years excellent service, both as a hard-tackling wing-half and club captain.

For 1898–99, Elcoat's season in charge, the League was increased to 18 clubs and Arsenal's final position of seventh was on a par with the previous season. Though the club was excused from having to play in the qualifying rounds of the FA Cup, they were beaten 6-0 at home by Derby County in the first round proper.

The club was still in a poor financial position and players had to be sold to keep the Gunners solvent. Attendances at Plumstead were also poor, averaging only around 4,000 and able to face the situation no longer,

Elcoat parted company with the club at the end of the season to be replaced by Harry Bradshaw.

♦ Arsenal's record under George Elcoat

P	W	D	L	F	A	Success Rate
43	23	6	14	92	55	60%

⊕ HARRY BRADSHAW
June 1899 – May 1904

Harry Bradshaw was Woolwich Arsenal's first successful manager. In five years in charge, he transformed the fortunes of the North London club, taking them from the verge of bankruptcy and building a side that, in 1903–04, was to win promotion to the First Division as runners-up to Preston North End.

A former player with Burnley, Bradshaw arrived at Plumstead to be met with a complete lack of local interest that showed itself in the club's falling attendances. With little funds available, Bradshaw brought in local talent, notably goalkeeper Jimmy Ashcroft from Gravesend, and full-back Jimmy Jackson from Scotland. In fact, Bradshaw adopted the Scottish style of a short, accurate passing game and with it the results improved. After finishing seventh the previous season, Arsenal rose to fourth in 1901–02, their best League finish to date. Following the improvement in playing results, there was an increase in support and with the club now able to afford new players, Bradshaw brought in Roddy McEachrane. The club finished third in 1902–03 and then the following season their hopes of top flight football were achieved.

Harry Bradshaw was a good administrator and a very clever tactician but, having put Arsenal on the map, he was surprisingly tempted away by a big money offer from Fulham rather than First Division football at Plumstead. Bradshaw's two young sons had been on the playing staff at Plumstead but they too followed him to Fulham.

Bradshaw was Fulham's first full-time manager and, in his time there, he took the club to two Southern League titles and eventually into the Football League. The Cottagers also reached the FA Cup semi-final and narrowly missed promotion to the First Division in 1908. Bradshaw was also instrumental in re-developing Craven Cottage into a modern stadium.

When his contract expired in 1909, he chose to become the secretary of the Southern League, a position he held until his death in 1921.

♈ Arsenal's record under Harry Bradshaw

P	W	D	L	F	A	Success Rate
189	96	39	54	329	173	61%

⚽ PHIL KELSO
March 1904 – February 1908

A stern, abrasive Scot, Phil Kelso was a man of firm views who had a reputation as a disciplinarian. He had been associated with Hibernian for a good number of years and, when he was appointed as successor to Harry Bradshaw, he was one of the best known men in footballing circles north of the border.

He had a paternalistic attitude towards the players of Woolwich Arsenal and discouraged both drinking and smoking. He also demanded that they live in London and he would often make them spend a week away before important games, which did not prove popular with all the players, many of whom left after clashes with Kelso.

One of his first priorities was to consolidate Arsenal's newly acquired status of playing in the First Division and he strengthened the side in all departments. The club not only progressed beyond the second round of the FA Cup but, in 1905–06 – Kelso's second season with the club – they reached the semi-final only to be beaten 2-0 by Newcastle United. The following season was the club's best so far as they finished seventh in Division One and reached the FA Cup semi-finals for a second successive season.

In 1907–08, results began to fall away and, as they did, attendances began to drop. With the club once again in a perilous financial position Kelso, unlike Bradshaw, found he couldn't cope and before the end of the season, he resigned. He returned north of the border to run a hotel in Largs.

Twelve months later he was persuaded by Fulham to return to the game as their manager. He stayed with the Cottagers throughout the First World War, parting company with them in 1924. During his 15 years at the helm, he brought some famous internationals to the club, adding a touch of glamour. He was just beginning to build a fine side in the early 1920s when Fulham was rocked by a bribery scandal following which the Cottagers' centre-forward Barney Travers was banned for life. Kelso, who became a publican in the area, lost some credibility after this episode.

♛ **Arsenal's record under Phil Kelso**

P	W	D	L	F	A	Success Rate
151	63	31	57	225	228	52%

⊙ GEORGE MORRELL
February 1908 – May 1915

George Morrell was committee man, secretary, treasurer, president and occasional player with Glenure Athletic, a Glasgow junior club. He later joined the staff of Glasgow Rangers and helped revive their fortunes as well as qualifying as a referee! In 1905, Morrell was appointed manager of Greenock Morton from a list of 85 applicants. The Scottish club were heavily in debt but Morrell soon made them solvent and they were voted into the Scottish First Division.

Morrell took up his appointment as Arsenal manager in February 1908, again being faced with a club experiencing poor support and therefore financial difficulties. Though the club finished sixth in his first full season in charge, he was later forced to sell a number of the club's excellent players such as Andy Ducat, Jimmy Sharp, Tim Coleman, Jimmy Ashcroft and Bert Freeman. Not surprisingly, after a few seasons of struggle, the club with the worst-ever playing record were relegated for the only time in their history in 1912–13.

Arsenal then moved across London from Plumstead to Highbury, in search of better support and Morrell therefore became the club's first manager at the famous ground. For two seasons, the club made a brave attempt to regain their top flight status but, with little change in the Gunners' financial situation, Morrell was forced to resign at the end of the 1914–15 season, as the club officially closed down because of the First World War.

♛ **Arsenal's record under George Morrell**

P	W	D	L	F	A	Success Rate
294	104	73	117	365	412	47%

⊙ LESLIE KNIGHTON
May 1919 – June 1925

Leslie Knighton enjoyed a long and relatively successful career as a manager after having his playing days cut short by an ankle injury. Appointed team manager of Castleford Town at the age of 20, he was offered the post of assistant secretary-manager of Huddersfield Town in 1909 and, after three years, a similar position with Manchester City. With both of these clubs, Knighton gained a reputation for developing fine young sides.

After the First World War, Sir Henry Norris, the Arsenal chairman, used his influence to ensure First Division status for the Gunners and his first step in his determination to make the North London club one of the most successful in the country, was to appoint Knighton as the Arsenal manager.

He was not in sole control at Arsenal. With the club were in debt after moving to Highbury, Norris instructed Knighton to build a successful side without spending any money! This was unrealistic and Knighton struggled to keep the Gunners in the First Division. He was rarely allowed to manage and Norris often interfered, making Knighton's task even more difficult. This was reflected in the club's playing record – in his six seasons in charge, not once did the goals 'for' exceed those 'against'. Although the club's best position was ninth in 1920–21, they did narrowly avoid relegation to the Second Division on two occasions.

Towards the end of the 1924–25 season, Knighton got fed up with the restrictions imposed by Norris and he challenged his authority with demands to buy key players. With the club having been knocked out of the FA Cup and lying in 20th place in Division One, Norris sacked the Arsenal manager.

Knighton soon took over the reins at Bournemouth where he rarely attended training sessions, allowing his assistants to look after team affairs, although some players took advantage of his good nature.

In 1928 he left to become manager of Birmingham and three years later helped the club to the FA Cup Final where they lost to West Bromwich Albion. He managed to keep the Blues in the top flight but left for Chelsea after they made him an offer he could not refuse.

Chelsea had an amazing run to avoid relegation at the end of his first season in charge. They also just avoided relegation again in 1938–39 but did reach the FA Cup quarter-finals.

After managing Midland League club Shrewsbury Town, Knighton's health broke down and he retired to Bournemouth where he took on the more genteel post of secretary of a local golf club.

♆ Arsenal's record under Leslie Knighton

P	W	D	L	F	A	Success Rate
267	92	62	114	330	380	46%

☺ HERBERT CHAPMAN
June 1925 – January 1934

One of the most successful and influential managers in the history of the
game, Herbert Chapman was a great innovator who changed the face of
football both on and off the field. He created two great sides at
Huddersfield Town and Arsenal and introduced tactical methods and many
other new ideas which had a far-reaching effect on the game.

The son of a coal miner, he was one of a family of six brothers and a
sister. He had a relatively undistinguished playing career with a number of
local league clubs before following experience with several minor League
clubs and Southern League Northampton, he joined his first League club
Tottenham Hotspur in 1905.

In April 1907, Northampton Town gave him his first stint in club
management and he retired from playing after guiding them to the
Southern League title in 1909. He joined Leeds City as secretary-manager
in May 1912, his first task being to successfully canvas for their re-
election to the Second Division but, as the club began to struggle
financially, so their playing fortunes also suffered. On his return to the club
after the First World War, investigations were carried out into illegal
payments to wartime guest players at Elland Road. Claiming a travesty of
justice by the FA commission, due to him not being in office at the time,
he quit the club. Although four other Leeds City officials were banned for
life, Chapman's appeal was upheld and, after feeling fully vindicated, was
enticed back into club management by Huddersfield Town.

Within five months of his arrival as secretary at Huddersfield, he had
risen to assistant-manager and assumed the full title from Ambrose
Langley in March 1921.Chapman's influence and astute transfer dealings
swiftly transformed the League's newest First Division team into a side
that would bring universal fame and reputation to the small wool-
producing town for years to come.

In 1922 he guided Town to their only FA Cup Final win – a 1-0 success
over Preston North End – and eclipsed that momentous feat by setting the
club on the road to their historic hat-trick by virtue of clinching two
successive First Division titles in 1923–24 and 1924–25.

However, in June 1925, following a meeting with the Huddersfield
directors, Chapman declined the club's offer to match Arsenal's financial
terms and he was allowed to join the Gunners. At Highbury, he continued
the trend of inspired signings by bringing Charlie Buchan, Alex James, Cliff

Bastin, Eddie Hapgood and David Jack to the club as well as introducing the 'stopper' centre-half Jack Butler and later Herbie Roberts.

Under Chapman, Arsenal's fortunes took off in spectacular fashion. At the end of his first season at Highbury, he had taken them to the runners-up spot in Division One, behind Huddersfield Town. Then, in 1930, he steered them to their first senior trophy, the FA Cup, which they won after beating Huddersfield Town at Wembley. The following year, the Gunners became the first southern club to win the League Championship, followed in 1932–33 by a second title success, only 12 months after they had finished runners-up in both League and FA Cup. He even persuaded the London Transport Passenger Board to change the name of their Gillespie Road underground station to that of Arsenal in November 1932.

Herbert Chapman died on the morning of 6 January 1934 – the apparent legacy of hectic scouting missions which had resulted in him contracting pneumonia – and the team he left behind equalled Huddersfield's feat by lifting a third successive title. On 22 October 1936, a bronze bust of the great man was unveiled in the main hall of Arsenal's plush new East Stand. For over two decades, a two minutes' silence was observed on the anniversary of his death.

♔ Arsenal's record under Herbert Chapman

P	W	D	L	F	A	Success Rate
403	201	97	105	864	598	62%

☺ JOE SHAW
January 1934 – June 1934

Upon the death of Herbert Chapman, the Arsenal directors were faced with the difficult task of finding a worthy successor to the great man. Until the end of that 1933–34 season, Joe Shaw became team manager and led the club to their third League Championship success in four seasons. John Peters was the secretary and George Allison took over the overall management duties. In the summer, Allison relinquished his position as 'manager-director' and became secretary-manager. Shaw later became general assistant at Highbury, leaving his post at the end of the 1955–56 season.

♔ Arsenal's record under Joe Shaw

P	W	D	L	F	A	Success Rate
23	14	3	6	44	29	67%

⊙ GEORGE ALLISON
June 1934 – May 1947

George Allison was to maintain the Gunners' great success of his illustrious predecessor, including winning the League Championship at the end of his first season in charge to complete three titles in successive seasons for Arsenal.

A journalist by profession, his first job in the world of football was at Middlesbrough, where he became assistant-secretary in 1905. A year later he moved to London to carry on his work as a journalist, often reporting on Woolwich Arsenal's matches. In 1920 he became the editor of the club's programme writing under the *nom de plume* of 'Gunners' Mate'. He joined the board of directors in 1926 and relinquished his position as managing director to take over as secretary-manager.

Under his managership, Arsenal won the League Championship in 1934–35 and 1937–38 and the FA Cup in 1936, beating Sheffield United in the final. He broke the British transfer record when he paid Wolves £14,500 for Bryan Jones in 1938. One of his first signings was Ted Drake, but, like most managers, he also made some mistakes. He considered Len Shackleton too frail for top-class football!

Allison's readiness to spend money earned Arsenal the nickname of the 'Bank of England Team'. He let things go on very much as they had under Chapman and interfered as little as possible on the playing side. Indeed, he left the management of the players to Joe Shaw and Tom Whittaker. Allison's brain child was Highbury's East Stand, built in 1936 and considered one of the finest stands in existence at that time. During World War Two, Allison practically ran Arsenal on his own and this probably took its toll, as he retired in May 1947.

He maintained his links with the media and was a pioneer broadcaster of football on both radio and television. He commentated on the first TV programme about football called *Soccer at Arsenal* which was broadcast in September 1937 and also appeared in the film *The Arsenal Stadium Mystery* in 1939.

Allison kept Arsenal in the headlines by continued success and his flamboyant methods and no reporter lacked help in getting a story. He died of a heart attack at his Golders Green home in 1957.

♛ Arsenal's record under George Allison

P	W	D	L	F	A	Success Rate
283	131	75	77	543	333	59%

☺ TOM WHITTAKER
June 1947 – October 1956

The son of a regular soldier, a sergeant-major in the 12th Lancers, Tom Whittaker was born in Aldershot, though he was brought up in the Newcastle area where he qualified as a marine engineer. He joined the Army in 1917 and later moved to the Navy, playing football for the Royal Garrison Artillery.

After his demob, Whittaker joined Arsenal in November 1919 as a promising centre-forward. His best season as a player came in 1921–22 in which he made 42 League and Cup appearances for The Gunners, appearing in a variety of positions. He gained two London Challenge Cup winners' medals and had made 70 appearances for the club when he was selected to tour Australia with the FA in 1925. Whilst playing in a game in Wollongong, a small township near Sydney, he broke his knee cap and was unable to play again.

Whittaker soon built up a reputation as one of the finest trainers in the game, working for Arsenal, England and the FA touring sides and travelling all over the world. He was the first modern physiotherapist-coach and had all the latest equipment to help look after players' injuries, encouraged by his manager Herbert Chapman.

During World War Two, Whittaker joined the RAF and on demob in 1946 became assistant-manager at Arsenal to George Allison. Between them they saved Arsenal from relegation with the inspired signings of Joe Mercer and the prolific Ronnie Rooke. In the summer of 1947, Whittaker succeeded Allison as manager and, after signing Don Roper and Archie Macaulay and adding Doug Lishman and Alex Forbes to his squad, Arsenal ran away with the League title in 1947–48 with Rooke scoring 33 goals.

Whittaker did not seek personal publicity and liked to keep a low profile but further honours were not far away and it became more difficult for him to achieve this. Arsenal won the FA Cup in 1950, beating Liverpool 2-0. They were back at Wembley again two years later but, after losing Walley Barnes through injury, the 10-men team fought a gallant losing battle with Newcastle United. In 1952–53, the Gunners won their last game of the season to take the League title again, but an ageing side was beginning to break up and the club entered a transitional period.

The lack of success caused Whittaker added strain and he became ill with nervous exhaustion. Following admission to hospital, this most popular and respected of all Arsenal servants died of a heart attack.

♟ Arsenal's record under Tom Whittaker

P	W	D	L	F	A	Success Rate
428	202	106	120	797	566	62%

⚽ JACK CRAYSTON
November 1956 – May 1958

Following the death of Tom Whittaker, Jack Crayston was appointed manager. For the first time in more than 30 years, the combined job of secretary-manager was split and the post of the club's secretary went to Bob Wall.

Crayston started his playing career in the Third Division (North) with Barrow, spending two seasons there before moving to Bradford Park Avenue, where he developed into a strong, dependable and aerially powerful right-half. Despite breaking a bone in his ankle and wrist during the 1933–34 season, Crayston recovered to sign for Arsenal. He scored on his competitive debut in an 8-1 thrashing of Liverpool and soon established himself as a regular in the Arsenal side. He won two League Championships and an FA Cup winners' medal whilst at Highbury but his playing career ended during the war because of a serious knee injury in a game against West Ham United.

After his premature retirement and his demobbing from the RAF, Crayston joined Arsenal's training staff and in 1947 became assistant to new Arsenal manager Tom Whittaker. After Whittaker's untimely death, Crayston was appointed the Gunners' new manager. In his first season in charge, Arsenal finished fifth and reached the quarter-finals of the FA Cup but things did not go so well after this. He was given little money to improve the side and, out of frustration, he resigned in May 1958.

Crayston later had a spell in charge of Doncaster Rovers but his stay at Belle Vue was brief and he left football to run a newsagents in Streetly, Birmingham.

♟ Arsenal's record under Jack Crayston

P	W	D	L	F	A	Success Rate
77	33	16	28	142	142	53%

☺ GEORGE SWINDIN
July 1958 – May 1962

One of Arsenal's best-ever goalkeepers, George Swindin won a League Championship medal in 1937–38 and was ever-present when the Gunners were again champions in 1947–48. He also appeared in 14 games when they won the title again in 1952–53. Swindin also appeared in two FA Cup finals, picking up a winners' medal in 1950 when Arsenal beat Liverpool 2-0.

He took Peterborough United to three Midlands League titles before returning to Highbury as manager. In his first season in charge, the club's playing staff underwent a drastic overhaul as he brought in players like Tommy Docherty, Jimmy Henderson and Bill McCullough, while players of the calibre of Derek Tapscott, Cliff Holton and Stan Charlton were among those allowed to leave Highbury. Arsenal finished the season in third place after heading the table for much of the campaign and, but for injuries to key players, may well have lifted the title.

In contrast to neighbours Spurs, who were winning just about everything in sight, Swindin was never as successful again, this in spite of signing players like George Eastham, Lawrie Brown and Johnny MacLeod. Swindin was justly criticised but accepted full responsibility for the club's lack of success and resigned at the end of the 1961–62 season.

On leaving Highbury he took over the reins at Norwich City but hadn't been in charge for long when he received a more lucrative offer to manage Cardiff City. At Ninian Park, John Charles was signed from Roma against his wishes and after 18 months of struggle, he was sacked. They did win the Welsh Cup though, entering Europe for the first time.

♉ Arsenal's record under George Swindin

P	W	D	L	F	A	Success Rate
179	70	43	66	320	320	51%

☺ BILLY WRIGHT
May 1962 – June 1966

An inspiring captain for both club and country, Billy Wright was a model professional, who was never sent off or booked in his career. He was the first player to make 100 appearances for England and was voted Footballer of the Year in 1952. Wright captained Wolves to three League titles and an FA Cup Final victory over Leicester City. He skippered England 90 times and played in the 1950, 1954 and 1958 World Cup Finals.

When he took over as Arsenal manager amid a blaze of publicity, Wright had no previous management experience. His signing of Joe Baker from Italian football demonstrated his intent but, though the club scored 86 goals in his first season, they conceded almost as many. Wright then signed centre-half Ian Ure from Dundee to boost the Gunners' defence but, unfortunately, his signing didn't have the desired effect. During the course of the 1964–65 season, Wright signed Don Howe and Frank McLintock but results and attendances deteriorated and the club were subjected to a shock FA Cup exit at Peterborough. The following season was even more disappointing and, after a mere 4,554 turned up to watch the match with Leeds United, it was clear that time was running out for Billy Wright.

Although he brought no honours to the club, he did bring in many fine players and developed a very promising youth team which were to form the foundation of successes to come. After being relieved of his duties, Wright worked for Midlands television franchise ATV as an anchorman and was later head of sport for that company and its successor, Central TV.

♉ Arsenal's record under Billy Wright

P	W	D	L	F	A	Success Rate
182	70	43	69	336	330	50%

☉ BERTIE MEE
June 1966 – March 1976

One of Arsenal's most successful post-war managers, Bertie Mee took over from Billy Wright on a temporary basis in the summer of 1966 before officially being appointed manager in March 1967.

Mee had a spell as a winger on Derby County's books before the war but did not play in the first team and joined Mansfield Town just before the outbreak of the hostilities. He made some guest appearances for Southampton during the war and appeared in a representative Army Wanderers side in the Middle East.

Forced to retire at the age of 27, he then spent six years as a sergeant in the RAMC, when he qualified as a physiotherapist and then spent 12 years as a rehabilitation officer for disabled servicemen. Mee also worked in the Health Service, running remedial centres in London.

In the summer of 1960 he became Arsenal's physiotherapist, replacing Billy Milne, who had retired. A coaching badge and his physiotherapy qualification seemed hardly enough for the challenge of managing the Gunners when he became boss.

A modest man, extremely efficient and knowledgeable in the arts of man-management and motivation, Mee gradually steered the Gunners from strength to strength, building a highly successful 'method' team within a disciplined framework. The team was far more important than the individual and Mee steered away from the media and avoided self publicity. He was well known for his dislike of swearing and poor behaviour by players.

After he took control, Mee was soon in action on the transfer market and in his first season brought George Graham and Bob McNab to Highbury. After two League Cup Final defeats at the hands of Leeds United and Swindon Town, the Gunners won their first major trophy for 17 years when they beat Anderlecht 4-3 on aggregate in the Inter Cities Fairs Cup Final.

The 1970–71 season was the greatest in the club's history when Mee, along with his right-hand man Don Howe, guided the Gunners to the League and FA Cup Double. Not surprisingly, Bertie Mee was voted Manager of the Year. Arsenal clinched the title against rivals Spurs on the Monday before the Cup Final, then went out and beat Liverpool at Wembley, thanks partly to a super strike from Charlie George.

Over the next couple of seasons, Mee was close to further honours. In 1972 Arsenal reached the FA Cup Final again but lost to Leeds United. The following season they were runners-up in Division One and knocked out of the FA Cup at the semi-final stage.

After this, the club's fortunes went into decline and, following two particularly difficult seasons, Mee announced in March 1976 that he would be retiring at the end of that season. Following a short break from the game, he joined Watford as general manager and later remained a director of the Vicarage Road club.

♈ Arsenal record under Bertie Mee

P	W	D	L	F	A	Success Rate
539	241	148	150	739	542	58%

⚽ TERRY NEILL
July 1976 – December 1983

Terry Neill served the Gunners as a player for 11 years, as a manager for seven and had most of his success in the game at Highbury.

Neill joined Arsenal as a wing-half but was later switched to centre-half by boss Billy Wright. He went on to both captain and manage Northern Ireland during his 59 international appearances, celebrating his final appearance by scoring the goal that beat England at Wembley in 1972. He did not win any domestic honours as a player but did pick up a losers' medal when the Gunners went down to Leeds United in the 1968 League Cup Final.

Neill was only 28 when he was appointed player-manager of Hull City in the summer of 1970. He was also chairman of the PFA at the time. On leaving Boothferry Park, he was appointed manager of Tottenham Hostpur as successor to Bill Nicholson. Spurs' fans could not take to him, however, due to his long association with Arsenal. At White Hart Lane, Neill pruned the playing staff and cleared the decks for the emergence of players like Glenn Hoddle. After narrowly avoiding relegation in 1974–75, Neill appointed Keith Burkinshaw as his coach and it was Burkinshaw who got most of the credit as Spurs reached the semi-finals of the League Cup only to lose to Newcastle United.

Neill resigned in the summer of 1976 to take up the manager's post at Arsenal and in his seven years in charge, the Gunners always finished in the top ten. After signing Malcolm Macdonald from Newcastle United, Neill experienced difficulties in managing former playing colleagues and made the mistake of making public his disagreements and criticisms of players.

During the course of the 1977–78 season, Don Howe returned as coach and forged a partnership with Neill that was to bring the club further honours. The Gunners reached the FA Cup Final in 1978, 1979 and 1980, their only victory coming in 1979 when they beat Manchester United 3-2. Arsenal's best season in the First Division came in 1980–81 when they finished third. In 1980 they beat Valencia in the European Cup Winners' Cup Final in Brussels on penalties. Neill took Arsenal to the FA and League Cup semi-finals in 1982–83 losing both to Manchester United.

Following mounting pressure from press and fans, and, a month after Arsenal had been beaten by Walsall in the League Cup, Neill was sacked. On leaving the game, he concentrated on work for charitable organisations.

♛ Arsenal's record under Terry Neill

P	W	D	L	F	A	Success Rate
416	187	117	112	601	446	59%

☉ DON HOWE
December 1983 – March 1986

Right-back Don Howe had a distinguished playing career with both West Bromwich Albion and England prior to joining Arsenal in April 1964. After 70 appearances for the Gunners, Howe had the misfortune to break his leg and never played again.

After being appointed reserve-team coach, he stepped up to chief coach in succession to Dave Sexton in October 1967. Howe and manager Bertie Mee formed a partnership that brought the Fairs Cup to Highbury and the League and Cup Double a year later. In the late 1970s, he coached Arsenal to three Wembley Cup Finals and a European Cup Winners' Cup Final appearance.

Howe left Arsenal to manage West Bromwich Albion but was not too successful as they lost their top flight status at the end of the 1972–73 season. After coaching spells with Turkish club Galatasaray and Leeds United, Howe returned to Highbury as chief coach and, following the departure of Terry Neill, was appointed caretaker-manager. He guided Arsenal to a final position of sixth in that 1983–84 season, just one place short of UEFA Cup qualification. Although the club finished seventh in both of the other seasons in which Howe was in charge, he was unable to sustain a challenge for honours. Amid the clamouring for success and rumours that the club were going to appoint Terry Venables, Howe resigned.

He continued as coach and assistant to Bobby Robson with the England team and was coach of Wimbledon when they won the FA Cup in 1988. Coach and later manager of Queen's Park Rangers, he later replaced Terry Butcher as manager of Coventry City before being appointed Ian Porterfield's assistant at Chelsea. On leaving Stamford Bridge he worked as a media commentator on Italian football for Channel 4.

♛ Arsenal's record under Don Howe

P	W	D	L	F	A	Success Rate
119	56	32	31	187	142	62%

☉ STEVE BURTENSHAW
March 1986 – May 1986

Steve Burtenshaw served Brighton and Hove Albion as a wing-half for 14 seasons, making 237 League appearances and winning a Third Division Championship medal in 1957–58. On hanging up his boots, he secured a job with Arsenal as reserve-team coach, taking over as chief coach when Don Howe left Highbury.

In 1973, Burtenshaw swapped jobs with Bobby Campbell at Queen's Park Rangers and later worked under Billy Bingham and Gordon Lee at Everton. Burtenshaw was appointed manager of Sheffield Wednesday in January 1974 but as boss at Hillsborough he experienced only 14 wins in more than 70 games in charge. The Owls just avoided relegation in 1973–74 by winning their last game but went down the following season as they finished bottom of the Second Division. After a poor start to the 1975–76 season, Burtenshaw's contract was terminated.

He then spent a disastrous season in charge of Queen's Park Rangers – being sacked after only ten months of a three-year contract following the Loftus Road club's relegation. Returning to Highbury as the club's chief scout, he was the club's caretaker-manager following Don Howe's decision to ask to be released from his contract.

♆ Arsenal's record under Steve Burtenshaw

P	W	D	L	F	A	Success Rate
11	3	2	6	7	15	36%

☺ GEORGE GRAHAM
May 1986 – February 1995

Under the astute management of George Graham, Arsenal again became one of the leading clubs in Britain as they won three League Championships in the space of five seasons.

A Scottish schoolboy international, Graham began his career in English football with Aston Villa, appearing in the 1963 League Cup Final before moving to Chelsea. Whilst at Stamford Bridge, Graham won a League Cup winners' medal and in 1966–67 helped the club reach the Fairs Cup semi-finals where they lost to Barcelona.

He then joined Arsenal and after a season in which he scored 21 goals, he switched to a midfield role. After two appearances in League Cup Finals, Graham was in the side that beat Anderlecht to lift the Fairs Cup and the following season helped the Gunners clinch the Double. Leaving Arsenal for Manchester United, he later played for Portsmouth and Crystal Palace.

Graham had done some coaching whilst at Selhurst Park and coached both Palace and Queen's Park Rangers before being appointed manager of Millwall. After saving them from relegation he led the Lions to success in the Football League Trophy, a competition for lower division clubs, and in 1984–85 took the club to promotion to Division Two as runners-up. After another good season in which Millwall consolidated their position in Division Two, Graham was offered the manager's job at Highbury.

This maintained the tradition with Arsenal appointing an old boy as their manager. At the end of his first season in charge, Arsenal tasted success as Liverpool were beaten 2-1 in the final of the League Cup. The following season the Gunners lost 3-2 in the final to Luton Town.

The 1988–89 season was a marvellous one for Arsenal, who clinched the League Championship in a never-to-be-forgotten final league match of the season at Anfield. Arsenal repeated this feat with Championship title wins in 1990–91 and 1992–93, when they became the first team ever to win the FA Cup and League Cup Double. In 1993–94, Arsenal beat Parma to lift the European Cup Winners' Cup, Graham writing himself into the record books as the first person to play for, and manage, European Cup winning sides.

In February 1995, Graham left Arsenal after speculation about player transfer irregularities. He then took charge of Leeds United before leaving to manage Tottenham Hotspur. Graham, who was replaced by Glenn Hoddle in April 2001, is still out of the game, though his name is still mentioned in connection with many vacant managerial positions.

♈ Arsenal's record under George Graham

P	W	D	L	F	A	Success Rate
460	225	133	102	711	403	63%

☉ STEWART HOUSTON
February 1995 – May 1995

Stewart Houston's first League club was Chelsea before moving on to Brentford where his outstanding displays at left-back led to Tommy Docherty signing him for Manchester United in December 1973.

A member of the United side beaten in the 1976 FA Cup Final, he missed the club's success at Wembley the following year with a broken ankle. Houston later played for Sheffield United and Colchester United before becoming a member of the Arsenal coaching staff.

Houston became the club's assistant-manager under both George Graham and Bruce Rioch. When Graham parted company with the club, Houston was installed as caretaker-manager until the end of the season. He took the Gunners to the final of the European Cup Winners' Cup but they were beaten by a spectacular last-minute goal by Nayim. He stepped in for a second spell as the club's caretaker-manager when Rioch lost his job but then surprised the club with a move across London to Queen's Park Rangers.

In his first season as the club's manager he led Rangers to within five points of the First Division play-offs but in November 1997 he paid the price for Rangers failing to offer a serious promotion challenge by getting the sack along with his assistant Bruce Rioch. He was later reunited with George Graham at White Hart Lane before having a spell as first team coach at Walsall.

♟ Arsenal's record under Stewart Houston

P	W	D	L	F	A	Success Rate
25	9	5	11	40	35	46%

⚽ BRUCE RIOCH
June 1995 – August 1996

The only English-born player to captain Scotland in a full international, Bruce Rioch began his career with Luton Town, helping the Hatters win the Fourth Division Championship in 1967–68, a season when he was the club's leading scorer with 24 goals. In 1969 Rioch moved to Aston Villa and after collecting a runners-up medal in the League Cup Final, won the Third Division Championship, too. In February 1974, a £200,000 offer took him to Derby County and in his first full season with the Rams he won a League Championship medal. He later had spells with Everton and Seattle Sounders in the NASL before becoming player-coach of Torquay United.

Appointed manager of Middlesbrough in February 1986, he guided the club out of a dire financial position, lifting them from the Third to the First Division within two seasons. But Boro were relegated in 1988–89 and in March 1990 he left Ayresome Park to take charge of Millwall.

He took the Lions to the Second Division play-offs but after their form slumped he resigned to manage Bolton Wanderers. He achieved promotion in his first season when the Wanderers finished runners-up in Division Two, whilst in 1994–95 he took the club to the League Cup Final and promotion to the Premiership via the play-offs.

In June 1995 Rioch left Bolton to manage Arsenal, the Gunners finishing fifth and reaching the League Cup semi-finals in his first season in charge. After 14 months in the job, Rioch announced that he had finally signed a contract after rumours he wouldn't be staying but within a matter of days of putting pen to paper – and William Hill stopping taking bets on wagers that he wouldn't survive the season – Rioch was sacked. His 61 weeks in charge was the briefest ever by a Highbury manager.

♆ Arsenal's record under Bruce Rioch

P	W	D	L	F	A	Success Rate
47	22	15	10	67	37	63%

☺ PAT RICE
September 1996

One of the most loyal players Arsenal has ever had, Pat Rice played in 527 League and Cup games for the Gunners – a total bettered only by George Armstrong and David O'Leary. On leaving Highbury he joined Watford, helping the Hornets gain promotion to the First Division in 1981–82 and then finish the next season as runners-up to Liverpool.

In 1984, Rice returned to Highbury as youth team coach and over the next ten years he helped the Gunners to two FA Youth Cup Finals win and discovered the likes of Andy Cole, Kevin Campbell, Paul Merson, David Rocastle and Michael Thomas, to name but a few.

Following the departure of Bruce Rioch, the running of the club was put in the hands of coaches Stewart Houston and Pat Rice but when Houston left to manage Queen's Park Rangers, Rice took charge until manager-elect Arsène Wenger had fulfilled his contract in Japan. He is now the club's assistant-manager.

♆ Arsenal's record under Pat Rice

P	W	D	L	F	A	Success Rate
4	3	0	1	10	4	75%

☺ ARSÈNE WENGER
September 1996 –

Arsène Wenger is a self-described football obsessive and since his arrival at Highbury in September 1996, his achievements have only been rivalled by Air Alex Ferguson at Old Trafford.

His attempts at forging a career as a player were for the most part limited to France's Third Division though he eventually managed a brief spell with top-flight club Strasbourg. During his time there, they captured the French title but during that Championship-winning season, Wenger's involvement was restricted to just three games.

Realising that he might not make it as a footballer, Wenger enrolled at the University of Strasbourg where he completed a master's degree in Economics. Despite this, he remained involved in the game and, in 1981, was appointed Strasbourg's youth team coach. After some impressive results he was appointed manager of Nancy but he didn't have the best of starts, as the club were relegated.

Wenger's first taste of managerial success came with his appointment as head coach of AS Monaco in 1987. He was to stay here for seven years, coinciding with one of the most successful periods for the club. During that time, they won the French League title, the French Cup and continually qualified for the latter knockout stages of the European Cup. Monaco's success led to a number of offers from other clubs including one from Bayern Munich. However, Wenger turned all these overtures down only to be sacked by Monaco in 1994.

A stint in charge of Japanese club Grampus Eight resulted in a manager of the year award and ultimately the attentions of the Gunners.

On his arrival at Highbury in September 1996, Wenger inherited a club struggling to recapture the successes it had enjoyed under George Graham in the 1980s. The arrival at Highbury of players such as Thierry Henry and Patrick Vieira cemented the Frenchman's reputation as a very shrewd judge of young talent and led to the club winning the League title and FA Cup Double in 1997–98.

Over the next few years, the North London club narrowly missed out on a variety of honours until 2001–02 saw the Gunners repeat the Double feat. After that the club embarked on a record-breaking 49-match unbeaten run that eventually came to an end in a game against Manchester United at Old Trafford – a most ill-tempered match!

☻ ARSENAL FACT ☻

Arsène Wenger is the first foreign manager to lead a team to the English League Championship.

In 2005–06, Wenger led his Arsenal side to the final of the Champions League – the one trophy to have eluded the popular Frenchman's grasp –

but though the 10-men Gunners put up a brave fight following Jens Lehmann's dismissal, they went down 2-1 to Barcelona.

♈ Arsenal's record under Arsène Wenger

*P	W	D	L	F	A	Success Rate
589	337	146	106	1062	537	70%

* up to 21/04/07

FAMOUS MATCHES

| WOOLWICH ARSENAL 2 | NEWCASTLE UNITED 2 |
2 September 1893
Woolwich Arsenal Williams; Powell; Jeffrey; Devine; Buist; Howat;
Gemmell; Henderson; Shaw; Elliott; Booth
Newcastle United Ramsay; Jeffrey; Miller; Crielly; Graham; McKane;
Bowman; Crate; Thompson; Sorley Wallace
Attendance 10,000
Referee T Stevenson (Birmingham)

Arsenal's first appearance as a Football League club took place at the
Manor Ground in Plumstead. Both Woolwich Arsenal and their opponents
on that historic day, Newcastle United, were newly-elected members of a
Second Division which had increased its membership for that 1893–94
season from 12 to 15 teams.

Joe Powell, captaining the Gunners for the very first time, won the toss
on a bright afternoon. The home side had the better of the early exchanges
and went ahead after 10 minutes when, following some fine interpassing
by Booth and Elliott, they set up a chance for Walter Shaw to shoot past
the advancing Ramsay.

The visitors seemed completely undaunted by this early setback and
pressed hard for an equaliser with both Bowman and Crate going close.
Williams saved well from a powerful Thompson shot and both Howat and
Buist got in strong challenges as the United forwards seemed likely to

score. Newcastle probably deserved to draw level but as the teams went in at half-time, Arsenal were still 1-0 up.

The second-half was only three minutes old when Booth made a brilliant run down the Arsenal left wing and crossed for Elliott to score the Gunners' second goal with an unstoppable shot which went in off the underside of the bar.

With a two-goal lead, Arsenal seemed to relax a little and play became very scrappy before the visitors forced their way back into the game with Crate forcing the ball over the line from close range. Arsenal defended in depth as Newcastle poured forward in search of the equaliser. The Gunners' defenders were under great pressure and one of them handled near his own goal. From the resultant free-kick, Sorley rose highest to head past Williams.

Both teams strove hard for the winning strike and though both goals had narrow escapes, it was thought that a draw was the fairest result.

ARSENAL 0	CARDIFF CITY 1

23 April 1927
Arsenal Lewis; Parker; Kennedy; Baker; Butler; John; Hulme; Buchan; Brain; Blyth; Hoar
Cardiff City Farquharson; Nelson; Watson; Keenor; Sloan; Hardy; Curtis; Irving; Ferguson; L Davies;
McLachlan
Attendance 91,206
Referee WF Bunnell (Lancashire)

This was Arsenal's first-ever appearance in an FA Cup Final but for their Welsh opponents it was their second final in three years. The Bluebirds were enjoying the most successful period in their history and three seasons earlier had been League Championship runners-up on goal average. In complete contrast, Arsenal were just beginning to reap the benefits of Herbert Chapman's management and were looking to win their first major honour.

Though Cardiff only had four players in their side that had played in the 1925 FA Cup Final, they did have eight internationals in their line-up, whilst the Gunners boasted five. Yet despite this plethora of talent, the game itself was something of a let down. Arsenal had the better of the early exchanges and with Joe Hulme's pace down the right flank causing problems for Watson, both Buchan and Brain went close. The only worthwhile attempt on goal in the first-half from the Cardiff side came from Ferguson whose header was well saved by Lewis.

The second-half continued in much the same vein as the first, with Brain, the Arsenal centre-forward, shooting into the side-netting when put through by Buchan. The game remained goalless until the 75th minute when, completely against the run of play, Cardiff took the lead. Ferguson, the Bluebirds' long-throw specialist hurled the ball into the Arsenal penalty area which Dan Lewis appeared to take comfortably. However, he had one eye on the onrushing Cardiff forwards and allowed the ball to spin from his grasp and over the line.

It was a real tragedy for Lewis, who would be forever remembered for this one unfortunate gaffe which presented Cardiff with the Cup. It also proved to be something of an historic goal for this was the first and only time that the FA Cup had been won by a team from outside England.

LEICESTER CITY 6   ARSENAL 6

21 April 1930
Leicester City Wright; Black; Brown; Duncan; Harrison; Watson; Adcock; Hine; Chandler; Lochhead; Barry
Arsenal Lewis; Parker; Cope; Baker; Haynes; John; Hulme; Jack; Halliday; James; Bastin
Attendance 27,241
Referee A Button (Wednesbury)

Arsenal and Leicester City created a record for the highest scoring draw in any English first-class game – it has been equalled by Charlton Athletic v Middlesborough in 1960 – in an amazing League match at Filbert Street on Easter Monday 1930.

The Gunners rested some regular first teamers because they had an FA Cup Final appointment with Huddersfield Town five days later but their side still contained some of the greats of the day: Cliff Bastin, Alex James, Joe Hulme and David Jack.

The Gunners set a blistering pace in the opening stages of the game and David Jack had the ball in the net after just two minutes only to have it ruled offside. However, the visitors were eventually rewarded with a goal after 21 minutes when Halliday found the net following a corner. But, by the interval, the home team had pulled back the deficit and had taken a 3-1 lead. An Adcock shot in the 26th minute was not held by Lewis and, though Parker seemed to hack it clear, the referee judged the ball had crossed the line. Two minutes later City were in front thanks to Lochhead and, three minutes before half-time, Adcock increased their lead when Lewis was again at fault, allowing the ball to slip through his hands.

Within two minutes of the restart, Cliff Bastin had reduced the arrears and in the 58th minute, Halliday scored his second goal of the game as Arsenal drew level at 3-3. Within four minutes, Arsenal were 5-3 in front with Halliday scoring both the goals which were as a result of magnificent wing play by Hulme. Hine pulled one back for Leicester in the 66th minute but the goalscoring spree was far from over. Bastin restored Arsenal's two-goal advantage 13 minutes from time, yet two minutes later City were back in it after Barry scored.

With the score 6-5 in Arsenal's favour and with 11 minutes remaining, the fans could not believe what was happening. The goal bonanza eventually came to an end in the 82nd minute when Lochhead scored his second goal of the game following good work from Adcock and Barry. Arsenal had two more chances to retake the lead in the closing minutes but were foiled by Wright and the Leicester defence. Mr Button eventually blew the final whistle and so brought to an end the First Division's only 6-6 draw.

Despite his four goals there was no place for Halliday in the FA Cup Final side the following week when Arsenal beat Huddersfield Town 2-0 to win the trophy for the first time in their history.

WALSALL 2	ARSENAL 0

14 January 1933
Walsall Cunningham; Bennett; Bird; Reed; Leslie; Salt; Coward; Ball; Alsop; Sheppard; Lee
Arsenal Moss; Male; Black; Hill; Roberts; Sidey; Warnes; Jack; Walsh; James; Bastin
Attendance 11,150
Referee A Taylor (Lancashire)

In one of the greatest giantkilling acts in the history of the FA Cup, Third Division (South) club Walsall accomplished a thoroughly deserved victory over an Arsenal side that were at that time top of the First Division.

Herbert Chapman obviously thought the Saddlers posted little threat because he 'rested' three internationals – Hapgood, John and Lambert –

although the official line was that they were either injured or stricken by a flu epidemic, and dropped winger Joe Hulme.

The Walsall pitch was narrow and muddy. Arsenal adapted to neither. Walsall tore into Arsenal from the off. Ball and Coward posed a constant threat and Arsenal keeper Moss was forced into making saves from Alsop and Lee. Arsenal's best effort of the first-half was a fine shot from Bastin shortly before the interval.

With the slope in their favour in the second-half, it seemed that the Gunners would finally take control. Warnes was presented with a good chance but delayed and was dispossessed by Salt. David Jack was robbed in front of an open goal when Walsh managed to get in his way and Walsh himself missed a decent opportunity. But only Bastin seriously tested Cunningham.

Having survived these attacks, Walsall broke out and, on the hour, the unthinkable happened when Gilbert Alsop headed in Lee's cross. Then five minutes later, the hapless Black hauled down Alsop and Billy Sheppard converted the resultant penalty. The second goal completely knocked the stuffing out of Arsenal. They offered little resistance in the remaining 25 minutes and were fortunate not to lose by a bigger margin.

At the final whistle, the Walsall players were carried off shoulder high by their jubilant fans. When the scoreline filtered through, it created such shock waves that some newspapers checked with their reporters to make sure it was not the wrong way round.

Chapman wasted no time in punishing the miscreants. So incensed was he by Black's reckless tackle on Alsop that he refused to allow the youngster to return to Highbury and within a week, had sold him to Plymouth Argyle.

Although Arsenal recovered to lift the first of three consecutive League Championships, for years the mere mention of Walsall was enough to send a shiver down the spines of the most hardened Gunners' fans.

ASTON VILLA 1	ARSENAL 7

14 December 1935
Aston Villa Morton; Blair; Cummings; Massie; Griffiths; Wood; Williams; Astley; Palethorpe; Dix; Houghton
Arsenal Wilson; Male; Hapgood; Crayston; Roberts; Copping; Rogers; Bowden; Drake; Bastin; Beasley
Attendance 58,469
Referee JM Wiltshire (Sherborne)

This was the day that England international centre-forward Ted Drake established a First Division record with a brilliant display of finishing. Eight shots yielded seven goals from the Arsenal No.9 and left Aston Villa to contemplate their worst-ever home League defeat.

A crowd of 58,469 had gathered to watch this encounter between two of the game's most famous clubs, although at the time of this meeting both clubs were far from chasing League honours – the Gunners were in mid-table and Villa were languishing at the foot of the table, this in spite of a team containing six internationals.

For the first half-hour, the home side were the better team with both Palethorpe and Dix going close but as the half-time whistle sounded, they were 3-0 down thanks to Drake's remarkable finishing powers. His opening goal came from a through ball by Beasley after quarter-of-an-hour. The second, after 28 minutes, was possibly the best of the afternoon as he took a long ball from Bastin and ran through the middle of the Villa defence with both Cummings and Griffiths in hot pursuit before shooting past Morton from outside the box. Drake completed his hat-trick in the 34th minute with a close range shot after Beasley's effort had been palmed out by Morton.

A minute after the restart, Drake chased a ball that appeared to be going out of play and surprised everyone by squeezing his shot from the most acute of angles between the Villa keeper and his near post. After 50 minutes, Bowden crossed for Drake to score again and then eight minutes later he netted his sixth when the ball rebounded to him off a Villa defender.

Villa did manage to pull a goal back after 61 minutes through Palethorpe but in the dying moments, Ted Drake scored again, this time off a cross-field pass by the enterprising Bastin. It was a remarkable performance by Ted Drake, for his seven goals had come from eight shots – the one that missed hit the woodwork!

NEWCASTLE UNITED 1   ARSENAL 0

3 May 1952
Newcastle United Simpson; Cowell; McMichael; Harvey; Brennan; E Robledo; Walker; Foulkes; Milburn; G Robledo; Mitchell
Arsenal Swindin; Barnes; L Smith; Forbes; Daniel; Mercer; Cox; Logie; Holton; Lishman; Roper
Attendance 100,000
Referee AE Ellis (Halifax)

Wembley Stadium has seldom seen a more heroic backs-to-the-wall performance than Arsenal's brave fight in the FA Cup Final of 1952. The Gunners, reduced to 10 men after 20 minutes following an injury to Welsh international full-back Walley Barnes, gave a defiant display against the then mighty Newcastle United and only the narrowest of margins separated the sides at the final whistle.

The Gunners were challenging for the League and Cup Double right up to the final Saturday of the Championship but a fixture congestion and a spate of niggling injuries saw the title slip from their grasp after they lost their last two games. This meant that the FA Cup was their only possible reward for a season of outstanding football.

On Cup Final day, Arsenal took to the field with Ray Daniel wearing a light plastic covering on a broken forearm, whilst Jimmy Logie had just spent three days in hospital with blood poisoning and Doug Lishman had also been hospitalised and was barely fit.

Despite these setbacks, Arsenal took charge from the start and could have taken the lead after only three minutes but Lishman's overhead kick scraped the bar. Logie was through on goal but with only Simpson to beat, pulled his shot wide. However, after 20 minutes, Arsenal's injury jinx struck again when Barnes badly twisted his knee as his studs stuck in the turf. After attempting to continue he left the field for good with Roper switching to full-back.

Inspired by their captain Joe Mercer, the Gunners turned in one of the greatest rearguard actions ever seen at the famous ground. Although Lionel Smith had to head off the line with Swindin beaten, Arsenal never really allowed the Magpies to gain the upper hand. The depleted Arsenal side did not just settle for survival and with 11 minutes to go, Lishman headed Cox's cross past Simpson but the ball ran along the crossbar and over the top.

Five minutes later, Arsenal conceded the goal that took the cup to Tyneside. With Roper lying injured on the ground, play continued and Mitchell crossed for George Robledo to head against the inside of the post before the ball rolled over the line.

BOLTON WANDERERS 4   ARSENAL 6

25 December 1952
Bolton Wanderers Hanson; Ball; Higgins; Wheeler; Barrass; Neill; Holden;
Moir; Lofthouse; Webster; Langton
Arsenal Kelsey; Wade; L Smith; Shaw; Daniel; Mercer; Milton; Logie; Holton;
Lishman; Roper
Attendance 47,344
Referee TW Glendenning (Sunderland)

If goals make football great, then the Christmas Day crowd at Burnden
Park for this First Division match saw the game at its best as the
Wanderers and Arsenal served up a real festive treat.

Inside a minute, Bolton inside-forward Willie Moir lost a great scoring
chance and then put the home side ahead, both being clinical moves.
Sparkling attacking play had Arsenal penned in their own half but in
characteristic Gunners fashion, they turned defence into attack when they
drew level after 12 minutes – Milton dribbling round two defenders before
shooting past Hanson. Webster shot against an upright for Bolton and Moir
saw his header beat Kelsey but curl away from an empty net. A powerful drive
from Cliff Holton hit the net and gave the Gunners a 2-1 half-time lead.

Two goals in five minutes after the break, from Roper and Logie
emphasised the Gunners' mastery of the goalmaking art and for a time the
visitors demonstrated a clear superiority of the game. Many a side would
have buckled at this stage, but not Bolton.

With the second-half, 10 minutes old, Lofthouse banged in a second goal
and although Arsenal promptly added two more, through a penalty from
Daniel and another powerful drive from Holton to make it 6-2, the
Wanderers attack battled back with spirit.

The margin was again reduced to two goals as Lofthouse, in the 78th,
and Moir in the 80th minute, beat Kelsey. The game was more alive than
ever with the crowd revelling in Bolton's attacking qualities. Five minutes
from time, Langton won a penalty. A fifth goal now from the home side
would mean that they could still save the day. However, Langton's spot-
kick was pushed away by Kelsey and though the Welsh international
keeper still had to make another outstanding save from a Lofthouse shot,
it was his penalty save that settled the issue.

Arsenal went on to win the League Championship whilst Bolton reached
the FA Cup Final where they lost to Blackpool in the 'Matthews Final'.

ARSENAL 3   BURNLEY 2

1 May 1953

Arsenal Swindin; Wade; L Smith; Forbes; Daniel; Mercer; Roper; Logie;
Goring; Lishman; Marden

Burnley Thompson; Aird; Winton; Adamson; Cummings; Brown; Stephenson;
McIlroy; Holden; Shannon; Elliott

Attendance 51,586

Referee RF Leafe (Nottingham)

A crowd of 51,586 crammed into Highbury on the eve of the 1953 FA Cup
Final, knowing that only a victory over Burnley would be enough to bring
the Football League Championship back to North London.

During the closing weeks of the campaign, the Gunners had battled it
out with Preston North End and on the penultimate weekend of the
League season, the Lancashire club beat Arsenal 2-0 at Deepdale and then
won their last game to go top of the table. They then embarked on an end-
of-season tour on the continent, leaving Arsenal needing victory in this,
their last match, to win the Championship.

Burnley, who had been in the top six for most of the season started the
brightest and took the lead after only eight minutes when a shot by Roy
Stephenson was deflected past George Swindin. The Gunners weren't
behind for long. Within a minute a powerful long-range shot from Alex
Forbes whistled past Thompson to level the scores.

The home side now took command of the game and after 13 minutes
they went ahead. Lishman lost his marker and volleyed Roper's cross past
Thompson and into the roof of the net. On 26 minutes, Jimmy Logie
extended Arsenal's lead when he rounded off a glorious move involving
four Arsenal players.

The Gunners held their 3-1 lead until the 74th minute when Billy Elliott
pulled a goal back for the Clarets to throw the game wide open again. In
a tense and exciting quarter-of-an-hour, Burnley laid siege to the Arsenal
goal in search of an equaliser. But some calm defending and an
outstanding save by George Swindin saw them hold out to become League
Champions for a record seventh time.

The title race had been so close. Arsenal's goal average was 1.516,
against North End's 1.417 – the Championship had been won by 0.099 of
a goal per game.

ARSENAL 4   MANCHESTER UNITED 5

1 February 1958

Arsenal Kelsey; S Charlton; Evans; Ward; Fotheringham; Bowen; Groves; Tapscott; Herd; Bloomfield; Nutt

Manchester United Gregg; Foulkes; Byrne; Colman; Jones; Edwards; Morgans; R Charlton; Taylor; Viollet; Scanlon

Attendance 63,578

Referee GW Pullen (Bristol)

Not only was this one of the greatest matches ever seen at Highbury but it was also Manchester United's final appearance in England before their magnificent team was destroyed by the Munich air disaster. The 'Busby Babes' were still showing the qualities which had seen them win the two previous League Championships, whilst the Gunners were still trying to regain the glories of the early post-war years.

United gave a marvellous first-half display before a packed Highbury Stadium and as the whistle sounded for half-time, they were 3-0 up. The game was just 10 minutes old when Duncan Edwards opened the scoring with a rising drive from the edge of the Arsenal penalty area and then, after Harry Gregg had made a superb save from a Vic Groves header in the 33rd minute, Albert Scanlon outpaced the Arsenal defence and crossed for Bobby Charlton to volley home. Two minutes before half-time, England centre-forward Tommy Taylor scored a third from close range.

If United felt that victory was assured, the home side had other ideas and in a breathtaking spell of three second-half minutes, they drew level. On 58 minutes, David Herd – later to join United – volleyed home a lob from Dave Bowen; less than two minutes later, Groves headed into the path of Bloomfield who made no mistake from six yards; and then a minute later, a hard cross from Nutt was met by the diving Bloomfield who headed his second past United's Northern Ireland keeper.

As the Gunners continued to press forward in search of a fourth goal, United showed their class by scoring two more goals. In the 65th minute, Viollet shot past Kelsey following good work by Scanlon and Charlton and then seven minutes later, Tommy Taylor beat Kelsey from a seemingly impossible angle.

Arsenal were still not finished and in the 77th minute, Derek Tapscott scored their fourth goal. United defended desperately for the rest of the match as the Gunners did their best to level the scores. Though United claimed both points, the honours were shared by the players of both sides who had given one of the finest exhibitions of football ever seen at the famous ground.

ARSENAL 3   ANDERLECHT 0

28 April 1970
Arsenal Wilson; Storey; McNab; Kelly; McLintock; Simpson; Armstrong; Sammels; Radford; George; Graham
Anderlecht Trappeniers; Heylens; Maaertens; Nordahl; Velkeneers; Kialunda; Desanghere; Devrindt; Mulder; Van Himst; Puis
Attendance 51,612
Referee Herr G Kunze (East Germany)

The first leg of Arsenal's first European final – the Inter Cities Fairs Cup – had seen Belgian side Anderlecht take a 3-0 lead before a late Ray Kennedy goal in the closing minutes gave the Gunners some hope for the second leg at Highbury.

Two goals from Mulder and one from Devrindt seemed to have given Anderlecht an unassailable lead but Kennedy's goal was a vital one because on the ruling that away goals count double in the event of a draw on aggregate, a 2-0 win at Highbury would be enough to give the Gunners overall victory. A goal by the visitors would of course cancel out those calculations.

Arsenal applied the pressure for the opening quarter of the game although the Belgian side caused one or two moments of panic in the Gunners' defence with a number of menacing counter attacks. On 26 minutes, Eddie Kelly collected a loose ball on the edge of the Anderlecht penalty area and fired past Trappeniers to give the Gunners a crucial first goal. Both sides had half-chances to score but half-time arrived with Arsenal still leading 1-0 on the night.

Arsenal continued to push forward and with Radford causing problems in the air and Armstrong's wing play a constant threat, it seemed the home side would soon extend their lead. On 71 minutes, McNab overlapped down the left flank and crossed for Radford to send a powerful header past the Anderlecht keeper. Two minutes later, Charlie George sent over a dipping cross and Jon Sammels came racing in to fire home a third goal. Arsenal did not have to rely on technicalities to lift the trophy.

TOTTENHAM HOTSPUR 0   ARSENAL 1

3 May 1971
Tottenham Hotspur Jennings; Kinnear; Knowles; Mullery; Collins; Beal;
Gilzean (Pearce); Perryman; Chivers; Peters; Neighbour
Arsenal Wilson; Rice; McNab; Kelly; McLintock; Simpson; Armstrong;
Graham; Radford; Kennedy; George
Attendanc 51,992
Referee Mr K Howley (Teeside)

As the 1970–71 season drew to a close, the Gunners were still in
contention for both the League Championship and the FA Cup Double, a
feat last achieved by their North London rivals Spurs 10 years previously.

Arsenal were locked at the top of the table with Leeds United who had
completed their League programme and again, as in other Arsenal League
Championship-winning seasons, mathematical permutations surrounded
the issue. Arsenal needed at least a goalless draw to take the title, whilst
an Arsenal defeat or a scoring draw at White Hart Lane would hand the
Championship to Leeds. Arsenal's first priority therefore was to try and
keep a clean sheet.

A crowd of 51,992 had crammed into White Hart Lane, with the gates
being locked a good hour before the scheduled kick-off. Also, it was
estimated that there were 100,000 left outside the ground.

It has to be said that the match was played in a tremendous
atmosphere throughout. Charlie George had a chance in the opening
minute but Pat Jennings produced a brilliant save. Then McLintock saw his
shot hit a defender with Jennings going the wrong way before Graham
went close with a header that passed just outside Jennings' right-hand
upright. At the other end, Spurs' Martin Peters almost scored with a
powerful header and Alan Gilzean failed by inches to get his foot to a
Jimmy Neighbour cross.

Despite both sides attacking throughout most of the game, there were
very few clear cut chances and a goalless draw seemed the likely outcome.
However, in the 87th minute, Jennings could only beat out Radford's shot
and Armstrong returned the ball into the middle for Kennedy to head just
under the bar.

Spurs threw everything into the final few minutes but the Gunners held
on and, as the final whistle blew, thousands of Arsenal fans invaded the
White Hart Lane pitch to congratulate their heroes.

ARSENAL 2   LIVERPOOL 1 after extra-time

8 May 1971

Arsenal Wilson; Rice; McNab; Storey (Kelly); McLintock; Simpson; Armstrong; George; Radford; Kennedy; Graham

Liverpool Clemence; Lawler; Lindsay; Smith; Lloyd; Hughes; Callaghan; Evans (Thompson); Toshack; Hall; Heighway

Attendance 100,000

Referee NCH Burtenshaw (Great Yarmouth)

Five days earlier, Arsenal had clinched the League Championship with the 1-0 at Spurs and now faced Liverpool in the FA Cup Final as they attempted to win the coveted Double.

In order to field the same team that had seen them through to Wembley, the Gunners took a chance with Peter Storey's fitness, while Liverpool were at full strength.

Both sides made a cautious approach to the match and chances at either end were few and far between. Kennedy and Armstrong had chances which on some days they would have put away and George Graham went close with a couple of headers – one hitting the bar and the other being cleared off the line by Lawler. Liverpool's best effort of the 90 minutes came from full-back Alec Lindsay whose low drive was well saved by Bob Wilson. Both sides decided to use their substitutes with Eddie Kelly replacing the drained Storey midway through the second-half and, minutes later, England winger Peter Thompson coming on for Evans. Despite these alterations there wasn't a change to the pattern of the game and at full-time the game was still goalless.

The first period of extra-time was only a couple of minutes old when Steve Heighway broke away down the left and scored with a shot that went inside Wilson's near post. The Arsenal keeper should really have saved it but he did redeem himself only moments later when he saved a point-blank shot from Brain Hall which most definitely kept the Gunners in the game.

With four minutes of the first-half of extra-time remaining, Arsenal drew level when Radford hooked the ball into the area where Eddie Kelly touched the ball past Clemence and though Graham followed the ball over the line, most sources give the goal to Kelly.

A replay was on the cards but nine minutes from the end of extra-time, Arsenal scored the goal that gave them the Double. Radford laid the ball off for Charlie George to give England keeper Ray Clemence absolutely no chance with a tremendous shot from 20 yards out.

Frank McLintock received the FA Cup on behalf of his team and a most momentous season was over.

ARSENAL 3	MANCHESTER UNITED 2

12 May 1979
Arsenal Jennings; Rice; Nelson; Talbot; O'Leary; Young; Brady; Sunderland; Stapleton; Price (Walford); Rix
Manchester United Bailey; Nicholl; Albiston; McIlroy; McQueen; Buchan; Coppell; J Greenhoff; Jordan; Macari; Thomas
Attendance 100,000
Referee RC Challis (Tonbridge)

In an FA Cup Final that only really came to life in the last five minutes, Arsenal beat Manchester United in one of Wembley's most memorable finishes.

United were contesting their third final at Wembley in four years, whilst the Gunners were determined to make amends after suffering a 1-0 defeat at the hands of Ipswich Town the previous year.

Arsenal made the best start and after 12 minutes, following some neat interplay between Brady and Stapleton, David Price broke clear on the right and drove a low cross into the United penalty area. Talbot and Sunderland arrived together but it was the former Ipswich man Brian Talbot who was adjudged to have made contact to put Arsenal 1-0 up. United pushed hard for an equaliser but Arsenal were always dangerous on the break and, two minutes before half-time, Liam Brady broke clear, slipped past two lunging tackles and hit a pin-point cross for Stapleton to head past Gary Bailey to send the Gunners in at half-time 2-0 ahead.

As the second-half wore on, the Gunners maintained their control of the match and even after Walford replaced Price it seemed that the Cup was securely in the North London club's grasp.

With just four minutes remaining, the game was completely transformed. Arsenal failed to clear a free-kick and, following a scramble in the Gunners' goalmouth, Gordon McQueen swung a boot at a loose ball and United were back in the match. Two minutes later, Sammy McIlroy cut in from the right, evaded a couple of challenges and then rolled the ball past Pat Jennings for the equaliser.

Extra-time now looked imminent but from the kick-off, Liam Brady kept possession and took the ball deep into United's half before releasing an inch-perfect pass to Rix on the left. Rix crossed to the far post where Alan Sunderland was running in. He stabbed the ball into the net and Arsenal had won the Cup.

JUVENTUS 0	ARSENAL 1

23 April 1980
Juventus Zoff; Gentile; Cabrini; Furino; Brio; Scirea; Causio; Tardelli; Bettega; Prandelli; Fanna
Arsenal Jennings; Rice; Devine; Talbot (Hollins); O'Leary; Young; Brady; Sunderland; Stapleton; Price (Vaessen); Rix
Attendance 66,386
Referee CGR Corver (Holland)

The Gunners produced one of the most outstanding results ever in European football history to reach their second European final with victory over Juventus in Turin.

In the first leg at Highbury, the Italians held Arsenal to a 1-1 draw. Bettega was brought down by Talbot and though Jennings saved the resultant spot-kick, Cabrini followed up to score. Juventus protected their lead with a display of brutal defending and though Tardelli was sent-off, others should have followed him, especially Bettega after an horrendous tackle on O'Leary. However, with four minutes to go, Stapleton forced Bettega into putting through his own goal.

Juventus hadn't lost at home in Europe for 10 years and with the advantage of an away goal and a draw, looked clear favourites to reach the final. Yet as the game got underway, Juventus didn't seem to know whether to attempt to extend their advantage or settle for a goalless draw. In the end they opted to try and keep a clean sheet and rarely ventured into the Arsenal half. These tactics suited Arsenal and, with Brady the main prompter, the Gunners came more and more into the game. With a little under a quarter-of-an-hour remaining, Vaessen replaced Price but as the minutes ticked away, the game remained goalless.

With just a minute to go, Rix on the left sent over another curling cross. Italian international keeper Dino Zoff, a Juventus defender and young substitute Paul Vaessen all jumped for the ball. Vaessen got there first and knocked the ball down and over the line. Juventus were staggered and

Arsenal held on for a couple of minutes of injury time to complete a most famous victory.

Unfortunately, the Gunners lost in the final to Valencia of Spain in a penalty shoot-out.

LIVERPOOL 0 ARSENAL 2

26 May 1989

Liverpool Grobbelaar; Ablett; Staunton; Nicol; Whelan; Hansen; Houghton; Aldridge; Rush (Beardsley); McMahon

Arsenal Lukic; Dixon; Winterburn; Thomas; O'Leary; Adams; Rocastle; Richardson; Smith; Bould (Groves); Merson (Hayes)

Attendance 41,783

Referee D Hutchinson (Abingdon)

It is highly unlikely that the League Championship will ever be decided in a more dramatic way than in the 1988–89 season. The final match of the campaign brought together the two leading teams, Liverpool and Arsenal, in an 'all or nothing' match. The fixture which had originally been scheduled for a month earlier had been postponed due to the Hillsborough tragedy.

Arsenal had led the table since Boxing Day but due to some unforeseen results and a 24-match unbeaten run by Liverpool, the Gunners had allowed the Anfield club to claw back a 19 point margin. Having already won the FA Cup, Liverpool had won their previous two League games convincingly to leave Arsenal needing to win this game by two clear goals to take the title. To add to the tension, the kick-off was delayed by 10 minutes to allow Arsenal's visiting fans to enter the ground. However, once the game was underway, it was the Gunners who made the early running.

As early as the ninth minute, a goalbound header from Steve Bould was cleared off the line by Steve Nicol, while moments later Alan Smith mistimed his header from a Lee Dixon cross. At the other end, Aldridge shot narrowly over the bar before Lukic made a good save from a Ronnie Whelan piledriver. After 33 minutes, Peter Beardsley replaced Ian Rush and though his first touch almost put Aldridge through, the first-half was goalless.

In the second-half Arsenal continued to dominate and in the 52nd minute, Alan Smith stole in behind a line of Liverpool defenders to score with a fine glancing header from Winterburn's free-kick. Another good move by the Gunners saw Kevin Richardson put Michael Thomas through with only Grobbelaar to beat but he shot straight at the Liverpool keeper.

In an all-out effort for that second goal, the Gunners brought on Hayes for Merson and then Groves for Bould.

Then, with the game entering injury-time, Lee Dixon received the ball from Lukic and sent a long pass to Alan Smith, who in turn played it superbly through for Michael Thomas. This time, Thomas calmly lifted the ball over the advancing Bruce Grobbelaar and into the net.

A few seconds later the referee blew the final whistle and Arsenal had won the League Championship by one of the narrowest of margins.

ARSENAL 2   SHEFFIELD WEDNESDAY 1 after extra-time
20 May 1993
Arsenal Seaman; Dixon; Winterburn; Davis; Linighan; Adams; Jensen; Wright (O'Leary); Smith;
Campbell; Merson
Sheffield Wednesday Woods; Nilsson (Bart-Williams); Worthington; Harkes; Palmer; Warhurst; Wilson (Hyde);
Waddle; Hirst; Bright; Sheridan
Attendance 62,267
Referee K Barrett (Coventry)

Though this FA Cup Final replay only attracted a crowd of 62,267, the lowest crowd ever for the fixture at Wembley and the lowest FA Cup Final attendance for more than seventy years, the fans saw a climax almost to rival that at Anfield in 1989.

With the kick-off delayed for half-an-hour and Wednesday fans jamming the BBC switchboard asking for more time to get to the ground following an accident on the M1 and massive tailbacks, the game kicked-off in heavy rain.

During the early stages of the game, tackles were flying in thick and fast with Adams on Hirst and Jensen on Chris Waddle given the benefit of the doubt by the referee. However, the worst challenge was inflicted by Wednesday's Mark Bright on Linighan which left the Arsenal central defender with a broken nose – though he carried on playing.

After these brutal exchanges, the game settled down and, after 33 minutes, Ian Wright scored his 30th goal of the season to put the Gunners ahead. It was Alan Smith whose through ball allowed Wright to gallop clear and chip Chris Woods from 12 yards out.

Chris Waddle equalised for the Owls after 66 minutes with a deflected volley and, with both sides showing tiredness, a great chance to win the game fell to Wednesday's Bright. However, his shot from 10 yards with only Seaman to beat scraped the outside of the upright. In the last minute of normal time, a Paul Merson shot squirmed from Wood's grasp but the Wednesday keeper just managed to snatch the ball before it trickled over the line.

It looked as though the game was heading to a penalty shoot-out but in the very last minute of extra-time, the Gunners won a left-wing corner. Up went Linighan and Adams and, as Merson swung the ball over, Linighan rose above his marker Bright to power a header through the grasp of Woods. Nigel Worthington tried to hack it clear but only succeeded in hitting it into the roof of the net to confirm impressions that it had already crossed the line.

Linighan was engulfed by his team-mates and will always be remembered as the man who scored the latest FA Cup goal of all time.

ARSENAL 1   PARMA 0
4 May 1994
Arsenal Seaman; Dixon; Winterburn; Davis; Bould; Adams; Campbell; Morrow; Smith; Merson (McGoldrick); Selley
Parma Buccci; Benarrivo; Di Chiara; Minotti; Apolloni; Sensini; Brolin; Pin (Melli); Crippa; Zola;Asprilla
Attendance 33,765
Referee Krondl (Czech Republic)

Arsenal's worries as they flew out to Copenhagen for this European Cup Winners' Cup match against Parma centred around a squad hit by both injury and suspension – Ian Wright, John Jensen, David Hillier and Martin Keown were all unavailable.

Parma were the reigning European Cup Winners' Cup champions, having defeated Royal Antwerp of Belgium 3-1 a year earlier. They had a rich benefactor and their star players were Thomas Brolin playing just behind a front two of Faustino Asprilla and Gianfranco Zola.

Arsenal's absentees meant that manager George Graham had to change the 4-3-3 formation he had introduced following the club's FA Cup defeat by Bolton Wanderers.

Parma had the better of the early exchanges and after coming close a couple of times in the opening five minutes, Brolin hit Seaman's right-hand post on the quarter-of-an-hour mark, the ball bouncing back from the inside and rolling along the line until collected by the Arsenal keeper.

Yet, on 21 minutes, Arsenal took the lead against the run of play. Lee Dixon took a throw 40 yards out and Minotti, one of Italy's best sweepers, attempted an unnecessary overhead clearance. The ball fell to Alan Smith, who chested it down and struck the ball on the volley. The shot flew off the post and into the net with Parma keeper Bucci completely beaten. The Arsenal fans in a packed Copenhagen stadium went wild.

Parma attacked in search of the goal that would get them back into the game and Brolin was outstanding, but they could not score. Tony Adams and, in particular, Steve Bould were brilliant and both were later called into the England squad. Parma continued to pass the ball around well and were the more clever team but Arsenal marked and harried their opponents and held out to record a famous victory.

Nevio Scala, the Parma manager, also praised Arsenal. 'Tactically and technically we did not function. This was because Arsenal were a better team.'

ARSENAL 4	EVERTON 0

3 May 1998
Arsenal Seaman; Dixon; Winterburn; Vieira; Adams; Keown; Parlour; Petit (Platt); Anelka (Wright); Wreh (Bould); Overmars
Everton Myhre; Tiler; Ball; Short; Watson; Bilic (Oster); Barmby; O'Kane (Farrelly); Ferguson; Hutchison; Beagrie (Madar)
Attendance 38,269
Referee G Ashby (Worcester)

The sun shone literally and metaphorically as Arsenal thrashed Everton 4-0 to win their 11th League Championship. The victory took them to 78 points, thus breaking the stranglehold on the title by Manchester United who now couldn't catch them. This was a remarkable success for Arsène Wenger in his first full season in charge.

Early in the game, the overlapping Winterburn took a pass from Overmars and sent a long penetrating cross to Wreh who hit it first time, forcing Myhre into making a good save. Petit then swung in a left footed free-kick from the right. Adams went up for it at the far post but it went into the net off the head of the unfortunate Croatian international Bilic.

Everton couldn't cope with Marc Overmars and after he came close, Nicolas Anelka and Nigel Winterburn played a one-two before the French striker shot just wide of Myhre's right-hand post. Then Parlour's header forced the Everton keeper into another good save. Myhre then raced out to smother the ball at the feet of Dixon. The Everton No.1 was having a good game but it was his mistake that led to Arsenal's second goal as he allowed Overmars' shot to creep under his body.

As half-time approached Petit was the victim of a two-footed tackle by Don Hutchison and he was taken off to be replaced by David Platt. Overmars scored again after 57 minutes, exploiting a lucky rebound to run on and place the ball past Myhre.

In the last minute, Steve Bould delivered a wonderful ball from midfield for Tony Adams to drive through and score with a great strike. The goal was practically the last kick of the game and Highbury erupted as Arsenal at last broke the northern domination of the Premiership.

MANCHESTER UNITED 0   ARSENAL 1

8 May 2002

Manchester United Barthez; P Neville; Blanc; Brown; Silvestre; Scholes; Keane; Veron (Van Nistelrooy); Giggs; Solskjaer; Forlan (Fortune)

Arsenal Seaman; Lauren; Keown; Campbell; Cole; Ljungberg; Parlour; Vieira; Edu; Wiltord; Kanu (Dixon)

Attendance 67,580

Referee PA Durkin (Dorset)

Arsenal sealed the Double in style as they added the Premiership title to the FA Cup with victory at Manchester United. Arsène Wenger's side repeated their feat of four years earlier by striding into enemy territory at Old Trafford and stamping their authority on Sir Alex Ferguson's side.

Sylvan Wiltord's goal in his 100th Arsenal appearance maintained their record of scoring in every League game this season. Arsenal kept their composure in the face of fierce early physical assault as United relinquished their crown in graceless fashion. It was a bitterly disappointing end to United's season as they saw their closest rivals take their title off them on home soil.

Manchester United boss Alex Ferguson sprang a surprise by leaving Van Nistelrooy on the bench but Arsenal were robbed of Henry, Bergkamp and Adams.

The opening 45 minutes were played in a frantic atmosphere and United were fortunate to survive the first half without losing at least one player to a red card. Paul Scholes was lucky not to be sent-off for a wild challenge on Edu and Phil Neville likewise for a senseless lunge at Wiltord. Roy Keane also decided to get in on the act by flattening Vieira.

Arsenal were penned in their own half, only breaking the shackles in the opening minute when Wiltord's close range shot was blocked by Lauren Blanc.

The North London side eventually tested the United rearguard when Wiltord's cross almost found Edu but the Brazilian's stretch was in vain. A poor clearance by Barthez almost let in Wiltord, but on 55 minutes but the French striker scored the goal that inched the Championship closer to London. Picking up a loose clearance by Silvestre, he found Freddie Ljungberg. His shot was parried by Barthez and Wiltord was on hand to steer the ball home.

Van Nistelrooy's introduction did little to knock Arsenal out of their mood of calm command – the Gunners showing resilience and demonstrating exactly why they were worthy champions by adding another Double to previous triumphs in 1971 and 1998.

BARCELONA 2	ARSENAL 1

20 May 2006
Barcelona Valdes; Oleguer (Belletti); Marquez; Puyol; Van Bronckhorst; Deco; Edmilson (Iniesta); Van Bommel (Larsson); Giuly; Eto'o Ronaldinho
Arsenal Lehmann; Eboue; Toure; Campbell; Cole; Pires (Almunia); Silva; Fabregas (Flamini); Hleb (Reyes); Ljungberg; Henry
Attendance 79,500
Referee T Hauge (Norway)

Arsenal started their first-ever Champions League final against Barcelona in Paris in sensational fashion and star striker Thierry Henry could have twice given the Gunners the lead in the opening three minutes. He turned brilliantly in the Barcelona box only to be denied by the diving Victor Valdes from point-blank range. From the resultant short corner, he fired in an angled rive which was pushed to safety by Valdes.

Lehmann had already shown his quality with two stops from Ludovic Giuly and Deco but the German international was shown the red card after 18 minutes – Eto'o bore down on goal after being played in by Ronaldinho but was upended by the Arsenal keeper as he tried to round him. The ball fell to Giuly who tapped home the loose ball but the referee had already blown for the foul. Referee Terje Hauge showed Lehmann the red card, prompting Arsène Wenger to replace Robert Pires with replacement goalkeeper Manuel Almunia.

Barcelona began to take control but were stunned after 37 minutes when Arsenal took the lead. A foul on Eboue saw the referee award a free-kick and Campbell headed home Thierry Henry's cross.

Barcelona's substitute Iniesta came close to equalising but Almunia did well to clutch his shot that skidded off the wet surface. Arsenal were still dangerous on the break and Henry and Fabregas combined to set up Hleb who fired wide. Freddie Ljungberg was also denied by a superb Valdes save. Henry had a glorious chance to extend Arsenal's lead but the Barcelona keeper again saved well.

Barcelona drew level when Eto'o tucked home Larsson's deft pass and then with 10 minutes to go, Belletti gave the Spanish side the lead. It was a killer blow from which Arsenal never looked likely to recover.

SEASON-BY-SEASON STATISTICS

	1893–94				
	Opposition	**H/A**	**Score**	**Scorers**	**Attendance**
1.	Newcastle United	H	2-2	Shaw Elliott	10,000
2.	Notts County	A	2-3	Elliott Shaw	7,000
3.	Walsall TS	H	4-0	Heath 3 Crawford	4,000
4.	Grimsby Town	H	3-1	Elliott Heath Booth	2,000
5.	Newcastle United	A	0-6		2,000
6.	Small Heath	A	1-4	Henderson	3,000
7.	Liverpool	H	0-5		9,000
8.	Ardwick	H	1-0	Henderson	4,500
9.	Rotherham Town	H	3-0	Shaw 2 Elliott	3,000
10.	Burton Swifts	A	2-6	Elliott Shaw	2,000
11.	Northwich Vic	A	2-2	Shaw Boyle	2,000
12.	Port Vale	H	4-1	Shaw Henderson Booth Crawford	10,000
13.	Grimsby Town	A	1-3	Buist (pen)	3,000
14.	Ardwick	A	1-0	Henderson	4,000
15.	Liverpool	A	0-2		5,000
16.	Port Vale	A	1-2	Elliott	900
17.	Lincoln City	A	0-3		2,000
18.	Rotherham Town	A	1-1	Worrall	2,000
19.	Crewe Alex	H	3-2	Henderson 3	4,000
20.	Walsall TS	A	2-1	Henderson Elliott	2,000
21.	Lincoln City	H	4-0	Elliott 2 Bryan Stothart og	3,000
22.	Middlesbrough I	A	6-3	Shaw 3 Henderson 2 Davis	500
23.	Crewe Alex	A	0-0		2,000
24.	Middlesbrough I	H	1-0	Shaw	5,000
25.	Northwich Vic	H	6-0	Jacques 2 Henderson 2 Elliott Howat	5,000
26.	Notts County	H	1-2	Crawford	13,000
27.	Small Heath	H	1-4	McNab	6,000
28.	Burton Swifts	H	0-2		2,000

Final League Position = 9th in Division Two

♀ FA Cup ♀

1Q	Ashford United	H	12-0	Elliott 3 Booth 2 Henderson 3 Crawford Heath 2 Powell	3,000
2Q	Clapton Orient	H	6-2	Henderson 2 Cooper 2 Shaw Elliott	2,500
3Q	Millwall Athletic	H	2-0	Davis, Booth	20,000
4Q	2nd Scots Guards	A	2-1*	Henderson 2	9,000
1	Sheffield Wed	H	1-2	Elliott	15,000
	*After extra-time				

	1894-95				
1.	Lincoln City	A	2-5	Heath Mortimer	2,000
2.	Grimsby Town	H	1-3	Boyd	4,000
3.	Burton Swifts	A	0-3		3,000
4.	Bury	H	4-2	Boyd 2 Henderson O'Brien	8,000
5.	Manchester City	H	4-2	Boyd 3 Mortimer	5,000
6.	Lincoln City	H	5-2	Boyd 2 Mortimer 2 O'Brien	8,000
7.	Newton Heath	A	3-3	Mortimer 2 Boyd	4,000
8.	Rotherham Town	A	2-1	Boyle Henderson	2,000
9.	Notts County	A	2-2	Howat Caldwell	2,000
10.	Notts County	H	2-1	Henderson O'Brien	11,000
11.	Walsall TS	A	1-4	Boyle	3,000
12.	Newcastle United	A	4-2	Sharpe Crawford Buchanan O'Brien	3,000
13.	Darwen	H	4-0	Mortimer O'Brien Henderson Davis	8,000
14.	Manchester City	A	1-4	Buchanan	5,000
15.	Port Vale	H	7-0	O'Brien 3 Davis Buchanan Sharpe Henderson	8,000
16.	Grimsby Town	A	2-4	Henderson O'Brien	5,000
17.	Darwen	A	1-3	Crawford	6,000
18.	Leicester Fosse	A	1-3	Mortimer	3,000
19.	Newcastle United	H	3-2	Buchanan Meade Crawford	5,000
20.	Port Vale	A	1-0	Crawford	700
21.	Burton W	H	1-1	Henderson	7,000
22.	Rotherham Town	H	1-1	Sharpe	3,000
23.	Burton Swifts	H*	3-0	Mortimer 2 Buchanan	5,000
24.	Bury	A	0-2		4,000
25.	Leicester Fosse	H*	3-3	O'Brien Sharpe Mortimer	4,000
26.	Crewe Alex	A	0-0		1,000
27.	Newton Heath	H	3-2	Mortimer Buchanan Crawford	6,000
28.	Crewe Alex	H	7-0	Buchanan 2 Davis Boyle O'Brien Crawford Hare	4,000
29.	Walsall TS	H	6-1	Hare 2 Mortimer 2 Buchanan Crawford	6,000
30.	Burton W	A	1-2	Hare	3,000

Final League Position = 8th in Division Two

* Following incidents against the referee on 26 January 1895, the Arsenal ground was closed for five weeks and therefore Match 23 was played at New Brompton and Match 25 at Leyton.

SEASON-BY-SEASON STATISTICS   269

♛ FA Cup ♛

1	Bolton Wands	A	0-1		7,000

1895–96

No.	Opponent	H/A	Score	Scorers	Att.
1.	Grimsby Town	H	3-1	Jenkyns O'Brien Gordon	6,000
2.	Manchester City	H	0-1		6,000
3.	Lincoln City	A	1-1	Buchanan	1,200
4.	Lincoln City	H	4-0	Jenkyns Mills Gordon Buchanan	6,000
5.	Manchester City	A	0-1	9,000	
6.	Rotherham Town	H	5-0	Gordon Mortimer Mills Jenkyns Buchanan	6,000
7.	Burton W	H	3-0	McAvoy Gordon Mortimer	8,000
8.	Burton Swifts	H	5-0	Mortimer 2 Mills Buchanan Boyd	8,000
9.	Rotherham Town	A	0-3		2,000
10.	Notts County	A	4-3	Hare Gordon 2 Boyd	8,000
11.	Newton Heath	H	2-1	Boyle Hare	9,000
12.	Liverpool	H	0-2		10,000
13.	Newton Heath	A	1-5	Hare	6,000
14.	Leicester Fosse	H	1-1	Boyd	5,000
15.	Burton W	A	1-4	Boyd	5,000
16.	Burton Swifts	A	2-3	Buchanan Boyd	2,000
17.	Crewe Alex	A	1-0	Boyd	3,000
18.	Port Vale	H	2-1	Buchanan Mortimer	2,000
19.	Loughborough T	H	5-0	Boyd 2 Jenkyns Powell Buchanan	4,000
20.	Liverpool	A	0-3		7,000
21.	Newcastle United	A	1-3	Jenkyns (pen)	8,000
22.	Leicester Fosse	A	0-1		6,000
23.	Port Vale	A	2-0	Boyd Haywood	1,000
24.	Loughborough T	A	1-2	Boyd	2,000
25.	Notts County	H	2-0	Jenkyns Haywood	6,000
26.	Darwen	A	1-1	Crawford	3,000
27.	Crewe Alex	H	7-0	Boyd 2 (1 pen) Mortimer 3 Haywood Brocks (og)	5,000
28.	Grimsby Town	A	1-1	Boyd	5,000
29.	Newcastle United	H	2-1	Mortimer O'Brien	14,000
30.	Darwen	H	1-3	Haywood	4,000

Final League Position = 7th in Division Two

♛ FA Cup ♛

1	Burnley	A	1-6	O'Brien	6,000

1896–97

No.	Opponent	H/A	Score	Scorers	Att.
1.	Manchester City	A	1-1	Haywood	8,000
2.	Walsall	H	1-1	Boyd	6,000
3.	Burton W	A	3-0	O'Brien Brock Boyd	4,000

4.	Loughborough T	H	2-0	O'Brien McAvoy	8,000
5.	Notts County	H	2-3	Meade McAvoy	9,000
6.	Burton W	H	3-0	Haywood Boyd 2	700
7.	Walsall	A	3-5	Meade Boyd (pen) Haywood	4,000
8.	Gainsborough T	A	6-1	Boyd 2 Brock 2 Haywood Russell	5,500
9.	Notts County	A	4-7	Brock Haywood O'Brien Boyd	3,000
10.	Small Heath	A	2-5	McAvoy Brock	3,000
11.	Grimsby Town	H	4-2	O'Brien 2 Boyd Brock	6,500
12.	Lincoln City	A	3-2	O'Brien 2 Boyd	2,000
13.	Loughborough T	A	0-8		500
14.	Blackpool	H	4-2	Crawford 2 Haywood 2	6,000
15.	Lincoln City	H	6-2	O'Brien 2 Boyle Meade 2 Russell	9,000
16.	Gainsborough T	A	1-4	Brock	3,000
17.	Darwen	A	1-4	Russell	5,000
18.	Blackpool	A	1-1	Brock	1,000
19.	Newcastle United	A	0-2		6,000
20.	Leicester Fosse	A	3-6	O'Brien 2 Haywood	6,000
21.	Burton Swifts	H	3-0	Haywood 2 Caie	5,000
22.	Burton Swifts	A	2-1	Caie 2	1,000
23.	Newton Heath	A	1-1	Brock	3,000
24.	Small Heath	H	2-3	Haywood McAvoy	2,500
25.	Newton Heath	H	0-2		6,000
26.	Grimsby Town	A	1-3	Hardie og	1,000
27.	Newcastle United	H	5-1	Brock Boyle O'Brien 2 Caldwell	7,000
28.	Leicester Fosse	H	2-1	Caie Brock	5,000
29.	Darwen	H	1-0	O'Brien	8,000
30.	Manchester City	H	1-2	Russell	2,000

Final League Position = 10th in Division Two

♆ FA Cup ♆

4Q	Leyton*	H	5-0	Meade McAvoy 2 Duff Farmer	3,000
5Q	Chatham	H	4-0	Haywood 2 Boyle Meade	4,500
Sup	Millwall	A	2-4	Boyle O'Brien	14,000

* As Arsenal were compelled to fulfil a League fixture at Loughborough on this date, they fielded a reserve team in the FA Cup tie. The reserves won handsomely, but the first team suffered Arsenal's record League defeat!

1897–98

1.	Grimsby Town	H	4-1	Monteith Steven Farrell White	6,000
2.	Newcastle United	A	1-4	McGeoch	10,000
3.	Burnley	A	0-5		3,000
4.	Lincoln City	H	2-2	Farrell McAvoy	8,000
5.	Gainsborough T	H	4-0	McGeoch 3 McAvoy	8,000
6.	Manchester City	A	1-4	Brock	7,000
7.	Luton Town	A	2-0	McAvoy Davis	5,000
8.	Luton Town	H	3-0	Stuart Brock Davis	14,000
9.	Newcastle United	H	0-0		12,000
10.	Leicester Fosse	H	0-3		7,000

11.	Walsall	A	2-3	Hannah Hunt	3,000
12.	Walsall	H	4-0	McGeoch 3 White	2,000
13.	Blackpool	H	2-1	Hannah Davis	6,500
14.	Leicester Fosse	A	1-2	Duff	8,000
15.	Loughborough T	A	3-1	Brock Hannah White	2,000
16.	Lincoln City	A	3-2	Hunt 2 Brock	4,000
17.	Blackpool	A	3-3	Devlin Cardwell 2 (og's)	1,500
18.	Newton Heath	H	5-1	Hunt Anderson White Brock Hannah	8,000
19.	Burton Swifts	A	2-1	Haywood Hannah	2,000
20.	Manchester City	H	2-2	Davis Brock	8,000
21.	Grimsby Town	A	4-1	Hunt 2 (1 pen) Hannah 2	3,500
22.	Newton Heath	A	1-5	Hunt	8,000
23.	Small Heath	H	4-2	Hannah 3 (1 pen) White	8,000
24.	Darwen	A	4-1	White Hunt Brock McGeoch	2,000
25.	Loughborough T	H	4-0	Hunt 2 Haywood McAuley	5,000
26.	Gainsborough T	A	0-1		2,000
27.	Burnley	H	1-1	Hunt	12,000
28.	Darwen	H	3-1	Brock 2 Haywood	5,000
29.	Burton Swifts	H	3-0	Hannah 2 Haywood	6,000
30.	Small Heath	A	1-2	Hunt	3,000

Final League Position = 5th in Division Two

♛ FA Cup ♛

3Q	St Albans	H	9-0	Hunt 3 Brock Haywood Steven McGeochDavis Farrell	3,000
4Q	Sheppey United	H	3-0	Crawford Haywood Brock	6,000
5Q	New Brompton	H	4-2	Haywood McAuley Crawford Janes og	5,500
1	Burnley	A	1-3	Brock	6,000

	1898–99				
1.	Luton Town	A	1-0	Mitchell	5,000
2.	Port Vale	A	0-3		5,000
3.	Leicester Fosse	H	4-0	White 2 Hunt 2	6,000
4.	Darwen	A	4-1	Hunt Dailly White Anderson	3,000
5.	Gainsborough T	H	5-1	Dailly 2 McGeoch 2 Hunt	7,000
6.	Manchester City	A	1-3	White	6,000
7.	Walsall	A	1-4	Haywood	4,000
8.	Burton Swifts	H	2-1	McGeoch Hunt (pen)	4,000
9.	Small Heath	H	2-0	White Hunt	7,000
10.	Loughborough T	A	0-0		2,500
11.	Grimsby Town	A	0-1		2,000
12.	Newton Heath	H	5-1	White 3 Hannah 2	7,000
13.	New Brighton	A	1-3	White	2,000
14.	Lincoln City	H	4-2	Mitchell Dailly McConnell Hunt	3,000
15.	Barnsley	A	1-2	Hunt	2,000
16.	Luton Town	H	6-2	Haywood 3 Hunt 3	4,000
17.	Leicester Fosse	A	1-2	Haywood	10,000

18.	Darwen	H	6-0	Haywood Hannah 2 Shaw White Hunt	3,000
19.	Gainsborough T	A	1-0	Haywood	2,000
20.	Glossop NE	A	0-2		2,000
21.	Walsall	H	0-0		3,000
22.	Glossop NE	H	3-0	Anderson Hunt McGeoch	2,000
23.	Burton Swifts	A	2-1	Shaw 2	4,000
24.	Port Vale	H	1-0	Shaw	6,000
25.	Small Heath	A	1-4	Haywood	3,000
26.	Loughborough T	H	3-1	Cottrell Shaw McGeoch	2,000
27.	Blackpool	H	6-0	Cottrell 3 Hunt Haywood 2	4,000
28.	Blackpool	A	1-1	Cottrell	2,000
29.	Grimsby Town	H	1-1	Hannah	3,500
30.	Newton Heath	A	2-2	Cottrell Haywood	5,000
31.	Manchester City	H	0-1		5,000
32.	New Brighton	H	4-0	Hunt Cottrell 2 Haywood	3,000
33.	Lincoln City	A	0-2		2,000
34.	Barnsley	H	3-0	Shaw 2 Cottrell	4,000

Final League Position = 7th in Division Two

♛ FA Cup ♛

1	Derby County	H	0-6		20,000

1899–1900					
1.	Leicester Fosse	H	0-2		10,000
2.	Luton Town	A	2-1	Logan Tennant	3,000
3.	Port Vale	H	1-0	Sanders	6,000
4.	Walsall	A	0-2	3,000	
5.	Middlesbrough	H	3-0	Shaw 2 McCowie	6,000
6.	Chesterfield	A	1-3	Aston	4,000
7.	Gainsborough T	H	2-1	Hartley Hunt (pen)	6,000
8.	Bolton Wands	A	0-1	5,000	
9.	Newton Heath	A	0-2	5,000	
10.	Sheffield Wed	H	1-2	McCowie	7,000
11.	Small Heath	H	3-0	Aston 2 Dick	4,000
12.	New Brighton	A	2-0	McCowie 2	4,000
13.	Burton Swifts	H	1-1	Gaudie	3,000
14.	Lincoln City	A	0-5	6,000	
15.	Leicester Fosse	A	0-0	8,500	
16.	Luton Town	H	3-1	Gaudie 2 Logan	2,500
17.	Port Vale	A	1-1	Gaudie	2,000
18.	Walsall	H	3-1	Logan 2 Gaudie	3,000
19.	Middlesbrough	A	0-1	6,000	
20.	Chesterfield	H	2-0	Dick McCowie	3,000
21.	Gainsborough T	A	1-1	McCowie	1,000
22.	Bolton Wands	H	0-1	5,500	
23.	Loughborough T	A	3-2	Logie Gaudie Tennant	800
24.	Newton Heath	H	2-1	Hunt Dick	4,000

25.	Loughborough T	H	12-0	Gaudie 3 Cottrell 2 Dick 2 Main 2 Tennant 2 Anderson	600
26.	Sheffield Wed	A	1-3	McNichol	3,000
27.	Lincoln City	H	2-1	McCowie Gaudie	2,500
28.	Small Heath	A	1-3	Gaudie	3,000
29.	New Brighton	H	5-0	Main Anderson Gaudie 2 Logan	2,000
30.	Grimsby Town	A	0-1		2,000
31.	Grimsby Town	H	2-0	Tennant 2	5,000
32.	Burton Swifts	A	0-2		2,000
33.	Barnsley	A	2-3	Anderson Lloyd	500
34.	Barnsley	H	5-1	Lloyd 2 Gaudie 2 Dick	3,000

Final League Position = 8th in Division Two

♛ FA Cup ♛

3Q	New Brompton	H	1-1	Hunt	5,500
R	New Brompton	A	0-0		2,000
2R	New Brompton*	N	2-2	Aston Hunt	2,000
3R	New Brompton**	N	1-1	Aston	2,000
4R	New Brompton***	N	0-1		3,000

* Played at Millwall   ** Played at Tottenham   *** Played at Gravesend

	1900–01				
1.	Gainsborough T	H	2-1	Turner Blackwood	8,000
2.	Walsall	H	1-1	Anderson	7,000
3.	Burton Swifts	A	0-1		1,300
4.	Barnsley	H	1-2	Main	700
5.	Chesterfield	H	1-0	Main	5,500
6.	Blackpool	A	1-1	Blackwood	3,000
7.	Stockport County	H	2-0	Dick Place	5,000
8.	Small Heath	A	1-2	Coles	8,000
9.	Grimsby Town	H	1-1	Turner	7,000
10.	Leicester Fosse	H	2-1	Blackwood Gaudie	7,000
11.	Newton Heath	H	2-1	Anderson Turner	8,000
12.	Glossop	A	1-0	Place	3,000
13.	Middlesbrough	H	1-0	Blackwood	8,000
14.	Burnley	A	0-3		4,000
15.	Port Vale	H	3-0	Blackwood Place 2	7,000
16.	Leicester Fosse	A	0-1		10,000
17.	New Brighton	H	2-1	Main Gaudie	6,000
18.	Walsall	A	0-1		4,000
19.	Gainsborough T	A	0-1		2,000
20.	Burton Swifts	H	3-1	Blackwood Main Turner	5,000
21.	Barnsley	A	0-3		3,000
22.	Lincoln City	A	3-3	Gaudie 2 Main	3,000
23.	Stockport County	A	1-3	Turner	3,000
24.	Chesterfield	A	1-0	Gaudie	2,000
25.	Grimsby Town	A	0-1		2,500
26.	Lincoln City	H	0-0		3,000
27.	Newton Heath	A	0-1		5,000

28.	Glossop	H	2-0	Place Tennant	3,000
29.	Middlesbrough	A	1-1	Main	6,000
30.	Burnley	H	3-1	Gaudie 2 Coles	7,000
31.	Blackpool	H	3-1	Gaudie Low Tennant	5,000
32.	Port Vale	A	0-1		1,000
33.	Small Heath	H	1-0	Cottrell	3,500
34.	New Brighton	A	0-1		2,000

Final League Position = 7th in Division Two

♈ FA Cup ♈

Sup	Darwen	A	2-0	Blackwood Tennant	5,000
1	Blackburn Rovers	H	2-0	Tennant Low	11,000
2	West Brom Alb	H	0-1		20,000

	1901–02				
1.	Barnsley	H	2-1	Foxall Swann	6,000
2.	Leicester Fosse	H	2-0	J Anderson Briercliffe	10,000
3.	Preston NE	A	0-2		6,000
4.	Burnley	H	4-0	Briercliffe 2 Laidlaw Foxall	10,000
5.	Port Vale	A	0-1		3,000
6.	Chesterfield	H	3-2	Laidlaw J Anderson (pen) Logan	8,000
7.	Gainsborough T	A	2-2	Main Owens	4,000
8.	Middlesbrough	H	0-3		8,000
9.	Bristol City	A	3-0	Briercliffe 2 Place	10,500
10.	Stockport County	A	0-0		3,000
11.	Newton Heath	H	2-0	Owens Briercliffe	5,000
12.	Glossop NE	A	1-0	Foxall	3,000
13.	Doncaster Rovers	H	1-0	Swann	10,000
14.	Lincoln City	A	0-0		4,000
15.	Burton United	H	0-1		4,000
16.	Blackpool	H	0-0		3,500
17.	Port Vale	H	3-1	Briercliffe Gooing Main	5,500
18.	Barnsley	A	0-2		3,000
19.	Leicester Fosse	A	1-2	Gooing	7,000
20.	Preston NE	H	0-0		8,000
21.	Burnley	A	0-0		4,000
22.	Chesterfield	A	3-1	Main Dick W Anderson	2,000
23.	Gainsborough T	H	5-0	Fitchie 2 Briercliffe 2 Gooing	7,000
24.	Middlesbrough	A	0-1		8,500
25.	Bristol City	H	2-0	Gooing 2	10,000
26.	Blackpool	A	3-1	W Anderson Dick Edgar	3,000
27.	Stockport County	H	3-0	Gooing W Anderson 2	6,000
28.	Newton Heath	A	1-0	W Anderson	4,000
29.	Glossop NE	H	4-0	Dick Gooing 2 Briercliffe	6,000
30.	Doncaster Rovers	A	0-1		3,000
31.	West Brom Alb	H	2-1	Gooing Main	10,000
32.	Lincoln City	H	2-0	Briercliffe Fitchie	6,000
33.	West Brom Alb	A	1-2	Main	8,878
34.	Burton United	A	0-2		3,000

Final League Position = 4th in Division Two

♆ FA Cup ♆

Sup	Luton Town	H	1-1	Jackson	10,000
R	Luton Town	A	2-0	Gooing Place	3,000
1	Newcastle United	H	0-2		15,000

	1902–03				
1.	Preston NE	A	2-2	Connor McMahon (og)	9,000
2.	Port Vale	H	3-0	Briercliffe Dick Coleman	12,000
3.	Barnsley	A	1-1	Coleman	5,000
4.	Gainsborough T	H	6-1	Gooing 3 Connor Coleman Lawrence	10,000
5.	Bristol City	A	0-1		12,024
6.	Bristol City	H	2-1	Gooing Hunt (pen)	16,000
7.	Glossop NE	A	2-1	Coleman 2	1,000
8.	Manchester Utd	H	0-1		12,000
9.	Manchester City	H	1-0	Gooing	12,000
10.	Blackpool	H	2-1	Bradshaw Lawrence	8,000
11.	Burnley	A	3-0	W Anderson Gooing Briercliffe	2,500
12.	Doncaster Rovers	A	1-0	Gooing	5,000
13.	Lincoln City	H	2-1	Coleman Briercliffe	14,000
14.	Small Heath	A	0-2		10,000
15.	Manchester City	A	1-4	Gooing	25,000
16.	Burton United	A	1-2	Briercliffe	4,000
17.	Burnley	H	5-1	Coleman 3 Briercliffe W Anderson	13.000
18.	Stockport County	A	1-0	Gooing	2,000
19.	Preston NE	H	3-1	Gooing W Anderson Linward	12,000
20.	Port Vale	A	1-1	Briercliffe	4,000
21.	Barnsley	H	4-0	Shanks 2 W Anderson Briercliffe	10,000
22.	Gainsborough T	A	1-0	W Anderson	3,000
23.	Burton United	H	3-0	Gooing Shanks Coleman	12,000
24.	Glossop NE	H	0-0		10,000
25.	Stockport County	H	3-1	Lawrence Coleman Shanks	8,000
26.	Blackpool	A	0-0		3,000
27.	Manchester Utd	A	0-3		5,000
28.	Chesterfield	A	2-2	Coleman 2	5,000
29.	Doncaster Rovers	H	3-0	Linward Coleman Langton (og)	10,000
30.	Lincoln City	A	2-2	Gooing Linward	3,000
31.	Small Heath	H	6-1	Coleman 2 Linward 2 Gooing 2	15,000
32.	Chesterfield	H	3-0	Briercliffe Gooing Thorpe og	14,000
33.	Leicester Fosse	A	2-0	Coleman Gooing	10,000
34.	Leicester Fosse	H	0-0		12,000

Final League Position = 3rd in Division Two

♆ FA Cup ♆

Sup	Brentford	A	1-1	Gooing	7,500
R	Brentford	H	5-0	Coleman 2 Connor Gooing J Anderson	3,000
1	Sheffield United	H	1-3	W Anderson	24,000

	1903–04				
1.	Blackpool	H	3-0	Gooing 2 Coleman	10,000
2.	Gainsborough T	A	2-0	Coleman 2	3,000
3.	Burton United	H	8-0	Briercliffe 3 Coleman 2 Gooing Shanks Linward	12,000
4.	Bristol City	A	4-0	Gooing 2 Coleman Linward	14,000
5.	Manchester Utd	H	4-0	Shanks Coleman Busby Briercliffe	20,000
6.	Glossop NE	A	3-1	Gooing 2 Coleman	1,000
7.	Port Vale	A	3-2	Briercliffe Shanks Gooing	3,000
8.	Leicester Fosse	H	8-0	Shanks 3 Pratt 2 Gooing Briercliffe Busby	5,000
9.	Barnsley	A	1-2	Briercliffe	6,000
10.	Lincoln City	H	4-0	Shanks 3 Coleman	16,000
11.	Chesterfield	H	6-0	Briercliffe Shanks 2 Coleman Linward Gooing	10,000
12.	Bolton Wands	A	1-2	Gooing	6,000
13.	Grimsby Town	H	5-1	Shanks 4 Coleman	14,000
14.	Bradford City	H	4-1	Shanks Sands Coleman 2	18,000
15.	Leicester Fosse	A	0-0		14,000
16.	Stockport County	A	0-0		4,000
17.	Blackpool	A	2-2	Shanks Sands	4,000
18.	Gainsborough T	H	6-0	Sands Briercliffe Gooing 2 Shanks Coleman	10,000
19.	Burton United	A	1-3	Briercliffe	2,000
20.	Manchester Utd	A	0-1		40,000
21.	Barnsley	H	3-0	Gooing Shanks Coleman	12,000
22.	Burnley	H	4-0	Shanks 3 Gooing	4,000
23.	Lincoln City	A	2-0	Dick Shanks	5,000
24.	Stockport County	H	5-2	Coleman 2 Gooing Linward 2	10,000
25.	Bristol City	H	2-0	Coleman 2	10,000
26.	Chesterfield	A	0-1		9,000
27.	Bolton Wands	H	3-0	Gooing 2 Coleman	18,000
28.	Preston NE	A	0-0		12,000
29.	Burnley	A	0-1		5,000
30.	Glossop NE	H	2-1	Coleman Shanks (pen)	17,000
31.	Preston NE	H	0-0		28,000
32.	Grimsby Town	A	2-2	Gooing Coleman	6,000
33.	Bradford City	A	3-0	Coleman Bradshaw Watson	12,000
34.	Port Vale	H	0-0		20,000

Final League Position = 2nd in Division Two

♗ FA Cup ♗

Sup	Bristol Rovers	A	1-1	Dick	14,000
R	Bristol Rovers	H	1-1	Tait og	12,000
2R	Bristol Rovers*	N	1-0	Briercliffe	10,000
1	Fulham	H	1-0	Shanks	15,000
2	Manchester City	H	0-2		30,000

* Played at Tottenham

1904–05

1.	Newcastle United	A	0-3		25,000
2.	Preston NE	H	0-0		25,000
3.	Middlesbrough	A	0-1		15,000
4.	Wolves	H	2-0	Satterthwaite Coleman	20,000
5.	Bury	A	1-1	Briercliffe	8,000
6.	Aston Villa	H	1-0	Gooing	32,850
7.	Blackburn Rovers	A	1-1	Satterthwaite	10,000
8.	Nottingham F	H	0-3		20,000
9.	Sheffield Wed	A	3-0	Crowe 2 Coleman	15,000
10.	Sunderland	H	0-0		30,000
11.	Stoke	H	2-1	Crowe Hunter	20,000
12.	Derby County	A	0-0		12,000
13.	Small Heath	A	1-2	Hunter	20,000
14.	Manchester City	H	1-0	Satterthwaite	16,000
15.	Notts County	A	5-1	Fitchie 3 Satterthwaite 2	15,000
16.	Sheffield United	H	1-0	Fitchie	20,000
17.	Aston Villa	A	1-3	Satterthwaite	40,000
18.	Nottingham F	A	3-0	Hunter Briercliffe Satterthwaite	16,000
19.	Sheffield United	A	0-4		30,000
20.	Newcastle United	H	0-2		30,000
21.	Preston NE	A	0-3		13,000
22.	Middlesbrough	H	1-1	Fitchie	15,000
23.	Wolves	A	1-4	Briercliffe	8,500
24.	Bury	H	2-1	Satterthwaite 2	20,000
25.	Blackburn Rovers	H	2-1	Fitchie Briercliffe	15,000
26.	Sheffield Wed	H	3-0	Satterthwaite Coleman 2	20,000
27.	Sunderland	A	1-1	Coleman	14,000
28.	Stoke	A	0-2		4,000
29.	Derby County	H	0-0		15,000
30.	Small Heath	H	1-1	Hunter	20,000
31.	Everton	A	0-1		12,000
32.	Manchester City	A	0-1		18,000
33.	Notts County	H	1-2	Templeton	12,000
34.	Everton	H	2-1	Satterthwaite Ducat	25,000

Final League Position = 10th in Division One

♛ FA Cup ♛

1	Bristol City	H	0-0		25,000
R	Bristol City	A	0-1		10,000

1905–06

1.	Liverpool	H	3-1	Coleman Satterthwaite Blair	20,000
2.	Sheffield United	A	1-3	Blair	16,000
3.	Notts County	H	1-1	Fitchie	16,000
4.	Preston NE	H	2-2	Fitchie 2	12,000
5.	Stoke	A	1-2	Fitchie	15,000
6.	Bolton Wands	H	0-0		20,000
7.	Wolves	A	2-0	Coleman 2	9,000

8.	Blackburn Rovers	A	0-2		10,000
9.	Sunderland	H	2-0	Blair Bellamy (pen)	13,000
10.	Birmingham	A	1-2	Crowe	16,000
11.	Everton	H	1-2	Coleman	18,000
12.	Derby County	A	1-5	Satterthwaite	6,000
13.	Sheffield Wed	H	0-2		20,000
14.	Nottingham F	A	1-3	Freeman	8,000
15.	Manchester City	H	2-0	Freeman 2	16,000
16.	Bury	A	0-2		8,000
17.	Middlesbrough	H	2-2	Bellamy Freeman	12,000
18.	Preston NE	A	2-2	Neave 2	6,000
19.	Newcastle United	H	4-3	Ducat 2 Fitchie 2	20,000
20.	Aston Villa	A	1-2	Fitchie	30,000
21.	Liverpool	A	0-3		15,000
22.	Bolton Wands	A	1-6	Satterthwaite	30,000
23.	Sheffield United	H	5-1	Coleman 2 Fitchie Garbutt Ducat	10,000
24.	Notts County	A	0-1		5,000
25.	Stoke	H	1-2	Neave	10,000
26.	Wolves	H	2-1	Freeman 2	10,000
27.	Blackburn Rovers	H	3-2	Coleman 2 Bellamy (pen)	8,000
28.	Birmingham	H	5-0	Satterthwaite 2 Coleman Sharp Freeman	25,000
29.	Derby County	H	1-0	Neave	20,000
30.	Everton	A	1-0	Garbutt	8,000
31.	Sheffield Wed	A	2-4	Sharp (pen) Fitchie	15,000
32.	Nottingham F	H	3-1	Neave 2 Freeman	10,000
33.	Manchester City	A	2-1	Satterthwaite	12,000
34.	Aston Villa	H	2-1	Coleman Freeman	30,000
35.	Bury	H	4-0	Ducat Coleman Satterthwaite 2	20,000
36.	Newcastle United	A	1-1	Garbutt	25,000
37.	Middlesbrough	A	0-2		12,000
38.	Sunderland	A	2-2	Satterthwaite Coleman	8,000

Final League Position = 12th in Division One

♛ FA Cup ♛

1	West Ham United	H	1-1	Sharp (pen)	18,000
R	West Ham United	A	3-2	Ducat Satterthwaite Garbutt	12,000
2	Watford	H	3-0	Freeman Coleman Fitchie	11,000
3	Sunderland	H	5-0	Garbutt 2 Fitchie Sands Coleman	30,000
4	Manchester Utd	A	3-2	Freeman 2 Coleman	26,500
SF	Newcastle United*	N	0-2		19,964

* Played at the Victoria Ground, Stoke

	1906–07				
1.	Manchester City	A	4-1	Kyle 2 Coleman Satterthwaite	18,000
2.	Bury	A	1-4	Kyle	9,000
3.	Middlesbrough	H	2-0	Satterthwaite 2	20,000
4.	Preston NE	A	3-0	Satterthwaite 2 Bellamy	12,000
5.	Newcastle United	H	2-0	Kyle 2	30,000

6.	Aston Villa	A	2-2	Satterthwaite Coleman	45,000
7.	Liverpool	H	2-1	Neave 2	30,000
8.	Bristol City	A	3-1	Bigden Ducat Neave	22,000
9.	Notts County	H	1-0	Coleman	25,000
10.	Sheffield United	A	2-4	Kyle Satterthwaite	18,816
11.	Bolton Wands	H	2-2	Satterthwaite 2	20,000
12.	Manchester Utd	A	0-1		25,000
13.	Stoke	H	2-1	Kyle Coleman	10,000
14.	Blackburn Rovers A	3-2		Freeman 2 Coleman	12,000
15.	Sunderland	H	0-1		20,000
16.	Birmingham	A	1-5	Sands	19,000
17.	Everton	H	3-1	Satterthwaite Kyle Coleman	12,000
18.	Derby County	A	0-0		7,000
19.	Bury	H	3-1	Kyle 2 Satterthwaite	8,000
20.	Manchester City	H	4-1	Coleman 2 Garbutt Kyle	15,000
21.	Sheffield Wed	A	1-1	Kyle	16,000
22.	Middlesbrough	A	3-5	Coleman Sharp Neave	15,000
23.	Preston NE	H	1-0	Coleman	12,000
24.	Newcastle United	A	0-1		35,000
25.	Liverpool	A	0-4		20,000
26.	Bristol City	H	1-2	Satterthwaite	18,000
27.	Sheffield United	H	0-1		12,000
28.	Manchester Utd	H	4-0	Satterthwaite 2 Kyle Coleman	6,000
29.	Bolton Wands	A	0-3		5,000
30.	Sheffield Wed	H	1-0	Satterthwaite	25,000
31.	Blackburn Rovers H	2-0		Sands Coleman	20,000
32.	Aston Villa	H	3-1	Garbutt Satterthwaite Freeman	20,000
33.	Sunderland	A	3-2	Freeman 2 Sands	12,000
34.	Everton	A	1-2	Satterthwaite	12,000
35.	Birmingham	H	2-1	Freeman Coleman	18,000
36.	Stoke	A	0-2		3,000
37.	Notts County	A	1-4	Freeman	3,000
38.	Derby County	H	3-2	Coleman Garbutt Freeman	2,000

Final League Position = 7th in Division One

♛ FA Cup ♛

1	Grimsby Town	A	1-1	Garbutt	10,000
R	Grimsby Town	H	3-0	Satterthwaite Sands Garbutt	13,269
2	Bristol City	H	2-1	Hynds Kyle	31,300
3	Bristol Rovers	H	1-0	Neave	22,000
4	Barnsley	A	2-1	Satterthwaite Neave	13,871
SF	Sheffield Wed*	N	1-3	Garbutt	36,000

* Played at St Andrew's, Birmingham

1907–08

1.	Notts County	H	1-1	Garbutt	10,000
2.	Bristol City	H	0-4		14,000
3.	Bury	A	2-3	Neave Kyle	10,000
4.	Notts County	A	0-2		10,000

5.	Manchester City	H	2-1	Sharp Coleman	12,000
6.	Preston NE	A	0-3		12,000
7.	Bury	H	0-0		14,000
8.	Aston Villa	A	1-0	Neave	25,000
9.	Liverpool	H	2-1	Lee 2	15,000
10.	Middlesbrough	A	0-0		18,000
11.	Sheffield United	H	5-1	Kyle 2 Coleman Neave C Satterthwaite	15,000
12.	Chelsea	A	1-2	C Satterthwaite	65,000
13.	Nottingham F	H	3-1	Kyle 2 Coleman	8,000
14.	Manchester Utd	A	2-4	Kyle Garbutt	15,000
15.	Blackburn Rovers	H	2-0	C Satterthwaite Sands	7,500
16.	Bolton Wands	A	1-3	Coleman	10,000
17.	Birmingham	H	1-1	Coleman	3,000
18.	Everton	A	1-1	Coleman	10,000
19.	Newcastle United	H	2-2	Kyle Freeman	25,000
20.	Sunderland	H	4-0	Lewis 2 Neave 2	6,000
21.	Sheffield Wed	A	0-6		9,000
22.	Sunderland	A	2-5	Kyle Neave	20,000
23.	Bristol City	A	2-1	Freeman Coleman	15,000
24.	Manchester City	A	0-4		25,000
25.	Preston NE	H	1-1	Sands	6,000
26.	Aston Villa	H	0-1		12,000
27.	Liverpool	A	1-4	Coleman	18,000
28.	Middlesbrough	H	4-1	Lewis 2 Lee Freeman	7,000
29.	Sheffield United	A	2-2	Freeman Lewis	8,000
30.	Chelsea	H	0-0		30,000
31.	Nottingham F	A	0-1		14,000
32.	Manchester Utd	H	1-0	Lee	18,000
33.	Blackburn Rovers	A	1-1	Ducat	12,000
34.	Bolton Wands	H	1-1	J Satterthwaite	10,000
35.	Birmingham	A	2-1	Lewis Lee	15,000
36.	Newcastle United	A	1-2	Neave	30,000
37.	Everton	H	2-1	Mordue Lewis	15,000
38.	Sheffield Wed	H	1-1	Lewis	16,000

Final League Position = 14th equal in Division One

♉ FA Cup ♉

1	Hull City	H	0-0		15,000
R	Hull City	A	1-4	Kyle	17,000

1908–09

1.	Everton	H	0-4		10,000
2.	Notts County	A	1-2	Neave	13,000
3.	Everton	A	3-0	Neave Lee Raybould	10,000
4.	Newcastle United	H	1-2	Greenaway	18,000
5.	Bristol City	A	1-2	Greenaway	16,000
6.	Preston NE	H	1-0	Fitchie	12,000
7.	Middlesbrough	A	1-1	Sands	20,000

8.	Manchester City	–	H	3-0	Raybould 2 Lee	12,000
9.	Liverpool		A	2-2	Satterthwaite Neave	20,000
10.	Bury		H	4-0	Raybould 3 Satterthwaite	9,500
11.	Sheffield United		A	1-1	Lee	15,000
12.	Aston Villa		H	0-1		20,000
13.	Nottingham F		A	1-0	Hoare	10,000
14.	Sunderland		H	0-4		12,000
15.	Chelsea		A	2-1	Greenaway Lewis	50,000
16.	Blackburn Rovers		H	0-1		12,000
17.	Bradford City		A	1-4	Fitchie	24,000
18.	Manchester Utd		H	0-1		10,000
19.	Leicester Fosse		A	1-1	Satterthwaite	16,000
20.	Leicester Fosse		H	2-1	Fitchie 2	20,000
21.	Sheffield Wed		A	2-6	Fitchie Hoare	12,000
22.	Notts County		H	1-0	Hoare	15,000
23.	Newcastle United		A	1-3	Fitchie	27,500
24.	Bristol City		H	1-1	Hoare	10,000
25.	Preston NE		A	0-0		8,000
26.	Manchester City		A	2-2	Lewis Ducat	20,000
27.	Liverpool		H	5-0	Beney 3 Satterthwaite (pen) Lewis	15,000
28.	Bury		A	1-1	Lewis	12,000
29.	Aston Villa		A	1-2	Fitchie	20,000
30.	Middlesbrough		H	1-1	Hoare	8,000
31.	Nottingham F		H	1-2	Neave	10,000
32.	Sunderland		A	0-1		7,500
33.	Sheffield United		H	1-0	Fitchie	6,000
34.	Chelsea		H	0-0		20,000
35.	Blackburn RoversA			3-1	Lee Neave Lewis	5,000
36.	Sheffield Wed		H	2-0	Lee Bartlett (og)	12,000
37.	Bradford City		H	1-0	Lee	14,000
38.	Manchester Utd		A	4-1	Lee 2 Fitchie Lewis	30,000

Final League Position = 6th in Division One

♛ FA Cup ♛

1	Croydon C*	A	1-1	Fitchie	16,578
R	CroydonC	H	2-0	Raybould Ducat	15,000
2	Millwall	H	1-1	Lewis	32,000
R	Millwall	A	0-1		16,285

* Played at the Crystal Palace, London

	1909–10					
1.	Aston Villa	A	1-5	Lewis	12,000
2.	Sheffield United	H	0-0		10,000
3.	Middlesbrough	A	2-5	Beney 2	12,000
4.	Bolton Wands	A	0-3		20,000
5.	Chelsea	H	3-2	Lee 2 Greenaway	15,000
6.	Blackburn Rovers	A	0-7		10,000
7.	Notts County	A	1-5	Neave	10,000

8.	Nottingham F	H	0-1		9,500
9.	Sunderland	A	2-6	Greenaway Lawrence	10,000
10.	Everton	H	1-0	Thomson	10,000
11.	Manchester Utd	A	0-1		20,000
12.	Bradford City	H	0-1		10,000
13.	Sheffield Wed	A	1-1	Lawrence	10,000
14.	Bristol City	H	2-2	Buckenham Greenaway	8,000
15.	Bury	A	2-1	Greenaway Steven	7,000
16.	Tottenham H	H	1-0	Lawrence	18,000
17.	Preston NE	A	4-3	Buckenham 2 Neave 2	6,000
18.	Notts County	H	1-2	Lewis	10,000
19.	Newcastle United	H	0-3		20,000
20.	Liverpool	H	1-1	McKellar	15,000
21.	Liverpool	A	1-5	Neave	25,000
22.	Sheffield United	A	0-2		17,000
23.	Middlesbrough	H	3-0	Buckenham Neave Lawrence	8,000
24.	Bolton Wands	H	2-0	Greenaway Ducat	7,000
25.	Blackburn Rovers	H	0-1		7,500
26.	Sunderland	H	1-2	Ducat	8,000
27.	Nottingham F	A	1-1	Buckenham	5,000
28.	Everton	A	0-1		6,000
29.	Manchester Utd	H	0-0		5,000
30.	Bradford City	A	1-0	Beney	14,000
31.	Newcastle United	A	1-1	Lewis	20,000
32.	Sheffield Wed	H	0-1		8,000
33.	Chelsea	A	1-0	McGibbon	40,000
34.	Bristol City	A	1-0	Lawrence	8,000
35.	Bury	H	0-0		10,000
36.	Aston Villa	H	1-0	McGibbon	8,000
37.	Tottenham H	A	1-1	McGibbon	39,800
38.	Preston NE	H	1-3	Ducat	10,000

Final League Position = 18th in Division One

♛ FA Cup ♛

1	Watford	H	3-0	McKellar Lewis 2	8,668
2	Everton	A	0-5		30,000

	1910–11				
1.	Manchester Utd	H	1-2	Rippon	15,000
2.	Bury	A	1-1	Rippon	10,000
3.	Sheffield United	H	0-0		14,000
4.	Aston Villa	A	0-3		20,000
5.	Sunderland	H	0-0		15,000
6.	Oldham Athletic	H	0-0		12,000
7.	Bradford City	A	0-3		26,000
8.	Blackburn Rovers	H	4-1	Neave 2 Lewis Chalmers	11,500
9.	Nottingham F	A	3-2	Chalmers 2 Greenaway	10,000
10.	Manchester City	H	0-1		10,000
11.	Everton	A	0-2		15,000

12.	Sheffield Wed	H	1-0	Chalmers	10,000
13.	Bristol City	A	1-0	Chalmers	8,000
14.	Newcastle United	H	1-2	Chalmers	14,000
15.	Tottenham H	A	1-3	Chalmers	16,000
16.	Middlesbrough	H	0-2		10,000
17.	Preston NE	A	1-4	Common	6,000
18.	Notts County	H	2-1	Chalmers Hoare	8,000
19.	Manchester Utd	A	0-5		35,000
20.	Bury	H	3-2	Ducat Hoare Chalmers	7,000
21.	Sheffield United	A	2-3	Hoare McGuire (og)	12,000
22.	Sunderland	A	2-2	Ducat (pen) Lewis	10,000
23.	Bradford City	H	0-0		10,000
24.	Blackburn Rovers	A	0-1		20,000
25.	Nottingham F	H	3-2	Ducat Chalmers Hoare	10,000
26.	Manchester City	A	1-1	Greenaway	20,000
27.	Oldham Athletic	A	0-3		7,000
28.	Everton	H	1-0	Chalmers	10,000
29.	Aston Villa	H	1-1	Hoare	6,000
30.	Sheffield Wed	A	0-0		7,000
31.	Bristol City	H	3-0	Common 2 Flanagan	10,977
32.	Newcastle United	A	1-0	Chalmers	18,000
33.	Tottenham H	H	2-0	Chalmers Common	24,583
34.	Liverpool	H	0-0		20,277
35.	Middlesbrough	A	1-1	Neave	14,000
36.	Liverpool	A	1-1	Chalmers	20,000
37.	Preston NE	H	2-0	Hoare Chalmers	9,092
38.	Notts County	A	2-0	Common 2	6,500

Final League Position = 10th in Division One

♔ FA Cup ♔

1	Clapton Orient	A	2-1	Chalmers Hoare	9,519
2	Swindon Town	A	0-1		14,861

1911–12

1.	Liverpool	H	2-2	Flanagan Chalmers	12,000
2.	Aston Villa	A	1-4	Common	24,000
3.	Newcastle United	H	2-0	Flanagan Common	17,000
4.	Sheffield United	A	1-2	Common	9,000
5.	Oldham Athletic	H	1-1	Lewis	11,000
6.	Bolton Wands	A	2-2	Chalmers 2	20,000
7.	Bradford City	H	2-0	Common Ducat	11,873
8.	Preston NE	A	1-0	Common	6,000
9.	Manchester City	A	3-3	Ducat Randall Common	25,000
10.	Everton	H	0-1		15,000
11.	West Brom Alb	A	1-1	Hoare	13,900
12.	Sunderland	H	3-0	Randall 3	3,000
13.	Blackburn Rovers	A	0-4		15,000
14.	Sheffield Wed	H	0-2		8,000
15.	Bury	A	1-3	Chalmers	10,000

16.	Middlesbrough	H	3-1	Chalmers 2 Randall	11,000
17.	Notts County	A	1-3	Calvert	6,000
18.	Tottenham H	A	0-5		47,100
19.	Tottenham H	H	3-1	Lewis Randall Winship	22,000
20.	Liverpool	A	1-4	Flanagan	16,000
21.	Manchester Utd	A	0-2		20,000
22.	Aston Villa	H	2-2	Winship Common	6,000
23.	Newcastle United	A	2-1	Common Flanagan	18,000
24.	Sheffield United	H	3-1	Common 2 Greenaway	10,299
25.	Bolton Wands	H	3-0	Flanagan Common Lewis	14,000
26.	Bradford City	A	1-1	Randall	10,000
27.	Middlesbrough	A	2-0	Common Ducat pen)	13,000
28.	Manchester City	H	2-0	Common Randall	12,000
29.	Oldham Athletic	A	0-0		8,000
30.	West Brom Alb	H	0-2		15,000
31.	Sunderland	A	0-1		5,000
32.	Everton	A	0-1		10,000
33.	Manchester Utd	H	2-1	Common 2	15,507
34.	Sheffield Wed	A	0-3		5,000
35.	Preston NE	H	4-1	Ducat Greenaway Common 2	10,066
36.	Bury	H	1-0	Ducat (pen)	8,000
37.	Blackburn RoversH	5-1		JW Grant 3 Flanagan 2	7,000
38.	Notts County	H	0-3		10,000

Final League Position = 10th in Division One

♈ FA Cup ♈

1	Bolton Wands	A	0-1		24,635

1912–13					
1.	Manchester Utd	H	0-0		10,000
2.	Liverpool	A	0-3		30,000
3.	Bolton Wands	H	1-2	Winship	13,000
4.	Aston Villa	H	0-3		6,805
5.	Sheffield United	A	3-1	Randall 2 McLaughlan	20,000
6.	Newcastle United	H	1-1	McLaughlan	18,000
7.	Oldham Athletic	A	0-0		7,500
8.	Chelsea	H	0-1		20,000
9.	Sunderland	H	1-3	McLaughlan	10,000
10.	Bradford City	A	1-3	Hanks	7,000
11.	Manchester City	H	0-4		8,000
12.	West Brom Alb	A	1-2	Greenaway	15,980
13.	Everton	H	0-0		10,000
14.	Sheffield Wed	A	0-2		14,000
15.	Blackburn Rovers	H	0-1		9,000
16.	Derby County	A	1-4	Flanagan	10,000
17.	Tottenham H	H	0-3		13,000
18.	Middlesbrough	A	0-2		10,000
19.	Notts County	H	0-0		7,000
20.	Notts County	A	1-2	Graham	12,000

21.	Liverpool	H	1-1	Graham (pen)	9,070
22.	Sunderland	A	1-4	Lewis	22,000
23.	Bolton Wands	A	1-5	Flanagan	10,000
24.	Sheffield United	H	1-3	Randall	6,000
25.	Newcastle United	A	1-3	Duncan	20,000
26.	Oldham Athletic	H	0-0		9,000
27.	Chelsea	A	1-1	Burrell	15,000
28.	Bradford City	H	1-1	Burrell	10,000
29.	Manchester City	A	1-0	Lewis	15,000
30.	West Brom Alb	H	1-0	Sands	8,000
31.	Manchester Utd	A	0-2		20,000
32.	Everton	A	0-3		10,000
33.	Aston Villa	A	1-4	Randall	30,000
34.	Sheffield Wed	H	2-5	Devine Grant	5,000
35.	Blackburn Rovers	A	1-1	Devine	6,000
36.	Derby County	H	1-2	Lewis	4,000
37.	Tottenham H	A	1-1	Grant	20,000
38.	Middlesbrough	H	1-1	Stonley	3,000

Final League Position = 20th in Division One

♆ FA Cup ♆

1	Croydon C	A	0-0		8,000
R	Croydon C	H	2-1	Duncan Graham	9,000
2	Liverpool	H	1-4	Lewis	8,653

	1913–14				
1.	Leicester Fosse	H	2-1	Jobey Devine (pen)	20,000
2.	Wolves	A	2-1	Winship Stonley (pen)	15,000
3.	Notts County	H	3-0	Stonley 2 Grant	20,000
4.	Hull City	H	0-0		25,000
5.	Barnsley	A	0-1		11,000
6.	Bury	H	0-1		30,000
7.	Huddersfield T	A	2-1	Stonley Burrell	8,000
8.	Lincoln City	H	3-0	Flanagan Stonley 2	25,000
9.	Blackpool	A	1-1	Jobey	18,000
10.	Nottingham F	H	3-2	Rutherford 2 Flanagan	25,000
11.	Fulham	A	1-6	Stonley	35,000
12.	Grimsby Town	A	1-1	Devine (pen)	8,000
13.	Birmingham	H	1-0	Flanagan	25,000
14.	Bristol City	A	1-1	Hardinge	15,000
15.	Leeds City	H	1-0	Benson (pen)	18,000
16.	Clapton Orient	A	0-1		27,000
17.	Glossop NE	H	2-0	Stonley Devine	14,500
18.	Bradford	A	3-2	Stonley 3	22,000
19.	Bradford	H	2-0	Flanagan Hardinge	30,000
20.	Leicester Fosse	A	2-1	Bell 2	10,000
21.	Notts County	A	0-1		7,000
22.	Wolves	H	3-1	Rutherford 2 Hardinge	20,000
23.	Hull City	A	2-1	Flanagan 2	10,000

24.	Barnsley	H	1-0	Rutherford	19,000
25.	Bury	A	1-1	Stonley	10,000
26.	Huddersfield T	H	0-1		25,000
27.	Lincoln City	A	2-5	Slade Hardinge	9,000
28.	Blackpool	H	2-1	Jobey Slade	20,000
29.	Nottingham F	A	0-0		10,000
30.	Fulham	H	2-0	Flanagan Slade	30,000
31.	Birmingham	A	0-2		18,000
32.	Bristol City	H	1-1	Winship	12,000
33.	Stockport County	A	0-2		15,000
34.	Leeds City	A	0-0		22,000
35.	Stockport County	H	4-0	Flanagan 2 Benson Rutherford	18,000
36.	Clapton Orient	H	2-2	Flanagan 2	35,000
37.	Grimsby Town	H	2-0	Stonley Flanagan	25,000
38.	Glossop NE	A	2-0	Slade Stapley (og)	4,000

Final League Position = 3rd in Division Two

♆ FA Cup ♆

| 1 | Bradford City | A | 0-2 | | 18,000 |

1914–15

1.	Glossop NE	H	3-0	King 2 Bradshaw	7,000
2.	Wolves	A	0-1		8,000
3.	Glossop NE	A	4-0	King 2 Flanagan Bradshaw	7,000
4.	Fulham	H	3-0	King 2 Rutherford	10,000
5.	Stockport County	A	1-1	King	6,000
6.	Hull City	H	2-1	Hardinge 2	20,000
7.	Leeds City	A	2-2	Bradshaw Hardinge	12,000
8.	Clapton Orient	H	2-1	King Bradshaw	30,000
9.	Blackpool	H	2-0	King 2	17,000
10.	Derby County	A	0-4		8,000
11.	Lincoln City	H	1-1	Hardinge	15,000
12.	Birmingham	A	0-3	15,000	
13.	Grimsby Town	H	6-0	King 3 Bradshaw Benson (pen) McKinnon	15,000
14.	Nottingham F	A	1-1	Benson (pen)	3,000
15.	Huddersfield T	A	0-3		9,000
16.	Bristol City	H	3-0	Hardinge 2 King	7,000
17.	Bury	A	1-3	Bradshaw	5,000
18.	Preston NE	H	1-2	Hardinge	10,000
19.	Leicester Fosse	A	4-1	Grant King Benson Blyth	13,000
20.	Leicester Fosse	H	6-0	Lewis 3 McKinnon King Flanagan	6,000
21.	Barnsley	A	0-1		5,000
22.	Wolves	H	5-1	King 4 Buckley	9,000
23.	Fulham	A	1-0	Bradshaw	10,000
24.	Stockport County	H	3-1	Flanagan 2 Bradshaw	6,000
25.	Leeds City	H	2-0	Rutherford Bradshaw	10,000
26.	Clapton Orient	A	0-1		4,000

27.	Blackpool	A	2-0	Winship King	6,000
28.	Derby County	H	1-2	King (pen)	18,000
29.	Lincoln City	A	0-1		6,000
30.	Birmingham	H	1-0	Bradshaw	19,000
31.	Grimsby Town	A	0-1		5,000
32.	Huddersfield T	H	0-3		14,000
33.	Hull City	A	0-1		8,000
34.	Bristol City	A	1-1	Winship	7,000
35.	Barnsley	H	1-0	Lewis	15,000
36.	Bury	H	3-1	Flanagan 2 Blyth	12,000
37.	Preston NE	A	0-3		14,000
38.	Nottingham F	H	7-0	Benson 2 King 4 Rutherford	10,000

Final League Position = 5th in Division Two

♆ FA Cup ♆

1	Merthyr Tydfil*	H	3-0	King 3	9,000
2	Chelsea	A	0-1		38,000

* Played at home by arrangement

1919–20

1.	Newcastle United	H	0-1		40,000
2.	Liverpool	A	3-2	White 2 Blyth	15,000
3.	Newcastle United	A	1-3	Groves	45,000
4.	Liverpool	H	1-0	Rutherford	20,000
5.	Sunderland	A	1-1	White	30,000
6.	Sunderland	H	3-2	White 3	42,000
7.	Blackburn Rovers	A	2-2	White Burgess	5,000
8.	Blackburn Rovers	H	0-1		30,000
9.	Everton	A	3-2	White 2 Blyth	35,000
10.	Everton	H	1-1	Groves	30,000
11.	Bradford City	H	1-2	Graham (pen)	35,000
12.	Bradford City	A	1-1	White	16,000
13.	Bolton Wands	H	2-2	Pagnam Rutherford	30,000
14.	Bolton Wands	A	2-2	Hardinge Pagnam	20,000
15.	Notts County	H	3-1	Pagnam 2 Toner	25,000
16.	Notts County	A	2-2	Buckley Pagnam	6,000
17.	Chelsea	H	1-1	White	50,000
18.	Chelsea	A	1-3	White	60,000
19.	Sheffield Wed	H	3-1	Hardinge Pagnam Butler	30,000
20.	Derby County	A	1-2	Pagnam (pen)	14,000
21.	Derby County	H	1-0	Groves	25,000
22.	Sheffield Wed	A	2-1	Hardinge White	23,000
23.	Manchester City	H	2-2	White Lewis	32,000
24.	Manchester City	A	1-4	Graham (pen)	25,000
25.	Aston Villa	H	0-1		55,000
26.	Oldham Athletic	H	3-2	North Graham Blyth	32,000
27.	Aston Villa	A	1-2	Graham (pen)	20,000
28.	Oldham Athletic	A	0-3		14,000
29.	Manchester Utd	H	0-3		25,000

30.	Manchester Utd	A	1-0	Rutherford	30,000
31.	Sheffield United	A	0-2		25,000
32.	Sheffield United	H	3-0	Graham Pagnam 2	35,000
33.	Middlesbrough	A	0-1		22,000
34.	Middlesbrough	H	2-1	Blyth Groves	25,000
35.	Burnley	A	1-2	Pagnam	20,000
36.	West Brom Alb	H	1-0	Blyth	40,000
37.	West Brom Alb	A	0-1		40,000
38.	Burnley	H	2-0	Bradshaw Pagnam	20,000
39.	Preston NE	A	1-1	White	13,000
40.	Preston NE	H	0-0		35,000
41.	Bradford	A	0-0		7,000
42.	Bradford	H	3-0	Groves Pagnam Bradshaw	30,000

Final League Position = 10th in Division One

♛ FA Cup ♛

1	Rochdale*	H	4-2	Rutherford Groves Graham Pagnam	26,596
2	Bristol City	A	0-1		25,900

* Played at home by arrangement

1920–21

1.	Aston Villa	A	0-5		50,000
2.	Manchester Utd	H	2-0	Pagnam Smith	25,000
3.	Aston Villa	H	0-1		45,000
4.	Manchester Utd	A	1-1	White	30,000
5.	Manchester City	H	2-1	Pagnam Groves	42,000
6.	Manchester City	A	1-3	Blyth	30,000
7.	Middlesbrough	H	2-0	Graham (pen) Pagnam	40,000
8.	Middlesbrough	A	1-2	White	25,000
9.	Bolton Wands	H	0-0		38,000
10.	Bolton Wands	A	1-1	White	35,000
11.	Derby County	A	1-1	White	18,000
12.	Derby County	H	2-0	Pagnam White	45,000
13.	Blackburn Rovers	A	2-2	McKinnon Buckley	20,000
14.	Blackburn Rovers	H	2-0	White Pagnam	40,000
15.	Huddersfield T	A	4-0	Pagnam 2 Blyth Graham (pen)	19,000
16.	Huddersfield T	H	2-0	Pagnam 2	35,000
17.	Chelsea	A	2-1	Pagnam 2	60,000
18.	Chelsea	H	1-1	Blyth	50,000
19.	Bradford City	A	1-3	Blyth	20,000
20.	Everton	A	4-2	White Toner Blyth Pagnam	35,000
21.	Everton	H	1-1	Pagnam	40,000
22.	Bradford City	H	1-2	Graham (pen)	20,000
23.	Tottenham H	A	1-2	Rutherford	39,721
24.	Tottenham H	H	3-2	Rutherford 2 White	60,600
25.	Sunderland	H	1-2	Pagnam	40,000
26.	Sunderland	A	1-5	Blyth	30,000
27.	Oldham Athletic	A	1-1	Graham (pen)	18,313
28.	Oldham Athletic	H	2-2	Rutherford Walden	40,000

29.	Preston NE	A	1-0	White	25,000
30.	Burnley	A	0-1		30,000
31.	Burnley	H	1-1	Baker (pen)	45,000
32.	Sheffield United	H	2-6	White Baker	30,000
33.	West Brom Alb	H	2-1	Graham (pen) Blyth	20,000
34.	West Brom Alb	A	4-3	North 2 Hopkins McKenzie	23,650
35.	Sheffield United	A	1-1	Rutherford	35,000
36.	Bradford	H	2-1	Toner Rutherford	30,000
37.	Bradford	A	1-0	Toner	14,000
38.	Newcastle United	H	1-1	Rutherford	20,000
39.	Preston NE	H	2-1	Hopkins McKinnon	12,000
40.	Newcastle United	A	0-1		35,000
41.	Liverpool	H	0-0		17,000
42.	Liverpool	A	0-3		20,000

Final League Position = 9th in Division One

♆ FA Cup ♆

1	Queen's Park R	A	0-2		18,000

1921–22

1.	Sheffield United	H	1-2	White	40,000
2.	Preston NE	A	2-3	White 2	25,000
3.	Sheffield United	A	1-4	White	25,000
4.	Preston NE	H	1-0	White	20,000
5.	Manchester City	A	0-2		25,000
6.	Manchester City	H	0-1		25,000
7.	Everton	A	1-1	Bradshaw	30,000
8.	Everton	H	1-0	White	35,000
9.	Sunderland	A	0-1		30,000
10.	Sunderland	H	1-2	Bradshaw	40,000
11.	Huddersfield T	A	0-2		12,000
12.	Huddersfield T	H	1-3	North	30,000
13.	Birmingham	A	1-0	North	30,000
14.	Birmingham	H	5-2	Whittaker Baker Hopkins 2 North	30,000
15.	Bolton Wands	A	0-1	20,000	
16.	Blackburn Rovers	A	1-0	Baker	25,000
17.	Blackburn Rovers	H	1-1	Hopkins	35,000
18.	Bolton Wands	H	1-1	Butler	10,000
19.	Oldham Athletic	A	1-2	Boreham	10,517
20.	Oldham Athletic	H	0-1		20,000
21.	Cardiff City	H	0-0		35,000
22.	Cardiff City	A	3-4	White Boreham 2	37,000
23.	Chelsea	A	2-0	White Boreham	40,000
24.	Chelsea	H	1-0	Boreham	40,000
25.	Burnley	H	0-0		23,000
26.	Newcastle United	H	2-1	Boreham Toner	30,000
27.	Newcastle United	A	1-3	Rutherford	30,000
28.	Burnley	A	0-1		15,000

29.	Liverpool	A	0-4		30,000
30.	Manchester Utd	A	0-1		25,000
31.	Aston Villa	A	0-2		30,000
32.	Liverpool	H	1-0	Baker	12,000
33.	Aston Villa	H	2-0	White Boreham	40,000
34.	Middlesbrough	H	2-2	White Boreham	30,000
35.	Manchester Utd	H	3-1	White Butler Boreham	25,000
36.	Middlesbrough	A	2-4	Baker White	20,000
37.	Tottenham H	A	0-2		40,394
38.	West Brom Alb	A	3-0	Boreham Young Graham	24,000
39.	West Brom Alb	H	2-2	White Graham (pen)	22,000
40.	Tottenham H	H	1-0	Graham (pen)	42,000
41.	Bradford City	A	2-0	White Young	35,000
42.	Bradford City	H	1-0	Blyth	32,000

Final League Position = 17th in Division One

♈ FA Cup ♈

1	Queen's Park R	H	0-0		31,000
R	Queen's Park R	A	2-1	Graham (pen) Milne	15,000
2	Bradford	A	3-2	White 2 Blyth	10,400
3	Leicester City	H	3-0	Rutherford White 2	39,421
4	Preston NE	H	1-1	White	37,517
R	Preston NE	A	1-2*	Blyth	30,000

* after extra-time

1922–23					
1.	Liverpool	A	2-5	Boreham Young	43,000
2.	Burnley	H	1-1	Young	25,000
3.	Liverpool	H	1-0	Hutchins	35,000
4.	Burnley	A	1-4	Hopkins	20,000
5.	Cardiff City	A	1-4	Whittaker	30,000
6.	Cardiff City	H	2-1	Young Boreham	40,000
7.	Tottenham H	A	2-1	Boreham 2	40,582
8.	Tottenham H	H	0-2		55,000
9.	Sheffield United	A	1-2	Boreham	15,000
10.	West Brom Alb	H	3-1	White Voysey Boreham	30,000
11.	West Brom Alb	A	0-7		21,730
12.	Newcastle United	A	1-1	Hopkins	30,000
13.	Newcastle United	H	1-2	Roe	35,000
14.	Everton	A	0-1		30,000
15.	Everton	H	1-2	Blyth	30,000
16.	Sunderland	A	3-3	Voysey 2 Turnbull	15,000
17.	Sunderland	H	2-3	Turnbull 2	30,000
18.	Birmingham	A	2-3	Voysey Turnbull	30,000
19.	Birmingham	H	1-0	Graham (pen)	30,000
20.	Huddersfield T	H	1-1	Rutherford	25,000
21.	Huddersfield T	A	0-4		10,000
22.	Bolton Wands	A	1-4	Turnbull	32,000
23.	Bolton Wands	H	5-0	Turnbull 4 Blyth	35,000

24.	Stoke	H	3-0	Blyth Boreham Turnbull	25,000
25.	Blackburn Rovers	A	5-0	Turnbull 4 Baker	20,000
26.	Stoke	A	0-1		15,000
27.	Manchester City	H	1-0	Turnbull	25,000
28.	Manchester City	A	0-0		30,000
29.	Nottingham F	A	1-2	Baker	15,000
30.	Nottingham F	H	2-0	Baker 2	20,000
31.	Chelsea	A	0-0		50,000
32.	Chelsea	H	3-1	Blyth 2 Baker	30,000
33.	Middlesbrough	A	0-2		20,000
34.	Middlesbrough	H	3-0	Turnbull 3	25,000
35.	Oldham Athletic	H	2-0	Blyth Freeman (og)	30,000
36.	Oldham Athletic	A	0-0		12,000
37.	Aston Villa	H	2-0	Baker Blyth	45,000
38.	Blackburn Rovers	H	1-1	McKenzie	32,000
39.	Aston Villa	A	1-1	Blyth	18,000
40.	Preston NE	H	1-1	Boreham	23,000
41	Preston NE	A	2-1	Earle Turnbull	15,000
42.	Sheffield United	H	2-0	Turnbull Blyth	25,000

Final League Position = 11th in Division One

♛ FA Cup ♛

1	Liverpool	A	0-0		37,000
R	Liverpool	H	1-4	Turnbull	39,000

1923–24

1.	Newcastle United	H	1-4	Turnbull	45,000
2.	West ham United	A	0-1		22,000
3.	Newcastle United	A	0-1		40,000
4.	West Brom Alb	A	0-4		25,000
5.	West Ham United	H	4-1	Earle 2 Woods Graham	36,000
6.	West Brom Alb	H	1-0	Voysey	36,004
7.	Birmingham	A	2-0	Turnbull Voysey	20,000
8.	Birmingham	H	0-0		35,000
9.	Manchester City	A	0-1		23,477
10.	Manchester City	H	1-2	Turnbull	32,000
11.	Bolton Wands	A	2-1	Woods Rutherford	20,000
12.	Bolton Wands	H	0-0		30,000
13.	Middlesbrough	H	2-1	Townrow Woods	25,000
14.	Middlesbrough	A	0-0		12,000
15.	Tottenham H	H	1-1	Townrow	50,000
16.	Tottenham H	A	0-3		31,624
17.	Blackburn Rovers	H	2-2	Young McIntyre (og)	20,000
18.	Blackburn Rovers	A	0-2		20,000
19.	Huddersfield T	H	1-3	Young	25,000
20.	Huddersfield T	A	1-6	Baker	15,000
21.	Notts County	A	2-1	Woods Blyth	25,000
22.	Notts County	H	0-0		16,000
23.	Chelsea	H	1-0	Turnbull	38,000

24.	Chelsea	A	0-0		38,000
25.	Cardiff City	H	1-2	Turnbull	30,000
26.	Cardiff City	A	0-4		20,000
27.	Sheffield United	A	1-3	Blyth	10,000
28.	Aston Villa	H	0-1		35,000
29.	Sheffield United	H	1-3	Milne	15,000
30.	Liverpool	H	3-1	Woods 2 Rutherford	35,000
31.	Aston Villa	A	1-2	Blyth	10,000
32.	Nottingham F	A	1-2	Ramsay	14,000
33.	Nottingham F	H	1-0	Neil	20,000
34.	Liverpool	A	0-0		30,000
35.	Burnley	H	2-0	Ramsay Neil	30,000
36.	Sunderland	H	2-0	Woods Haden	18,000
37.	Everton	A	1-3	Haden	30,000
38.	Sunderland	A	1-1	Woods	20,000
39.	Everton	H	0-1		25,000
40.	Preston NE	A	2-0	Haden Ramsay	12,000
41.	Burnley	A	1-4	Woods	9,000
42.	Preston NE	H	1-2	Turnbull	25,000

Final League Position = 19th in Division One

♆ FA Cup ♆

1	Luton Town	H	4-1	Blyth Woods Turnbull Milne	37,500
2	Cardiff City	A	0-1		35,000

1924–25					
1.	Nottingham F	A	2-0	Ramsay Woods	20,000
2.	Manchester City	H	1-0	Neil	25,000
3.	Liverpool	H	2-0	Woods 2	45,000
4.	Newcastle United	A	2-2	Rutherford Woods	30,000
5.	Manchester City	A	0-2		34,000
6.	Sheffield United	H	2-0	Butler Rutherford	40,000
7.	West Ham United	A	0-1		31,000
8.	Blackburn Rovers	H	1-0	Neil	40,000
9.	Huddersfield T	A	0-4		15,000
10.	Bury	H	0-1		20,000
11.	Aston Villa	H	1-1	Butler	40,000
12.	Tottenham H	H	1-0	Brain	51,000
13.	Bolton Wands	A	1-4	Brain	18,000
14.	Notts County	H	0-1		35,000
15.	Everton	A	3-2	Ramsay 2 Young	20,000
16.	Sunderland	H	0-0		35,000
17.	Cardiff City	A	1-1	Young	20,000
18.	Preston NE	H	4-0	Woods 3 Toner	30,000
19.	Burnley	A	0-1		6,000
20.	Leeds United	H	6-1	Brain 4 Woods Ramsay	30,000
21.	Birmingham	A	1-2	Woods	36,000
22.	Birmingham	H	0-1		40,000
23.	Nottingham F	H	2-1	Butler Ramsay	12,000

24.	Liverpool	A	1-2	Hoar	24,000
25.	Newcastle United	H	0-2		30,000
26.	Sheffield United	A	1-2	Ramsay	12,000
27.	Blackburn Rovers	A	0-1		20,000
28.	Huddersfield T	H	0-5		25,000
29.	Tottenham H	A	0-2		29,457
30.	Bolton Wands	H	1-0	Blyth	35,000
31.	Notts County	A	1-2	Brain	12,000
32.	Everton	H	3-1	Woods 2 Baker	20,000
33.	West Ham United	H	1-2	Baker	10,000
34.	Sunderland	A	0-2		18,000
35.	Aston Villa	A	0-4		10,000
36.	Cardiff City	H	1-1	Brain	35,000
37.	Preston NE	A	0-2		12,000
38.	West Brom Alb	A	0-2		24,000
39.	West Brom Alb	H	2-0	Brain John	21,000
40.	Burnley	H	5-0	Brain 3 Haden Woods	25,000
41.	Leeds United	A	0-1		20,000
42.	Bury	A	0-2		15,000

Final League Position = 20th in Division One

♔ FA Cup ♔

1	West Ham United	A	0-0		26,000
R	West Ham United	H	2-2*	Brain 2	34,160
2R	West Ham United	N**	0-1		36,955

* after extra-time   ** played at Stamford Bridge, London

1925–26

1.	Tottenham H	H	0-1		53,183
2.	Leicester City	H	2-2	Neil Brain	23,823
3.	Manchester Utd	A	1-0	Brain	32,288
4.	Leicester City	A	1-0	Brain	25,401
5.	Liverpool	H	1-1	Buchan	32,553
6.	Burnley	A	2-2	Haden Baker	12,334
7.	West Ham United	H	3-2	Buchan 2 Neil	24,800
8.	Leeds United	H	4-1	Brain 2 Buchan Neil	32,531
9.	Newcastle United	A	0-7		40,683
10.	West Ham United	A	4-0	Buchan 2 Brain 2	18,769
11.	Bolton Wands	H	2-3	Buchan Baker	41,076
12.	Cardiff City	H	5-0	Brain 3 Neil Blyth	38,130
13.	Sheffield United	A	0-4		27,555
14.	Everton	H	4-1	Brain 3 Hoar	24,926
15.	Manchester City	A	5-2	Brain 2 Buchan Hoar Haden	11,384
16.	Bury	H	6-1	Brain 3 Buchan 2 Baker	22,566
17.	Blackburn Rovers	A	3-2	Buchan Brain Rollo (og)	11,386
18.	Sunderland	H	2-0	Buchan Brain	44,870
19.	Huddersfield T	A	2-2	Neil Buchan	22,115
20.	West Brom Alb	H	1-0	Blyth	34,178
21.	Birmingham	A	0-1		26,843

22.	Notts County	H	3-0	Neil Buchan Hoar	33,398
23.	Notts County	A	1-4	Baker	32,045
24.	Tottenham H	A	1-1	Baker	42,221
25.	Manchester Utd	H	3-2	Brain 2 Buchan	25,252
26.	Liverpool	A	0-3		38,232
27.	Burnley	H	1-2	Buchan	14,800
28.	Leeds United	A	2-4	Brain Johnson (og)	26,239
29.	Newcastle United	H	3-0	Buchan Blyth Paterson	48,346
30.	Cardiff City	A	0-0		21,684
31.	Everton	A	3-2	Brain 3	30,515
32.	Sheffield United	H	4-0	Brain 2 Buchan Blyth	15,609
33.	Manchester City	H	1-0	Blyth	34,974
34.	Bury	A	2-2	Brain Hulme	18,078
35.	Aston Villa	A	0-3		26,177
36.	Blackburn Rovers	H	4-2	Baker Blyth Lawson Buchan	31,031
37.	Aston Villa	H	2-0	Brain 2	25,990
38.	Sunderland	A	1-2	Brain	20.990
39.	Huddersfield T	H	3-1	Lawson Hulme Parker (pen)	34,110
40.	West Brom Alb	A	1-2	Blyth	14,226
41.	Bolton Wands	A	1-1	Parker	22,198
42.	Birmingham	H	3-0	Brain 2 Parker (pen)	22,240

Final League Position = 2nd in Division One

♈ FA Cup ♈

3	Wolves	A	1-1	Brain	42,083
R	Wolves	H	1-0	Baker	42,823
4	Blackburn Rovers	H	3-1	Haden Brain Hope (og)	44,836
5	Aston Villa	A	1-1	Buchan	55,400
R	Aston Villa	H	2-0	Paterson Brain	71,446
6	Swansea Town	A	1-2	Mackie	25,198

1926–27					
1.	Derby County	H	2-1	Parker (pen) Buchan	32,990
2.	Bolton Wands	H	2-1	Hulme 2	23,002
3.	Sheffield United	A	0-4		21,942
4.	Bolton Wands	A	2-2	Brain Hulme	19,717
5.	Leicester City	H	2-2	Brain Hulme	30,800
6.	Manchester Utd	A	2-2	Brain 2	15,259
7.	Liverpool	H	2-0	Brain Hoar	35,497
8.	Leeds United	A	1-4	Buchan	20,544
9.	Newcastle United	H	2-2	Buchan Parker (pen)	38,842
10.	Burnley	A	0-2		17,709
11.	West Ham United	H	2-2	Lambert Brain	35,534
12.	Sheffield Wed	H	6-2	Brain 4 Haden 2	27,846
13.	Everton	A	1-3	Brain	34,153
14.	Blackburn Rovers	H	2-2	Buchan Brain	29,439
15.	Huddersfield T	A	3-3	Blyth Haden Ramsay	16,219
16.	Sunderland	H	2-3	Buchan Ramsay	20,087
17.	West Brom Alb	A	3-1	Hulme Haden Brain	20,815

18.	Bury	H	1-0	Brain	30,375
19.	Birmingham	A	0-0		22,982
20.	Tottenham H	H	2-4	Butler Brain	49,429
21.	Cardiff City	A	0-2		25,386
22.	Manchester Utd	H	1-0	Blyth	30,111
23.	Cardiff City	H	3-2	Brain 3	30,000
24.	Derby County	A	2-0	Buchan Parker	21,999
25.	Sheffield United	H	1-1	Buchan	16,831
26.	Liverpool	A	0-3		30,618
27.	Leicester City	A	1-2	Brain	16,736
28.	Leeds United	H	1-0	Buchan	25,961
29.	Burnley	H	6-2	Brain 4 Buchan Hoar	29,070
30.	West Ham United	A	0-7		11,764
31.	Sheffield Wed	A	2-4	Buchan Brain	21,252
32.	Everton	H	1-2	Buchan	33,788
33.	Huddersfield T	H	0-2		24,409
34.	Newcastle United	A	1-6	Buchan	33,635
35.	Sunderland	A	1-5	Shaw	23,163
36.	Aston Villa	H	2-1	Brain 2	38,096
37.	West Brom Alb	H	4-1	Brain Parker (pen) Buchan 2	24,506
38.	Aston Villa	A	3-2	John 2 Barley	22,542
39.	Blackburn Rovers	A	2-1	Hulme Brain	13,833
40.	Birmingham	H	3-0	Brain Tricker John	22,619
41.	Bury	A	2-3	Hulme 2	8,513
42.	Tottenham H	A	4-0	Brain 2 Tricker 2	29,555

Final League Position = 11th in Division One

♛ FA Cup ♛

3	Sheffield United	A	3-2	Brain Buchan Hulme	28,137
4	Port Vale	A	2-2	Buchan Brain	18,000
R	Port Vale	H	1-0	Buchan	35,781
5	Liverpool	H	2-0	Brain Buchan	43,000
6	Wolves	H	2-1	Blyth Butler	52,821
SF	Southampton*	N	2-1	Hulme Buchan	52,133
F	Cardiff City**	N	0-1		91,206

** played at Stamford Bridge, London ** played at Wembley Stadium.*

	1927–28				
1.	Bury	A	1-5	Brain	17,614
2.	Burnley	H	4-1	Buchan Brain 2 Blyth	19,910
3.	Sheffield United	H	6-1	Hulme Blyth Buchan 2 Brain Parker	30,910
4.	Burnley	A	2-1	Blyth Brain	14,668
5.	Aston Villa	A	2-2	Blyth 2	42,136
6.	Sunderland	H	2-1	Baker Brain	45,501
7.	Derby County	A	0-4		16,539
8.	West Ham United	H	2-2	Brain 2	34,931
9.	Portsmouth	A	3-2	Blyth Hulme Brain	27,261
10.	Leicester City	H	2-2	Brain Hoar	36,640

11.	Sheffield Wed	A	1-1	Buchan	12,698
12.	Bolton Wands	H	1-2	Buchan	35,787
13.	Blackburn Rovers	A	1-4	Parker (pen)	9,656
14.	Middlesbrough	H	3-1	Buchan 2 Hulme	25,921
15.	Birmingham	A	1-1	Hoar	10,030
16.	Huddersfield T	A	1-2	Brain	15,140
17.	Newcastle United	H	4-1	Hulme Brain Parker Hoar	42,630
18.	Manchester Utd	A	1-4	Wilson (og)	18,120
19.	Everton	H	3-2	Hulme Buchan Blyth	27,995
20.	Liverpool	A	2-0	Hoar Brain	41,024
21.	Bury	H	3-1	Lambert John Parker (pen)	20,742
22.	Tottenham H	H	1-1	Hoar	13,518
23.	Sheffield United	A	4-6	Hoar 2 Brain 2	18,158
24.	Aston Villa	H	0-3		32,505
25.	Derby County	H	3-4	Brain 3	21,405
26.	West Ham United	A	2-2	Brain 2	28,086
27.	Leicester City	A	2-3	Hoar Buchan	25,835
28.	Liverpool	H	6-3	Brain 3 Hulme Buchan Lambert	14,037
29.	Bolton Wands	A	1-1	Buchan	15,546
30.	Sunderland	A	1-5	Lambert	9,478
31.	Blackburn Rovers	H	3-2	Buchan 2 Hoar	33,446
32.	Portsmouth	H	0-2		15,416
33.	Birmingham	H	2-2	Buchan 2	13,990
34.	Cardiff City	H	3-0	Hulme Buchan Brain	36,828
35.	Tottenham H	A	0-2		39,193
36.	Cardiff City	A	2-2	Tricker 2	17,699
37.	Huddersfield T	H	0-0		38,707
38.	Middlesbrough	A	2-2	Baker Hulme	16,731
39.	Newcastle United	A	1-1	Shaw	22,819
40.	Manchester Utd	H	0-1		22,452
41.	Sheffield Wed	H	1-1	Brain	15,818
42.	Everton	A	3-3	Shaw 2 O'Donnell (og)	48,715

Final League Position = 10th in Division One

♆ FA Cup ♆

3	West Brom Alb	H	2-0	Brain Hulme	43,322
4	Everton	H	4-3	Hulme 2 Brain Buchan	44,328
5	Aston Villa	H	4-1	Blyth 2 Lambert Hulme	58,505
6	Stoke City	H	4-1	Blyth 2 Hoar 2	41,974
SF	Blackburn Rovers	N*	0-1		25,633

* played at Filbert Street, Leicester

1928–29					
1.	Sheffield Wed	A	2-3	Jones Brain	23,684
2.	Derby County	H	1-3	Blyth	20,064
3.	Bolton Wands	H	2-0	Peel Brain	35,124
4.	Portsmouth	A	0-2		24,846
5.	Birmingham	H	0-0		30,118
6.	Manchester City	A	1-4	Brain	36,223

7.	Derby County	A	0-0		16,754
8.	Huddersfield T	H	2-0	Lambert John	39,938
9.	Everton	A	2-4	Brain Jones	37,846
10.	West Ham United	H	2-3	Jones 2	43,327
11.	Newcastle United	A	3-0	Thompson 2 (1 pen) Brain	30,121
12.	Liverpool	H	4-4	Thompson 2 (1 pen) Brain Davidson (og)	33,782
13.	Cardiff City	A	1-1	Jones	18,757
14.	Sheffield United	H	2-0	Hulme Jack	28,560
15.	Bury	A	0-1		10,957
16.	Aston Villa	H	2-5	Jack 2	30,491
17.	Leicester City	A	1-1	Brain	26,851
18.	Manchester Utd	H	3-1	Jack 2 Brain	18,923
19.	Leeds United	A	1-1	Brain	20,293
20.	Burnley	H	3-1	Hulme Peel Brain	14,990
21.	Blackburn Rovers	A	2-5	Jack Brain	30,828
22.	Sunderland	H	1-1	Peel	15,747
23.	Sheffield Wed	H	2-2	Brain Hulme	39,255
24.	Sunderland	A	1-5	Parkin	32,843
25.	Bolton Wands	A	2-1	Jack 2	17,597
26.	Portsmouth	H	4-0	Jack 2 Peel Brain	32,224
27.	Manchester City	H	0-0		13,764
28.	Huddersfield T	A	1-0	Jack	14,697
29.	West Ham United	A	4-3	Brain Jack Hoar Hulme	28,931
30.	Liverpool	A	4-2	Hulme 2 Brain Jones	26,195
31.	Birmingham	A	1-1	Jack	11,001
32.	Cardiff City	H	2-1	Brain Jack	28,393
33.	Sheffield United	A	2-2	Parker (pen) Jack	20,266
34.	Blackburn Rovers	H	1-0	Brain	39,038
35.	Bury	H	7-1	Jack 4 Parkin 2 Thompson	22,577
36.	Newcastle United	H	1-2	Jack	21,699
37.	Aston Villa	A	2-4	Brain Jack	26,664
38.	Leicester City	H	1-1	Parker (pen)	19,139
39.	Manchester Utd	A	1-4	Jack	22,858
40.	Everton	H	2-0	Jack Parker (pen)	11,696
41.	Leeds United	H	1-0	Peel	21,465
42.	Burnley	A	3-3	Jack 2 Brain	7,400

Final League Position = 9th in Division One

♛ FA Cup ♛

3	Stoke City	H	2-1	Brain Hulme	30,762
4	Mansfield Town	H	2-0	Jack Peel	44,493
5	Swindon Town	A	0-0	.	16,692
R	Swindon Town	H	1-0	Brain	44,582
6	Aston Villa	A	0-1		73,300

	1929–30				
1.	Leeds United	H	4-0	Jack 2 Hulme Parker (pen)	41,885
2.	Manchester City	A	1-3	Jack	38,458

3.	Sheffield Wed	A	2-0	Jack Hulme	31,735
4.	Manchester City	H	3-2	Jack 2 Johnstone	23,057
5.	Burnley	H	6-1	Lambert 2 Hulme	38,556
				Jack James Waterfield (og)	
6.	Sunderland	A	1-0	Lambert	34,804
7.	Aston Villa	A	2-5	James Thompson	33,850
8.	Bolton Wands	H	1-2	Jones	42,723
9.	Everton	A	1-1	Hulme	45,015
10.	Derby County	H	1-1	Parker (pen)	42,448
11.	Grimsby Town	H	4-1	Lambert 3 Hulme	43,794
12.	Manchester Utd	A	0-1		12,662
13.	West Ham United	H	0-1		44,828
14.	Birmingham	A	3-2	Hulme 2 Jack	33,904
15.	Blackburn Rovers	A	1-1	Halliday	25,591
16.	Middlesbrough	H	1-2	Jack	28,326
17.	Newcastle United	H	0-1		40,365
18.	Huddersfield T	H	2-0	Hulme Jack	34,097
19.	Sheffield United	A	1-4	Halliday	16,134
20.	Liverpool	A	0-1		32,819
21.	Portsmouth	A	1-0	James	27,475
22.	Portsmouth	H	1-2	Hulme	49,433
23.	Leeds United	A	0-2		29,167
24.	Sheffield Wed	H	2-3	Bastin Parker	40,766
25.	Burnley	A	2-2	Bastin Jack	22,566
26.	Bolton Wands	A	0-0		27,336
27.	Everton	H	4-0	Lambert 3 Williams	27,302
28.	Derby County	A	1-4	Halliday	11,136
29.	Grimsby Town	A	1-1	Lambert	17,151
30.	West Ham United	A	2-3	Jack 2	31,268
31.	Manchester Utd	H	4-2	Bastin Williams Lambert Hulme	18,082
32.	Birmingham	H	1-0	James	32,174
33.	Blackburn Rovers	H	4-0	Williams Hulme Lambert 2	40,459
34.	Liverpool	H	0-1		18,824
35.	Newcastle United	A	1-1	Halliday	36,309
36.	Middlesbrough	A	1-1	Hulme	9,287
37.	Sheffield United	H	8-1	Lambert 3 Johnstone	24,217
				2 Hulme Bastin James	
38.	Leicester City	H	1-1	James	46,663
39.	Huddersfield T	A	2-2	Bastin Hulme	11,988
40.	Leicester City	A	6-6	Halliday 4 Bastin 2	27,241
41.	Sunderland	H	0-1		31,250
42.	Aston Villa	H	2-4	Lambert 2	37,020

Final League Position = 14th in Division One

♈ FA Cup ♈

3	Chelsea	H	2-0	Lambert Bastin	55,579
4	Birmingham	H	2-2	Bastin Jack	43,274
R	Birmingham	A	1-0	Baker (pen)	47,521
5	Middlesbrough	A	2-0	Lambert Bastin	42,073

6	West Ham United	A	3-0	Lambert 2 Baker	40,797
SF	Hull City*	N	2-2	Jack Bastin	47,549
R	Hull City**	N	1-0	Jack	46,200
F	Huddersfield T***N	2-0		Lambert James	92,486

*played at Elland Road Leeds   ** played at Villa Park, Birmingham   *** played at Wembley Stadium*

1930–31

1.	Blackpool	A	4-1	Bastin 2 (1 pen) Jack 2	28,723
2.	Bolton Wands	A	4-1	Lambert 3 Hulme	20,684
3.	Leeds United	H	3-1	Lambert 2 Jack	40,828
4.	Blackburn Rovers	H	3-2	Bastin 2 Johnstone	20,863
5.	Sunderland	A	4-1	Lambert 3 Hulme	26,525
6.	Blackburn Rovers	A	2-2	Hulme Lambert	25,572
7.	Leicester City	H	4-1	Hulme Lambert 2 Bastin	37,851
8.	Birmingham	A	4-2	Lambert 3 Bastin	31,693
9.	Sheffield United	H	1-1	Lambert	47,113
10.	Derby County	A	2-4	Bastin Roberts	29,783
11.	Manchester Utd	A	2-1	Williams Lambert	23,406
12.	West Ham United	H	1-1	Bastin	51,918
13.	Huddersfield T	A	1-1	Jack	25,772
14.	Aston Villa	H	5-2	Bastin 2 Jack 2 Lambert	56,417
15.	Sheffield Wed	A	2-1	Lambert 2	43,671
16.	Middlesbrough	H	5-3	Lambert 3 Bastin 2 (1 pen)	32,517
17.	Chelsea	A	5-1	Jack 3 Lambert Williams	74,667
18.	Liverpool	A	1-1	Jack	44,342
19.	Newcastle United	H	1-2	Jack	32,212
20.	Manchester City	A	4-2	Bastin Jack Lambert Hulme	56,750
21.	Manchester City	H	3-1	Hulme Bastin John	17,624
22.	Blackpool	H	7-1	Jack 3 Brain 3 Bastin	35,113
23.	Sunderland	H	1-3	James	35,975
24.	Grimsby Town	H	9-1	Jack 4 Lambert 3 Bastin Hulme	15,751
25.	Birmingham	H	1-1	Lambert	30,913
26.	Leicester City	A	7-2	Lambert 3 Bastin 2 Jack Hulme	17,416
27.	Sheffield United	A	1-1	Hulme	49,602
28.	Derby County	H	6-3	Bastin 3 (1 pen) James Hulme Jack	34,785
29.	Manchester Utd	H	4-1	Hulme Jack Brain Bastin	41,510
30.	West Ham United	A	4-2	John Jack 2 Bastin	30,361
31.	Huddersfield T	H	0-0	31,058	
32.	Leeds United	A	2-1	Bastin James	12,212
33.	Aston Villa	A	1-5	Jack	60,997
34.	Sheffield Wed	H	2-0	Jack Bastin	47,872
35.	Middlesbrough	A	5-2	Lambert 3 Jack 2	23,476
36.	Portsmouth	A	1-1	Bastin	31,398
37.	Chelsea	H	2-1	Hulme Bastin	53,867
38.	Portsmouth	H	1-1	James	40,490
39.	Grimsby Town	A	1-0	Lambert	22,394
40.	Liverpool	H	3-1	Lambert Bastin Jack	39,143
41.	Newcastle United	A	3-1	Jones Hulme 2	21,747
42.	Bolton Wands	H	5-0	Lambert 2 Jack 2 James	35,406

Final League Position = 1st in Division One

♛ FA Cup ♛

3	Aston Villa	H	2-2	Lambert Jack	40,864
R	Aston Villa	A	3-1	Hulme 2 Jack	73,668
4	Chelsea	A	1-2	Bastin	62,945

1931–32

1.	West Brom Alb	H	0-1		52,478
2.	Blackburn Rovers	A	1-1	Hulme	22,138
3.	Birmingham	A	2-2	Lambert Hulme	26,810
4.	Portsmouth	H	3-3	Lambert 2 Bastin	25,403
5.	Sunderland	H	2-0	Hulme 2	22,926
6.	Portsmouth	A	3-0	Bastin 2 Parkin	22,977
7.	Manchester City	A	3-1	Jack 2 Lambert	46,756
8.	Everton	H	3-2	Hulme Jack Lambert	47,637
9.	Grimsby Town	A	1-3	Lambert	17,840
10.	Blackpool	A	5-1	Bastin 3 (1 pen) Hulme Lambert	29,516
11.	Bolton Wands	H	1-1	Hulme	42,141
12.	Leicester City	A	2-1	Jack Osborne (og)	26,233
13.	Aston Villa	H	1-1	Jack	54,951
14.	Newcastle United	A	2-3	Lambert Jack	28,949
15.	West Ham United	H	4-1	Jack 3 Hulme	41,028
16.	Chelsea	A	1-2	Jack	64,427
17.	Liverpool	H	6-0	Jack 2 Lambert 3 Hulme	29,220
18.	Sheffield Wed	A	3-1	Jack 2 Bastin	27,265
19.	Huddersfield T	H	1-1	Jack	39,748
20.	Middlesbrough	A	5-2	Jack 2 Bastin 2 Lambert	17,083
21.	Sheffield United	A	1-4	Hulme	49,737
22.	Sheffield United	H	0-2		55,207
23.	West Brom Alb	A	0-1		25,823
24.	Birmingham	H	3-0	Hulme Bastin Booton (og)	37,843
25.	Manchester City	H	4-0	Parkin 3 James	39,834
26.	Everton	A	3-1	Bastin Hulme John	56,698
27.	Grimsby Town	H	4-0	Bastin Jack Parkin James	20,980
28.	Blackpool	H	2-0	Jack Parkin	39,045
29.	Bolton Wands	A	0-1		20,922
30.	Leicester City	H	2-1	Bastin (pen) Hulme	53,920
31.	Newcastle United	H	1-0	Hulme	57,516
32.	Derby County	H	2-1	Lambert 2	56,435
33.	West Ham United	A	1-1	Lambert	34,852
34.	Derby County	A	1-1	Jack	25,790
35.	Chelsea	H	1-1	Lambert	56,124
36.	Sunderland	A	0-2		30,443
37.	Liverpool	A	1-2	Lambert	30,100
38.	Sheffield Wed	H	3-1	John 2 Jack	25,220
39.	Aston Villa	A	1-1	Parkin	25,959
40.	Huddersfield T	A	2-1	Coleman Lambert	13,370
41.	Middlesbrough	H	5-0	Bastin 2 Lambert 2 Webster (og)	30,714
42.	Blackburn Rovers	H	4-0	Lambert 2 Stockill Hutton (og)	23,127

Final League Position = 2nd in Division One

♏ FA Cup ♏

3	Darwen	H	11-1	Bastin 4 Jack 3 Lambert 2 Hulme 2	37,486
4	Plymouth Argyle	H	4-2	Lambert 2 Hulme Roberts (og)	65,386
5	Portsmouth	A	2-0	Bastin Hulme	38,918
6	Huddersfield T	A	1-0	Roberts	67,037
SF	Manchester City	N*	1-0	Bastin	50,337
F	Newcastle United	N**	1-2	John	92,298

*played at Villa Park, Birmingham ** played at Wembley Stadium*

1932–33

1.	Birmingham	A	1-0	Stockill	31,592
2.	West Brom Alb	H	1-2	Stockill	37,748
3.	Sunderland	H	6-1	Hulme 3 Coleman Jack Bastin	28,896
4.	Manchester City	A	3-2	Jack Coleman 2	36,542
5.	West Brom Alb	A	1-1	Jack	45,038
6.	Bolton Wands	H	3-2	Hulme Coleman Bastin	42,395
7.	Everton	H	2-1	Jack Coleman	51,182
8.	Blackpool	A	2-1	Bastin Coleman	30,218
9.	Derby County	H	3-3	Coleman 2 Hulme	32,055
10.	Blackburn Rovers	A	3-2	Bastin Jack Coleman	28,799
11.	Liverpool	A	3-2	Bastin 2 Coleman	38,548
12.	Leicester City	H	8-2	Hulme 3 Bastin 2 Coleman 2 Jack	36,714
13.	Wolves	A	7-1	Jack 3 Bastin 2 Lambert 2	43,570
14.	Newcastle United	H	1-0	Hulme	56,498
15.	Aston Villa	A	3-5	Jack Lambert Bastin	58,066
16.	Middlesbrough	H	4-2	Coleman 2 Hulme Jack	34,640
17.	Portsmouth	A	3-1	Bastin 2 Jack	31,401
18.	Chelsea	H	4-1	Bastin 2 Coleman Hulme	53,206
19.	Huddersfield T	A	1-0	Coleman	23,198
20.	Sheffield United	H	9-2	Lambert 5 Bastin 3 Jack	41,520
21.	Leeds United	H	1-2	Hulme	55,876
22.	Leeds United	A	0-0		56,776
23.	Birmingham	H	3-0	Jack James Bastin	37,800
24.	Sheffield Wed	A	2-3	Jack Bastin (pen)	64,492
25.	Sunderland	A	2-3	Lambert 2	36,707
26.	Manchester City	H	2-1	Bastin 2	32,456
27.	Bolton Wands	A	4-0	Coleman 3 Bastin	13,401
28.	Everton	A	1-1	Coleman	55,463
29.	Blackpool	H	1-1	Coleman	35,180
30.	Derby County	A	2-2	Jack Bastin	23,148
31.	Blackburn Rovers	H	8-0	Coleman 3 Hulme 2 Bastin 2 Stockill	27,576
32.	Liverpool	H	0-1		42,868
33.	Leicester City	A	1-1	James	32,228
34.	Wolves	H	1-2	Bowden	44,711
35.	Newcastle United	A	1-2	Hulme	51,215
36.	Aston Villa	H	5-0	Lambert 2 Jack Bowden James	54,265
37.	Middlesbrough	A	4-3	Hulme 3 Bastin	22,137

38.	Sheffield Wed	H	4-2	Hulme 2 Lambert Bastin	61,945
39.	Portsmouth	H	2-0	Lambert Bastin	42,809
40.	Chelsea	A	3-1	Bastin 2 Jack	72,260
41.	Huddersfield T	H	2-2	Bastin 2	30,799
42.	Sheffield United	A	1-3	Hill	18,620

Final League Position = 1st in Division One

♔ FA Cup ♔

| 3 | Walsall | A | 0-2 | | 11,150 |

1933–34					
1.	Birmingham	H	1-1	Jack	44,662
2.	Sheffield Wed	A	2-1	Bastin Jack	23,186
3.	West Brom Alb	H	3-1	Bastin 2 (1 pen) Lambert	34,688
4.	Manchester City	H	1-1	Coleman	43,412
5.	West Brom Alb	A	0-1		29,429
6.	Tottenham H	A	1-1	Bowden	56,612
7.	Everton	A	1-3	Bowden	53,792
8.	Middlesbrough	H	6-0	Birkett 2 Jack 2 Bastin Bowden	28,293
9.	Balckburn Rovers	A	2-2	Bastin Bowden	31,636
10.	Newcastle United	H	3-0	Birkett Bowden Fairhurst (og)	32,821
11.	Leicester City	H	2-0	Dunne 2	44,014
12.	Aston Villa	A	3-2	Dunne 2 Bastin	54,323
13.	Portsmouth	H	1-1	Bastin	51,765
14.	Wolves	A	1-0	Bowden	37,210
15.	Stoke City	H	3-0	Hulme Dunne John	32,972
16.	Huddersfield T	A	1-0	Dunne	29,407
17.	Liverpool	H	2-1	Hulme Dunne	38,362
18.	Sunderland	A	0-3		35,166
19.	Chelsea	H	2-1	Beasley 2	43,897
20.	Sheffield United	A	3-1	Beasley 2 Bowden	31,453
21.	Leeds United	A	1-0	Bastin	33,193
22.	Leeds United	H	2-0	Bowden Dunne	22,817
23.	Birmingham	A	0-0		34,771
24.	Sheffield Wed	H	1-1	Dunne	45,156
25.	Manchester City	A	1-2	Beasley	60,401
26.	Tottenham H	H	1-3	Bastin	68,828
27.	Everton	H	1-2	Birkett	24,025
28.	Middlesbrough	A	2-0	Birkett Bowden	15,894
29.	Blackburn Rovers	H	2-1	Bastin Beasley	29,886
30.	Newcastle United	A	1-0	Beasley	40,065
31.	Leicester City	A	1-4	Bowden	23,976
32.	Aston Villa	H	3-2	Jack Roberts Hulme	41,169
33.	Wolves	H	3-2	Drake James Bastin	41,143
34.	Derby County	H	1-0	James	69,070
35.	Stoke City	A	1-1	Bastin	43,163
36.	Derby County	A	4-2	Drake 2 Bowden 2	32,180
37.	Huddersfield T	H	3-1	Beasley Bowden Drake	55,930
38.	Liverpool	A	3-2	Beasley Hulme 2	43,027

39.	Portsmouth	A	0-1		28,442
40.	Sunderland	H	2-1	Drake Beasley	37,783
41.	Chelsea	A	2-2	James Bastin	65,344
42.	Sheffield United	H	2-0	Drake 2	25,265

Final League Position = 1st in Division One

♆ FA Cup ♆

3	Luton Town	A	1-0	Dunne	18,641
4	Crystal Palace	H	7-0	Dunne 2 Bastin 2 Beasley 2 Birkett	56,177
5	Derby County	H	1-0	Jack	66,905
6	Aston Villa	H	1-2	Dougall	67,366

	1934–35				
1.	Portsmouth	A	3-3	Bowden Drake Bastin	39,710
2.	Liverpool	H	8-1	Drake 3 Bowden 3 Bastin Crayston	54,062
3.	Blackburn Rovers	H	4-0	Drake 2 Bowden Bastin	39,654
4.	Leeds United	A	1-1	Drake	29,447
5.	West Brom Alb	H	4-3	Bowden James Bastin Drake	40,016
6.	Blackburn Rovers	A	0-2		25,472
7.	Sheffield Wed	A	0-0		24,751
8.	Birmingham	H	5-1	Drake 4 Bastin	47,868
9.	Stoke City	A	2-2	Bastin 2	45,348
10.	Manchester City	H	3-0	Bowden 2 Bastin	68,145
11.	Tottenham H	H	5-1	Drake 3 Beasley T Evans (og)	70,544
12.	Sunderland	A	1-2	Drake	43,744
13.	Everton	H	2-0	Bastin 2	50,350
14.	Grimsby Town	A	2-2	Drake Hulme	26,288
15.	Aston Villa	H'	1-2	Bastin (pen)	54,226
16.	Chelsea	A	5-2	Drake 4 Hulme	43,419
17.	Wolves	H	7-0	Drake 4 Birkett 2 Bowden	39,532
18.	Huddersfield T	A	1-1	Roughton (og)	36,113
19.	Leicester City	H	8-0	Drake 3 Hulme 3 Bastin 2	23,689
20.	Derby County	A	1-3	Bowden	26,091
21.	Preston NE	H	5-3	Hulme 2 Bowden Bastin Hough (og)	40,201
22.	Preston NE	A	1-2	Hill	39,411
23.	Portsmouth	H	1-1	Drake	36,054
24.	Liverpool	A	2-0	Drake Hapgood	55,794
25.	Leeds United	H	3-0	Bowden 2 Bastin	37,026
26.	West Brom Alb	A	3-0	Drake Bastin Hulme	30,713
27.	Sheffield Wed	H	4-1	James 3 Bastin	57,922
28.	Birmingham	A	0-3		50,188
29.	Stoke City	H	2-0	Davidson Hill	27,067
30.	Manchester City	A	1-1	Bowden	79,491
31.	Tottenham H	A	6-0	Kirchen 2 Drake 2 Dougall Bastin (pen)	47,714
32.	Sunderland	H	0-0		73,295
33.	Everton	A	2-0	Moss Drake	50,389

34.	Grimsby Town	H	1-1	Drake	33,591
35.	Aston Villa	A	3-1	Beasley Drake Bastin (pen)	59,572
36.	Chelsea	H	2-2	Drake Compton (pen)	54,020
37.	Wolves	A	1-1	Hill	40,888
38.	Middlesbrough	H	8-0	Drake 4 Rogers 2 Bastin Beasley	45,719
39.	Huddersfield T	H	1-0	Beasley	41,892
40.	Middlesbrough	A	1-0	Drake	29,171
41.	Leicester City	A	5-3	Beasley 2 Crayston 2 Davidson	26,958
42.	Derby County	H	0-1		36,421

Final League Position = 1st in Division One

♛ FA Cup ♛

3	Brighton & HA	A	2-0	Hulme Drake	22,343
4	Leicester City	A	1-0	Hulme	39,494
5	Reading	A	1-0	Bastin	30,621
6	Sheffield Wed	A	1-2	Catlin (og)	66,945

1935–36

1.	Sunderland	H	3-1	Drake 2 Bastin	66,428
2.	Grimsby Town	A	0-1		25,978
3.	Birmingham	A	1-1	Drake	42,804
4.	Grimsby Town	H	6-0	Milne 3 Beasley Bowden Drake	33,633
5.	Sheffield Wed	H	2-2	Drake Milne	59,492
6.	Leeds United	A	1-1	Drake	24,283
7.	Manchester City	H	2-3	Bastin (pen) James	61,290
8.	Stoke City	A	3-0	Bastin 2 Crayston	45,570
9.	Blackburn Rovers	H	5-1	Bowden 3 Bastin Milne	45,981
10.	Chelsea	A	1-1	Crayston	82,905
11.	Portsmouth	A	1-2	Milne	34,165
12.	Preston NE	H	2-1	Drake Bastin	42,126
13.	Brentford	A	1-2	Parkin	26,330
14.	Derby County	H	1-1	Drake	54,027
15.	Everton	A	2-0	Drake Bastin	46,990
16.	Wolves	H	4-0	Rogers Drake 2 Hulme	39,860
17.	Huddersfield T	A	0-0		35,816
18.	Middlesbrough	H	2-0	Rogers 2	23,365
19.	Aston Villa	A	7-1	Drake 7	58,469
20.	Liverpool	A	1-0	Hulme	45,899
21.	Liverpool	H	1-2	Hulme	57,035
22.	Sunderland	A	4-5	Bowden Drake Bastin (pen) Clarke (og)	58,773
23.	Birmingham	H	1-1	Drake	44,534
24.	Sheffield Wed	A	2-3	Drake Roberts	35,576
25.	Stoke City	H	1-0	Drake	49,347
26.	Blackburn Rovers	A	1-0	Crayston	24,988
27.	Portsmouth	H	2-3	Compton Dougall	21,728
28.	Derby County	A	4-0	Dougall Kirchen Cox Crayston	17,930
29.	Huddersfield T	H	1-1	Bastin	43,930
30.	Manchester City	A	0-1		32,750

31.	Preston NE	A	0-1		30,039
32.	Everton	H	1-1	Hulme	18,593
33.	Wolves	A	2-2	Beasley Kirchen	32,330
34.	Bolton Wands	H	1-1	Westcott	10,485
35.	Brentford	H	1-1	Dougall	28,303
36.	West Brom Alb	H	4-0	Crayston Dunne Hulme James	59,245
37.	Middlesbrough	A	2-2	Bowden Bastin (pen)	31,006
38.	West Brom Alb	A	0-1		42,286
39.	Aston Villa	H	1-0	Drake	55,431
40.	Chelsea	H	1-1	Drake	40,402
41.	Bolton Wands	A	1-2	Hulme	29,479
42.	Leeds United	H	2-2	Bastin Kirchen	25,920

Final League Position = 6th in Division One

♔ FA Cup ♔

3	Bristol Rovers	A	5-1	Bastin 2 Drake 2 Bowden	24,234
4	Liverpool	A	2-0	Bowden Hulme	53,720
5	Newcastle United	A	3-3	Bowden 2 Hulme	65,484
R	Newcastle United	H	3-0	Bastin 2 pens Beasley	62,391
6	Barnsley	H	4-1	Beasley 2 Bowden Bastin (pen)	60,420
SF	Grimsby Town	N*	1-0	Bastin	63,210
F	Sheffield United	N**	1-0	Drake	93,384

*played at Leeds Road, Huddersfield ** played at Wembley Stadium

1936–37

1.	Everton	H	3-2	Hapgood Bowden James	50,321
2.	Brentford	A	0-2		31,056
3.	Huddersfield T	A	0-0		32,013
4.	Brentford	H	1-1	Drake	44,010
5.	Sunderland	H	4-1	Crayston Beasley Bastin Roberts	56,820
6.	Wolves	A	0-2		53,097
7.	Derby County	H	2-2	D Compton Drake	61,390
8.	Manchester Utd	A	0-2		55,884
9.	Sheffield Wed	H	1-1	Drake	46,421
10.	Charlton Ath	A	2-0	Davidson D Compton	68,160
11.	Grimsby Town	H	0-0		51,202
12.	Liverpool	A	1-2	Kirchen	39,251
13.	Leeds United	H	4-1	Kirchen Drake Milne Davidson	32,535
14.	Birmingham	A	3-1	Drake 2 Kirchen	39,940
15.	Middlesbrough	H	5-3	Milne 2 Drake Bastin Bowden	44,829
16.	West Brom Alb	A	4-2	Drake 2 Milne 2	27,609
17.	Manchester City	H	1-3	Drake	41,783
18.	Portsmouth	A	5-1	Davidson 4 Drake	32,184
19.	Chelsea	H	4-1	Kirchen 2 Drake Davidson	49,917
20.	Preston NE	H	4-1	Drake 2 Kirchen Milne	42,781
21.	Everton	A	1-1	Kirchen	59,440
22.	Preston NE	A	3-1	Kirchen Nelson Milne	25,787
23.	Bolton Wands	A	5-0	Drake 4 Milne	42,171
24.	Huddersfield T	H	1-1	Kirchen	44,224

25.	Sunderland	A	1-1	Milne	54,694
26.	Wolves	H	3-0	Bastin (pen) Drake Bowden	33,896
27.	Derby County	A	4-5	Drake Bastin (pen)	22,064
				Kirchen Howe (og)	22,064
28.	Manchester Utd	H	1-1	Davidson	37,236
29.	Sheffield Wed	A	0-0		35,813
30.	Charlton Ath	H	1-1	Kirchen	60,568
31.	Grimsby Town	A	3-1	Kirchen 3	18,216
32.	Liverpool	H	1-0	Kirchen	16,145
33.	Leeds United	A	4-3	Kirchen 2 Bastin (pen) Bowden	25,148
34.	Birmingham	H	1-1	Bowden	46,086
35.	Stoke City	H	0-0		59,495
36.	Middlesbrough	A	1-1	Bowden	44,523
37.	Stoke City	A	0-0		51,480
38.	West Brom Alb	H	2-0	Davidson Nelson	38,773
39.	Manchester City	A	0-2		74,918
40.	Portsmouth	H	4-0	D Compton 2 Nelson Kirchen	29,098
41.	Chelsea	A	0-2		53,325
42.	Bolton Wands	H	0-0		22,875

Final League Position = 3rd in Division One

♛ FA Cup ♛

3	Chesterfield	A	5-1	Drake 2 Kirchen 2 Davidson	21,786
4	Manchester Utd	H	5-0	Bastin Davidson Drake	45,637
				Kirchen Brown (og)	
5	Burnley	A	7-1	Drake 4 Crayston Bastin Kirchen	54,445
6	West Brom Alb	A	1-3	Bastin	64,815

	1937–38				
1.	Everton	A	4-1	Drake 3 Bastin	53,856
2.	Huddersfield T	H	3-1	Drake Crayston Bastin	32,758
3.	Wolves	H	5-0	Drake 2 Crayston Hulme	67,311
				Bastin (pen)	
4.	Huddersfield T	A	1-2	Bowden	28,405
5.	Leicester City	A	1-1	Drake	39,106
6.	Bolton Wands	A	0-1		39,750
7.	Sunderland	H	4-1	Milne Drake Hulme Davidson	65,635
8.	Derby County	A	0-2		33,101
9.	Manchester City	H	2-1	Milne Kirchen	68,353
10.	Chelsea	A	2-2	Kirchen 2	75,952
11.	Portsmouth	H	1-1	Hunt	45,150
12.	Stoke City	A	1-1	Davidson	35,684
13.	Middlesbrough	H	1-2	Milne	39,066
14.	Grimsby Town	A	1-2	L Jones	20,244
15.	West Brom Alb	H	1-1	L Compton	34,324
16.	Charlton Ath	A	3-0	Bastin Drake Ford (og)	55,078
17.	Leeds United	H	4-1	Drake 2 Bastin (pen) Kirchen	34,350
18.	Birmingham	A	2-1	Kirchen Cartwright	18,440
19.	Preston NE	H	2-0	Bastin Milne	35,679

20.	Liverpool	A	0-2		32,093
21.	Blackpool	A	1-2	Bastin (pen)	23,229
22.	Blackpool	H	2-1	Bastin Cartwright	54,163
23.	Everton	H	2-1	Lewis Hunt	36,953
24.	Wolves	A	1-3	Drake	39,383
25.	Sunderland	A	1-1	Hunt	42,638
26.	Leicester City	H	3-1	Drake Bastin L Jones	23,839
27.	Derby County	H	3-0	Crayston 2 Lewis	47,286
28.	Manchester City	A	2-1	Drake D Compton	34,299
29.	Chelsea	H	2-0	Griffiths Drake	49,573
30.	Portsmouth	A	0-0		43,991
31.	Stoke City	H	4-0	Carr Griffiths 2 Drake	35,296
32.	Middlesbrough	A	1-2	Bastin	46,747
33.	Grimsby Town	H	5-1	Bastin 2 (1 pen) Griffiths 2 L Jones	40,701
34.	West Brom Alb	A	0-0		33,954
35.	Charlton Ath	H	2-2	Drake Carr	52,858
36.	Leeds United	A	1-0	Bremner	29,365
37.	Brentford	H	0-2		51,299
38.	Birmingham	H	0-0		35,161
39.	Brentford	A	0-3		34,601
40.	Preston NE	A	3-1	Carr 2 Bastin	42,684
41.	Liverpool	H	1-0	Carr	34,703
42.	Bolton Wands	H	5-0	Bastin 2 Carr 2 Kirchen	40,500

Final League Position = 1st in Division One

♆ FA Cup ♆

3	Bolton Wands	H	3-1	Bastin 2 Kirchen	64,016
4	Wolves	A	2-1	Kirchen Drake	61,267
5	Preston NE	H	0-1		72,121

	1938–39				
1.	Portsmouth	H	2-0	B Jones Rochford (og)	54,940
2.	Huddersfield T	A	1-1	B Jones	26,126
3.	Brentford	A	0-1		38,535
4.	Everton	H	1-2	B Jones	64,555
5.	Derby County	H	1-2	Drake	25,756
6.	Wolves	A	1-0	Cumner	45,364
7.	Aston Villa	H	0-0		66,456
8.	Sunderland	A	0-0		51,042
9.	Grimsby Town	H	2-0	Bremner Kirchen	39,174
10.	Chelsea	A	2-4	Cumner Kirchen	65,443
11.	Preston NE	H	1-0	A Beattie (og)	40,296
12.	Bolton Wands	A	1-1	B Jones	46,611
13.	Leeds United	H	2-3	Bastin Drake	39,092
14.	Liverpool	A	2-2	Drake Kirchen	42,540
15.	Leicester City	H	0-0		36,407
16.	Middlesbrough	A	1-1	Drury	29,147
17.	Birmingham	H	3-1	Drake Crayston Nelson	33,710

18.	Manchester Utd	A	0-1		42,008
19.	Stoke City	H	4-1	Lewis 2 Bastin Drury	30,006
20.	Portsmouth	A	0-0		21,344
21.	Charlton Ath	A	0-1		51,479
22.	Huddersfield T	H	1-0	Drake	34,146
23.	Everton	A	0-2		47,178
24.	Charlton Ath	H	2-0	Crayston Lewis	39,702
25.	Aston Villa	A	3-1	Lewis 2 Kirchen	57,453
26.	Wolves	H	0-0		33,103
27.	Sunderland	H	2-0	Bastin Lewis	45,875
28.	Chelsea	H	1-0	Bremner	54,510
29.	Grimsby Town	A	1-2	Kirchen	10,845
30.	Preston NE	A	1-2	Lewis	29,678
31.	Bolton Wands	H	3-1	Drake 2 Winter (og)	29,814
32.	Leeds United	A	2-4	Drake L Compton (pen)	22,160
33.	Liverpool	H	2-0	Kirchen Drake	31,495
34.	Leicester City	A	2-0	Kirchen Drake	22,565
35.	Middlesbrough	H	1-2	Bremner	34,669
36.	Blackpool	A	0-1		31,497
37.	Birmingham	A	2-1	Kirchen Drury	33,250
38.	Blackpool	H	2-1	Drake L Compton (pen)	30,760
39.	Manchester Utd	H	2-1	Drake Crayston	25,741
40.	Stoke City	A	0-1		26,039
41.	Derby County	A	2-1	Farr Drake	10,186
42.	Brentford	H	2-0	Kirchen Drake	30,928

Final League Position = 5th in Division One

♛ FA Cup ♛

3	Chelsea	A	1-2	Bastin	58,095

	1946–47				
1.	Wolves	A	1-6	Lewis	50,845
2.	Blackburn Rovers	H	1-3	Lewis	28,700
3.	Sunderland	H	2-2	Lewis 2	60,000
4.	Everton	A	2-3	Lewis 2	40,000
5.	Aston Villa	A	2-0	Lewis O'Flanagan	40,000
6.	Blackburn Rovers	A	2-1	Lewis 2	28,000
7.	Derby County	H	0-1		63,000
8.	Manchester Utd	A	2-5	Lewis McPherson	62,718
9.	Blackpool	A	1-2	Logie	24,039
10.	Brentford	H	2-2	Lewis Logie	45,000
11.	Stoke City	H	1-0	O'Flanagan	62,000
12.	Chelsea	A	1-2	Lewis	56,568
13.	Sheffield United	H	2-3	Lewis Logie	45,000
14.	Preston NE	A	0-2		29,971
15.	Leeds United	H	4-2	Lewis 2 (1 pen) Logie McPherson	40,000
16.	Liverpool	A	2-4	Lewis Logie	51,435
17.	Bolton Wands	H	2-2	Lewis (pen) O'Flanagan	47,000

18.	Middlesbrough	A	0-2		35,000
19.	Charlton Ath	H	1-0	Rooke	45,000
20.	Grimsby Town	A	0-0		17,000
21.	Portsmouth	H	2-1	Rooke Logie	38,000
22.	Portsmouth	A	2-0	Rooke 2	38,000
23.	Wolves	A	1-1	Rooke	63,000
24.	Sunderland	A	4-1	Rooke 2 Lewis 2	36,812
25.	Aston Villa	H	0-2		61,000
26.	Manchester Utd	H	6-2	Rooke 3 Rudkin Logie McPherson	38,000
27.	Blackpool	H	1-1	Rooke	36,000
28.	Stoke City	A	1-3	Rooke	30,000
29.	Chelsea	H	1-2	Rudkin	57,000
30.	Preston NE	H	4-1	Lewis 3 Rooke	50,000
31.	Leeds United	A	1-1	Lewis	32,000
32.	Huddersfield T	H	1-2	B Jones	50,000
33.	Bolton Wands	A	3-1	Rooke 2 Lewis	34,398
34.	Huddersfield T	A	0-0		33,381
35.	Middlesbrough	H	4-0	Rooke 4 (1 pen)	50,000
36.	Charlton Ath	A	2-2	McPherson Logie	55,000
37.	Grimsby Town	H	5-3	Lewis 4 D Compton	50,000
38.	Derby County	A	1-0	Rooke	19,153
39.	Liverpool	H	1-2	McPherson	48,000
40.	Brentford	A	1-0	Sloan	17,599
41.	Everton	H	2-1	Rooke Lewis	30,000
42.	Sheffield United	A	1-2	McPherson	20,000

Final League Position = 13th in Division One

♆ FA Cup ♆

3	Chelsa	A	1-1	McPherson	70,195
R	Chelsea	H	1-1*	Rooke	53,350
2R	Chelsea**	N	0-2		59,590

* after extra-time   ** played at White Hart Lane, London.

1947–48					
1.	Sunderland	H	3-1	McPherson Logie Rooke	60,000
2.	Charlton Ath	A	4-2	McPherson Roger Lewis Logie	60,000
3.	Sheffield United	A	2-1	Rooke Roper	39,130
4.	Charlton Ath	H	6-0	Lewis 4 Rooke 2	58,000
5.	Manchester Utd	H	2-1	Rooke Lewis	62,000
6.	Bolton Wands	H	2-0	McPherson Rooke (pen)	50,000
7.	Preston NE	A	0-0		40,061
8.	Stoke City	H	3-0	Logie McPherson 2	62,000
9.	Burnley	A	1-0	Lewis	47,258
10.	Portsmouth	H	0-0		62,000
11.	Aston Villa	H	1-0	Rooke	61,000
12.	Wolves	A	1-1	Rooke (pen)	55,998
13.	Everton	H	1-1	Lewis	59,000
14.	Chelsea	A	0-0		67,277
15.	Blackpool	H	2-1	Rooke (pen) Roper	62,000

16.	Blackburn Rovers	A	1-0	Rooke	37,423
17.	Huddersfield T	H	2-0	Rooke Logie	50,000
18.	Derby County	A	0-1		35,605
19.	Manchester City	H	1-1	Rooke (pen)	43,000
20.	Grimsby Town	A	4-0	Rooke 2 Logie Roper	20,000
21.	Sunderland	A	1-1	B Jones	58,391
22.	Liverpool	A	3-1	Rooke 2 Roper	53,604
23.	Liverpool	H	1-2	Lewis	59,000
24.	Bolton Wands	A	1-0	Lewis	30,028
25.	Sheffield United	H	3-2	Rooke 2 Lewis	50,000
26.	Manchester Utd	A	1-1	Lewis	81,962
27.	Preston NE	H	3-0	Lewis 2 Rooke	62,000
28.	Stoke City	A	0-0		41,000
29.	Burnley	H	3-0	Rooke 2 Roper	62,000
30.	Aston Villa	A	2-4	Rooke Moss (og)	65,690
31.	Wolves	H	5-2	Rooke 2 Forbes Roper Logie	58,000
32.	Everton	A	2-0	D Compton 2	64,059
33.	Chelsea	H	0-2		59,000
34.	Middlesbrough	H	7-0	Rooke 3 D Compton 2 Roper Robinson (og)	60,000
35.	Blackpool	A	0-1		32,678
36.	Middlesbrough	A	1-1	Rooke	38,469
37.	Blackburn Rovers	H	2-0	Logie Rooke	48,000
38.	Huddersfield T	A	1-1	Roper	38,110
39.	Derby County	H	1-2	Roper	52,000
40.	Portsmouth	A	0-0		42,813
41.	Manchester City	A	0-0		20,782
42.	Grimsby Town	H	8-0	Rooke 4 D Compton 2 Forbes Logie (pen)	35,000

Final League Position = 1st in Division One

♈ FA Cup ♈

3	Bradford	H	0-1		47,738

	1948–49				
1.	Huddersfield T	A	1-1	Rooke	30,620
2.	Stoke City	H	3-0	Logie Forbes Roper	47,000
3.	Manchester Utd	H	0-1		62,000
4.	Stoke City	A	0-1		39,534
5.	Sheffield United	A	1-1	Cox (og)	38,111
6.	Liverpool	H	1-1	Rooke	48,000
7.	Aston Villa	H	3-1	Rooke 2 (pens) Roper	58,000
8.	Liverpool	A	1-0	Lewis	46,714
9.	Sunderland	A	1-1	B Jones	64,436
10.	Wolves	H	3-1	Lewis 2 D Compton	59,000
11.	Bolton Wands	A	0-1		43,110
12.	Burnley	H	3-1	Lewis 2 Logie	57,000
13.	Preston NE	A	1-1	Rooke	31,443
14.	Everton	H	5-0	Rooke 2 Logie 2 Forbes	53,000

15.	Chelsea	A	1-0	Rooke (pen)	56,476
16.	Birmingham	H	2-0	Forbes Lewis	62,000
17.	Middlesbrough	A	1-0	Lewis	35,727
18.	Newcastle United	H	0-1		62,000
19.	Portsmouth	A	1-4	Lewis (pen)	42,687
20.	Manchester City	H	1-1	Rooke	45,000
21.	Charlton Ath	A	3-4	Roper McPherson Lewis	52,549
22.	Huddersfield T	H	3-0	Rooke 3	40,000
23.	Derby County	H	3-3	Logie Rooke McPherson	43,000
24.	Derby County	A	1-2	Lewis	33,378
25.	Manchester Utd	A	0-2		61,288
26.	Sheffield United	H	5-3	Logie 2 Lishman Rooke McPherson	45,000
27.	Aston Villa	A	0-1		65,000
28.	Sunderland	H	5-0	Lewis Macaulay Lishman Vallance McPherson	55,000
29.	Wolves	A	3-1	Lewis 2 Logie	54,536
30.	Bolton Wands	H	5-0	Logie 2 Lewis Vallance McPherson	53,000
31.	Burnley	A	1-1	Lishman	20,303
32.	Preston NE	H	0-0		59,000
33.	Newcastle United	A	2-3	Lewis Forbes (pen)	60,000
34.	Birmingham	A	1-1	Lishman	38,503
35.	Middlesbrough	H	1-1	Lishman	55,000
36.	Blackpool	A	1-1	Lewis	28,718
37.	Everton	A	0-0		56,987
38.	Blackpool	H	2-0	Lishman 2	47,000
39.	Chelsea	H	1-2	D Compton	58,000
40.	Manchester City	A	3-0	Lishman2 Roper	27,955
41.	Portsmouth	H	3-2	Lishman 2 Logie	60,000
42.	Charlton Ath	H	2-0	Roper Lishman	50,000

Final League Position = 5th in Division One

♛ FA Cup ♛

3	Tottenham H	H	3-0	McPherson Roper Lishman	47,314
4	Derby County	A	0-1		31,073

1949–50

1.	Burnley	H	0-1		50,000
2.	Chelsea	A	2-1	Lishman Goring	63,124
3.	Sunderland	A	2-4	Logie Hudgell (og)	56,500
4.	Chelsea	H	2-3	Goring 2	56,000
5.	Liverpool	H	1-2	Lishman	56,000
6.	West Brom Alb	A	2-1	Lewis Barnes (pen)	43,000
7.	Huddersfield T	A	2-2	Lewis Goring	20,882
8.	West Brom Alb	H	4-1	Lewis Goring Roper Barnes (pen)	44,000 44,000
9.	Bolton Wands	A	2-2	Lewis Barnes (pen)	35,000
10.	Birmingham City	H	4-2	Goring 2 Logie Lewis	53,000

11.	Derby County	A	2-1	Lewis 2	29,000
12.	Everton	H	5-2	Goring 2 Lewis 2 Roper	56,000
13.	Middlesbrough	A	1-1	Roper	43,000
14.	Blackpool	H	1-0	Lewis	65,000
15.	Newcastle United	A	3-0	Roper 3	55,000
16.	Fulham	H	2-1	McPherson Barnes (pen)	43,000
17.	Manchester City	A	2-0	Logie Cox	28,288
18.	Charlton Ath	H	2-3	Logie Lewis	60,000
19.	Aston Villa	A	1-1	Lewis	45,000
20.	Wolves	H	1-1	Roper	60,000
21.	Portsmouth	A	1-2	Goring	39,537
22.	Burnley	A	0-0		25,661
23.	Sunderland	H	5-0	Lewis Forbes Goring Logie McPherson	45,000
24.	Manchester Utd	A	0-2		53,928
25.	Manchester Utd	H	0-0		65,000
26.	Liverpool	A	0-2		55,020
27.	Huddersfield T	H	1-0	Lewis	50,000
28.	Bolton Wands	H	1-1	Lewis	49,000
29.	Birmingham City	A	1-2	Goring	35,000
30.	Derby County	H	1-0	Logie	67,000
31.	Everton	A	1-0	Cox	43,632
32.	Middlesbrough	H	1-1	Forbes (pen)	37,000
33.	Charlton Ath	A	1-1	D Compton	52,000
34.	Fulham	A	2-2	Logie Cox	40,000
35.	Aston Villa	H	1-3	Lishman	27,000
36.	Manchester City	H	4-1	Lewis 2 Lishman Goring	42,000
37.	Blackpool	A	1-2	Goring	32,000
38.	Stoke City	H	6-0	Goring 2 Lishman2 Barnes (pen) Franklin (og)	30,000
39.	Newcastle United	H	4-2	Goring 3 Lewis	54,000
40.	Wolves	A	0-3		53,082
41.	Portsmouth	H	2-0	Goring 2	65,000
42.	Stoke City	A	5-2	Lishman 3 Lewis McPherson	18,000

Final League Position = 6th in Division One

♕ FA Cup ♕

3	Sheffield Wed	H	1-0	Lewis	54,193
4	Swansea Town	H	2-1	Logie Barnes (pen)	57,305
5	Burnley	H	2-0	Lewis D Compton	55,458
6	Leeds United	H	1-0	Lewis	62,573
SF	Chelsea*	N	2-2	Cox L Compton	67,752
R	Chelsea*	N	1-0**	Cox	66,482
F	Liverpool***	N	2-0	Lewis 2	100,000

* played at White Hart Lane, London   ** after extra-time   *** played at Wembley Stadium

1950–51					
1.	Burnley	A	1-0	Roper	32,957
2.	Chelsea	H	0-0		63,000

3.	Tottenham H	H	2-2	Roper Barnes (pen)	64,500
4.	Chelsea	A	1-0	Cox	48,792
5.	Sheffield Wed	H	3-0	Logie 2 Lishman	48,300
6.	Everton	H	2-1	Cox Barnes (pen)	40,000
7.	Middlesbrough	A	1-2	Lishman	45,000
8.	Everton	A	1-1	Goring	47,518
9.	Huddersfield T	H	6-2	Goring 3 Logie 2 Lishman	54,200
10.	Newcastle United	A	1-2	Logie	65,000
11.	West Brom Alb	H	3-0	Lishman 2 Logie	53,700
12.	Charlton Ath	A	3-1	Goring Forbes Roper	64,000
13.	Manchester Utd	H	3-0	Lishman Goring Cockburn (og)	66,150
14.	Aston Villa	A	1-1	Logie	45,000
15.	Derby County	H	3-1	Logie Forbes Goring	64,750
16.	Wolves	A	1-0	Lishman	55,548
17.	Sunderland	H	5-1	Lishman 4 Roper	66,250
18.	Liverpool	A	3-1	Lishman Logie Roper	44,193
19.	Fulham	H	5-1	Lishman 3 Goring Forbes	45,450
20.	Bolton Wands	A	0-3		40,489
21.	Blackpool	H	4-4	Lishman Forbes Goring Barnes (pen)	57,445
22.	Burnley	H	0-1		35,300
23.	Tottenham H	A	0-1		54,898
24.	Stoke City	H	0-3		38,800
25.	Stoke City	A	0-1		45,000
26.	Sheffield Wed	A	2-0	Goring 2	39,583
27.	Middlesbrough	H	3-1	Lewis 2 Goring	65,038
28.	Huddersfield T	A	2-2	Lewis 2	37,175
29.	Newcastle United	H	0-0		55,073
30.	West Brom Alb	A	0-2		38,000
31.	Charlton Ath	H	2-5	Goring 2	58,137
32.	Manchester Utd	A	1-3	Holton	46,202
33.	Aston Villa	H	2-1	Lewis 2	43,747
34.	Derby County	A	2-4	Lewis Goring	22,168
35.	Portsmouth	H	0-1		52,051
36.	Wolves	H	2-1	Holton 2	54,213
37.	Portsmouth	A	1-1	Marden	39,189
38.	Sunderland	A	2-0	Marden Roper	31,515
39.	Liverpool	H	1-2	Holton	42,000
40.	Fulham	A	2-3	Holton Lewis	35,000
41.	Bolton Wands	H	1-1	Lishman	45,040
42.	Blackpool	A	1-0	Roper	25,000

Final League Position = 5th in Division One

♆ FA Cup ♆

3	Carlisle United	H	0-0		57,932
R	Carlisle United	A	4-1	Lewis 2 Logie Goring	21,215
4	Northampton T	H	3-2	Lewis 2 Roper	72,408
5	Manchester Utd	A	0-1		55,058

1951–52

1.	Huddersfield T	H	2-2	Marden Holton	54,072
2.	Chelsea	A	3-1	Holton Marden Roper	59,143
3.	Wolves	A	1-2	Holton	40,000
4.	Chelsea	H	2-1	Holton Lishman	48,768
5.	Sunderland	H	3-0	Lishman 3	66,137
6.	Liverpool	H	0-0		50,483
7.	Aston Villa	A	0-1		60,000
8.	Liverpool	A	0-0		39,853
9.	Derby County	H	3-1	Holton 2 Lishman	50,181
10.	Manchester City	A	2-0	Holton Lishman	48,367
11.	Tottenham H	H	1-1	Holton	68,164
12.	Preston NE	A	0-2		39,000
13.	Burnley	H	1-0	Lewis	48,531
14.	Charlton Ath	A	3-1	Holton 2 Milton	57,000
15.	Fulham	H	4-3	Lishman 3 Holton	54,178
16.	Middlesbrough	A	3-0	Holton Lishman Milton	36,000
17.	West Brom Alb	H	6-3	Lishman 3 Holton 2 Logie	53,432
18.	Newcastle United	A	0-2		61,192
19.	Bolton Wands	H	4-2	Lishman 3 Roper	53,790
20.	Stoke City	A	1-2	Lewis	26,000
21.	Manchester Utd	H	1-3	Logie	55,451
22.	Huddersfield T	A	3-2	Roper 2 Lewis	22,427
23.	Wolves	H	2-2	Lewis 2	45,644
24.	Portsmouth	H	4-1	Cox Goring Lewis Logie	54,241
25.	Portsmouth	A	1-1	Cox	41,305
26.	Sunderland	A	1-4	Goring	47,045
27.	Aston Villa	H	2-1	Roper 2	53,540
28.	Derby County	A	2-1	Logie Roper	28,791
29.	Manchester City	H	2-1	Lishman 2	54,527
30.	Tottenham H	A	2-1	Roper Forbes	66,438
31.	Preston NE	H	3-3	Lewis 2 Roper	61,849
32.	Burnley	A	1-0	Milton	41,000
33.	Charlton Ath	H	2-1	Goring 2	37,985
34.	Fulham	A	0-0		46,000
35.	Middlesbrough	H	3-1	Holton Lishman Milton	52,000
36.	Blackpool	A	0-0		32,186
37.	Bolton Wands	A	1-2	Forbes	44,722
38.	Blackpool	H	4-1	Lishman 2 Barnes (pen) Crosland (og)	50,445
39.	Newcastle United	H	1-1	Milton	53,203
40.	Stoke City	H	4-1	Holton 2 Barnes (pen) Lishman	47,962
41.	West Brom Alb	A	1-3	Lishman	29,700
42.	Manchester Utd	A	1-6	Cox	53,651

Final League Position = 3rd in Division One

FA Cup

3	Norwich City	A	5-0	Lishman 2 Logie Goring Roper	38,964
4	Barnsley	H	4-0	Lewis 3 Lishman	69,466
5	Leyton Orient	A	3-0	Lishman 2 Lewis	30,000

6	Luton Town	A	3-2	Cox 2 Milton	28,433
SF	Chelsea*	N	1-1	Cox	68,084
R	Chelsea*	N	3-0	Cox 2 Lishman	57,450
F	Newcastle United N**		0-1		100,000

*played at White Hart Lane, London   ** played at Wembley Stadium

	1952–53				
1.	Aston Villa	A	2-1	Lishman Oakes	55,000
2.	Manchester Utd	H	2-1	Cox Goring	58,831
3.	Sunderland	H	1-2	Lishman	57,873
4.	Manchester Utd	A	0-0		37,367
5.	Wolves	A	1-1	Roper	43,371
6.	Portsmouth	H	3-1	Goring Milton Roper	40,743
7.	Charlton Ath	H	3-4	Milton Goring Daniel	61,102
8.	Portsmouth	A	2-2	Holton 2	37,256
9.	Tottenham H	A	3-1	Goring Milton Logie	69,220
10.	Derby County	A	0-2		24,582
11.	Blackpool	H	3-1	Roper 2 Logie	66,682
12.	Sheffield Wed	H	2-2	Roper Logie	55,678
13.	Newcastle United	H	3-0	Roper 2 Lishman	63,744
14.	West Brom Alb	A	0-2		41,000
15.	Middlesbrough	H	2-1	Milton Holton	49,564
16.	Liverpool	A	5-1	Holton 3 Marden 2	45,010
17.	Manchester City	H	3-1	Logie 2 Lishman	39,161
18.	Stoke City	A	1-1	Holton	24,033
19.	Burnley	A	1-1	Milton	32,840
20.	Aston Villa	H	3-1	Lishman Holton Roper	32,064
21.	Bolton Wands	A	6-4	Holton 2 Milton Logie Roper Daniel	47,344
22.	Sunderland	A	1-3	Lishman	54,912
23.	Wolves	H	5-3	Lishman 2 Daniel Logie Milton	58,983
24.	Charlton Ath	A	2-2	Lishman Roper	66,426
25.	Tottenham H	H	4-0	Holton 2 Lishman Logie	69,051
26.	Derby County	H	6-2	Daniel 2 Holton 2 Lishman 2	32,681
27.	Blackpool	A	2-3	Mercer Goring	27,000
28.	Sheffield Wed	A	4-1	Holton 4	30,452
29.	Cardiff City	H	0-1		59,580
30.	Newcastle United	A	2-2	Lishman 2	51,560
31.	Preston NE	H	1-1	Mercer	33,697
32.	West Brom Alb	H	2-2	Holton Roper	50,078
33.	Middlesbrough	A	0-2		35,000
34.	Chelsea	A	1-1	Goring	72,614
35.	Liverpool	H	5-3	Roper 2 Lishman Goring Hughes (og)	39,564
36.	Chelsea	H	2-0	Lishman Marden	40,536
37.	Manchester City	A	4-2	Goring 2 Logie Roper	53,418
38.	Bolton Wands	H	4-1	Lishman 2 Goring Marden	35,006
39.	Stoke City	H	3-1	Lishman 3	47,376
40.	Cardiff City	A	0-0		57,800

| 41. | Preston NE | A | 0-2 | | 40,000 |
| 42. | Burnley | H | 3-2 | Forbes Lishman Logie | 51,586 |

Final League Position = 1st in Division One

♈ FA Cup ♈

3	Doncaster Rovers	H	4-0	Lishman Holton Logie Roper	57,443
4	Bury	H	6-2	Holton Lishman Logie	45,071
				Milton Roper T Daniel (og)	
5	Burnley	A	2-0	Holton Lishman	52,122
6	Blackpool	H	1-2	Logie	69,158

1953–54

1.	West Brom Alb	A	0-2		39,710
2.	Huddersfield T	H	0-0		54,847
3.	Sheffield United	A	0-1		51,070
4.	Aston Villa	A	1-2	Forbes	40,000
5.	Sheffield United	H	1-1	Shaw (og)	41,077
6.	Wolves	H	2-3	Roper Holton	60,450
7.	Chelsea	H	1-2	Holton	55,086
8.	Sunderland	A	1-7	Lishman	59,808
9.	Chelsea	A	2-0	Lishman 2	60,652
10.	Manchester City	H	2-2	Lishman 2	65,869
11.	Cardiff City	A	3-0	Lishman 2 Mansell (og)	55,000
12.	Preston NE	H	3-2	Roper 2 Barnes (pen)	61,807
13.	Tottenham H	A	4-1	Logie 2 Milton Forbes	69,821
14.	Burnley	H	2-5	Forbes Roper	47,373
15.	Charlton Ath	A	5-1	Marden 3 Holton Roper	60,245
16.	Sheffield Wed	H	4-1	Holton 2 Logie 2	52,543
17.	Manchester Utd	A	2-2	Holton Roper	28,141
18.	Bolton Wands	H	4-3	Holton 3 Lishman	52,319
19.	Liverpool	A	2-1	Logie Lishman	47,814
20.	Newcastle United	H	2-1	Holton Forbes	62,456
21.	Middlesbrough	A	0-2		35,000
22.	West Brom Alb	H	2-2	Lishman 2	55,264
23.	Huddersfield T	A	2-2	Milton Lishman	34,018
24.	Blackpool	A	2-2	Lishman Roper	29,347
25.	Blackpool	H	1-1	Roper	62,900
26.	Wolves	A	2-0	Logie Lishman	45,974
27.	Sunderland	H	1-4	Holton	60,218
28.	Manchester City	A	0-0		39,026
29.	Cardiff City	H	1-1	Lishman	45,497
30.	Preston NE	A	1-0	Lishman	23,000
31.	Tottenham H	H	0-3		64,211
32.	Burnley	A	1-2	Holton	22,726
33.	Charlton Ath	H	3-3	Holton Lishman Dickson	41,256
34.	Sheffield Wed	A	1-2	Holton	42,072
35.	Manchester Utd	H	3-1	Logie 2 Holton	42,735
36.	Bolton Wands	A	1-3	Holton	30,473
37.	Aston Villa	H	1-1	Lawton	14,519

38.	Liverpool	H	3-0	Tapscott 2 Roper	33,178
39.	Portsmouth	H	3-0	Tapscott 2 Roper	44,948
40.	Newcastle United	A	2-5	Milton Holton	48,540
41.	Portsmouth	A	1-1	Roper	30,958
42.	Middlesbrough	H	3-1	Roper Lishman Tapscott	35,196

Final League Position = 12th in Division One

♈ FA Cup ♈

3	Aston Villa	H	5-1	Roper 2 Holton Logie Milton	50,990
4	Norwich City	H	1-2	Logie	55,767

	1954–55				
1.	Newcastle United	H	1-3	Lishman	65,334
2.	Everton	A	0-1		69,134
3.	West Brom Alb	A	1-3	Lishman	50,000
4.	Everton	H	2-0	Lishman Roper	42,146
5.	Tottenham H	H	2-0	Logie Lishman	53,977
6.	Manchester City	A	1-2	Lishman	38,146
7.	Sheffield United	H	4-0	Forbes Lishman Tapscott Roper	41,679
8.	Manchester City	H	2-3	Tapscott Lishman	33,898
9.	Preston NE	A	1-3	Logie	36,000
10.	Burnley	H	4-0	Lawton 2 Lishman Roper	46,190
11.	Leicester City	A	3-3	Lawton 2 Logie	42,486
12.	Sheffield Wed	A	2-1	Roper Bloomfield	38,167
13.	Portsmouth	H	0-1		44,866
14.	Aston Villa	A	1-2	Roper	40,000
15.	Sunderland	H	1-1	Roper	65,424
16.	Bolton Wands	A	2-2	Goring Lishman	31,222
17.	Huddersfield T	H	3-5	Milton 2 Lishman	42,950
18.	Manchester Utd	A	1-2	Tapscott	33,373
19.	Wolves	H	1-1	Roper	55,055
20.	Blackpool	A	2-2	Tapscott Roper	16,348
21.	Charlton Ath	H	3-1	Roper 2 Milton	40,498
22.	Newcastle United	A	1-5	Wills (pen)	35,060
23.	Chelsea	H	1-0	Lawton	47,178
24.	Chelsea	A	1-1	Tapscott	66,922
25.	West Brom Alb	H	2-2	Tapscott Lishman	40,246
26.	Tottenham H	A	1-0	Lawton	36,263
27.	Preston NE	H	2-0	Tapscott Roper	41,228
28.	Burnley	A	0-3		24,940
29.	Leicester City	H	1-1	Roper	27,384
30.	Sheffield Wed	H	3-2	Tapscott 3	26,910
31.	Charlton Ath	A	1-1	Bloomfield	42,064
32.	Aston Villa	H	2-0	Tapscott Roper	30,136
33.	Sunderland	A	1-0	Bloomfield	40,279
34.	Bolton Wands	H	3-0	Lishman 2 Roper	33,852
35.	Huddersfield T	A	1-0	Roper	22,853
36.	Cardiff City	H	2-0	Tapscott 2	39,052
37.	Blackpool	H	3-0	Lishman 2 Roper	60,741

38.	Cardiff City	A	2-1	Bloomfield Lishman	38,000
39.	Wolves	A	1-3	Lishman	34,985
40.	Sheffield United	A	1-1	Roper	21,380
41.	Manchester Utd	H	2-3	Lishman 2	42,754
42.	Portsmouth	A	1-2	Herd	28,156

Final League Position = 9th in Division One

♆ FA Cup ♆

| 3 | Cardiff City | H | 1-0 | Lawton | 51,298 |
| 4 | Wolves | A | 0-1 | | 52,857 |

1955–56

1.	Blackpool	A	1-3	Tapscott	30,928
2.	Cardiff City	H	3-1	Lawton 3	31,352
3.	Chelsea	H	1-1	Lawton	55,011
4.	Manchester City	A	2-2	Roper Lawton	36,955
5.	Bolton Wands	A	1-4	Lawton	22,690
6.	Manchester City	H	0-0		30,864
7.	Tottenham H	A	1-3	Roper	51,029
8.	Portsmouth	H	1-3	Lishman	48,816
9,	Sunderland	A	1-3	Lishman	55,397
10.	Aston Villa	H	1-0	Nutt	43,824
11.	Everton	A	1-1	Lishman	47,794
12.	Newcastle United	H	1-0	Roper	46,093
13.	Luton Town	A	0-0		23,997
14.	Charlton Ath	H	2-4	Lishman Clapton	47,038
15.	Manchester Utd	A	1-1	Lishman	41,586
16.	Sheffield United	H	2-1	Groves Roper	46,647
17.	Preston NE	A	1-0	Holton	23,000
18.	Burnley	H	0-1		37,583
19.	Birmingham City	A	0-4		35,765
20.	West Brom Alb	H	2-0	Tapscott Williams (og)	33,217
21.	Blackpool	H	4-1	Groves Holton Tapscott Bloomfield	45,086
22.	Chelsea	A	0-2		43,022
23.	Wolves	A	3-3	Groves 2 Bloomfield	43,738
24.	Wolves	H	2-2	Tapscott 2	61,814
25.	Bolton Wands	H	3-1	Tapscott 2 Groves	42,677
26.	Tottenham H	H	0-1		59,603
27.	Portsmouth	A	2-5	Tapscott 2	30,513
28.	Sunderland	H	3-1	Herd 2 Bloomfield	38,780
29.	Aston Villa	A	1-1	Groves	28,000
30.	Everton	H	3-2	Tapscott 2 Groves	16,039
31.	Newcastle United	A	0-2		50,800
32.	Preston NE	H	3-2	Tapscott 2 Groves	34,672
33.	Charlton Ath	A	0-2		39,553
34.	Manchester Utd	H	1-1	Holton	50,758
35.	Sheffield United	A	2-0	Holton Tapscott	26,556
36.	Luton Town	H	3-0	Holton 2 Haverty	45,968

37.	Huddersfield T	H	2-0	Haverty Holton	30,836
38.	Huddersfield T	A	1-0	Clapton	24,469
39.	Burnley	A	1-0	Swallow	24,403
40.	Birmingham City	H	1-0	Tapscott	31,733
41.	West Brom Alb	A	1-2	Tapscott	22,400
42.	Cardiff City	A	2-1	Holton Tapscott	20,000

Final League Position = 5th in Division One

♗ FA Cup ♗

3	Bedford Town	H	2-2	Tapscott Groves	55,178
R	Bedford Town	A	2-1	Groves Tapscott	15,306
4	Aston Villa	H	4-1	Tapscott 2 Groves Charlton	43,052
5	Charlton Ath	A	2-0	Groves Bloomfield	71,758
6	Birmingham City	H	1-3	Charlton	67,872

1956–57					
1.	Cardiff City	H	0-0		51,069
2.	Burnley	H	2-0	Tiddy Bloomfield	38,321
3.	Birmingham City	A	2-4	Holton Roper	37,200
4.	Burnley	A	1-3	Tiddy	18,829
5.	West Brom Alb	H	4-1	Roper 2 Tiddy Tapscott	39,973
6.	Preston NE	H	1-2	Bloomfield	40,470
7.	Portsmouth	A	3-2	Bloomfield Tiddy Holton	30,768
8.	Preston NE	A	0-3		35,450
9.	Newcastle United	H	0-1		46,318
10.	Sheffield Wed	A	4-2	Bloomfield 2 Tapscott Tiddy	40,629
11.	Manchester Utd	H	1-2	Evans (pen)	62,429
12.	Manchester City	H	7-3	Holton 4 Evans (pen) Bloomfield Haverty	33,651
13.	Charlton Ah	A	3-1	Tapscott 2 Clapton	40,051
14.	Tottenham H	H	3-1	Herd 2 Haverty	60,580
15.	Everton	A	0-4		52,478
16.	Aston Villa	H	2-1	Groves 2	40,045
17.	Wolves	A	2-5	Tapscott Haverty	34,019
18.	Bolton Wands	H	3-0	Tapscott 2 Haverty	33,377
19.	Leeds United	A	3-3	Tapscott 2 Holton	39,000
20.	Sunderland	H	1-1	Tapscott	36,442
21.	Luton Town	A	2-1	Haverty Tapscott	22,000
22.	Cardiff City	A	3-2	Herd 2 Haverty	15,000
23.	Birmingham City	H	4-0	Evans (pen) Holton B loomfield Watts (og)	28,644
24.	Chelsea	A	1-1	Bloomfield	32,094
25.	Chelsea	H	2-0	Clapton Tapscott	22,526
26.	West Brom Alb	A	2-0	Haverty Tapscott	25,000
27.	Portsmouth	H	1-1	Herd	48,949
28.	Newcastle United	A	1-3	Evans (pen)	45,990
29.	Sheffield Wed	H	6-3	Herd 3 Tapscott 2 Bloomfield	40,217
30.	Manchester Utd	A	2-6	Herd 2	60,384
31.	Everton	H	2-0	Holton Tapscott	30,562

32.	Luton Town	H	1-1	Tapscott	41,288
33.	Tottenham H	A	3-1	Bowen 2 Tapscott	65,455
34.	Aston Villa	A	0-0		40,000
35.	Manchester City	A	3-2	Tiddy Bloomfield Tapscott	27,974
36.	Wolves	H	0-0		51,021
37.	Bolton Wands	A	1-2	Tapscott	23,879
38.	Leeds United	H	1-0	Herd	40,388
39.	Sunderland	A	0-1		34,749
40.	Blackpool	H	1-1	Tapscott	50,270
41.	Charlton Ath	H	3-1	Tapscott 2 Holton	26,364
42.	Blackpool	A	4-2	Tapscott 2 Herd Haverty	24,118

Final League Position = 5th in Division One

♛ FA Cup ♛

3	Stoke City	H	4-2	Herd 2 Tapscott Haverty	56,173
4	Newport County	A	2-0	Tapscott Herd	22,450
5	Preston NE	A	3-3	Clapton Herd Dunn (og)	39,608
R	Preston NE	H	2-1	Dodgin Herd	61,501
6	West Brom Alb	A	2-2	Herd Charlton	58,000
R	West Brom Alb	H	1-2	Holton	58,757

1957–58

1.	Sunderland	A	1-0	Groves	56,493
2.	West Brom Alb	H	2-2	Herd 2	45,988
3.	Luton Town	H	2-0	Groves Holton	50,111
4.	West Brom Alb	A	2-1	Bloomfield Swallow	25,600
5.	Blackpool	A	0-1		31,486
6.	Everton	H	2-3	Groves 2	42,010
7.	Leicester City	H	3-1	Groves 2 Herd	45,321
8.	Manchester Utd	A	2-4	Tiddy Herd	47,142
9.	Leeds United	H	2-1	Herd 2	39,347
10.	Aston Villa	H	4-0	Swallow Tiddy Bloomfield Herd	18,472
11.	Bolton Wands	A	1-0	Herd	20,212
12.	Tottenham H	A	1-3	Holton	60,671
13.	Everton	A	2-2	Bloomfield Herd	54,345
14.	Birmingham City	H	1-1	Swallow	39,006
15.	Chelsea	A	0-0		66,007
16.	Manchester City	H	2-1	Tapscott Bloomfield	43,664
17.	Nottingham F	A	0-4		34,216
18.	Portsmouth	H	3-2	Herd 2 Clapton	40,528
19.	Sheffield Wed	A	0-2		25,200
20.	Newcastle United	H	2-3	Holton Clapton	41,694
21.	Burnley	A	1-2	Holton	18,530
22.	Preston NE	H	4-2	Nutt Herd Bloomfield Dunn (og)	31,830
23.	Sunderland	H	3-0	Herd 2 Groves	28,105
24.	Aston Villa	A	0-3		41,000
25.	Luton Town	A	0-4		27,291
26.	Blackpool	H	2-3	Herd 2	38,667

27.	Leicester City	A	1-0	Groves	31,778
28.	Manchester Utd	H	4-5	Bloomfield 2 Herd Tapscott	63,578
29.	Bolton Wands	H	1-2	Bloomfield	28,420
30.	Tottenham H	H	4-4	Clapton Herd Nutt Henry (og)	59,116
31.	Birmingham City	A	1-4	Bloomfield	26,824
32.	Chelsea	H	5-4	Herd 3 Clapton Bloomfield	41,570
33.	Manchester City	A	4-2	Bloomfield 3 Herd	31,645
34.	Leeds United	A	0-2		26,000
35.	Sheffield Wed	H	1-0	Herd	28,074
36.	Portsmouth	A	4-5	Bloomfield Clapton Nutt Gunter (og)	23,000
37.	Wolves	H	0-2		51,318
38.	Wolves	A	2-1	Groves Wills (pen)	47,501
39.	Newcastle United	A	3-3	Herd Groves Bloomfield	42,700
40.	Burnley	H	0-0		31,440
41.	Nottingham F	H	1-1	Bloomfield	23,217
42.	Preston NE	A	0-3		21,528

Final League Position = 12th in Division One

♕ FA Cup ♕

3	Northampton T	A	1-3	Clapton	21,344

1958–59

1.	Preston NE	A	1-2	Bloomfield	30,578
2.	Burnley	H	3-0	Bloomfield Holton Docherty	41,305
3.	Leicester City	H	5-1	Holton 2 Evans Clapton Nutt	35,411
4.	Burnley	A	1-3	Groves	28,240
5.	Everton	A	6-1	Groves Herd 4 Bloomfield	40,557
6.	Bolton Wands	H	6-1	Herd Nutt 2 Bloomfield Clapton Evans (pen)	45,255
7.	Tottenham H	H	3-1	Nutt Herd 2	65,565
8.	Bolton Wands	A	1-2	Bloomfield	42,391
9.	Manchester City	H	4-1	Herd 2 Evans (pen) Bloomfield	47,878
10.	Leeds United	A	1-2	Herd	34,000
11.	West Brom Alb	H	4-3	Henderson 2 Herd Barlow (og)	57,770
12.	Manchester Utd	A	1-1	Ward	55,909
13.	Wolves	H	1-1	Biggs	49,393
14.	Aston Villa	A	2-1	Ward Nutt	30,000
15.	Blackburn Rovers	A	2-4	Evans (pen) Ward	37,600
16.	Newcastle United	H	3-2	Groves Henderson 2	62,801
17.	West Ham United	A	0-0		38,250
18.	Nottingham F	H	3-1	Herd Henderson McKinlay (og)	49,106
19.	Chelsea	A	3-0	Henderson Clapton Barnwell	57,910
20.	Blackpool	H	1-4	Clapton	54,792
21.	Portsmouth	A	1-0	Nutt	33,321
22.	Aston Villa	H	1-2	Henderson	32,170
23.	Preston NE	H	1-2	Henderson	32,860
24.	Luton Town	A	3-6	Julians Evans (pen) Bloomfield	21,870
25.	Luton Town	H	1-0	Bloomfield	56,501

26.	Leicester City	A	3-2	Julians 2 Bloomfield	33,979
27.	Everton	H	3-1	Groves 2 Bloomfield	39,474
28.	Tottenham H	A	4-1	Groves Herd Henderson 2	60,241
29.	Manchester City	A	0-0		31,819
30.	West Brom Alb	A	1-1	Julians	32,700
31.	Leeds United	H	1-0	Herd	30,244
32.	Manchester Utd	H	3-2	Barnwell 2 Herd	67,386
33.	Wolves	A	1-6	Haverty	40,080
34.	Blackburn Rovers	H	1-1	Wills (pen)	40,155
35.	Newcastle United	A	0-1		32,620
36.	West Ham United	H	1-2	Henderson	52,452
37.	Nottingham F	A	1-1	Haverty	32,558
38.	Chelsea	H	1-1	Ward	40,900
39.	Birmingham City	A	1-4	Clapton	25,791
40.	Blackpool	A	2-1	Haverty Julians	17,118
41.	Portsmouth	H	5-2	Groves 3 Henderson Gunter (og)	24,569
42.	Birmingham City	H	2-1	Clapton Groves	26,129

Final League Position = 3rd in Division One

♆ FA Cup ♆

3	Bury	A	1-0	Herd	29,880
4	Colchester Utd	A	2-2	Groves 2	16,000
R	Colchester Utd	H	4-0	Herd 2 Julians Evans (pen)	62,686
5	Sheffield United	H	2-2	Evans (pen) Julians	55,407
R	Sheffield United	A	0-3		48,763

	1959–60				
1.	Sheffield Wed	H	0-1		47,585
2.	Nottingham F	A	3-0	Clapton 3	32,386
3.	Wolves	A	3-3	Clapton Herd 2	45,885
4.	Nottingham F	H	1-1	Herd	41,585
5.	Tottenham H	H	1-1	Barnwell	61,011
6.	Bolton Wands	A	1-0	Herd	32,571
7.	Manchester City	H	3-1	Clapton Barnwell Haverty	38,392
8.	Bolton Wands	H	2-1	Herd Clapton	38,795
9.	Blackburn Rovers	A	1-1	Herd	31,800
10.	Blackpool	H	2-1	Barnwell Herd	47,473
11.	Everton	A	1-3	Barnwell	40,587
12.	Manchester Utd	A	2-4	Henderson Herd	51,872
13.	Preston NE	H	0-3		44,073
14.	Leicester City	A	2-2	Barnwell Bloomfield	29,152
15.	Birmingham City	H	3-0	Herd Barnwell Henderson	34,605
16.	Leeds United	A	2-3	Herd Henderson	21,500
17.	West Ham United	H	1-3	Bloomfield	49,760
18.	Chelsea	A	3-1	Haverty 2 Bloomfield	52,748
19.	West Brom Alb	H	2-4	Groves Bloomfield	41,157
20.	Newcastle United	A	1-4	Haverty	39,940
21.	Burnley	H	2-4	Haverty Bloomfield	26,249
22.	Sheffield Wed	A	1-5	Julians	25,135

23.	Luton Town	H	0-3		31,466
24.	Luton Town	A	1-0	Julians	27,055
25.	Wolves	H	4-4	Evans Haverty Charles Wills (pen)	47,854
26.	Tottenham H	A	0-3		58,962
27.	Manchester City	A	2-1	Charles Barnes (og)	28,441
28.	Blackburn Rovers	H	5-2	Charles 3 Haverty Herd	35,633
29.	Blackpool	A	1-2	Charles	14,868
30.	Everton	H	2-1	Charles 2	28,872
31.	Newcastle United	H	1-0	Barnwell	47,657
32.	Preston NE	A	3-0	Haverty Henderson Bloomfield	23,635
33.	Leicester City	H	1-1	Herd	27,838
34.	Burnley	A	2-3	Henderson 2	20,166
35.	Leeds United	H	1-1	Herd	19,735
36.	West Ham United	A	0-0		29,000
37.	Chelsea	H	1-4	Bloomfield	40,700
38.	Fulham	H	2-0	Henderson Herd	37,873
39.	Birmingham City	A	0-3		27,216
40.	Fulham	A	0-3		31,058
41.	Manchester Utd	H	5-2	Bloomfield 3 Clapton Ward	41,057
42.	West Brom Alb	A	0-1		25,600

Final League Position = 13th in Division One

♆ FA Cup ♆

3	Rotherham Utd	A	2-2	Julians Williams (og)	24,750
R	Rotherham Utd	H	1-1	Bloomfield	57,598
2R	Rotherham Utd	N*	0-2		56,290

* played at Hillsborough, Sheffield.

1960–61

1.	Burnley	A	2-3	Herd Bloomfield	23,653
2.	Preston NE	H	1-0	Everitt	31,612
3.	Nottingham F	H	3-0	Henderson Skirton 2	28,878
4.	Preston NE	A	0-2		20,105
5.	Manchester City	A	0-0		36,656
6.	Birmingham City	H	2-0	Herd Kane	20,285
7.	Tottenham H	H	2-3	Herd Ward	60,088
8.	Birmingham City	A	0-2		22,904
9.	Newcastle United	H	5-0	Herd 3 Strong Clapton	34,885
10.	Cardiff City	A	0-1		35,000
11.	West Brom Alb	H	1-0	Herd	27,176
12.	Leicester City	A	1-2	Henderson	22,501
13.	Aston Villa	H	2-1	Herd Strong	34,048
14.	Blackburn Rovers	A	4-2	Strong 2 Charles Herd	21,500
15.	Manchester Utd	H	2-1	Barnwell Herd	45,715
16.	West Ham United	A	0-6		29,375
17.	Chelsea	H	1-4	Charles	38,886
18.	Blackpool	A	1-1	Herd	15,417
19.	Everton	H	3-2	Herd 3	36,709

20.	Wolves	A	3-5	Herd 2 Barnwell	25,658
21.	Bolton Wands	H	5-1	Barnwell Strong 2 Eastham 2	30,818
22.	Burnley	H	2-3	Strong Herd	37,209
23.	Sheffield Wed	A	1-1	Neill	29,311
24.	Sheffield Wed	H	1-1	Eastham	43,555
25.	Nottingham F	A	5-3	Herd 3 Eastham Henderson	30,735
26.	Manchester City	H	5-4	Herd 3 Henderson Clapton	36,440
27.	Tottenham H	A	2-4	Henderson Haverty	65,251
28.	Newcastle United	A	3-3	Strong 2 Eastham	34,780
29.	Cardiff City	H	2-3	Herd 2	33,754
30.	West Brom Alb	A	3-2	Haverty 2 Skirton	21,500
31.	Leicester City	H	1-3	Henderson	31,721
32.	Aston Villa	A	2-2	Haverty Barnwell	35,000
33.	Blackburn Rovers	H	0-0		34,250
34.	Manchester Utd	A	1-1	Charles	29,732
35.	West Ham United	H	0-0		27,665
36.	Fulham	A	2-2	Herd 2	35,476
37.	Bolton Wands	A	1-1	Henderson	18,618
38.	Fulham	H	4-2	Henderson 2 Barnwell 2	20,142
39.	Blackpool	H	1-0	Herd	36,301
40.	Chelsea	A	1-3	Strong	38,233
41.	Wolves	H	1-5	Henderson	34,429
42.	Everton	A	1-4	Herd	39,810

Final League Position = 11th in Division One

♆ FA Cup ♆

| 3 | Sunderland | A | 1-2 | Herd | 58,575 |

1961–62

1.	Burnley	H	2-2	Charles 2	42,856
2.	Leicester City	A	1-0	Eastham	29,396
3.	Tottenham H	A	3-4	Charles 2 Skirton	59,371
4.	Leicester City	H	4-4	MacLeod Eastham Skirton Charles	35,055
5.	Bolton Wands	A	1-2	Charles	18,414
6.	Manchester City	H	3-0	Griffiths Skirton Sears (og)	41,478
7.	West Brom Alb	A	0-4		20,560
8.	Sheffield Wed	A	1-1	Charles	35,903
9.	Birmingham City	H	1-1	Skirton	31,749
10.	Everton	A	1-4	Charles	41,289
11.	Blackpool	H	3-0	Charles 2 Ward	41,166
12.	Blackburn Rovers	A	0-0		14,000
13.	Manchester Utd	H	5-1	Skirton 2 Eastham Barnwell Ward	54,099
14.	Cardiff City	A	1-1	Charles	25,400
15.	Chelsea	H	0-3		37,590
16.	Aston Villa	A	1-3	Skirton	24,200
17.	Sheffield Wed	H	1-0	Strong	19,331
18.	Nottingham F	H	2-1	Strong MacLeod	34,217
19.	Wolves	A	3-2	Ward 2 Skirton	28,882

20.	West Ham United	H	2-2	Strong Skirton	47,206
21.	Sheffield United	A	1-2	Strong	19,213
22.	Burnley	A	2-0	Skirton Charles	22,887
23.	Tottenham H	H	2-1	Charles Skirton	63,440
24.	Fulham	H	1-0	Charles	32,969
25.	Bolton Wands	H	1-2	Charles	33,351
26.	Manchester City	A	2-3	Skirton 2	20,414
27.	West Brom Alb	H	0-1		29,597
28.	Birmingham City	A	0-1		27,797
29.	Blackpool	A	1-0	Strong	13,728
30.	Blackburn Rovers	H	0-0		25,744
31.	Cardiff City	H	1-1	Strong	25,059
32.	Chelsea	A	3-2	Skirton Barnwell MacLeod	31,016
33.	Aston Villa	H	4-5	Skirton 2 Strong 2	20,107
34.	Nottingham F	A	1-0	Strong	21,129
35.	Fulham	A	2-5	Skirton MacLeod	26,517
36.	Wolves	H	3-1	Skirton Strong 2	24,367
37.	Manchester Utd	A	3-2	Eastham Skirton Cantwell (og)	24,788
38.	Ipswich Town	A	2-2	MacLeod Eastham	30,649
39.	West Ham United	A	3-3	Clapton Strong MacLeod	31,912
40.	Ipswich Town	H	0-3		44,694
41.	Sheffield United	H	2-0	Barnwell Eastham	18,761
42.	Everton	H	2-3	Griffiths Armstrong	20,034

Final League Position = 10th in Division One

♆ FA Cup ♆

| 3 | Bradford City | H | 3-0 | Charles 2 Lawlor (og) | 40,232 |
| 4 | Manchester Utd | A | 0-1 | | 54,082 |

1962–63

1.	Leyton Orient	A	2-1	Strong Baker	26,300
2.	Birmingham City	H	2-0	Baker McCullough	34,004
3.	Manchester Utd	H	1-3	Clamp	62,308
4.	Birmingham City	A	2-2	Strong 2	27,135
5.	Burnley	A	1-2	Skirton	26,231
6.	Aston Villa	H	1-2	Skirton	33,861
7.	Sheffield Wed	H	1-2	Baker	31,115
8.	Aston Villa	A	1-3	Baker	36,705
9.	Fulham	A	3-1	Skirton MacLeod Baker	31,442
10.	Leicester City	H	1-1	Baker	31,291
11.	Bolton Wands	A	0-3		16,572
12.	Tottenham H	A	4-4	Court 2 MacLeod Skirton	61,749
13.	West Ham United	H	1-1	Baker	49,597
14.	Wolves	H	5-4	Baker 3 Eastham 2	43,002
15.	Blackburn Rovers	A	5-5	Baker 2 Skirton 2 Eastham	15,400
16.	Sheffield United	H	1-0	Strong	25,503
17.	Liverpool	A	1-2	Strong	38,452
18.	Nottingham F	A	0-3		24,804
19.	Ipswich Town	H	3-1	Baker Armstrong Barnwell	25,056

20.	Manchester City	A	4-2	MacLeod 2 Baker Strong	25,454
21.	Blackpool	H	2-0	Strong Martin (og)	23,767
22.	Leyton Orient	H	2-0	Baker 2	29,075
23.	Leicester City	A	0-2		26,320
24.	Bolton Wands	H	3-2	MacLeod Brown Armstrong	25,204
25.	Tottenham H	H	2-3	Strong Baker	59,980
26.	West Ham United	A	4-0	Baker 2 McCullough Strong	31,467
27.	Liverpool	H	2-2	MacLeod McCullough	30,496
28.	Blackburn Rovers	H	3-1	Strong 2 MacLeod	21,467
29.	Everton	H	4-3	Strong Baker MacLeod Skirton	38,061
30.	Ipswich Town	A	1-1	Thrower (og)	16,686
31.	Nottingham F	H	0-0		25,134
32.	Wolves	A	0-1		18,593
33.	West Brom Alb	H	3-2	Strong 2 Skirton	28,219
34.	Sheffield United	A	3-3	Baker Anderson Barnwell	21,487
35.	West Brom Alb	A	2-1	Baker 2	16,600
36.	Manchester City	H	2-3	MacLeod Strong	20,539
37.	Everton	A	1-1	Strong	56,034
38.	Blackpool	A	2-3	Sammels Skirton	13,864
39.	Manchester Utd	A	3-2	Baker Strong Skirton	36,000
40.	Burnley	H	2-3	Skirton Baker	23,256
41.	Fulham	H	3-0	Baker 3	17,389
42.	Sheffield Wed	A	3-2	Baker Eastham Court	20,514

Final League Position = 7th in Division One

♀ FA Cup ♀

3	Oxford United	H	5-1	Baker 2 Strong 2 MacLeod	14,649
4	Sheffield Wed	H	2-0	MacLeod Strong	40,367
5	Liverpool	H	1-2	MacLeod	55,245

	1963–64				
1.	Wolves	H	1-3	Strong	50,302
2.	West Brom Alb	H	3-2	Baker 2 Strong	31,381
3.	Leicester City	A	2-7	Barnwell (pen) MacLeod	29,620
4.	West Brom Alb	A	0-4		24,500
5.	Bolton Wands	H	4-3	Skirton 2 Baker Ure	26,016
6.	Aston Villa	H	3-0	Baker 3	29,189
7.	Fulham	A	4-1	Strong 2 Baker MacLeod	34,910
8.	Manchester Utd	H	2-1	Eastham Baker	56,776
9.	Burnley	A	3-0	Strong 2 Eastham	20,618
10.	Everton	A	1-2	Strong	51,829
11.	Ipswich Town	H	6-0	Strong 3 Baker 2 MacLeod	31,803
12.	Stoke City	A	2-1	Baker 2	31,014
13.	Tottenham H	H	4-4	Eastham 2 Baker Strong	67,986
14.	Aston Vila	A	1-2	MacLeod	22,981
15.	Nottingham F	H	4-2	Strong 2 Anderson McKinlay (og)	41,124
16.	Sheffield United	A	2-2	Baker Strong	33,908
17.	Birmingham City	H	4-1	Baker 3 Strong	23,499
18.	West Ham United	H	3-3	MacLeod Eastham Anderson	52,742

19.	Chelsea	A	1-3	Eastham	47,050
20.	Blackpool	H	5-3	Strong 2 Barnwell Brown Eastham	33,847
21.	Blackburn Rovers	A	1-4	Baker	21,000
22.	Liverpool	H	1-1	Baker	40,551
23.	Everton	H	6-0	Baker 2 Eastham 2 Armstrong Strong	33,644
24.	Wolves	A	2-2	Strong 2	18,952
25.	Leicester City	H	0-1		28,019
26.	Birmingham City	A	4-1	MacLeod 2 Baker Armstrong	23,329
27.	Bolton Wands	A	1-1	Baker	14,651
28.	Fulham	H	2-2	Baker Strong	35,895
29.	Manchester Utd	A	1-3	McCullough	48,340
30.	Burnley	H	3-2	Strong Armstrong Anderson	30,863
31.	Ipswich Town	A	2-1	Eastham Strong	17,486
32.	Tottenham H	A	1-3	Strong	57,358
33.	Stoke City	H	1-1	Baker	26,208
34.	Nottingham F	A	0-2		18,416
35.	Chelsea	H	2-4	Neill Baker	25,513
36.	West Ham United	A	1-1	Skirton	28,170
37.	Sheffield Wed	H	1-1	Strong	18,221
38.	Sheffield United	H	1-3	Strong	21,001
39.	Sheffield Wed	A	4-0	Skirton 3 Court	26,433
40.	Blackpool	A	1-0	Skirton	14,067
41.	Blackburn Rovers	H	0-0		26,164
42.	Liverpool	A	0-5		48,623

Final League Position = 8th in Division One

♛ FA Cup ♛

3	Wolves	H	2-1	Strong Baker	40,803
4	West Brom Alb	A	3-3	MacLeod Armstrong Baker	39,597
R	West Brom Alb	H	2-0	Armstrong Strong	57,698
5	Liverpool	H	0-1		61,295

1964-65

1.	Liverpool	A	2-3	Baker Strong	47,620
2.	Sheffield Wed	H	1-1	Simpson	35,590
3.	Aston Villa	H	3-1	Armstrong MacLeod Strong	28,732
4.	Sheffield Wed	A	1-2	Baker	22,555
5.	Wolves	A	1-0	Skirton	23,000
6.	Blackburn Rovers	H	1-1	Baker	29,510
7.	Sunderland	H	3-1	Eastham 2 Strong	34,291
8.	Blackburn Rovers	A	2-1	Armstrong Baker	17,675
9.	Leicester City	A	3-2	Baker Court Eastham	21,364
10.	Chelsea	H	1-3	Court	54,936
11.	Nottingham F	H	0-3		35,041
12.	Tottenham H	A	1-3	Baker	55,959
13.	Burnley	H	3-2	Baker Simpson Sammels	24,962
14.	Sheffield United	A	0-4		16,906

15.	Everton	H	3-1	Baker 2 Anderson	33,561
16.	Birmingham City	A	3-2	Baker Eastham Sammels	20,210
17.	Leeds United	A	1-3	Sammels	38,620
18.	West Ham United	H	0-3		36,026
19.	West Brom Alb	A	0-0		18,000
20.	Manchester Utd	H	2-3	Anderson Eastham	59,637
21.	Fulham	A	4-3	Baker 2 Skirton Armstrong	13,764
22.	Liverpool	H	0-0		25,171
23.	Aston Villa	A	1-3	Baker	16,000
24.	Stoke City	H	3-2	Baker Sammels McLintock	27,663
25.	Stoke City	A	1-4	Sammels	20,491
26.	Wolves	H	4-1	Radford 3 Baker	25,561
27.	Sunderland	A	2-0	Radford Baker	42,158
28.	Leicester City	H	4-3	Baker 2 Eastham Armstrong	31,063
29.	Chelsea	A	1-2	Radford	46,798
30.	Leeds United	H	1-2	Eastham	32,132
31.	Fulham	H	2-0	Radford Baker	22,101
32.	Tottenham H	H	3-1	Baker 2 Radford	48,367
33.	Burnley	A	1-2	Court	12,841
34.	Sheffield United	H	1-1	Ure	22,001
35.	Nottingham F	A	0-3		24,497
36.	West Ham United	A	1-2	Baker	24,665
37.	West Brom Alb	H	1-1	Eastham	18,797
38.	Birmingham City	H	3-0	Baker Skirton McLintock	16,048
39.	Blackpool	A	1-1	Eastham	18,620
40.	Blackpool	H	3-1	Baker 2 Neill	17,063
41.	Everton	A	0-1		32,643
42.	Manchester Utd	A	1-3	Eastham	51,625

Final League Position = 13th in Division One

♆ FA Cup ♆

3	Darlington	A	2-0	Radford Armstrong	19,717
4	Peterborough U	A	1-2	Radford	32,000

1965–66					
1.	Stoke City	H	2-1	Baker 2	30,107
2.	Northampton T	A	1-1	Baldwin	17,352
3.	Burnley	A	2-2	Eastham Baker	16,737
4.	Chelsea	H	1-3	Baker	45,456
5.	Nottingham F	A	1-0	Sammels	30,431
6.	Tottenham H	A	2-2	Baker L Brown (og)	53,962
7.	Nottingham F	H	1-0	Eastham	34,542
8.	Everton	A	1-3	Baker	38,935
9.	Manchester Utd	H	4-2	Baker Radford Armstrong Eastham	56,757
10.	Northampton T	H	1-1	Radford	33,240
11.	Newcastle Utd	A	1-0	McLintock	42,790
12.	Fulham	H	2-1	Sammels Baker	32,318
13.	Blackpool	A	3-5	Armstrong Radford Armfield (og)	19,533

14.	Blackburn Rovers	H	2-2	McLintock Baker	27,703
15.	Leicester City	A	1-3	Armstrong	22,528
16.	Sheffield United	H	6-2	Baker 2 Skirton 2 Armstrong 2	28,541
17.	Leeds United	A	0-2		36,383
18.	West Ham United	H	3-2	Skirton 2 Baker	35,855
19.	Aston Villa	H	3-3	Skirton 2 Eastham	25,880
20.	Liverpool	A	2-4	Radford Baldwin	43,727
21.	Sheffield Wed	A	0-4		33,101
22.	Sheffield Wed	H	5-2	Eastham 2 Skirton Sammels Baker	21,035
23.	Fulham	A	0-1		25,801
24.	Liverpool	H	0-1		43,917
25.	Blackburn Rovers	A	1-2	Radford	12,532
26.	Stoke City	A	3-1	Radford 2 Howe	21,883
27.	Burnley	H	1-1	Sammels	28,652
28.	Chelsea	A	0-0		48,641
29.	Blackpool	H	0-0		21,881
30.	Tottenham H	H	1-1	Court	51,805
31.	Everton	H	0-1		24,821
32.	Manchester Utd	A	1-2	Walley	47,246
33.	Newcastle Utd	H	1-3	Noble (og)	13,979
34.	West Brom Alb	H	1-1	Skirton	8,738
35.	West Brom Alb	A	4-4	Baldwin 2 Radford Armstrong	20,000
36.	West Ham United	A	1-2	Baldwin	26,022
37.	Sunderland	A	2-0	Skirton Sammels	32,349
38.	Sunderland	H	1-1	Sammels	25,699
39.	Sheffield United	A	0-3		15,045
40.	Aston Villa	A	0-3		18,866
41.	Leeds United	H	0-3		4,554
42.	Leicester City	H	1-0	Rodrigues (og)	16,435

Final League Position = 14th in Division One

♟ FA Cup ♟

3	Blackburn Rovers	A	0-3		22,951

1966–67

1.	Sunderland	A	3-1	Skirton 2 Armstrong	33,304
2.	West Ham United	H	2-1	Radford Baldwin	40,614
3.	Aston Villa	H	1-0	Baldwin	26,762
4.	West Ham United	A	2-2	McLintock Sammels	34,964
5.	Tottenham H	A	1-3	Sammels	56,271
6.	Sheffield Wed	H	1-1	Sammels	28,898
7.	Manchester City	A	1-1	Sammels	27,948
8.	Blackpool	H	1-1	Coakley	28,946
9.	Chelsea	A	1-3	Addison	48,001
10.	Leicester City	H	2-4	Addison Graham	33,945
11.	Newcastle Utd	H	2-0	Boot Clark (og)	24,595
12.	Leeds United	A	1-3	Boot	31,481
13.	West Brom Alb	H	2-3	Armstrong 2	31,606

14.	Manchester Utd	A	0-1		45,387
15.	Leeds United	H	0-1		24,227
16.	Everton	A	0-0		45,745
17.	Fulham	H	1-0	McLintock	25,755
18.	Nottingham F	A	1-2	Neilson	20,482
19.	Burnley	H	0-0		23,220
20.	Sheffield United	A	1-1	Graham	15,488
21.	Sunderland	H	2-0	McLintock Sammels	20,482
22.	Southampton	H	4-1	Radford 2 Armstrong 2	29,527
23.	Southampton	A	1-2	Addison	27,781
24.	Aston Villa	A	1-0	McLintock	19,431
25.	Tottenham H	H	0-2		49,851
26.	Manchester City	H	1-0	McLintock	22,392
27.	Blackpool	A	3-0	Sammels 2 Neilson	12,028
28.	Chelsea	H	2-1	Graham Armstrong	52,467
29.	Leicester City	A	1-2	Graham	24,587
30.	Newcastle Utd	A	1-2	Graham	27,460
31.	Manchester Utd	H	1-1	Sammels	63,563
32.	West Brom Alb	A	1-0	McLintock	16,500
33.	Sheffield United	H	2-0	Sammels McLintock	23,099
34.	Liverpool	A	0-0		46,168
35.	Liverpool	H	1-1	Graham	35,877
36.	Stoke City	A	2-2	Graham 2	14,606
37.	Fulham	A	0-0		27,690
38.	Nottingham F	H	1-1	Storey	36,196
39.	Everton	H	3-1	Sammels Graham McLintock	20,567
40.	Burnley	A	4-1	Addison Graham Armstrong Simpson	10,947
41.	Stoke City	H	3-1	Radford McLintock Allen (og)	24,611
42.	Sheffield Wed	A	1-1	Graham	23,222

Final League Position = 7th in Division One

♆ FA Cup ♆

3	Bristol Rovers	A	3-0	Graham Neilson Armstrong	35,420
4	Bolton Wands	A	0-0		31,870
R	Bolton Wands	H	3-0	Radford 3	47,050
5	Birmingham City	A	0-1		40,665

League Cup
2	Gillingham	H	1-1	Baldwin	13,029
R	Gillingham	A	1-1	Baldwin	20,566
2R	Gillingham	H	5-0	Baldwin 2 McLintock 2 Coakley	18,409
3	West Ham United	H	1-3	Jenkins	33,647

1967–68
1.	Stoke City	A	2-0	Graham Sammels	27,048
2.	Liverpool	A	0-2		52,033
3.	Nottingham F	A	0-2		33,991
4.	Liverpool	H	2-0	Sammels Hateley (og)	33,420

5.	Coventry City	H	1-1	Graham	30,404
6.	West Brom Alb	A	3-1	Armstrong Sammels Addison	19,232
7.	Sheffield United	A	4-2	Addison Graham 2 McLintock	14,939
8.	Tottenham H	H	4-0	Radford Neill (pen)	62,836
				Graham Addison	62,836
9.	Manchester City	H	1-0	Radford	41,466
10.	Newcastle Utd	A	1-2	Graham	33,350
11.	Manchester Utd	A	0-1		60,197
12.	Sunderland	H	2-1	Radford Graham	30,864
13.	Wolves	A	2-3	Graham Armstrong	36,664
14.	Fulham	H	5-3	Radford 3 Addison 2	29,974
15.	Leeds United	A	1-3	McLintock	31,362
16.	Everton	H	2-2	Johnston Sammels	36,371
17.	Leicester City	A	2-2	Radford Johnston	28,150
18.	West Ham United	H	0-0		42,029
19.	Burnley	A	0-1		15,381
20.	Stoke City	A	1-0	Graham	16,119
21.	Nottingham F	H	3-0	Graham 2 Armstrong	32,512
22.	Chelsea	A	1-2	Neill (pen)	51,672
23.	Chelsea	H	1-1	Radford	47,157
24.	Coventry City	A	1-1	Graham	32,839
25.	Sheffield United	H	1-1	Graham	27,447
26.	Tottenham H	A	0-1		57,885
27.	Manchester City	A	1-1	Graham	42,392
28.	Newcastle Utd	H	0-0		36,996
29.	Manchester Utd	H	0-2		46,417
30.	Wolves	H	0-2		25,983
31.	Fulham	A	3-1	Graham Gould Court	20,612
32.	West Ham United	A	1-1	Armstrong	33,986
33.	Everton	A	0-2		40,029
34.	Southampton	A	0-2		23,207
35.	Leicester City	H	2-1	Gould Graham	19,108
36.	Southampton	H	0-3		23,165
37.	Sunderland	A	0-2		31,255
38.	Burnley	H	2-0	Court Armstrong	15,278
39.	Sheffield Wed	H	3-2	Court Radford Gould	11,262
40.	Sheffield Wed	A	2-1	Radford Gould	25,066
41.	Leeds United	H	4-3	Gould McLintock Johnston Madeley (og)	25,043
42.	West Brom Alb	H	2-1	Gould McLintock	24,896

Final League Position = 9th in Division One

♆ FA Cup ♆

3	Shrewsbury T	A	1-1	Radford	18,280
R	Shrewsbury T	H	2-0	Sammels Jenkins	41,958
4	Swansea Town	A	1-0	Gould	31,919
5	Birmingham City	H	1-1	Radford	45,515
R	Birmingham City	A	1-2	Gould	51,586

League Cup

2	Coventry City	A	2-1	Sammels Graham	22,605
3	Reading	H	1-0	Simpson	27,866
4	Blackburn Rovers	H	2-1	Graham Addison	20,044
5	Burnley	A	3-3	Graham 2 McLintock	16,033
R	Burnley	H	2-1	Radford Neill	36,570
SF	Huddersfield T	H	3-2	Graham Radford McNab	39,986
SF	Huddersfield T	A	3-1	Sammels Jenkins McLintock	27,312
F	Leeds United	N*	0-1		97,887

* played at Wembley Stadium

1968–69

1.	Tottenham H	A	2-1	Radford Beal (og)	56,280
2.	Leicester City	H	3-0	Court Gould 2	32,164
3.	Liverpool	H	1-1	Radford	43,535
4.	Wolves	A	0-0	36,006	
5.	Ipswich Town	A	2-1	Radford Jenkins	25,825
6.	Manchester City	H	4-1	Jenkins 2 Sammels Radford	40,776
7.	Queen's Park R	H	2-1	McLintock Neill (pen)	44,407
8.	Southampton	A	2-1	Radford 2	25,126
9.	Stoke City	H	1-0	Neill	28,275
10.	Leeds United	A	0-2		39,946
11.	Sunderland	H	0-0		35,277
12.	Manchester Utd	A	0-0		61,843
13.	Manchester City	A	1-1	Radford	33,830
14.	Coventry City	H	2-1	Court Radford	35,240
15.	West Brom Alb	A	0-1		29,324
16.	West Ham United	H	0-0		59,533
17.	Newcastle United	H	0-0		34,277
18.	Nottingham F	A	2-0	Armstrong Radford	24,550
19.	Chelsea	H	0-1		45,588
20.	Burnley	A	1-0	Robertson	16,264
21.	Everton	H	3-1	Radford Court Graham	40,108
22.	Coventry City	A	1-0	Gould	27,332
23.	West Brom Alb	H	2-0	Gould Fraser (og)	30,765
24.	Manchester Utd	H	3-0	Armstrong Court Radford	62,300
25.	Sheffield Wed	H	2-0	Gould Radford	39,008
26.	Newcastle United	A	1-2	Gould	34,227
27.	Nottingham F	H	1-1	Gould	35,585
28.	Burnley	H	2-0	Gould 2	27,614
29.	Ipswich Town	H	0-2		23,891
30.	Sheffield Wed	A	5-0	Radford 3 Sammels Gould	21,436
31.	Queen's Park R	A	1-0	Armstrong	23,076
32.	Tottenham H	H	1-0	Sammels	43,972
33.	Southampton	H	0-0		28,990
34.	Liverpool	A	1-1	Robertson	44,843
35.	Sunderland	A	0-0		23,214
36.	Wolves	H	3-1	Robertson Armstrong Graham	31,011
37.	Leicester City	A	0-0		35,573
38.	Leeds United	H	1-2	Graham	44,715

39.	Chelsea	A	1-2	Court	38,905
40.	Stoke City	A	3-1	Armstrong Court Stevenson (og)	14,996
41.	West Ham United	A	2-1	Sammels Graham	34,941
42.	Everton	A	0-1		39,689

Final League Position = 4th in Division One

♆ FA Cup ♆

3	Cardiff City	A	0-0		55,316
R	Cardiff City	H	2-0	Armstrong Gould	52,681
4	Charlton Ath	H	2-0	Sammels Robertson	55,760
5	West Brom Alb	A	0-1		46,000

League Cup

2	Sunderland	H	1-0	Neill	28,460
3	Scunthorpe Utd	A	6-1	Jenkins 3 Gould Sammels Court	17,450
4	Liverpool	H	2-1	Simpson Radford	39,299
5	Blackpool	H	5-1	Armstrong 2 Radford Gould Simpson	32,321
SF	Tottenham H	H	1-0	Radford	55,237
SF	Tottenham H	A	1-1	Radford	55,923
F	Swindon Town	N*	1-3	Gould	98,189

* played at Wembley Stadium

1969-70

1.	Everton	H	0-1		44,364
2.	Leeds United	A	0-0		37,164
3.	West Brom Alb	A	1-0	George	32,215
4.	Leeds United	H	1-1	Rice	44,923
5.	Nottingham F	H	2-1	McNab Graham	30,290
6.	West Ham United	A	1-1	Lampard (og)	39,590
7.	Newcastle United	A	1-3	Robertson	47,208
8.	Sheffield Wed	H	0-0		28,605
9.	Burnley	A	1-0	Graham	14,721
10.	Tottenham H	H	2-3	Robertson Radford	55,280
11.	Manchester Utd	H	2-2	Graham Sammels	59,489
12.	Chelsea	A	0-3		46,370
13.	Coventry City	H	0-1		28,877
14.	West Brom Alb	H	1-1	Radford	21,165
15.	Stoke City	A	0-0		25,801
16.	Sunderland	A	1-1	Sammels	17,864
17.	Ipswich Town	H	0-0		22,458
18.	Crystal Palace	A	5-1	Radford 3 Armstrong Graham	34,894
19.	Derby County	H	4-0	Sammels 2 George Armstrong	49,763
20.	Wolves	A	0-2		26,796
21.	Manchester City	H	1-1	Neill (pen)	42,923
22.	Liverpool	A	1-0	Robertson	40,295
23.	Southampton	H	2-2	Sammels Radford	24,509
24.	Burnley	H	3-2	Robertson Radford Armstrong	21,404
25.	Sheffield Wed	A	1-1	Sammels	17,101

26.	Nottingham F	A	1-1	McNab	38,915
27.	Newcastle United	H	0-0		39,637
28.	Manchester Utd	A	1-2	Marinello	41,055
29.	Chelsea	H	0-3		53,793
30.	Coventry City	A	0-2		31,661
31.	Stoke City	H	0-0		26,601
32.	Everton	A	2-2	George Radford	48,564
33.	Manchester City	A	1-1	Graham	25,508
34.	Derby County	A	2-3	Radford Roberts	35,284
35.	Sunderland	H	3-1	Storey (pen) Kennedy Kelly	21,826
36.	Liverpool	H	2-1	Sammels Radford	32,295
37.	Southampton	A	2-0	Sammels George	23,902
38.	Wolves	H	2-2	Graham 2	32,353
39.	Crystal Palace	H	2-0	Radford George	34,144
40.	Ipswich Town	A	1-2	George	25,713
41.	West Ham United	H	2-1	Kelly Radford	36,212
42.	Tottenham H	A	0-1		46,969

Final League Position = 12th in Division One

♆ FA Cup ♆

3	Blackpool	H	1-1	Radford	32,210
R	Blackpool	A	2-3	Sammels Radford	24,801

League Cup

2	Southampton	A	1-1	McNab	21,111
R	Southampton	H	2-0	Graham 2	26,362
3	Everton	H	0-0		36,102
R	Everton	A	0-1		41,140

1970–71

1.	Everton	A	2-2	George Graham	49,684
2.	West Ham United	A	0-0		39,904
3.	Manchester Utd	H	4-0	Radford 3 Graham	54,117
4.	Huddersfield	H	1-0	Kennedy	34,848
5.	Chelsea	A	1-2	Kelly	53,722
6.	Leeds United	H	0-0		47,749
7.	Tottenham H	H	2-0	Armstrong 2	48,713
8.	Burnley	A	2-1	Kennedy Radford	12,675
9.	West Brom Alb	H	6-2	Kennedy 2 Graham 2 Armstrong Cantello (og)	33,326
10.	Stoke City	A	0-5		18,153
11.	Nottingham F	H	4-0	Kennedy 3 Armstrong	32,053
12.	Newcastle United	A	1-1	Graham	38,024
13.	Everton	H	4-0	Kennedy 2 Kelly Storey (pen)	50,012
14.	Coventry City	A	3-1	Kennedy Radford Graham	30,017
15.	Derby County	H	2-0	Kelly Radford	43,013
16.	Blackpool	A	1-0	Radford	17,115
17.	Crystal Palace	H	1-1	Radford	34,503
18.	Ipswich Town	A	1-0	Armstrong	22,856

19.	Liverpool	H	2-0	Graham Radford	45,097
20.	Manchester City	A	2-0	Armstrong Radford	33,027
21.	Wolves	H	2-1	Radford Graham	38,816
22.	Manchester Utd	A	3-1	McLintock Graham Kennedy	33,182
23.	Southampton	H	0-0		34,169
24.	West Ham United	H	2-0	Graham Kennedy	49,007
25.	Huddersfield T	A	1-2	Kennedy	30,455
26.	Liverpool	A	0-2		43,847
27.	Manchester City	H	1-0	Radford	46,122
28.	Ipswich Town	H	3-2	George Radford McLintock	39,822
29.	Derby County	A	0-2		35,875
30.	Wolves	A	3-0	Armstrong Kennedy Radford	33,644
31.	Crystal Palace	A	2-0	Graham Sammels	35,022
32.	Blackpool	H	1-0	Storey	37,372
33.	Chelsea	H	2-0	Kennedy 2	62,087
34.	Coventry City	H	1-0	Kennedy	37,029
35.	Southampton	A	2-1	Radford McLintock	30,231
36.	Nottingham F	A	3-0	McLintock Kennedy George	40,727
37.	Newcastle United	H	1-0	George	48,106
38.	Burnley	H	1-0	George (pen)	47,484
39.	West Brom Alb	A	2-2	McLintock Harford (og)	36,858
40.	Leeds United	A	0-1		48,350
41.	Stoke City	H	1-0	Kelly	55,011
42.	Tottenham H	A	1-0	Kennedy	51,992

Final League Position = 1st in Division One

♆ FA Cup ♆

3	Yeovil Town	A	3-0	Radford 2 Kennedy	4,374
4	Portsmouth	A	1-1	Storey (pen)	39,659
R	Portsmouth	H	3-2	George Simpson Storey (pen)	47,865
5	Manchester City	A	2-1	George 2	45,105
6	Leicester City	A	0-0		42,000
R	Leicester City	H	1-0	George	57,443
SF	Stoke City	N*	2-2	Storey 2 (1 pen)	53,436
R	Stoke City	N**	2-0	Graham Kennedy	62,500
F	Liverpool	N***	2-1	Kelly George	100,000

*played at Hillsborough, Sheffield ** played at Villa Park, Birmingham *** played at Wembley Stadium*

	League Cup				
2	Ipswich Town	A	0-0		21,564
R	Ipswich Town	H	4-0	Kennedy 2 Radford Roberts	26,379
3	Luton Town	A	1-0	Graham	27,023
4	Crystal Palace	A	0-0		40,451
R	Crystal Palace	H	0-2		45,026

	1971–72				
1.	Chelsea	H	3-0	McLintock Kennedy Radford	49,174
2.	Huddersfield T	A	1-0	Kennedy	21,279
3.	Manchester Utd	A*	1-3	McLintock	27,649

4.	Sheffield United	H	0-1		45,395
5.	Stoke City	H	0-1		37,637
6.	West Brom Alb	A	1-0	Roberts	29,922
7.	Leeds United	H	2-0	Graham Storey (pen)	51,196
8.	Everton	A	1-2	Kennedy	39,710
9.	Leicester City	H	3-0	Radford 2 Rice	40,201
10.	Southampton	A	1-0	Simpson	23,738
11.	Newcastle United	H	4-2	Graham Kennedy Armstrong Kelly	40,509
12,	Chelsea	A	2-1	Kennedy 2	52,338
13.	Derby County	A	1-2	Graham	36,480
14.	Ipswich Town	H	2-1	George Sivell (og)	39,065
15.	Liverpool	A	2-3	Kennedy Smith (og)	46,929
16.	Manchester City	H	1-2	Nelson	47,443
17.	Wolves	A	1-5	Kennedy	28,851
18.	Tottenham H	A	1-1	Kennedy	52,884
19.	Crystal Palace	H	2-1	Kelly Radford	32,461
20.	West Ham United	A	0-0		35,155
21.	Coventry City	H	2-0	Radford 2	28,599
22.	West Brom Alb	H	2-0	Roberts 2	28,177
23.	Nottingham F	A	1-1	Graham	42,750
24.	Everton	H	1-1	Simpson	47,031
25.	Stoke City	A	0-0		18,965
26.	Huddersfield T	H	1-0	Armstrong	36,670
27.	Sheffield United	A	5-0	George 2 Graham Simpson Kennedy	30,778
28.	Derby County	H	2-0	George 2 (1 pen)	52,055
29.	Ipswich Town	A	1-0	George	28,657
30.	Manchester City	A	0-2		44,213
31.	Newcastle United	A	0-2		31,920
32.	Leeds United	A	0-3		45,055
33.	Southampton	H	1-0	Marinello	27,172
34.	Nottingham F	H	3-0	Kennedy George (pen) Graham	33,895
35.	Leicester City	A	0-0		27,431
36.	Wolves	H	2-1	Graham 2	38,189
37.	Crystal Palace	A	2-2	Radford Ball	34,384
38.	West Ham United	H	2-1	Ball 2	45,251
39.	Manchester Utd	H	3-0	Radford Kennedy Simpson	49,125
40.	Coventry City	A	1-0	McLintock	23,509
41.	Liverpool	H	0-0		39,285
42.	Tottenham H	H	0-2		42,038

Final League Position = 5th in Division One   *played at Wembley Stadium

♕ FA Cup ♕

3	Swindon Town	A	2-0	Armstrong Ball	32,000
4	Reading	A	2-1	Rice Morgan (og)	25,756
5	Derby County	A	2-2	George 2	39,622
R	Derby County	H	0-0		63,077
2R	Derby County	N*	1-0	Kennedy	36,534

6	Orient	A	1-0	Ball	31,768
SF	Stoke City	N**	1-1	Armstrong	56,576
R	Stoke City	N***	2-1	George Radford	38,970
F	Leeds United	N****	0-1		100,000

*played at Filbert Street, Leicester **played at Villa Park, Birmingham ***played at Goodison Park
****played at Wembley Stadium

League Cup

2	Barnsley	H	1-0	Kennedy	27,294
3	Newcastle United	H	4-0	Radford 2 Kennedy Graham	34,071
4	Sheffield United	H	0-0		44,061
R	Sheffield United	A	0-2		35,461

1972–73

1.	Leicester City	A	1-0	Ball (pen)	28,009
2.	Wolves	H	5-2	Radford 2 Kennedy Simpson McNab	38,524
3.	Stoke City	H	2-0	Kennedy 2	42,146
4.	Coventry City	A	1-1	Rice	24,670
5.	Manchester Utd	A	0-0		48,108
6.	West Ham United	H	1-0	Ball (pen)	43,802
7.	Chelsea	H	1-1	Webb (og)	46,675
8.	Newcastle United	A	1-2	Kennedy	23,849
9.	Liverpool	H	0-0		47,597
10.	Norwich City	A	2-3	Storey Radford	32,273
11.	Birmingham City	H	2-0	Storey George	30,003
12.	Southampton	H	1-0	Graham	34,694
13.	Sheffield United	A	0-1		24,478
14.	Ipswich Town	H	1-0	Graham	34,196
15.	Crystal Palace	A	3-2	George (pen) Radford Rice	35,865
16.	Manchester City	H	0-0		45,536
17.	Coventry City	H	0-2		33,699
18.	Wolves	A	3-1	Radford 2 Marinello	25,988
19.	Everton	H	1-0	Radford	35,728
20.	Derby County	A	0-5		31,034
21.	Leeds United	H	2-1	Ball (pen) Radford	39,108
22.	Tottenham H	A	2-1	Storey Radford	47,505
23.	West Brom Alb	H	2-1	Radford Nisbet (og)	27,119
24.	Birmingham City	A	1-1	Kelly	32,721
25.	Norwich City	H	2-0	Radford Ball	39,038
26.	Stoke City	A	0-0		24,586
27.	Manchester Utd	H	3-1	Kennedy Armstrong Ball	56,194
28.	Chelsea	A	1-0	Kennedy	36,292
29.	Newcastle United	H	2-2	Kennedy Ball	37,906
30.	Liverpool	A	2-0	Ball (pen) Radford	49,898
31.	Leicester City	H	1-0	Manley (og)	42,047
32.	West Brom Alb	A	0-1		23,515
33.	Sheffield United	H	3-2	George 2 Ball	33,346
34.	Ipswich Town	A	2-1	Radford Ball (pen)	34,636
35.	Manchester City	A	2-1	George Kennedy	32,031

36.	Crystal Palace	H	1-0	Ball	41,879
37.	Derby County	H	0-1		45,217
38.	Tottenham H	H	1-1	Storey	50,863
39.	Everton	A	0-0		42,888
40.	Southampton	A	2-2	George Radford	23,919
41.	West Ham United	A	2-1	Kennedy Radford	37,366
42.	Leeds United	A	1-6	Armstrong	25,088

Final League Position = 2nd in Division One

♆ FA Cup ♆

3	Leicester City	H	2-2	Kennedy Armstrong	36,433
R	Leicester City	A	2-1	Radford Kelly	32,973
4	Bradford City	H	2-0	Ball George	40,407
5	Carlisle United	A	2-1	Ball McLintock	23,922
6	Chelsea	A	2-2	Ball George	37,685
R	Chelsea	H	2-1	Ball (pen) Kennedy	62,746
SF	Sunderland	N*	1-2	George	53,301

*played at Hillsborough, Sheffield

FA Cup third place play-off (played at beginning of 1973–74 season)					
PO	Wolves	H	1-3	Hornsby	21,038

League Cup					
2	Everton	H	1-0	Storey	35,230
3	Rotherham Utd	H	5-0	Radford 2 George Storey Marinello	25,241
4	Sheffield United	A	2-1	Radford George	20,128
5	Norwich City	H	0-3		37,671

1973–74					
1.	Manchester Utd	H	3-0	Kennedy Radford Ball	51,501
2.	Leeds United	H	1-2	Blockley	47,429
3.	Newcastle United	A	1-1	George	28,697
4.	Sheffield United	A	0-5		27,839
5.	Leicester City	H	0-2		28,558
6.	Sheffield United	H	1-0	Kennedy	29,434
7.	Norwich City	A	4-0	George McNab Ball (pen) Kennedy	29,278
8.	Stoke City	H	2-1	Radford Ball	30,578
9.	Everton	A	0-1		31,359
10.	Birmingham City	H	1-0	Kennedy	23,915
11.	Tottenham H	A	0-2		41,855
12.	Ipswich Town	H	1-1	Simpson	28,344
13.	Queen's Park R	A	0-2		29,115
14.	Liverpool	H	0-2		39,837
15.	Manchester City	A	2-1	Kelly Hornsby	31,041
16.	Chelsea	H	0-0		38,677
17.	West Ham United	A	3-1	George Ball 2	28,287
18.	Coventry City	H	2-2	Hornsby Nelson	22,340

19.	Wolves	H	2-2	George Hornsby	13,482
20.	Derby County	A	1-1	Newton (og)	25,161
21.	Burnley	A	1-2	Radford	13,200
22.	Everton	H	1-0	Ball	19,886
23.	Southampton	A	1-1	Ball	24,133
24.	Leicester City	A	0-2		25,860
25.	Newcastle United	H	0-1		29,258
26.	Norwich City	H	2-0	Ball 2	22,084
27.	Manchester Utd	A	1-1	Kennedy	38,589
28.	Burnley	H	1-1	Ball	30,789
29.	Leeds United	A	1-3	Ball	26,778
30.	Tottenham H	H	0-1		38,804
31.	Birmingham City	A	1-3	Kennedy	29,822
32.	Southampton	H	1-0	Ball	19,210
33.	Ipswich Town	A	2-2	Kennedy Simpson	22,297
34.	Manchester City	H	2-0	Radford 2	25,319
35.	Stoke City	A	0-0		18,532
36.	West Ham United	H	0-0		37,868
37.	Chelsea	A	3-1	Kennedy 2 Radford	29,152
38.	Wolves	A	1-3	Kennedy	25,881
39.	Derby County	H	2-0	Ball (pen) George	26,017
40.	Liverpool	A	1-0	Kennedy	47,997
41.	Coventry City	A	3-3	Rice Kennedy Radford	19,945
42.	Queen's Park R	H	1-1	Brady	40,396

Final League Position = 10th in Division One

♆ FA Cup ♆

3	Norwich City	A	1-0	Kelly	21,500
4	Aston Villa	H	1-1	Kennedy	41,682
R	Aston Villa	A	0-2		47,821

League Cup

| 2 | Tranmere Rovers | H | 0-1 | | 20,337 |

1974–75

1.	Leicester City	A	1-0	Kidd	26,448
2.	Ipswich Town	H	0-1		31,027
3.	Manchester City	H	4-0	Kidd 2 Radford 2	27,143
4.	Ipswich Town	A	0-3		28,036
5.	Everton	A	1-2	Kidd	42,438
6.	Burnley	H	0-1		23,586
7.	Chelsea	A	0-0		34,596
8.	Luton Town	H	2-2	Kidd 2	21,629
9.	Birmingham City	A	1-3	George	25,584
10.	Leeds United	A	0-2		32,784
11.	Queen's Park R	H	2-2	Kidd Radford	29,690
12.	Manchester City	A	1-2	Radford	26,658
13.	Tottenham H	A	0-2		36,194
14.	West Ham United	H	3-0	Radford Brady Kidd	41,004

15.	Wolves	H	0-0		27,572
16.	Liverpool	A	3-1	Ball 2 Brady	43,850
17.	Derby County	H	3-1	Ball 2 (1 pen) Kidd	32,286
18.	Coventry City	A	0-3		15,669
19.	Middlesbrough	H	2-0	Brady Ball (pen)	25,283
20.	Carlisle United	A	1-2	Kidd	12,926
21.	Leicester City	H	0-0		20,849
22.	Stoke City	A	2-0	Kidd 2	23,292
23.	Chelsea	H	1-2	Ball (pen)	33,784
24.	Sheffield United	A	1-1	George	19,967
25.	Carlisle United	H	2-1	Radford Cropley	21,538
26.	Middlesbrough	A	0-0		27,996
27.	Liverpool	H	2-0	Ball 2 (1 pen)	43,028
28.	Wolves	A	0-1		19,807
29.	Derby County	A	1-2	Radford	24,002
30.	Everton	H	0-2		32,216
31.	Birmingham City	H	1-1	Kidd	17,845
32.	Newcastle United	H	3-0	Kidd Ball (pen) Rostron	16,540
33.	Burnley	A	3-3	Rostron Hornsby 2	17,539
34.	Luton Town	A	0-2		22,101
35.	Stoke City	H	1-1	Kelly	26,852
36.	Sheffield United	H	1-0	Kidd	24,338
37.	Coventry City	H	2-0	Kidd 2	17,291
38.	Leeds United	H	1-2	Kidd	36,619
39.	Queen's Park R	A	0-0		24,362
40.	Newcastle United	A	1-3	Hornsby	21,895
41.	Tottenham H	H	1-0	Kidd	43,752
42.	West Ham United	A	0-1		30,195

Final League Position = 16th in Division One

♛ FA Cup ♛

3	York City	H	1-1	Kelly	27,029
R	York City	A	3-1	Kidd 3	15,362
4	Coventry City	A	1-1	Ball	31,165
R	Coventry City	H	3-0	Armstrong 2 Matthews	30,867
5	Leicester City	H	0-0		43,841
R	Leicester City	A	1-1	Radford	35,009
2R	Leicester City	A	1-0	Radford	39,025
6	West Ham United	H	0-2		56,742

League Cup					
2	Leicester City	H	1-1	Kidd	20,788
R	Leicester City	A	1-2	Brady	17,303

1975–76					
1.	Burnley	A	0-0		18,603
2.	Sheffield United	A	3-1	Brady Rice Kidd	23,344
3.	Stoke City	H	0-1		28,025
4.	Norwich City	H	2-1	Ball (pen) Kelly	22,613

5.	Wolves	A	0-0		18,144
6.	Leicester City	H	1-1	Stapleton	22,005
7.	Aston Villa	A	0-2		34,474
8.	Everton	H	2-2	Kidd Stapleton	24,864
9.	Tottenham H	A	0-0		37,092
10.	Manchester City	H	2-3	Ball Cropley	24,928
11.	Coventry City	H	5-0	Cropley 2 Ball Kidd 2	19,234
12.	Manchester Utd	A	1-3	Kelly	52,958
13.	Middlesbrough	H	2-1	Stapleton Cropley	23,591
14.	Newcastle United	A	0-2		32,824
15.	Derby County	H	0-1		32,012
16.	Birmingham City	A	1-3	Ball	21,652
17.	Manchester Utd	H	3-1	Ball Armstrong Greenhoff (og)	40,102
18.	West Ham United	A	0-1		31,012
19.	Liverpool	A	2-2	Ball (pen) Kidd	27,447
20.	Leeds United	H	1-2	Brady	36,003
21.	Stoke City	A	1-2	Armstrong	18,628
22.	Burnley	H	1-0	Radford	16,459
23.	Ipswich Town	A	0-2		28,457
24.	Queen's Park R	H	2-0	Ball Kidd	39,021
25.	Aston Villa	H	0-0		24,501
26.	Leicester City	A	1-2	Ross	21,331
27.	Sheffield United	H	1-0	Brady	14,477
28.	Norwich City	A	1-3	Kidd	23,038
29.	Derby County	A	0-2		24,875
30.	Birmingham City	H	1-0	Brady	20,907
31.	Liverpool	H	1-0	Radford	36,127
32.	Middlesbrough	A	1-0	Radford	20,000
33.	Coventry City	A	1-1	Powling	13,938
34.	Newcastle United	H	0-0		18,424
35.	West Ham United	H	6-1	Kidd 3 Ball 2 (1 pen) Armstrong	34,011
36.	Leeds United	A	0-3		26,657
37.	Tottenham H	H	0-2		42,134
38.	Everton	A	0-0		20,774
39.	Wolves	H	2-1	Brady Mancini	19,518
40.	Ipswich Town	H	1-2	Stapleton	26,973
41.	Queen's Park R	A	1-2	Kidd	30,362
42.	Manchester City	A	1-3	Armstrong	31,003

Final League Position = 17th in Division One

♆ FA Cup ♆

3	Wolves	A	0-3		22,215

League Cup

2	Everton	A	2-2	Cropley Stapleton	17,174
R	Everton	H	0-1	21,813	

1976–77

1.	Bristol City	H	0-1		41,082

2.	Norwich City	A	3-1	Nelson Macdonald Stapleton	26,769
3.	Sunderland	A	2-2	Ross Macdonald	41,211
4.	Manchester City	H	0-0		35,132
5.	West Ham United	A	2-0	Ross Stapleton	32,415
6.	Everton	H	3-1	Brady Stapleton Macdonald	34,076
7.	Ipswich Town	A	1-3	Hunter (og)	25,505
8.	Queen's Park R	H	3-2	Rice Brady Stapleton	39,442
9.	Stoke City	H	2-0	Rice Macdonald	28,745
10.	Aston Villa	A	1-5	Ball	33,860
11.	Leicester City	A	1-4	Stapleton	19,351
12.	Leeds United	A	1-2	Matthews	33,556
13.	Birmingham City	H	4-0	Stapleton Nelson Macdonald (pen) Ross	23,063
14.	Liverpool	H	1-1	Armstrong	45,016
15.	Coventry City	A	2-1	Macdonald Stapleton	18,313
16.	Newcastle United	H	5-3	Macdonald 3 Ross Stapleton	34,053
17.	Derby County	A	0-0		24,016
18.	Manchester Utd	H	3-1	Macdonald 2 Brady	39,572
19.	Tottenham H	A	2-2	Macdonald 2	47,751
20.	Leeds United	H	1-1	Macdonald	44,090
21.	Norwich City	H	1-0	Rice	30,537
22.	Birmingham City	A	3-3	Macdonald 3	23,247
23.	Bristol City	A	0-2		26,282
24.	Sunderland	H	0-0		30,925
25.	Manchester City	A	0-1		45,368
26.	Middlesbrough	A	0-3		26,083
27.	West Ham United	H	2-3	Brady Stapleton	38,221
28.	Everton	A	1-2	Macdonald	29,802
29.	Ipswich Town	H	1-4	Macdonald (pen)	34,688
30.	West Brom Alb	H	1-2	Macdonald	19,517
31.	Queen's Park R	A	1-2	Young	26,191
32.	Stoke City	A	1-1	Price	13,951
33.	Leicester City	H	3-0	Rix O'Leary 2	23,013
34.	West Brom Alb	A	2-0	Stapleton Macdonald	24,275
35.	Tottenham H	H	1-0	Macdonald	47,432
36.	Liverpool	A	0-2		48,174
37.	Coventry City	H	2-0	Stapleton Macdonald	22,790
38.	Aston Villa	H	3-0	Macdonald Armstrong Nelson	24,011
39.	Newcastle United	A	2-0	Macdonald Matthews	44,763
40.	Derby County	H	0-0		26,659
41.	Middlesbrough	H	1-1	Stapleton	23,911
42.	Manchester Utd	A	2-3	Brady Stapleton	53,232

Final League Position = 8th in Division One

♔ FA Cup ♔

3	Notts County	A	1-0	Ross	17,328
4	Coventry City	H	3-1	Macdonald 2 Stapleton	41,078
5	Middlesbrough	A	1-4	Macdonald	35,208

League Cup

2	Carlisle United	H	3-2	Ross 2 Macdonald	21,550
3	Blackpool	A	1-1	Armstrong	18,893
R	Blackpool	H	0-0		27,195
2R	Blackpool	H	2-0	Stapleton O'Leary	26,791
4	Chelsea	H	2-1	Ross Stapleton	52,285
5	Queen's Park R	A	1-2	Stapleton	27,621

1977–78

1.	Ipswich Town	A	0-1		30,384
2.	Everton	H	1-0	Powling	32,924
3.	Wolves	A	1-1	Powling	22,909
4.	Nottingham F	H	3-0	Stapleton 2 Brady (pen)	40,810
5.	Aston Villa	A	0-1		36,929
6.	Leicester City	H	2-1	Stapleton Macdonald	27,371
7.	Norwich City	A	0-1		19,312
8.	West Ham United	H	3-0	Stapleton Rice Brady (pen)	41,245
9.	Liverpool	H	0-0		47,110
10.	Manchester City	A	1-2	Macdonald	43,177
11.	Queen's Park R	H	1-0	Macdonald	36,290
12.	Bristol City	A	2-0	Rix Macdonald	25,497
13.	Birmingham City	H	1-1	Rice	31,355
14.	Manchester Utd	A	2-1	Macdonald Stapleton	53,055
15.	Coventry City	H	1-1	Coop (og)	31,653
16.	Newcastle United	A	2-1	Stapleton Sunderland	22,880
17.	Derby County	H	1-3	Nelson	31,989
18.	Middlesbrough	A	1-0	Cooper (og)	17,422
19.	Leeds United	H	1-1	Young	40,162
20.	Coventry City	A	2-1	Stapleton 2	20,993
21.	Chelsea	H	3-0	Price Rix O'Leary	46,074
22.	West Brom Alb	A	3-1	Sunderland Macdonald Brady (pen)	27,723
23.	Everton	A	0-2		47,039
24.	Ipswich Town	H	1-0	Price	43,705
25.	Wolves	H	3-1	Brady Macdonald Stapleton	34,784
26.	Nottingham F	A	0-2		35,743
27.	Aston Villa	H	0-1		30,127
28.	Leicester City	A	1-1	Brady (pen)	15,780
29.	West Ham United	A	2-2	Macdonald 2	31,675
30.	Norwich City	H	0-0		23,506
31.	Manchester City	H	3-0	Sunderland Young Price	34,003
32.	Bristol City	H	4-1	Stapleton 2 Sunderland Price	28,463
33.	Birmingham City	A	1-1	Brady (pen)	22,087
34.	West Brom Alb	H	4-0	Macdonald 3 Young	36,763
35.	Chelsea	A	0-0		40,764
36.	Manchester Utd	H	3-1	Macdonald 2 Brady	40,739
37.	Queen's Park R	A	1-2	Brady (pen)	25,683
38.	Newcastle United	H	2-1	Brady Price	33,353
39.	Leeds United	A	3-1	Stapleton Macdonald Hart (og)	33,263
40.	Liverpool	A	0-1		38,318

| 41. | Middlesbrough | H | 1-0 | Stapleton | 32,138 |
| 42. | Derby County | A | 0-3 | | 21,189 |

Final League Position = 5th in Division One

♛ FA Cup ♛

3	Sheffield United	A	5-0	Macdonald 2 Stapleton O'Leary	32,156
4	Wolves	H	2-1	Sunderland Macdonald	49,373
5	Walsall	H	4-1	Stapleton 2 Macdonald Sunderland	43,789
6	Wrexham	A	3-2	Macdonald Sunderland Young	25,547
SF	Orient	N*	3-0	Macdonald 2 Rix	49,698
F	Ipswich Town	N**	0-1		100,000

* played at Stamford Bridge, London   ** played at Wembley Stadium

League Cup

2	Manchester Utd	H	3-2	Macdonald 2 Brady	36,171
3	Southampton	H	2-0	Brady (pen) Stapleton	40,749
4	Hull City	H	5-1	Matthews 2 Brady Macdonald Stapleton	25,922
5	Manchester City	A	0-0		42,435
R	Manchester City	H	1-0	Brady	57,960
SF	Liverpool	A	1-2	Macdonald	44,764
SF	Liverpool	H	0-0		49,561

1978–79

1.	Leeds United	H	2-2	Brady 2 (1 pen)	42,057
2.	Manchester City	A	1-1	Macdonald	39,506
3.	Everton	A	0-1		41,179
4.	Queen's Park R	H	5-1	Rix 2 Brady Stapleton 2	33,883
5.	Nottingham F	A	1-2	Brady	28,124
6.	Bolton Wands	H	1-0	Stapleton	31,120
7.	Manchester Utd	H	1-1	Price	45,393
8.	Middlesbrough	A	3-2	O'Leary Price Walford	14,404
9.	Aston Villa	H	1-1	Sunderland	34,537
10.	Wolves	A	0-1		19,664
11.	Southampton	H	1-0	Brady	33,074
12.	Bristol City	A	3-1	Brady 2 (1 pen) Stapleton	27,016
13.	Ipswich Town	H	4-1	Stapleton 3 Nelson	35,269
14.	Leeds United	A	1-0	Gatting	33,961
15.	Everton	H	2-2	Brady 2 (1 pen)	39,801
16.	Coventry City	A	1-1	Stapleton	26,786
17.	Liverpool	H	1-0	Price	51,902
18.	Norwich City	A	0-0		20,165
19.	Derby County	H	2-0	Price Stapleton	26,943
20.	Tottenham H	A	5-0	Sunderland 3 Stapleton Brady	42,273
21.	West Brom Alb	H	1-2	Brady (pen)	40,055
22.	Birmingham City	H	3-1	Stapleton Rice Sunderland	27,877
23.	Nottingham F	H	2-1	Price Stapleton	52,158
24.	Manchester Utd	A	2-0	Sunderland 2	45,460

25.	Middlesbrough	H	0-0		28,371
26.	Queen's Park R	A	2-1	Price Brady	21,125
27.	Wolves	H	0-1		32,215
28.	Southampton	A	0-2		25,052
29.	Bristol City	H	2-0	Rix Stapleton	24,288
30.	Ipswich Town	A	0-2		26,407
31.	Manchester City	H	1-1	Sunderland	35,014
32.	Bolton Wands	A	2-4	Price Heeley	20,704
33.	Coventry City	H	1-1	Nelson	30,091
34.	Liverpool	A	0-3		47,297
35.	Tottenham H	H	1-0	Stapleton	53,896
36.	West Brom Alb	A	1-1	Brady	28,353
37.	Chelsea	H	5-2	Stapleton 2 O'Leary Sunderland Price	37,232
38.	Derby County	A	0-2		18,674
39.	Aston Villa	A	1-5	Stapleton	26,168
40.	Norwich City	H	1-1	Walford	28,885
41.	Birmingham City	A	0-0		14,015
42.	Chelsea	A	1-1	Macdonald	30,705

Final League Position = 7th in Division One

♆ FA Cup ♆

3	Sheffield Wed	A	1-1	Sunderland	33,635
R	Sheffield Wed	H	1-1	Brady	37,987
2R	Sheffield Wed	N*	2-2	Brady Sunderland	25,011
3R	Sheffield Wed	N*	3-3	Stapleton 2 Young	17,088
4R	Sheffield Wed	N*	2-0	Gatting Stapleton	30,275
4	Notts County	H	2-0	Young Talbot	39,195
5	Nottingham F	A	1-0	Stapleton	35,906
6	Southampton	A	1-1	Price	24,536
R	Southampton	H	2-0	Sunderland 2	44,820
SF	Wolves	N**	2-0	Stapleton Sunderland	46,244
F	Manchester Utd	N***	3-2	Talbot Stapleton Sunderland	100,000

* played at Filbert Street, Leicester   ** played at Villa Park, Birmingham   *** played at Wembley Stadium

League Cup					
2	Rotherham Utd	A	1-3	Stapleton	10,481

1979–80					
1.	Brighton & HA	A	4-0	Sunderland 2 Stapleton Brady (pen)	28,604
2.	Ipswich Town	H	0-2		33,255
3.	Manchester Utd	H	0-0		44,380
4.	Leeds United	A	1-1	Nelson	23,245
5.	Derby County	A	2-3	Sunderland Stapleton	16,429
6.	Middlesbrough	H	2-0	Sunderland Stapleton	30,341
7.	Aston Villa	A	0-0		27,277
8.	Wolves	H	2-3	Stapleton Hollins	41,844
9.	Manchester City	H	0-0		34,688

10.	Ipswich Town	A	2-1	Sunderland Rix	21,527
11.	Bolton Wands	A	0-0		17,032
12.	Stoke City	H	0-0		31,591
13.	Bristol City	A	1-0	Sunderland	23,029
14.	Brighton & HA	H	3-0	Rix Brady (pen) Sunderland	34,400
15.	Crystal Palace	A	0-1		42,887
16.	Everton	H	2-0	Stapleton 2	33,450
17.	Liverpool	H	0-0		55,546
18.	Nottingham F	A	1-1	Stapleton	27,925
19.	Coventry City	H	3-1	Stapleton Sunderland O'Leary	27,563
20.	West Brom Alb	A	2-2	Nelson Stapleton	18,280
21.	Norwich City	H	1-1	Stapleton	18,869
22.	Tottenham H	H	1-0	Sunderland	44,560
23.	Manchester Utd	A	0-3		54,295
24.	Southampton	A	1-0	Young	22,473
25.	Leeds United	H	0-1		35,945
26.	Derby County	H	2-0	Brady (pen) Young	22,091
27.	Aston Villa	H	3-1	Sunderland 2 Rix	33,816
28.	Bolton Wands	H	2-0	Young Stapleton	24,383
29.	Stoke City	A	3-2	Sunderland Price Brady	19,752
30.	Bristol City	H	0-0		21,559
31.	Manchester City	A	3-0	Brady 2 (1 pen) Stapleton	33,792
32.	Crystal Palace	H	1-1	Brady	37,606
33.	Everton	A	1-0	Gatting	28,184
34.	Norwich City	A	1-2	Rix	16,923
35.	Southampton	H	1-1	Sunderland	34,593
36.	Tottenham H	A	2-1	Vaessen Sunderland	41,369
37.	Liverpool	A	1-1	Talbot	46,.878
38.	West Brom Alb	H	1-1	Stapleton	30,027
39.	Coventry City	A	1-0	Vaessen	16,817
40.	Nottingham F	H	0-0		34,632
41.	Wolves	A	2-1	Walford Stapleton	23,619
42.	Middlesbrough	A	0-5		15,603

Final League Position = 4th in Division One

♛ FA Cup ♛

3	Cardiff City	A	0-0		21,972
R	Cardiff City	H	2-1	Sunderland 2	36,155
4	Brighton & HA	H	2-0	Nelson Talbot	43,202
5	Bolton Wands	A	1-1	Stapleton	23,530
R	Bolton Wands	H	3-0	Sunderland 2 Stapleton	40,564
6	Watford	A	2-1	Stapleton 2	27,975
SF	Liverpool	N*	0-0		50,174
R	Liverpool	N**	1-1	Sunderland	40,679
2R	Liverpool	N**	1-1	Sunderland	42,975
3R	Liverpool	N***	1-0	Talbot	35,335
F	West Ham United	N****	0-1		100,000

* played at Hillsborough, Sheffield ** played at Villa Park, Birmingham *** played at Highfield Road
**** played at Wembley Stadium

	League Cup				
2	Leeds United	A	1-1	Stapleton	23,421
R	Leeds United	H	7-0	Sunderland 3 Brady (1 pen) Nelson Stapleton	235,133
3	Southampton	H	2-1	Stapleton Brady	37,348
4	Brighton & HA	A	0-0		25,231
R	Brighton & HA	H	4-0	Stapleton 2 Vaessen 2	30,351
5	Swindon Town	H	1-1	Sunderland (pen)	38,024
R	Swindon Town	A	3-4	Brady 2 Talbot	21,795

	1980–81				
1.	West Brom Alb	A	1-0	Stapleton	22,364
2.	Southampton	H	1-1	Stapleton	43,050
3.	Coventry City	A	1-3	Stapleton	15,399
4.	Tottenham H	H	2-0	Price Stapleton	54,045
5.	Manchester City	A	1-1	Young	32,233
6.	Stoke City	H	2-0	Hollins Sansom	27,183
7.	Middlesbrough	A	1-2	Rix	14,680
8.	Nottingham F	H	1-0	Rix	37,582
9.	Leicester City	H	1-0	Stapleton	28,490
10.	Birmingham City	A	1-3	Sunderland	15,511
11.	Manchester Utd	A	0-0		49,036
12.	Sunderland	H	2-2	Gatting Young	32,135
13.	Norwich City	H	3-1	Talbot McDermott Sansom	21,839
14.	Liverpool	A	1-1	Sunderland	40,310
15.	Brighton & HA	H	2-0	Rix McDermott	28,569
16.	Leeds United	A	5-0	Hollins 2 Gatting Talbot Sunderland	20,855
17.	Southampton	A	1-3	Rix	21,244
18.	West Brom Alb	H	2-2	Sunderland Batson (og)	25,858
19.	Everton	H	2-1	McDermott Stapleton	30,911
20.	Aston Villa	A	1-1	Talbot	30,140
21.	Wolves	H	1-1	Stapleton	26,050
22.	Sunderland	A	0-2		21,595
23.	Manchester Utd	H	2-1	Rix Vaessen	33,730
24.	Crystal Palace	A	2-2	Stapleton McDermott	29,850
25.	Ipswich Town	H	1-1	Sunderland	42,818
26.	Everton	A	2-1	Gatting Vaessen	29,362
27.	Tottenham H	A	0-2		32,994
28.	Coventry City	H	2-2	Talbot Stapleton	24,876
29.	Stoke City	A	1-1	Stapleton	14,428
30.	Nottingham F	A	1-3	Stapleton	25,357
31.	Manchester City	H	2-0	Talbot Sunderland	24,790
32.	Middlesbrough	H	2-2	Stapleton Hollins (pen)	24,504
33.	Leicester City	A	0-1		20,198
34.	Norwich City	A	1-1	Talbot	19,569
35.	Liverpool	H	1-0	Sunderland	47,058
36.	Birmingham City	H	2-1	Stapleton O'Leary	17,431
37.	Brighton & HA	A	1-0	Hollins	21,015
38.	Leeds United	H	0-0		29,339

39.	Ipswich Town	A	2-0	Sansom Nicholas	30,935
40.	Crystal Palace	H	3-2	Talbot Davis Young	24,346
41.	Wolves	A	2-1	Stapleton Berry (og)	15,160
42.	Aston Villa	H	2-0	Young McDermott	57,472

Final League Position = 3rd in Division One

FA Cup

3	Everton	A	0-2	34,236	

League Cup					
2	Swansea City	A	1-1	Stapleton	17,036
2	Swansea City	H	3-1	Hollins (pen) Sunderland Walford	26,399
3	Stockport County	A	3-1	Hollins Sunderland Stapleton	11,635
4	Tottenham H	A	0-1		42,511

1981–82					
1.	Stoke City	H	0-1		28,012
2.	West Brom Alb	A	2-0	Talbot Sunderland	17,104
3.	Liverpool	A	0-2		35,269
4.	Sunderland	H	1-1	Sunderland	26,527
5.	Leeds United	A	0-0		21,410
6.	Birmingham City	H	1-0	Talbot	19,588
7.	Mancheter Utd	H	0-0		39,797
8.	Notts County	A	1-2	Hawley	10,840
9.	Swansea City	A	0-2		20,591
10.	Manchester City	H	1-0	Meade	25,466
11.	Ipswich Town	A	1-2	Sunderland	24,362
12.	Coventry City	H	1-0	Thomas (og)	23,102
13.	Aston Villa	A	2-0	Talbot Rix	27,316
14.	Nottingham F	A	2-1	Talbot Sunderland	20,912
15.	Everton	H	1-0	McDermott	25,860
16.	West Ham United	A	2-1	Hollins (pen) Whyte	33,833
17.	Stoke City	A	1-0	Sunderland	9,625
18.	Southampton	A	1-3	O'Leary	22,263
19.	Brighton & HA	H	0-0		17,922
20.	Leeds United	H	1-0	Vaessen	22,408
21.	Wolves	H	2-1	Rix Vaessen	15,163
22.	Sunderland	A	0-0		16,345
23.	Notts County	H	1-0	Meade	18,229
24.	Middlesbrough	H	1-0	Rix	13,738
25.	Manchester Utd	A	0-0		43,833
26.	Swansea City	H	0-2		29,724
27.	Manchester City	A	0-0		30,288
28.	Ipswich Town	H	1-0	Robson	25,977
29.	West Brom Alb	H	2-2	Meade Sunderland	15,799
30.	Coventry City	A	0-1		11,965
31.	Aston Villa	H	4-3	Sunderland Rix 2 Meade	24,756
32.	Tottenham H	A	2-2	Sunderland 2	40,940
33.	Wolves	A	1-1	Davis	11,532

34.	Brighton & HA	A	1-2	Talbot	21,019
35.	Tottenham H	H	1-3	Hawley	48,897
36.	Nottingham F	H	2-0	Talbot Rix	21,986
37.	Everton	A	1-2	Rix	19,136
38.	West Ham United	H	2-0	Rix Sunderland	34,977
39.	Birmingham City	A	1-0	Whyte	13,133
40.	Middlesbrough	A	3-1	Talbot Davis Rix	9,565
41.	Liverpool	H	1-1	Sunderland	30,932
42.	Southampton	H	4-1	Davis 2 Robson Hawley	28,534

Final League Position = 5th in Division One

♛ FA Cup ♛

3	Tottenham H	A	0-1		38,421

League Cup

2	Sheffield United	A	0-1		19,101
2	Sheffield United	H	2-0	Sunderland Young	22,301
3	Norwich City	H	1-0	Nicholas	19,899
4	Liverpool	H	0-0		37,917
R	Liverpool	A	0-3		21,375

1982–83

1.	Stoke City	A	1-2	Sunderland	15,532
2.	Norwich City	H	1-1	Woodcock	22,652
3.	Liverpool	H	0-2		36,429
4.	Brighton & HA	A	0-1		13,507
5.	Coventry City	A	2-0	Chapman Woodcock	10,246
6.	Notts County	H	2-0	Rix Hollins (pen)	20,556
7.	Manchester Utd	A	0-0		43,198
8.	West Ham United	H	2-3	Talbot Davis	30,484
9.	Ipswich Town	A	1-0	Woodcock	20,792
10.	West Brom Alb	H	2-0	Sunderland Woodcock	21,666
11.	Nottingham F	A	0-3		17,161
12.	Birmingham City	H	0-0		20,699
13.	Luton Town	A	2-2	Rix Talbot	16,597
14.	Everton	H	1-1	McDermott	23,067
15.	Swansea City	A	2-1	Woodcock Chapman	12,389
16.	Watford	H	2-4	Robson Talbot	34,287
17.	Manchester City	A	1-2	McDermott	23,057
18.	Aston Villa	H	2-1	Whyte Woodcock	17,384
19.	Sunderland	A	0-3		11,753
20.	Tottenham H	H	2-0	Sunderland Woodcock	51,497
21.	Southampton	A	2-2	Woodcock Chapman	22,025
22.	Swansea City	H	2-1	Sunderland Woodcock	25,237
23.	Liverpool	A	1-3	Talbot	37,713
24.	Stoke City	H	3-0	Rix Petrovic Hollins (pen)	19,428
25.	Notts County	A	0-1		9,731
26.	Brighton & HA	H	3-1	Meade 2 Rix	17,972
27.	West Brom Alb	A	0-0		13,923

28.	Nottingham F	H	0-0		21,698
29.	Birmingham City	A	1-2	Sunderland	11,276
30.	Luton Town	H	4-1	Woodcock 3 Davis	23,987
31.	Ipswich Town	H	2-2	Rix Whyte	17,639
32.	Everton	A	3-2	Sunderland Robson Woodcock	16,318
33.	Southampton	H	0-0		24,911
34.	Tottenham H	A	0-5		43,642
35.	Coventry City	H	2-1	Rix Woodcock	19,152
36.	Norwich City	A	1-3	Davis	16,858
37.	Manchester City	H	3-0	Talbot 3	16,810
38.	Watford	A	1-2	McDermott	20,043
39.	Manchester Utd	H	3-0	O'Leary Talbot 2	23,602
40.	Sunderland	H	0-1		18,053
41.	West Ham United	A	3-1	Whyte Petrovic McDermott	28,930
42.	Aston Villa	A	1-2	Davis	24,647

Final League Position = 10th in Division One

♆ FA Cup ♆

3	Bolton Wands	H	2-1	Davis Rix	22,576
4	Leeds United	H	1-1	Sunderland	33,930
R	Leeds United	A	1-1	Rix	24,410
2R	Leeds United	H	2-1	Woodcock Rix	26,802
5	Middlesbrough	A	1-1	Rix	20,580
R	Middlesbrough	H	3-2	Talbot Woodcock Davis	28,689
6	Aston Villa	H	2-0	Woodcock Petrovic	41,774
SF	Manchester Utd	N*	1-2	Woodcock	46,535

* played at Villa Park, Birmingham

League Cup

2	Cardiff City	H	2-1	Hollins Davis	15,115
2	Cardiff City	A	3-1	Sunderland Woodcock Davis	11,632
3	Everton	A	1-1	Robson	13,089
R	Everton	H	3-0	Sunderland 3	19,547
4	Huddersfield T	H	1-0	Sunderland (pen)	17,742
5	Sheffield Wed	H	1-0	Woodcock	30,937
SF	Manchester Utd	H	2-4	Nicholas Woodcock	43,136
SF	Manchester Utd	A	1-2	Meade	56,635

1983–84

1.	Luton Town	H	2-1	Woodcock McDermott	39,348
2.	Wolves	A	2-1	Nicholas 2 (1 pen)	18,571
3.	Southampton	A	0-1		19,377
4.	Manchester Utd	H	2-3	Woodcock Talbot	42,704
5.	Liverpool	H	0-2		41,896
6.	Notts County	A	4-0	Rix Woodcock Talbot Hunt (og)	10,217
7.	Norwich City	H	3-0	Chapman Sunderland 2	24,438
8.	Queen's Park R	A	0-2		26,293
9.	Coventry City	H	0-1		20,290
10.	Nottingham F	H	4-1	Woodcock 2 Hill Sunderland	22,870

11.	Aston Villa	A	6-2	Woodcock 5 McDermott	23,678
12.	Sunderland	H	1-2	Woodcock	26,064
13.	Ipswich Town	A	0-1		21,652
14.	Everton	H	2-1	Sunderland Robson	24,330
15.	Leicester City	A	0-3		14,777
16.	West Brom Alb	H	0-1		22,271
17.	West Ham United	A	1-3	Whyte	25,118
18.	Watford	H	3-1	Meade 3	25,104
19.	Tottenham H	A	4-2	Nicholas 2 Meade 2	38,756
20.	Birmingham City	H	1-1	Nicholas (pen)	25,642
21.	Southampton	H	2-2	Cork Nicholas (pen)	27,596
22.	Norwich City	A	1-1	Woodcock	20,482
23.	Luton Town	A	2-1	Sansom Woodcock	16,320
24.	Notts County	H	1-1	Nicholas	20,110
25.	Stoke City	A	0-1		12,840
26.	Queen's Park R	H	0-2		31,014
27.	Liverpool	A	1-2	Rix	34,642
28.	Aston Villa	H	1-1	Rix	26,640
29.	Nottingham F	A	1-0	Mariner	20,045
30.	Sunderland	A	2-2	Nicholas (pen) Woodcock	15,370
31.	Ipswich Town	H	4-1	Mariner 2 Talbot Woodcock	24,000
32.	Manchester Utd	A	0-4		48,942
33.	Wolves	H	4-1	Robson Woodcock Nicholas (pen) Rix2	18,612
34.	Coventry City	A	4-1	Talbot Whyte Robson Mariner	10,550
35.	Stoke City	H	3-1	Nicholas Mariner Woodcock	21,211
36.	Everton	A	0-0		21,174
37.	Tottenham H	H	3-2	Robson Nicholas Woodcock	48,831
38.	Birmingham City	A	1-1	Woodcock	11,164
39.	Leicester City	H	2-1	Woodcock Davis	24,143
40.	West Brom Alb	A	3-1	Talbot Mariner Robson	13,566
41.	West Ham United	H	3-3	Talbot Woodcock Mariner	33,347
42.	Watford	A	1-2	Robson	22,007

Final League Position = 6th in Division One

♆ FA Cup ♆

3	Middlesbrough	A	2-3	Woodcock Nicholas	17,813

League Cup

2	Plymouth Argyle	A	1-1	Rix	20,983
2	Plymouth Argyle	H	1-0	Sunderland	22,640
3	Tottenham H	A	2-1	Nicholas Woodcock	48,200
4	Walsall	H	1-2	Robson	22,406

1984–85

1.	Chelsea	H	1-1	Mariner	45,329
2.	Nottingham F	A	0-2		17,972
3.	Watford	A	4-3	Nicholas 2 Talbot Woodcock	21,320
4.	Newcastle United	H	2-0	Talbot Anderson	37,078

5.	Liverpool	H	3-1	Talbot 2 Woodcock	50,006
6.	Ipswich Town	A	1-2	Nicholas	24,508
7.	Stoke City	H	4-0	Woodcock 2 (1 pen) Mariner Sansom	26,758
8.	Coventry City	A	2-1	Woodcock Mariner	14,394
9.	Everton	H	1-0	Nicholas (pen)	37,049
10.	Leicester City	A	4-1	Talbot 2 (1 pen) Anderson Rix	19,944
11.	Sunderland	H	3-2	Caton Allinson Talbot	36,944
12.	West Ham United	A	1-3	Allinson	33,218
13.	Manchester Utd	A	2-4	Allinson Woodcock	32,379
14.	Aston Villa	H	1-1	Mariner	33,193
15.	Queen's Park R	H	1-0	Woodcock	34,953
16.	Sheffield Wed	A	1-2	Woodcock	25,575
17.	Luton Town	H	3-1	Allinson Woodcock Anderson	26,366
18.	Southampton	A	0-1		20,243
19.	West Brom Alb	H	4-0	Allinson 2 Talbot Davis (pen)	23,728
20.	Watford	H	1-1	Allinson	31,302
21.	Norwich City	A	0-1		17,702
22.	Newcastle United	A	3-1	Nicholas 2 Talbot	27,349
23.	Tottenham H	H	1-2	Woodcock	48,714
24.	Chelsea	A	1-1	Mariner	34,752
25.	Coventry City	H	2-1	Meade Allinson	21,791
26.	Liverpool	A	0-3		28,645
27.	Manchester Utd	H	0-1		48,612
28.	West Ham United	H	2-1	Mariner Robson	25,818
29.	Sunderland	A	0-0		27,694
30.	Aston Villa	A	0-0		15,487
31.	Leicester City	H	2-0	Williams Meade	20,663
32.	Ipswich Town	H	1-1	Meade	18,365
33.	Everton	A	0-2		36,387
34.	Stoke City	A	0-2		7,371
35.	Norwich City	H	2-0	Nicholas Robson	19,597
36.	Nottingham F	H	1-1	Allinson	24,152
37.	Tottenham H	A	2-0	Nicholas Talbot	40,399
38.	Queen's Park R	A	0-1		20,189
39.	Sheffield Wed	H	1-0	Mariner	23,803
40.	Luton Town	A	1-3	Nicholas (pen)	12,251
41.	Southampton	H	1-0	Rix	21,214
42.	West Brom Alb	A	2-2	Allinson Robertson (og)	13,485

Final League Position = 7th in Division One

♆ FA Cup ♆

3	Hereford United	A	1-1	Woodcock	15,777
R	Hereford United	H	7-2	Mariner 2 Talbot 2 Nicholas Anderson Woodcock	26,023
4	York City	A	0-1		10,840

League Cup

2	Bristol Rovers	H	4-0	Woodcock Anderson Nicholas 2	23,871
2	Bristol Rovers	A	1-1	Caton	10,408
3	Oxford United	A	2-3	Rix Allinson	14,393

1985–86

1.	Liverpool	A	0-2		38,261
2.	Southampton	H	3-2	Caton Robson Woodcock	21,895
3.	Manchester Utd	H	1-2	Allinson (pen)	37,145
4.	Luton Town	A	2-2	Woodcock Donaghy (og)	10,012
5.	Leicester City	H	1-0	Woodcock	18,207
6.	Queen's Park R	A	1-0	Allinson	15,993
7.	Coventry City	A	2-0	Woodcock Nicholas	12,189
8.	Sheffield Wed	H	1-0	Allinson (pen)	23,108
9.	Chelsea	A	1-2	Nicholas	33,241
10.	Newcastle United	H	0-0		24,104
11.	Aston Villa	H	3-2	Woodcock Anderson Whyte	18,881
12.	West Ham United	A	0-0		24,057
13.	Ipswich Town	H	1-0	Davis	19,523
14.	Nottingham F	A	2-3	Rix Davis	17,756
15.	Manchester City	H	1-0	Davis	22,264
16.	Everton	A	1-6	Nicholas	28,620
17.	Oxford United	H	2-1	Davis Woodcock	19,632
18.	West Brom Alb	A	0-0		9,165
19.	Birmingham City	H	0-0		16,673
20.	Southampton	A	0-3		15,052
21.	Liverpool	H	2-0	Nicholas Quinn	35,048
22.	Manchester Utd	A	1-0	Nicholas	44,386
23.	Queen's Park R	H	3-1	Rix Nicholas Woodcock	25,770
24.	Tottenham H	H	0-0		45,109
25.	Leicester City	A	2-2	Robson Nicholas	11,246
26.	Luton Town	H	2-1	Allinson (pen) Rix	22,473
27.	Newcastle United	A	0-1		21,860
28.	Aston Villa	A	4-1	Nicholas Hayes Rocastle Elliott (og)	10,584
29.	Ipswich Town	A	2-1	Nicholas Woodcock	13,967
30.	West Ham United	H	1-0	Woodcock	31,240
31.	Coventry City	H	3-0	Woodcock Hayes McInally (og)	17,189
32.	Tottenham H	A	0-1		33,427
33.	Watford	H	0-2		19,599
34.	Watford	A	0-3		18,635
35.	Manchester City	A	1-0	Robson	19,590
36.	Nottingham F	H	1-1	Allinson (pen)	15,098
37.	Everton	H	0-1		28,251
38.	Sheffield Wed	A	0-2		16,344
39.	West Brom Alb	H	2-2	Robson Allinson (pen)	14,843
40.	Chelsea	H	2-0	Anderson Nicholas	24,025
41.	Birmingham City	A	1-0	Woodcock	6,234
42.	Oxford United	A	0-3		13,651

Final League Position = 7th in Division One

♈ FA Cup ♈

3	Grimsby Town	A	4-3	Rix Nicholas 3	12,829
4	Rotherham Utd	H	5-1	Rix Nicholas Allinson 2 (1 pen) Robson	28,490
5	Luton Town	A	2-2	Allinson Rocastle	15,799
R	Luton Town	H	0-0		26,547
2R	Luton Town	A	0-3		13,251

League Cup

2	Hereford United	A	0-0		6,049
2	Hereford United	H	2-1	Anderson Nicholas	15,789
3	Manchester City	A	2-1	Nicholas Allinson	18,279
4	Southampton	H	0-0		18,244
R	Southampton	A	3-1	Hayes Nicholas Robson	14,010
5	Aston Villa	A	1-1	Nicholas	26,093
R	Aston Villa	H	1-2	Mariner	33,091

1986–87

1.	Manchester Utd	H	1-0	Nicholas	41,382
2.	Coventry City	A	1-2	Anderson	11,182
3.	Liverpool	A	1-2	Adams	38,637
4.	Sheffield Wed	H	2-0	Adams Quinn	20,101
5.	Tottenham H	H	0-0		44,707
6.	Luton Town	A	0-0		9,876
7.	Oxford United	H	0-0		20,676
8.	Nottingham F	A	0-1		25,371
9.	Everton	A	1-0	Williams	30,007
10.	Watford	H	3-1	Groves Hayes (pen) Quinn	24,076
11.	Newcastle United	A	2-1	Anderson Williams	22,368
12.	Chelsea	H	3-1	Rocastle Hayes 2 (1 pen)	32,990
13.	Charlton Ath	A	2-0	Adams Hayes	19,614
14.	West Ham United	H	0-0		36,084
15.	Southampton	A	4-0	Hayes (pen) Quinn Groves Anderson	18,728
16.	Manchester City	H	3-0	Quinn Anderson Adams	29,009
17.	Aston Villa	A	4-0	Hayes Rocastle Groves Keown (og)	21,658
18.	Queen's Park R	H	3-1	Hayes 2 Quinn	34,049
19.	Norwich City	A	1-1	Hayes (pen)	21,409
20.	Luton Town	H	3-0	Quinn Adams Hayes	28,217
21.	Leicester City	A	1-1	Hayes (pen)	19,205
22.	Southampton	H	1-0	Quinn	38,138
23.	Wimbledon	H	3-1	Nicholas 2 Hayes (pen)	36,144
24.	Tottenham H	A	2-1	Adams Davis	37,723
25.	Coventry City	H	0-0		17,561
26.	Manchester Utd	A	0-2		51,367
27.	Sheffield Wed	A	1-1	Quinn	24,792
28.	Oxford United	A	0-0		13,296
29.	Chelsea	A	0-1		29,301
30.	Liverpool	H	0-1		47,777

31.	Nottingham F	H	0-0		18,352
32.	Watford	A	0-2		18,172
33.	Everton	H	0-1		36,218
34.	West Ham United	A	1-3	Hayes (pen)	26,174
35.	Charlton Ath	H	2-1	Davis Hayes	26,111
36.	Newcastle United	H	0-1		17,353
37.	Wimbledon	A	2-1	Davis Merson	8,515
38.	Leicester City	H	4-1	Davis Hayes 2 (1 pen) Nicholas	18,767
39.	Manchester City	A	0-3		18,072
40.	Aston Villa	H	2-1	Hayes 2 (1 pen)	18,463
41.	Queen's Park R	A	4-1	Rix 2 Merson Hayes	13,387
42.	Norwich City	H	1-2	Merson	24,001

Final League Position = 4th in Division One

♆ FA Cup ♆

3	Reading	A	3-1	Nicholas 2 Hayes (pen)	16,822
4	Plymouth Argyle	H	6-1	Nicholas Davis Quinn Rocastle Anderson 2	39,029
5	Barnsley	H	2-0	Hayes (pen) Nicholas	28,302
6	Watford	H	1-3	Allinson	43,276

League Cup					
2	Huddersfield T	H	2-0	Davis Quinn	15,194
2	Huddersfield T	A	1-1	Hayes	8,713
3	Manchester City	H	3-1	Rocastle Hayes (pen) Davis	21,604
4	Charlton Ath	H	2-0	Quinn Curbishley (og)	28,301
5	Nottingham F	H	2-0	Nicholas Hayes	38,617
SF	Tottenham H	H	0-1		41,306
SF	Tottenham H	A	2-1	Anderson Quinn	37,099
R	Tottenham H	A	2-1	Allinson Rocastle	41,055
F	Liverpool	N*	2-1	Nicholas 2	96,000

played at Wembley Stadium

1987–88					
1.	Liverpool	H	1-2	Davis	54,703
2.	Manchester Utd	A	0-0		42,890
3.	Queen's Park R	A	0-2		18,981
4.	Portsmouth	H	6-0	Smith 3 Adams Rocastle Davis	30,865
5.	Luton Town	A	1-1	Davis	8,745
6.	Nottingham F	A	1-0	Smith	18,490
7.	Wimbledon	H	3-0	Rocastle Smith Thomas (pen)	27,752
8.	West Ham United	H	1-0	Sansom	40,127
9.	Charlton Ath	A	3-0	Thomas Adams Groves	15,326
10.	Oxford United	H	2-0	Davis Williams	25,244
11.	Tottenham H	A	2-1	Rocastle Thomas	36,680
12.	Derby County	H	2-1	Richardson Thomas (pen)	32,374
13.	Newcastle United	A	1-0	Smith	23,622
14.	Chelsea	H	3-1	Richardson 2 Wegerle (og)	40,230
15.	Norwich City	A	4-2	Rocastle 2 Thomas Groves	20,558

16.	Southampton	H	0-1		32,477
17.	Watford	A	0-2		19,598
18.	Sheffield Wed	H	3-1	Groves Richardson Merson	23,670
19.	Coventry City	A	0-0		17,557
20.	Everton	H	1-1	Rocastle	34,857
21.	Nottingham F	H	0-2		31,211
22.	Wimbledon	A	1-3	Quinn	12,473
23.	Portsmouth	A	1-1	Smith	17,366
24.	Queen's Park R	H	0-0		28,271
25.	Liverpool	A	0-2		44,294
26.	Manchester Utd	H	1-2	Quinn	29,392
27.	Luton Town	H	2-1	Thomas Rocastle	22,615
28.	Charlton Ath	H	4-0	Merson 2 Thomas Smith	25,394
29.	Tottenham H	H	2-1	Smith Groves	37,143
30.	Newcastle United	H	1-1	Groves	25,889
31.	Derby County	A	0-0		18,382
32.	Oxford United	A	0-0		9,088
33.	Chelsea	A	1-1	McLaughlin (og)	26,084
34.	Norwich City	H	2-0	Smith Groves	19,341
35.	Southampton	A	2-4	Davis Bond (og)	14,521
36.	West Ham United	A	1-0	Thomas	26,746
37.	Watford	H	0-1		19,541
38.	Sheffield Wed	A	3-3	Merson 2 Smith	16,681
39.	Coventry City	H	1-1	Marwood (pen)	16,963
40.	Everton	A	2-1	Thomas Hayes	22,445

Final League Position = 6th in Division One

♼ FA Cup ♼

3	Millwall	H	2-0	Hayes Rocastle	42,083
4	Brighton & HA	A	2-1	Richardson Groves	26,467
5	Manchester Utd	H	2-1	Smith Duxbury (og)	54,161
6	Nottingham F	H	1-2	Rocastle	50,157

League Cup

2	Doncaster Rovers	A	3-0	Groves Smith Williams	5,469
2	Doncaster Rovers	H	1-0	Rocastle	18,321
3	Bournemouth	H	3-0	Richardson Smith Thomas (pen)	26,050
4	Stoke City	H	3-0	O'Leary Rocastle Richardson	30,058
5	Sheffield Wed	A	1-0	Winterburn	34,535
SF	Everton	A	1-0	Groves	25,476
SF	Everton	H	3-1	Thomas Rocastle Smith	51,148
F	Luton Town	N*	2-3	Hayes Smith	95,732

* played at Wembley Stadium

1988–89

1.	Wimbledon	A	5-1	Smith 3 Marwood Merson	15,710
2.	Aston Villa	H	2-3	Marwood Smith	37,417
3.	Tottenham H	A	3-2	Winterburn Marwood Smith	32,261
4.	Southampton	H	2-2	Marwood (pen) Smith	31,384

5.	Sheffield Wed	A	1-2	Smith	17,830
6.	West Ham United	A	4-1	Smith 2 Thomas Rocastle	27,658
7.	Queen's Park R	H	2-1	Adams Smith	33,202
8.	Luton Town	A	1-1	Smith	10,548
9.	Coventry City	H	2-0	Thomas Adams	31,273
10.	Nottingham F	A	4-1	Smith Bould Adams Marwood	19,038
11.	Newcastle United	A	1-0	Bould	24,003
12.	Middlesbrough	H	3-0	Merson 2 Rocastle	32,294
13.	Derby County	A	1-2	Thomas	21,209
14.	Liverpool	H	1-1	Smith	31,863
15.	Norwich City	A	0-0		23,069
16.	Manchester Utd	H	2-1	Thomas Merson	37,422
17.	Charlton Ath	A	3-2	Marwood 2 (1 pen) Merson	18,439
18.	Aston Villa	A	3-0	Smith Rocastle Groves	32,486
19.	Tottenham H	H	2-0	Merson Thomas	45,129
20.	Everton	A	3-1	Merson Smith Richardson	34,825
21.	Sheffield Wed	H	1-1	Merson	33,490
22.	West Ham United	H	2-1	Groves Smith	40,139
23.	Millwall	A	2-1	Marwood Smith	21,854
24.	Queen's Park R	A	0-0		20,543
25.	Coventry City	A	0-1		21,390
26.	Luton Town	H	2-0	Groves Smith	31,012
27.	Millwall	H	0-0		37,524
28.	Nottingham F	H	1-3	Smith	39,639
29.	Charlton Ath	H	2-2	Rocastle Davis	30,259
30.	Southampton	A	3-1	Groves Rocastle Merson	19,202
31.	Manchester Utd	A	1-1	Adams	37,977
32.	Everton	H	2-0	Dixon Quinn	37,608
33.	Newcastle United	H	1-0	Marwood	38,023
34.	Norwich City	H	5-0	Winterburn Smith 2	28,449
				Rocastle Thomas	28,449
35.	Middlesbrough	A	1-0	Hayes	21,803
36.	Derby County	H	1-2	Smith	41,008
37.	Wimbledon	H	2-2	Winterburn Merson	39,132
38.	Liverpool	A	2-0	Smith Thomas	41,728

Final League Position = 1st in Division One

♔ FA Cup ♔

3	West Ham United	A	2-2	Merson 2	22,017
R	West Ham United	H	0-1		44,124

League Cup

2	Hull City	A	2-1	Winterburn Marwood	11,450
2	Hull City	H	3-0	Merson Smith 2	17,885
3	Liverpool	A	1-1	Rocastle	31,951
R	Liverpool	H	0-0		54,029
2R	Liverpool	N*	1-2	Merson	21,708

*played at Villa Park, Birmingham

	1989–90				
1.	Manchester Utd	A	1-4	Rocastle	47,245
2.	Coventry City	H	2-0	Thomas Marwood	33,886
3.	Wimbledon	H	0-0		32,279
4.	Sheffield Wed	H	5-0	Merson Smith Thomas	30,058
				Adams Marwood	30,058
5.	Nottingham F	A	2-1	Marwood Merson	22,216
6.	Charlton Ath	H	1-0	Marwood (pen)	34,583
7.	Chelsea	A	0-0		31,833
8.	Manchester City	H	4-0	Groves 2 Merson Thomas	40,414
9.	Tottenham H	A	1-2	Thomas	33,944
10.	Everton	A	0-3		32,917
11.	Derby County	H	1-1	Smith	33,189
12.	Norwich City	H	4-3	Quinn O'Leary Dixon 2 (1 pen)	35,338
13.	Millwall	A	2-1	Quinn Thomas	17,265
14.	Queen's Park R	H	3-0	Dixon (pen) Smith Jonsson	38,236
15.	Liverpool	A	1-2	Smith	35,983
16.	Manchester Utd	H	1-0	Groves	34,484
17.	Coventry City	A	1-0	Merson	16,255
18.	Luton Town	H	3-2	Smith Marwood Merson	28,761
19.	Southampton	A	0-1		20,229
20.	Aston Villa	A	1-2	Adams	40,665
21.	Crystal Palace	H	4-1	Smith 2 Dixon Adams	38,711
22.	Wimbledon	A	0-1		13,793
23.	Tottenham H	H	1-0	Adams	46,132
24.	Sheffield Wed	A	0-1		20,640
25.	Charlton Ath	A	0-0		17,504
26.	Queen's Park R	A	0-2		18,067
27.	Nottingham F	H	3-0	Groves Adam Campbell	31,879
28.	Manchester City	A	1-1	Marwood	29,087
29.	Chelsea	H	0-1		33,805
30.	Derby County	A	3-1	Hayes 2 Campbell	17,514
31.	Everton	H	1-0	Smith	35,223
32.	Aston Villa	H	0-1		30,060
33.	Crystal Palace	A	1-1	Hayes	28,094
34.	Liverpool	H	1-1	Merson	33,395
35.	Luton Town	A	0-2		11,595
36.	Millwall	H	2-0	Davis Merson	25,607
37.	Southampton	H	2-1	Dixon (pen) Rocastle	23,732
38.	Norwich City	A	2-2	Smith 2	19,256

Final League Position = 4th in Division One

♛ FA Cup ♛

3	Stoke City	A	1-0	Quinn	23,827
4	Queen's Park R	H	0-0		43,483
R	Queen's Park R	A	0-2		21,547

	League Cup				
2	Plymouth Argyle	H	2-0	Smith Rocastle	26,865

2	Plymouth Argyle	A	6-1	Thomas 3 Smith Groves Rocastle	17,360
3	Liverpool	H	1-0	Smith	40,814
4	Oldham Athletic	A	1-3	Quinn	14,924

1990–91

1.	Wimbledon	A	3-0	Merson Smith Groves	13,733
2.	Luton Town	H	2-1	Merson Thomas	32,723
3.	Tottenham H	H	0-0		40,009
4.	Everton	A	1-1	Groves	29,919
5.	Chelsea	H	4-1	Limpar Dixon (pen) Merson Rocastle	40,475
6.	Nottingham F	A	2-0	Rocastle Limpar	26,013
7.	Leeds United	A	2-2	Limpar 2	30,085
8.	Norwich City	H	2-0	Davis 2	36,737
9.	Manchester Utd	A	1-0	Limpar	47,232
10.	Sunderland	H	1-0	Dixon (pen)	38,485
11.	Coventry City	A	2-0	Limpar 2	15,336
12.	Crystal Palace	A	0-0		28,282
13.	Southampton	H	4-0	Merson Limpar Smith 2	36,229
14.	Queen's Park R	A	3-1	Merson Smith Campbell	18,555
15.	Liverpool	H	3-0	Merson Dixon (pen) Smith	40,419
16.	Luton Town	A	1-1	Smith	12,506
17.	Wimbledon	H	2-2	Merson Adams	30,164
18.	Aston Villa	A	0-0		22,687
19.	Derby County	H	3-0	Smith 2 Merson	25,558
20.	Sheffield United	H	4-1	Dixon (pen) Smith 2 Thomas	37,810
21.	Manchester City	A	1-0	Smith	30,579
22.	Tottenham H	A	0-0		34,753
23.	Everton	H	1-0	Merson	35,349
24.	Chelsea	A	1-2	Smith	29,094
25.	Crystal Palace	H	4-0	O'Leary Merson Smith Campbell	42,162
26.	Liverpool	A	1-0	Merson	37,221
27.	Leeds United	H	2-0	Campbell 2	26,218
28.	Nottingham F	H	1-1	Campbell	34,152
29.	Norwich City	A	0-0		20,131
30.	Derby County	A	2-0	Smith 2	18,397
31.	Aston Villa	H	5-0	Campbell 2 Davis Smith 2	41,868
32.	Sheffield United	A	2-0	Campbell Smith	26,920
33.	Southampton	A	1-1	Adams (og)	21,200
34.	Manchester City	H	2-2	Campbell Merson	38,412
35.	Queen's Park R	H	2-0	Dixon (pen) Merson	42,393
36.	Sunderland	A	0-0		22,606
37.	Manchester Utd	H	3-1	Smith 3	40,229
38.	Coventry City	H	6-1	Peake (og) Limpar 3 Smith Groves	41,039

Final League Position = 1st in Division One

♛ FA Cup ♛

3	Sunderland	H	2-1	Smith Limpar	35,128
4	Leeds United	H	0-0		30,905
R	Leeds United	A	1-1	Limpar	27,763
2R	Leeds United	H	0-0		30,433
3R	Leeds United	A	2-1	Merson Dixon	27,190
5	Shrewsbury Town	A	1-0	Thomas	12,536
6	Cambridge Utd	H	2-1	Campbell Adams	42,960
SF	Tottenham H	N*	1-3	Smith	41,868

played at Wembley Stadium

League Cup

2	Chester City	A	1-0	Merson	4,135
2	Chester City	H	5-0	Groves 2 Smith Adams Merson	22,890
3	Manchester City	A	2-1	Groves Adams	26,825
4	Manchester Utd	H	2-6	Smith 2	40,884

1991–92

1.	Queen's Park R	H	1-1	Merson	38,099
2.	Everton	A	1-3	Winterburn	31,200
3.	Aston Villa	A	1-3	Smith	29,684
4.	Luton Town	H	2-0	Merson Smith	25,898
5.	Manchester City	H	2-1	Smith Limpar	35,009
6.	Leeds United	A	2-2	Smith 2	29,396
7.	Coventry City	H	1-2	Adams	28,142
8.	Crystal Palace	A	4-1	Campbell 2 Smith Thomas	24,228
9.	Sheffield United	H	5-2	Smith Dixon (pen) Groves Rocastle Campbell	30,244
10.	Southampton	A	4-0	Rocastle Wright 3	18,050
11.	Chelsea	H	3-2	Dixon (pen) Wright Campbell	42,074
12.	Manchester Utd	A	1-1	Rocastle	46,594
13.	Notts County	H	2-0	Smith Wright	30,011
14.	West Ham United	H	0-1		33,539
15.	Oldham Athletic	A	1-1	Wright	15,681
16.	Sheffield Wed	A	1-1	Bould	32,174
17.	Tottenham H	H	2-0	Wright Campbell	38,892
18.	Nottingham F	A	2-3	Merson Smith	22,095
19.	Everton	H	4-2	Wright 4	29,684
20.	Luton Town	A	0-1		12,655
21.	Manchester City	A	0-1		32,325
22.	Wimbledon	H	1-1	Merson	26,839
23.	Aston Villa	H	0-0		31,413
24.	Queen's Park R	A	0-0		20,497
25.	Liverpool	A	0-2		33,753
26.	Manchester Utd	H	1-1	Rocastle	41,703
27.	Notts County	A	1-0	Smith	11,221
28.	Norwich City	H	1-1	Merson	22,352
29.	Sheffield Wed	H	7-1	Smith Campbell 2 Limpar 2 Merson Wright	26,805

30.	Tottenham H	A	1-1	Wright —	33,124
31.	Oldham Athletic	H	2-1	Wright Merson	22,096
32.	West Ham United	A	2-0	Wright 2	22,640
33.	Leeds United	H	1-1	Merson	27,844
34.	Wimbledon	A	3-1	Parlour Wright Campbell	11,299
35.	Nottingham F	H	3-3	Dixon (pen) Merson Adams	27,036
36.	Coventry City	A	1-0	Campbell	14,133
37.	Norwich City	A	3-1	Wright 2 (1 pen) Campbell	12,971
38.	Crystal Palace	H	4-1	Merson 3 Campbell	36,016
39.	Sheffield United	A	1-1	Campbell	25,034
40.	Liverpool	H	4-0	Hillier Wright 2 Limpar	38,517
41.	Chelsea	A	1-1	Dixon	26,003
42.	Southampton	H	5-1	Campbell Wright 3 (1 pen) Smith	37,702

Final League Position = 4th in Division One

♆ FA Cup ♆

| 3 | Wrexham | A | 1-2 | Smith | 13,342 |

League Cup

2	Leicester City	A	1-1	Wright	20,679
2	Leicester City	H	2-0	Wright Merson	28,580
3	Coventry City	A	0-1		15,337

1992–93

1.	Norwich City	H	2-4	Bould Campbell	24,036
2.	Blackburn Rovers	A	0-1		16,454
3.	Liverpool	A	2-0	Limpar Wright	34,961
4.	Oldham Athletic	H	2-0	Winterburn Wright	20,795
5.	Sheffield Wed	H	2-1	Parlour Merson	23,389
6.	Queen's Park R	A	0-0		20,868
7.	Wimbledon	A	2-3	Wright 2	12,906
8.	Blackburn Rovers	H	0-1		28,643
9.	Sheffield United	A	1-1	Wright	23,000
10.	Manchester City	H	1-0	Wright	21,504
11.	Chelsea	H	2-1	Merson Wright	27,780
12.	Nottingham F	A	1-0	Smith	24,862
13.	Everton	H	2-0	Wright Limpar	28,052
14.	Crystal Palace	A	2-1	Merson Wright	20,247
15.	Coventry City	H	3-0	Smith Wright Campbell	27,693
16.	Leeds United	A	0-3		30,516
17.	Manchester Utd	H	0-1		29,739
18.	Southampton	A	0-2		17,286
19.	Tottenham H	A	0-1		33,709
20.	Middlesbrough	H	1-1	Wright	23,197
21.	Ipswich Town	H	0-0		26,198
22.	Aston Villa	A	0-1		35,170
23.	Sheffield United	H	1-1	Hillier	23,818
24.	Manchester City	A	1-0	Merson	25,041
25.	Liverpool	H	0-1		27,580

26.	Wimbledon	H	0-1		18,253
27.	Oldham Athletic	A	1-0	Linighan	12,311
28.	Leeds United	H	0-0		21,061
29.	Chelsea	A	0-1		17,725
30.	Norwich City	A	1-1	Wright	14,803
31.	Coventry City	A	2-0	Campbell Wright	15,437
32.	Southampton	H	4-3	Linighan Merson Carter 2	24,149
33.	Manchester Utd	A	0-0		37,301
34.	Middlesbrough	A	0-1		12,726
35.	Ipswich Town	A	2-1	Smith Merson	20,358
36.	Aston Villa	H	0-1		27,125
37.	Nottingham F	H	1-1	Wright	19,024
38.	Everton	A	0-0		19,044
39.	Queen's Park R	H	0-0		18,817
40.	Sheffield Wed	A	0-1		23,645
41.	Crystal Palace	H	3-0	Wright Dickov Campbell	25,225
42.	Tottenham H	H	1-3	Dickov	26,393

Final League Position = 10th in the Premiership

♆ FA Cup ♆

3	Yeovil Town	A	3-1	Wright 3	8,612
4	Leeds United	H	2-2	Parlour Merson	26,516
R	Leeds United	A	3-2	Smith Wright 2	26,449
5	Nottingham F	H	2-0	Wright 2	27,591
6	Ipswich Town	A	4-2	Adams Wright (pen) Whelan (og) Campbell	22,054
SF	Tottenham H	N*	1-0	Adams	76,263
F	Sheffield Wed	N*	1-1	Wright	79,346
R	Sheffield Wed	N*	2-1	Wright Linighan	62,267

* played at Wembley Stadium

League Cup

2	Millwall	H	1-1	Campbell	20,940
2	Millwall	A*	1-1	Campbell	16,994
3	Derby County	A	1-1	Campbell	22,208
R	Derby County	H	2-1	Wright Campbell	24,587
4	Scarborough	A	1-0	Winterburn	6,261
5	Nottingham F	H	2-0	Wright 2	25,600
SF	Crystal Palace	A	3-1	Wright (pen) Smith 2	26,508
SF	Crystal Palace	H	2-0	Linighan Wright	28,584
F	Sheffield Wed	N*	2-1	Merson Morrow	74,007

* played at Wembley Stadium

1993–94

1.	Coventry City	H	0-3		26,397
2.	Tottenham H	A	1-0	Wright	28,355
3.	Sheffield Wed	A	1-0	Wright	26,023
4.	Leeds United	H	2-1	Newsome (og) Merson	29,042
5.	Everton	H	2-0	Wright 2	29,063

6.	Blackburn Rovers	A	1-1	Campbell	14,410
7.	Ipswich Town	H	4-0	Wright Campbell 3	28,563
8.	Manchester Utd	A	0-1		44,009
9.	Southampton	H	1-0	Merson	26,902
10.	Liverpool	A	0-0		42,750
11.	Manchester City	H	0-0		29,567
12.	Oldham Athletic	A	0-0		12,105
13.	Norwich City	H	0-0		30,516
14.	Aston Villa	H	1-2	Wright	31,773
15.	Chelsea	A	2-0	Smith Wright (pen)	26,839
16.	West Ham United	A	0-0		20,279
17.	Newcastle United	H	2-1	Wright Smith	36,091
18.	Coventry City	A	0-1		12,632
19.	Tottenham H	H	1-1	Wright	35,669
20.	Sheffield Wed	H	1-0	Wright	22,026
21.	Leeds United	A	1-2	Campbell	37,289
22.	Swindon Town	A	4-0	Campbell 3 Wright	17,214
23.	Sheffield United	H	3-0	Campbell 2 Wright	27,035
24.	Wimbledon	A	3-0	Campbell Parlour Wright	16,584
25.	Queen's Park R	H	0-0		34,935
26.	Manchester City	A	0-0		25,642
27.	Oldham Athletic	H	1-1	Wright (pen)	26,524
28.	Norwich City	A	1-1	Campbell	17,667
29.	Everton	A	1-1	Merson	19,760
30.	Blackburn Rovers	H	1-0	Merson	35,030
31.	Ipswich Town	A	5-1	Wright 3 (1 pen) Youds (og) Parlour	18,803
32.	Southampton	A	4-0	Wright 3 (1 pen) Campbell	16,790
33.	Manchester Utd	H	2-2	Pallister (og) Merson	36,203
34.	Liverpool	H	1-0	Merson	35,556
35.	Swindon Town	H	1-1	Smith	31,635
36.	Sheffield United	A	1-1	Campbell	20,019
37.	Chelsea	H	1-0	Wright	34,314
38.	Wimbledon	H	1-1	Bould	21,292
39.	Aston Villa	A	2-1	Wright 2 (1 pen)	31,580
40.	Queen's Park R	A	1-1	Merson	11,442
41.	West Ham United	H	0-2		33,700
42.	Newcastle United	A	0-2		32,216

Final League Position = 4th in the Premiership

♔ FA Cup ♔

3	Millwall	A	1-0	Adams	20,093
4	Bolton Wands	A	2-2	Wright Adams	18,891
R	Bolton Wands	H	1-3	Smith	33,863

League Cup

2	Huddersfield T	A	5-0	Wright 3 Campbell Merson	14,275
2	Huddersfield T	H	1-1	Smith	18,789
3	Norwich City	H	1-1	Wright	24,539

R	Norwich City	A	3-0	Wright 2 Merson	16,319
4	Aston Villa	H	0-1		26,453

1994–95

1.	Manchester City	H	3-0	Campbell Coton (og) Wright	38,368
2.	Leeds United	A	0-1		34,318
3.	Liverpool	A	0-3		30,017
4.	Blackburn Rovers	H	0-0		37,629
5.	Norwich City	A	0-0		17,768
6.	Newcastle United	H	2-3	Adams Wright	36,819
7.	West Ham United	A	2-0	Adams Wright	18,495
8.	Crystal Palace	H	1-2	Wright	34,146
9.	Wimbledon	A	3-1	Wright Smith Campbell	10,842
10.	Chelsea	H	3-1	Wright 2 Campbell	38,234
11.	Coventry City	H	2-1	Wright 2	31,725
12.	Everton	A	1-1	Schwarz	32,005
13.	Sheffield Wed	H	0-0		33,705
14.	Southampton	A	0-1		15,201
15.	Leicester City	A	1-2	Wright (pen)	20,774
16.	Manchester Utd	H	0-0		38,301
17.	Nottingham F	A	2-2	Keown Davis	21,662
18.	Manchester City	A	2-1	Smith Schwarz	20,500
19.	Leeds United	H	1-3	Linighan	38,100
20.	Aston Villa	H	0-0		34,452
21.	Ipswich Town	A	2-0	Wright Campbell	22,047
22.	Queen's Park R	H	1-3	Jensen	32,393
23.	Tottenham H	A	0-1		28,747
24.	Everton	H	1-1	Wright	34,743
25.	Coventry City	A	1-0	Hartson	14,557
26.	Southampton	H	1-1	Hartson	27,213
27.	Sheffield Wed	A	1-3	Linighan	23,468
28.	Leicester City	H	1-1	Merson	31,373
29.	Nottingham F	H	1-0	Kiwomya	35,441
30.	Crystal Palace	A	3-0	Merson Kiwomya 2	17,063
31.	West Ham United	H	0-1		36,295
32.	Blackburn Rovers	A	1-3	Morrow	23,452
33.	Newcastle United	A	0-1		35,611
34.	Manchester Utd	A	0-3		43,623
35.	Norwich City	H	5-1	Hartson 2 Dixon Merson Newman (og)	36,942
36.	Queen's Park R	A	1-3	Adams	16,341
37.	Liverpool	H	0-1		38,036
38.	Ipswich Town	H	4-1	Merson Wright 3	36,818
39.	Aston Villa	A	4-0	Hartson 2 Wright 2 (1 pen)	32,005
40.	Tottenham H	H	1-1	Wright (pen)	38,377
41.	Wimbledon	H	0-0		32,822
42.	Chelsea	A	1-2	Hartson	29,542

Final League Position = 12th in the Premiership

♛ FA Cup ♛

3	Millwall	A	0-0		17,715
R	Millwall	H	0-2		32,319

	League Cup				
2	Hartlepool Utd	A	5-0	Adams Smith Wright 2 Merson	4,421
2	Hartlepool Utd	H	2-0	Campbell Dickov	20,520
3	Oldham Athletic	A	0-0		9,303
R	Oldham Athletic	H	2-0	Dickov 2	22,746
4	Sheffield Wed	H	2-0	Morrow Wright	27,390
5	Liverpool	A	0-1	35,026	

	1995–96				
1.	Middlesbrough	H	1-1	Wright	37,308
2.	Everton	A	2-0	Platt Wright	35,775
3.	Coventry City	A	0-0		20,081
4.	Nottingham F	H	1-1	Platt	38,248
5.	Manchester City	A	1-0	Wright	23,994
6.	West Ham United	H	1-0	Wright (pen)	38,065
7.	Southampton	H	4-2	Bergkamp 2 Adams Wright	38,136
8.	Chelsea	A	0-1		31,048
9.	Leeds United	A	3-0	Merson Bergkamp Wright	38,332
10.	Aston Villa	H	2-0	Merson Wright	38,271
11.	Bolton Wands	A	0-1		18,682
12.	Manchester Utd	H	1-0	Bergkamp	38,317
13.	Tottenham H	A	1-2	Bergkamp	32,894
14.	Sheffield Wed	H	4-2	Bergkamp Winterburn Dickov Hartson	34,556
15.	Blackburn Rovers	H	0-0		37,695
16.	Aston Villa	A	1-1	Platt	37,770
17.	Southampton	A	0-0		15,238
18.	Chelsea	H	1-1	Dixon	38,295
19.	Liverpool	A	1-3	Wright (pen)	39,806
20.	Queen's Park R	H	3-0	Wright Merson 2	38,259
21.	Wimbledon	H	1-3	Wright	37,640
22.	Newcastle United	A	0-2		36,530
23.	Middlesbrough	A	3-2	Merson Platt Helder	29,359
24.	Everton	H	1-2	Wright	38,275
25.	Coventry City	H	1-1	Bergkamp	35,623
26.	Nottingham F	A	1-0	Bergkamp	27,222
27.	West Ham United	A	1-0	Hartson	24,217
28.	Queen's Park R	A	1-1	Bergkamp	17,970
29.	Manchester City	H	3-1	Hartson 2 Dixon	34,519
30.	Wimbledon	A	3-0	Winterburn Platt Bergkamp	18,335
31.	Manchester Utd	A	0-1		50,028
32.	Newcastle United	H	2-0	Marshall Wright	38,271
33.	Leeds United	H	2-1	Wright 2	37,619
34.	Sheffield Wed	A	0-1		24,349
35.	Tottenham H	H	0-0		38,273

36.	Blackburn Rovers	A	1-1	Wright (pen)	29,834
37.	Liverpool	H	0-0		38,323
38.	Bolton Wands	H	2-1	Platt Bergkamp	38,104

Final League Position = 5th in the Premiership

♆ FA Cup ♆

| 3 | Sheffield United | H | 1-1 | Wright | 33,453 |
| R | Sheffield United | A | 0-1 | | 22,255 |

League Cup

2	Hartlepool Utd	A	3-0	Adams 2 Wright	4,945
2	Hartlepool Utd	H	5-0	Bergkamp 2 Wright 3	27,194
3	Barnsley	A	3-0	Bould Bergkamp Keown	18,429
4	Sheffield Wed	H	2-1	Wright (pen) Hartson	35,361
5	Newcastle United	H	2-0	Wright 2	37,857
SF	Aston Villa	H	2-2	Bergkamp 2	37,562
SF	Aston Villa	A	0-0		39,334

1996–97

1.	West Ham United	H	2-0	Hartson Bergkamp (pen)	38,056
2.	Liverpool	A	0-2		38,103
3.	Leicester City	A	2-0	Bergkamp (pen) Wright	20,429
4.	Chelsea	H	3-3	Merson Keown Wright	38,132
5.	Aston Villa	A	2-2	Merson Linighan	37,944
6.	Sheffield Wed	H	4-1	Platt Wright 3 (1 pen)	33,461
7.	Middlesbrough	A	2-0	Hartson Wright	29,629
8.	Sunderland	H	2-0	Hartson Parlour	38,016
9.	Blackburn Rovers	A	2-0	Wright 2	24,303
10.	Coventry City	H	0-0		38,141
11.	Leeds United	H	3-0	Dixon Bergkamp Wright	38,076
12.	Wimbledon	A	2-2	Wright Merson	25,521
13.	Manchester Utd	A	0-1		55,210
14.	Tottenham H	H	3-1	Wright (pen) Adams Bergkamp	38,264
15.	Newcastle United	A	2-1	Dixon Wright	36,565
16.	Southampton	H	3-1	Merson Wright (pen) Shaw	38,033
17.	Derby County	H	2-2	Adams Vieira	38,018
18.	Nottingham F	A	1-2	Wright	27,384
19.	Sheffield Wed	A	0-0		23,245
20.	Aston Villa	H	2-2	Wright Merson	38,130
21.	Middlesbrough	H	2-0	Bergkamp Wright	37,573
22.	Sunderland	A	0-1		21,074
23.	Everton	H	3-1	Bergkamp Vieira Merson	38,095
24.	West Ham United	A	2-1	Parlour Wright	24,382
25.	Leeds United	A	0-0		35,596
26.	Tottenham H	A	0-0		33,039
27.	Manchester Utd	H	1-2	Bergkamp	38,172
28.	Wimbledon	H	0-1		37,854
29.	Everton	A	2-0	Bergkamp Wright	36,980
30.	Nottingham F	H	2-0	Bergkamp 2 (1 pen)	38,206

31.	Southampton	A	2-0	Hughes Shaw	15,144
32.	Liverpool	H	1-2	Wright	38,068
33.	Chelsea	A	3-0	Wright Platt Bergkamp	26,923
34.	Leicester City	H	2-0	Adams Platt	38,044
35.	Blackburn Rovers	H	1-1	Platt	38,086
36.	Coventry City	A	1-1	Wright (pen)	20,004
37.	Newcastle United	H	0-1		38,179
38.	Derby County	A	3-1	Wright 2 Bergkamp	18,297

Final League Position = 3rd in the Premiership

♆ FA Cup ♆

3	Sunderland	H	1-1	Hartson	37,793
R	Sunderland	A	2-0	Bergkamp Hughes	15,277
4	Leeds United	H	0-1		38,115

League Cup

3	Stoke City	A	1-1	Wright	20,804
R	Stoke City	H	5-2	Wright 2 Platt Bergkamp Merson	33,962
4	Liverpool	A	2-4	Wright 2 (2 pens)	32,814

1997-98

1.	Leeds United	A	1-1	Wright	37,993
2.	Coventry City	H	2-0	Wright 2	37,324
3.	Southampton	A	3-1	Overmars Bergkamp 2	15,246
4.	Leicester City	A	3-3	Bergkamp 3	21,089
5.	Tottenham H	H	0-0		38,102
6.	Bolton Wands	H	4-1	Wright 3 Parlour	38,138
7.	Chelsea	A	3-2	Bergkamp 2 Winterburn	31,290
8.	West Ham United	H	4-0	Bergkamp Overmars 2 Wright (pen)	38,012
9.	Everton	A	2-2	Wright Overmars	35,457
10.	Barnsley	H	5-0	Bergkamp 2 Parlour Platt Wright	38,049
11.	Crystal Palace	A	0-0		26,180
12.	Aston Villa	H	0-0		38,061
13.	Derby County	A	0-3		30,004
14.	Manchester Utd	H	3-2	Anelka Vieira Platt	38,205
15.	Sheffield Wed	A	0-2		34,373
16.	Liverpool	H	0-1		38,094
17.	Newcastle United	A	1-0	Wright	36,751
18.	Blackburn Rovers	H	1-3	Overmars	38,147
19.	Leicester City	H	2-1	Platt Walsh (og)	38,023
20.	Tottenham H	A	1-1	Parlour	29,601
21.	Leeds United	H	2-1	Overmars 2	38,018
22.	Coventry City	A	2-2	Bergkamp Anelka	22,777
23.	Southampton	H	3-0	Bergkamp Adams Anelka	38,056
24.	Chelsea	H	2-0	Hughes 2	38,083
25.	Crystal Palace	H	1-0	Grimandi	38,094

26.	West Ham United	A	0-0		25,717
27.	Wimbledon	A	1-0	Wreh	22,291
28.	Manchester Utd	A	1-0	Overmars	55,174
29.	Sheffield Wed	H	1-0	Bergkamp	38,087
30.	Bolton Wands	A	1-0	Wreh	25,000
31.	Newcastle United	H	3-1	Anelka 2 Vieira	38,102
32.	Blackburn Rovers	A	4-1	Bergkamp Parlour 2 Anelka	28,212
33.	Wimbledon	H	5-0	Adams Overmars Bergkamp Petit Wreh	38,024
34.	Barnsley	A	2-0	Bergkamp Overmars	18,691
35.	Derby County	H	1-0	Petit	38,121
36.	Everton	H	4-0	Bilic (og) Overmars 2 Adams	38,269
37.	Liverpool	A	0-4		44,417
38.	Aston Villa	A	0-1		39,372

Final League Position = 1st in the Premiership

♆ FA Cup ♆

3	Port Vale	H	0-0		37,471
R	Port Vale	A	1-1*	Bergkamp	14,964
4	Middlesbrough	A	2-1	Overmars Parlour	28,264
5	Crystal Palace	H	0-0		37,164
R	Crystal Palace	A	2-1	Anelka Bergkamp	15,674
6	West Ham United	H	1-1	Bergkamp (pen)	38,077
R	West Ham United	A	1-1*	Anelka	25,859
SF	Wolves	N**	1-0	Wreh	39,372
F	Newcastle United	N***	2-0	Overmars Anelka	79,183

* won 4-3 on penalties   ** played at Villa Park, Birmingham   *** played at Wembley Stadium

League Cup

3	Birmingham City	H	4-1	Boa Morte 2 Platt (pen) Mendez	27,097
4	Coventry City	H	1-0	Bergkamp	30,199
5	West Ham United	A	2-1	Wright Overmars	24,770
SF	Chelsea	H	2-1	Overmars Hughes	38,114
SF	Chelsea	A	1-3	Bergkamp (pen)	34,330

1998–99

1.	Nottingham F	H	2-1	Petit Overmars	38,064
2.	Liverpool	A	0-0		44,429
3.	Charlton Ath	H	0-0		38,014
4.	Chelsea	A	0-0		34,647
5.	Leicester City	A	1-1	Hughes	21,628
6.	Manchester Utd	H	3-0	Adams Anelka Ljungberg	38,142
7.	Sheffield Wed	A	0-1		27,949
8.	Newcastle United	H	3-0	Bergkamp 2 (1 pen) Anelka	38,102
9.	Southampton	H	1-1	Anelka	38,027
10.	Blackburn Rovers	A	2-1	Anelka Petit	27,012
11.	Coventry City	A	1-0	Anelka	23,039
12.	Everton	H	1-0	Anelka	38,088
13.	Tottenham H	H	0-0		38,278

14.	Wimbledon	A	0-1		26,003
15.	Middlesbrough	H	1-1	Anelka	38,075
16.	Derby County	A	0-0		29,018
17.	Aston Villa	A	2-3	Bergkamp 2	39,217
18.	Leeds United	H	3-1	Bergkamp Vieira Petit	38,025
19.	West Ham United	H	1-0	Overmars	38,098
20.	Charlton Ath	A	1-0	Overmars (pen)	20,043
21.	Liverpool	H	0-0		38,107
22.	Nottingham F	A	1-0	Keown	26,021
23.	Chelsea	H	1-0	Bergkamp	38,121
24.	West Ham United	A	4-0	Bergkamp Overmars Anelka Parlour	26,042
25.	Manchester Utd	A	1-1	Anelka	55,171
26.	Leicester City	H	5-0	Anelka 3 Parlour 2	38,069
27.	Newcastle United	A	1-1	Anelka	36,708
28.	Sheffield Wed	H	3-0	Bergkamp 2 Kanu	37,792
29.	Everton	A	2-0	Parlour Bergkamp (pen)	38,049
30.	Coventry City	H	2-0	Parlour Overmars	38,074
31.	Southampton	A	0-0		15,255
32.	Blackburn Rovers	H	1-0	Bergkamp	37,762
33.	Wimbledon	H	5-1	Parlour Vieira Thatcher (og) Bergkamp Kanu	37,982
34.	Middlesbrough	A	6-1	Overmars (pen) Anelka 2 Kanu 2 Vieira	34,630
35.	Derby County	H	1-0	Anelka	37,323
36.	Tottenham H	A	3-1	Petit Anelka Kanu	36,019
37.	Leeds United	A	0-1	40,124	
38.	Aston Villa	H	1-0	Kanu	38,308

Final League Position = 2nd in the Premiership

♛ FA Cup ♛

3	Preston NE	A	4-2	Boa Morte Petit 2 Overmars	21,099
4	Wolves	A	2-1	Overmars Bergkamp	27,511
5	Sheffield United	H	2-1	Vieira Overmars	38,020
6	Derby County	H	1-0	Kanu	38,046
SF	Manchester Utd	N*	0-0		39,217
R	Manchester Utd	N*	1-2	Bergkamp	30,223

* played at Villa Park, Birmingham

League Cup

3	Derby County	A	2-1	Carsley (og) Vivas	25,621
4	Chelsea	H	0-5		37,562

1999–2000

1.	Leicester City	H	2-1	Bergkamp Sinclair (og)	38,026
2.	Derby County	A	2-1	Petit Bergkamp	25,901
3.	Sunderland	A	0-0		40,037
4.	Manchester Utd	H	1-2	Ljungberg	38,147
5.	Bradford City	H	2-0	Vieira Kanu (pen)	38,073

6.	Liverpool	A	0-2		44,886
7.	Aston Villa	H	3-1	Suker 2 Kanu	38,093
8.	Southampton	A	1-0	Henry	15,242
9.	Watford	H	1-0	Kanu	38,127
10.	West Ham United	A	1-2	Suker	26,009
11.	Everton	H	4-1	Dixon Suker 2 Kanu	38,042
12.	Chelsea	A	3-2	Kanu 3	34,958
13.	Newcastle United	H	0-0		38,106
14.	Tottenham H	A	1-2	Vieira	36,085
15.	Middlesbrough	H	5-1	Overmars 3 Bergkamp 2	38,082
16.	Derby County	H	2-1	Henry 2	37,964
17.	Leicester City	A	3-0	Grimandi Dixon Overmars	20,495
18.	Wimbledon	H	1-1	Henry	38,052
19.	Coventry City	A	2-3	Ljungberg Suker	22,750
20.	Leeds United	H	2-0	Ljungberg Henry	38,096
21.	Sheffield Wed	A	1-1	Petit	26,155
22.	Sunderland	H	4-1	Henry 2 Suker 2	38,039
23.	Manchester Utd	A	1-1	Ljungberg	58,293
24.	Bradford City	A	1-2	Henry	18,276
25.	Liverpool	H	0-1		38,098
26.	Southampton	H	3-1	Ljungberg 2 Bergkamp	38,044
27.	Aston Villa	A	1-1	Dixon	36,930
28.	Middlesbrough	A	1-2	Bergkamp	32,244
29.	Tottenham H	H	2-1	Armstrong (og) Henry (pen)	38,131
30.	Coventry City	H	3-0	Henry Grimandi Kanu	38,027
31.	Wimbledon	A	3-1	Kanu 2 Henry (pen)	25,858
32.	Leeds United	A	4-0	Henry Keown Kanu Overmars	39,307
33.	Watford	A	3-2	Henry 2 Parlour	19,670
34.	Everton	A	1-0	Overmars	35,919
35.	West Ham United	H	2-1	Overmars Petit	38,093
36.	Chelsea	H	2-1	Henry 2	38,119
37.	Sheffield Wed	H	3-3	Dixon Silvinho Henry	37,271
38.	Newcastle United	A	2-4	Kanu Malz	36,450

Final League Position = 2nd in the Premiership

♟ FA Cup ♟

3	Blackpool	H	3-1	Grimandi Adams Overmars	34,143
4	Leicester City	H	0-0		35,710
R	Leicester City	A	0-0*		15,235

* lost 6-5 on penalties

League Cup

3	Preston NE	H	2-1	Kanu Malz	15,239
4	Middlesbrough	A	2-2**	Henry Suker	23,157

** lost 3-1 on penalties

2000–01

1.	Sunderland	A	0-1	45,820	
2.	Liverpool	H	2-0	Lauren Henry	38,014

3.	Charlton Ath	H	5-3	Vieira 2 Henry 2 Silvinho	38,025
4.	Chelsea	A	2-2	Henry Silvinho	34,923
5.	Bradford City	A	1-1	Cole	17,160
6.	Coventry City	H	2-1	Wiltord Vernazza	37,794
7.	Ipswich Town	A	1-1	Bergkamp	22,028
8.	Manchester Utd	H	1-0	Henry	38,146
9.	Aston Villa	H	1-0	Henry	38,042
10.	West Ham United	A	2-1	Pires Ferdinand (og)	26,034
11.	Manchester City	H	5-0	Cole Bergkamp Wiltord Henry 2	38,049
12.	Middlesbrough	A	1-0	Henry (pen)	29,541
13.	Derby County	H	0-0		37,679
14.	Everton	A	0-2		33,106
15.	Leeds United	A	0-1		38,084
16.	Southampton	H	1-0	Kachloul (og)	38,036
17.	Newcastle United	H	5-0	Henry Parlour 3 Kanu	38,052
18.	Tottenham H	A	1-1	Vieira	36,062
19.	Liverpool	A	0-4		44,144
20.	Leicester City	H	6-1	Henry 3 Vieira Ljungberg Adams	38,007
21.	Sunderland	H	2-2	Vieira Dixon	38,026
22.	Charlton Ath	A	0-1		20,043
23.	Chelsea	H	1-1	Pires	38,071
24.	Leicester City	A	0-0		21,872
25.	Bradford City	H	2-0	Parlour Lauren	37,318
26.	Coventry City	A	1-0	Bergkamp	22,034
27.	Ipswich Town	H	1-0	Henry	38,011
28.	Manchester Utd	A	1-6	Henry	67,535
29.	West Ham United	H	3-0	Wiltord 3	38,076
30.	Aston Villa	A	0-0		36,111
31.	Tottenham H	H	2-0	Pires Henry	38,121
32.	Manchester City	A	4-0	Ljungberg 2 Wiltord Kanu	33,444
33.	Middlesbrough	H	0-3		37,879
34.	Everton	H	4-1	Ljungberg Grimandi Wiltord Henry	38,029
35.	Derby County	A	2-1	Kanu Pires	29,567
36.	Leeds United	H	2-1	Ljungberg Wiltord	38,142
37.	Newcastle United	A	0-0		50,729
38.	Southampton	A	2-3	Cole Ljungberg	15,252

Final League Position = 2nd in the Premiership

♆ FA Cup ♆

3	Carlisle United	A	1-0	Wiltord	15,300
4	Queen's Park R	A	6-0	Plummer (og) Wiltord 2 Rose (og) Pires Bergkamp	19,003
5	Chelsea	H	3-1	Henry (pen) Wiltord 2	38,096
6	Blackburn Rovers	H	3-0	Wiltord Adams Pires	36,304
SF	Tottenham H	N*	2-1	Vieira Pires	63,541
F	Liverpool	N**	1-2	Ljungberg	74,200

* played at Old Trafford, Manchester   ** played at the Millennium Stadium, Cardiff

League Cup

3	Ipswich Town	H	1-2	Stepanovs	26,105

2001–02

1.	Middlesbrough	A	4-0	Henry Pires (pen) Bergkamp 2	31,557
2.	Leeds United	H	1-2	Wiltord	38,062
3.	Leicester City	H	4-0	Ljungberg Wiltord Henry Kanu	37,909
4.	Chelsea	A	1-1	Henry	40,883
5.	Fulham	A	3-1	Ljungberg Henry Bergkamp	20,805
6.	Bolton Wands	H	1-1	Jeffers	38,014
7.	Derby County	A	2-0	Henry 2 (1 pen)	29,200
8.	Southampton	A	2-0	Pires Henry	29,759
9.	Blackburn Rovers	H	3-3	Pires Bergkamp Henry	38,108
10.	Sunderland	A	1-1	Kanu	45,989
11.	Charlton Ath	H	2-4	Henry 2 (1 pen)	38,010
12.	Tottenham H	A	1-1	Pires	36,066
13.	Manchester Utd	H	3-1	Ljungberg Henry 2	38,174
14.	Ipswich Town	A	2-0	Ljungberg Henry (pen)	24,631
15.	Aston Villa	H	3-2	Wiltord Henry 2	38,074
16.	West Ham United	A	1-1	Cole	34,523
17.	Newcastle United	H	1-3	Pires	38,012
18.	Liverpool	A	2-1	Henry (pen) Ljungberg	44,297
19.	Chelsea	H	2-1	Campbell Wiltord	38,079
20.	Middlesbrough	H	2-1	Pires Cole	37,928
21.	Liverpool	H	1-1	Ljungberg	38,132
22.	Leeds United	A	1-1	Pires	40,143
23.	Leicester City	A	3-1	Van Bronckhorst Henry Wiltord	21,344
24.	Blackburn Rovers	A	3-2	Bergkamp 2 Henry	25,983
25.	Southampton	H	1-1	Wiltord	38,024
26.	Everton	A	1-0	Wiltord	30,859
27.	Fulham	H	4-1	Lauren Vieira Henry 2	38,029
28.	Newcastle United	A	2-0	Bergkamp Campbell	30,859
29.	Derby County	H	1-0	Pires	37,898
30.	Aston Villa	A	2-1	Edu Pires	41,520
31.	Sunderland	H	3-0	Vieira Bergkamp Wiltord	38,047
32.	Charlton Ath	A	3-0	Henry 2 Ljungberg	26,336
33.	Tottenham H	H	2-1	Ljungberg Lauren (pen)	38,186
34.	Ipswich Town	H	2-0	Ljungberg 2	38,058
35.	West Ham United	H	2-0	Ljungberg Kanu	38,038
36.	Bolton Wands	A	2-0	Ljungberg Wiltord	27,351
37.	Manchester Utd	A	1-0	Wiltord	67,580
38.	Everton	H	4-3	Bergkamp Henry 2 Jeffers	38,240

Final League Position = 1st in the Premiership

♛ FA Cup ♛

3	Watford	A	4-2	Henry Ljungberg Kanu Bergkamp	20,105
4	Liverpool	H	1-0	Bergkamp	38,092
5	Gillingham	H	5-2	Wiltord 2 Kanu Adams Parlour	38,003
6	Newcastle United	A	1-1	Edu	51,027

R	Newcastle United	H	3-0	Pires Bergkamp Campbell	38,073
SF	Middlesbrough	N*	1-0	Festa (og)	61,168
F	Chelsea	N**	2-0	Parlor Ljungberg	73,963

*played at Old Trafford, Manchester ** played at the Millennium Stadium, Cardiff*

League Cup

3	Manchester Utd	H	4-0	Wiltord 3 (1 pen) Kanu (pen)	30,693
4	Grimsby Town	H	2-0	Edu Wiltord	16,917
5	Blackburn Rovers	A	0-4		13,278

2002–03

1.	Birmingham City	H	2-0	Henry Wiltord	38,018
2.	West Ham United	A	2-2	Henry Wiltord	35,046
3.	West Brom Alb	H	5-2	Cole Lauren Wiltord 2 Aliadiere	37,920
4.	Chelsea	A	1-1	Toure	40,107
5.	Manchester City	H	2-1	Wiltord Henry	37,878
6.	Charlton Ath	A	3-0	Henry Wiltord Edu	26,080
7.	Bolton Wands	H	2-1	Henry Kanu	37,974
8.	Leeds United	A	4-1	Kanu 2 Toure Henry	40,199
9.	Sunderland	H	3-1	Kanu 2 Vieira	37,902
10.	Everton	A	1-2	Ljungberg	39,038
11.	Blackburn Rovers	H	1-2	Edu	38,064
12.	Fulham	A	1-0	Marlet (og)	17,810
13.	Newcastle United	H	1-0	Wiltord	38,121
14.	Tottenham H	H	3-0	Henry Ljungberg Wiltord	38,121
15.	Southampton	A	2-3	Bergkamp Pires	31,797
16.	Aston Villa	H	3-1	Pires Henry 2 (1 pen)	38,090
17.	Manchester Utd	A	0-2		67,650
18.	Tottenham H	A	1-1	Pires (pen)	36,077
19.	Middlesbrough	H	2-0	Campbell Pires	38,003
20.	West Brom Alb	A	2-1	Jeffers Henry	26,782
21.	Liverpool	H	1-1	Henry (pen)	38,074
22.	Chelsea	H	3-2	Desailly (og) Van Bronckhorst Henry	38,096
23.	Birmingham City	A	4-0	Henry 2 Pires Johnson M (og)	29,505
24.	West Ham United	H	3-1	Henry 3 (1 pen)	38,053
25.	Liverpool	A	2-2	Pires Bergkamp	43,668
26.	Fulham	H	2-1	Pires 2	38,050
27.	Newcastle United	A	1-1	Henry	52,157
28.	Manchester City	A	5-1	Bergkamp Pires Henry Campbell Vieira	34,900
29.	Charlton Ath	H	2-0	Jeffers Pires	38,015
30.	Blackburn Rovers	A	0-2		29,840
31.	Everton	H	2-1	Cygan Vieira	38,042
32.	Aston Villa	A	1-1	Ljungberg	42,602
33.	Manchester Utd	H	2-2	Henry 2	38,164
34.	Middlesbrough	A	2-0	Wiltord Henry	34,724
35.	Bolton Wands	A	2-2	Wiltord Pires	27,253
36.	Leeds United	H	2-3	Henry Bergkamp	38,127

| 37. | Southampton | H | 6-1 | Pires 3 Pennant 3 | 38,052 |
| 38. | Sunderland | A | 4-0 | Henry Ljungberg 3 | 40,188 |

Final League Position = 2nd in the Premiership

♛ FA Cup ♛

3	Oxford United	H	2-0	Bergkamp McNiven (og)	35,432
4	Farnborough T	A*	5-1	Campbell Jeffers 2 Bergkamp Lauren8	35,10
5	Manchester Utd	A	2-0	Edu Wiltord	67,209
6	Chelsea	H	2-2	Jeffers Henry	38,104
R	Chelsea	A	3-1	Terry (og) Wiltord Lauren	41,456
SF	Sheffield United	N**	1-0	Ljungberg	59,170
F	Southampton	N***	1-0	Pires	73,726

* played at Highbury * * played at Old Trafford, Manchester   *** played at the Millennium Stadium,, Cardiff

League Cup

| 3 | Sunderland | H | 2-3 | Pires Jeffers | 19,059 |

2003–04

1.	Everton	H	2-1	Henry (pen) Pires	38,014
2.	Middlesbrough	A	4-0	Henry Silva Wiltord 2	29,450
3.	Aston Villa	H	2-0	Campbell Henry	38,010
4.	Manchester City	A	2-1	Wiltord Ljungberg	46,436
5.	Portsmouth	H	1-1	Henry (pen)	38,052
6.	Manchester Utd	A	0-0		67,639
7.	Newcastle United	H	3-2	Henry 2 (1 pen) Silva	38,112
8.	Liverpool	A	2-1	Hyypia (og) Pires	44,374
9.	Chelsea	H	2-1	Edu Henry	38,172
10.	Charlton Ath	A	1-1	Henry	26,639
11.	Leeds United	A	4-1	Henry 2 Pires Silva	36,491
12.	Tottenham H	H	2-1	Pires Ljungberg	38,101
13.	Birmingham City	A	3-0	Ljungberg Bergkamp Pires	29,588
14.	Fulham	H	0-0		38,063
15.	Leicester City	A	1-1	Silva	32,108
16.	Blackburn Rovers	H	1-0	Bergkamp	37,677
17.	Bolton Wands	A	1-1	Pires	27,492
18.	Wolves	H	3-0	Craddock (og) Henry 2	38,003
19.	Southampton	A	1-0	Pires	32,151
20.	Everton	A	1-1	Kanu	38,726
21.	Middlesbrough	H	4-1	Henry (pen) Queudrue (og) Pires Ljungberg	38,117
22.	Aston Villa	A	2-0	Henry 2 (1 pen)	39,380
23.	Manchester City	H	2-1	Tarnat (og) Henry	38,103
24.	Wolves	A	3-1	Bergkamp Henry Toure	29,392
25.	Southampton	H	2-0	Henry 2	38,007
26.	Chelsea	A	2-1	Vieira Edu	41,926
27.	Charlton Ath	H	2-1	Pires Henry	38,137
28.	Blackburn Rovers	A	2-0	Henry Pires	28,627
29.	Bolton Wands	H	2-1	Pires Bergkamp	38,053

30.	Manchester Utd	H	1-1	Henry	38,184
31.	Liverpool	H	4-2	Henry 3 Pires	38,119
32.	Newcastle United	A	0-0		52,141
33.	Leeds United	H	5-0	Pires Henry 4 (1 pen)	38,094
34.	Tottenham H	A	2-2	Vieira Pires	36,097
35.	Birmingham City	H	0-0		38,061
36.	Portsmouth	A	1-1	Reyes	20,140
37.	Fulham	A	1-0	Reyes	18,102
38.	Leicester City	H	2-1	Henry (pen) Vieira	38,419

Final League Position = 1st in the Premiership

♛ FA Cup ♛

3	Leeds United	A	4-1	Henry Edu Pires Toure	31,207
4	Middlesbrough	H	4-1	Bergkamp Ljungberg 2 Bentley	37,256
5	Chelsea	H	2-1	Reyes 2	38,136
6	Portsmouth	A	5-1	Henry 2 Ljungberg 2 Toure	20,137
SF	Manchester Utd	N*	0-1		39,939

* played at Villa Park, Birmingham

League Cup

3	Rotherham Utd	H	1-1**	Aliadiere	27,451
4	Wolves	H	5-1	Aliadiere 2 Kanu Wiltord Fabregas	28,161
5	West Brom Alb	A	2-0	Kanu Aliadiere	20,369
SF	Middlesbrough	H	0-1		31,070
SF	Middlesbrough	A	1-2	Edu	28,781

* won 9-8 on penalties

2004–05

1.	Everton	A	4-1	Bergkamp Reyes Ljungberg Pires	35,521
2.	Middlesbrough	H	5-3	Henry 2 Bergkamp Pires Reyes	37,415
3.	Blackburn Rovers	H	3-0	Henry Fabregas Reyes	37,496
4.	Norwich City	A	4-1	Reyes Henry Pires Bergkamp	23,944
5.	Fulham	A	3-0	Ljungberg Knight (og) Reyes	21,681
6.	Bolton Wands	H	2-2	Henry Pires	37,010
7.	Manchester City	A	1-0	Cole	47,015
8.	Charlton Ath	H	4-0	Ljungberg Henry 2 Reyes	38,103
9.	Aston Villa	H	3-1	Pires 2 (1 pen) Henry	38,137
10.	Manchester Utd	A	0-2		67,862
11.	Southampton	H	2-2	Henry Van Persie	38,141
12.	Crystal Palace	A	1-1	Henry	26,193
13.	Tottenham H	A	5-4	Henry Lauren (pen) Vieira Ljungberg Pires	36,095
14.	West Brom Alb	H	1-1	Pires	38,109
15.	Liverpool	A	1-2	Vieira	43,730
16.	Birmingham City	H	3-0	Pires Henry 2	38,064
17.	Chelsea	H	2-2	Henry 2	38,153
18.	Portsmouth	A	1-0	Campbell	20,170
19.	Fulham	H	2-0	Henry Pires	38,047

20.	Newcastle United	A	1-0	Vieira	52,320
21.	Charlton Ath	A	3-1	Ljungberg 2 Van Persie	26,711
22.	Manchester City	H	1-1	Ljungberg	38,066
23.	Bolton Wands	A	0-1		27,514
24.	Newcastle United	H	1-0	Bergkamp	38,137
25.	Manchester Utd	H	2-4	Vieira Bergkamp	38,164
26.	Aston Villa	A	3-1	Ljungberg Henry Cole	42,593
27.	Crystal Palace	H	5-1	Bergkamp Reyes Henry 2 Vieira	38,056
28.	Southampton	A	1-1	Ljungberg	31,815
29.	Portsmouth	H	3-0	Henry 3	38,079
30.	Blackburn Rovers	A	1-0	Van Persie	22,992
31.	Norwich City	H	4-1	Henry 3 Ljungberg	38,066
32.	Middlesbrough	A	1-0	Pires	33,874
33.	Chelsea	A	0-0		41,621
34.	Tottenham H	H	1-0	Reyes	38,147
35.	West Brom Alb	A	2-0	Van Persie Edu	27,351
36.	Liverpool	H	3-1	Pires Reyes Fabregas	38,119
37.	Everton	H	7-0	Van Persie Pires 2 Vieira Edu (pen) Bergkamp Flamini	38,073
38.	Birmingham City	A	1-2	Bergkamp	29,302

Final League Position = 2nd in the Premiership

♛ FA Cup ♛

3	Stoke City	H	2-1	Reyes Van Persie	36,579
4	Wolves	H	2-0	Vieira (pen) Ljungberg	37,153
5	Sheffield United	H	1-1	Pires	36,891
R	Sheffield United	A	0-0*		27,595
6	Bolton Wands	A	1-0	Ljungberg	23,523
SF	Blackburn Rovers	N**	3-0	Pires Van Persie 2	52,077
F	Manchester Utd	N**	0-0***		71,896

* won 4-2 on penalties   ** played at the Millennium Stadium, Cardiff   *** won 5-4 on penalties

League Cup

3	Manchester City	A	2-1	Van Persie Karbassiyoon	21,708
4	Everton	H	3-1	Owusu-Abeyie Lupoli 2	27,791
5	Manchester Utd	A	0-1		67,103

2005-06

1.	Newcastle United	H	2-0	Henry (pen) Van Persie	38,072
2.	Chelsea	A	0-1		42,136
3.	Fulham	H	4-1	Cygan 2 Henry 2	37,867
4.	Middlesbrough	A	1-2	Reyes	28,075
5.	Everton	H	2-0	Campbell 2	38,121
6.	West Ham United	A	0-0		34,742
7.	Birmingham City	H	1-0	Clemence (og)	37,891
8.	West Brom Alb	A	1-2	Senderos	26,604
9.	Manchester City	H	1-0	Pires (pen)	38,189
10.	Tottenham H	A	1-1	Pires	36,154
11.	Sunderland	H	3-1	Van Persie Henry 2	38,210

12.	Wigan Athletic	A	3-2	Van Persie Henry 2	25,004
13.	Blackburn Rovers	H	3-0	Fabregas Henry Van Persie	38,192
14.	Bolton Wands	A	0-2		26,792
15.	Newcastle United	A	0-1		52,297
16.	Chelsea	H	0-2		38,347
17.	Charlton Ath	A	1-0	Reyes	27,111
18.	Portsmouth	H	4-0	Bergkamp Reyes Henry 2 (1 pen)	38,223
19.	Aston Villa	A	0-0		37,114
20.	Manchester Utd	H	0-0		38,313
21.	Middlesbrough	H	7-0	Henry 3 Senderos Pires Silva Hleb	38,186
22.	Everton	A	0-1		36,920
23.	West Ham United	H	2-3	Henry Pires	38,216
24.	Birmingham City	A	2-0	Adebayor Henry	27,075
25.	Bolton Wands	H	1-1	Silva	38,193
26.	Liverpool	A	0-1		44,065
27.	Blackburn Rovers	A	0-1		22,504
28.	Fulham	A	4-0	Henry 2 Adebayor Fabregas	22,397
29.	Liverpool	H	2-1	Henry 2	38,221
30.	Charlton Ath	H	3-0	Pires Adebayor Hleb	38,223
31.	Aston Villa	H	5-0	Adebayor Henry 2 Van Persie Diaby	38,183
32.	Manchester Utd	A	0-2		70,908
33.	Portsmouth	A	1-1	Henry	20,230
34.	West Brom Alb	H	3-1	Hleb Pires Ljungberg	38,167
35.	Tottenham H	H	1-1	Henry	38,326
36.	Sunderland	A	3-0	Collins D (og) Fabregas Henry	44,003
37.	Manchester City	A	3-1	Ljungberg Reyes 2	41,875
38.	Wigan Athletic	H	4-2	Pires Henry 3 (1 pen)	38,389

Final League Position = 4th in the Premiership

☬ FA Cup ☬

3	Cardiff City	H	2-1	Pires 2	36,552
4	Bolton Wands	A	0-1		13,326

League Cup

3	Sunderland	A	3-0	Eboue Van Persie 2 (1 pen)	47,366
4	Reading	H	3-0	Reyes Van Persie Lupoli	36,167
5	Doncaster Rovs	A	2-2*	Owusu-Abeyie Silva	10,006
SF	Wigan Athletic	A	0-1		12,181
SF	Wigan Athletic	H	2-1	Henry Van Persie	34,692

* won 3-1 on penalties

2006–07

1	Aston Villa	H	1-1	Silva	60,023
2	Manchester City	A	0-1		40,699
3	Middlesbrough	H	1-1	Henry	60,007
4	Manchester United	A	1-0	Adebayor	75,595
5	Sheffield United	H	3-0	Gallas Jagielka og Henry	59,912
6	Charlton Athletic	A	2-1	Van Persie 2	26,770

7	Watford	H	3-0	Stewart og Henry Adebayor	60,018
8	Reading	A	4-0	Henry 2 Hleb Van Persie	24,004
9	Everton	H	1-1	Van Persie	60,047
10	West Ham United	A	0-1		34,969
11	Liverpool	H	3-0	Flamini Toure Gallas	60,110
12	Newcastle United	H	1-1	Henry	60,058
13	Bolton Wanderers	A	1-3	Silva	24,409
14	Fulham	H	3-0	Silva 2 Adebayor	24,510
15	Tottenham Hotspur	H	1-1	Flamini	60,115
16	Chelsea	A	1-1	Flamini	41,917
17	Wigan Athletic	A	1-0	Adebayor	15,311
18	Portsmouth	H	2-2	Adebayor Silva	60,037
19	Blackburn Rovers	H	6-2	Van Persie 2 Silva Hleb Adebayor Flamini	59,913
20	Watford	A	2-1	Silva van Persie	19,750
21	Sheffield United	A	0-1		32,086
22	Charlton Athletic	H	4-0	Van Persie 2 Henry Hoyte	60,057
23	Blackburn Rovers	A	2-0	Toure Henry	21,852
24	Manchester United	H	2-1	Van Persie Henry	60,128
25	Middlesbrough	A	1-1	Henry	31,112
26	Wigan Athletic	H	2-1	Hall og Rosicky	60,049
27	Reading	H	2-1	Silva Baptista	60,132
28	Everton	A	0-1		37,162
29	Liverpool	A	1-4	Gallas	43,958

♛ FA Cup ♛

3	Liverpool	A	3-1	Rosicky 2 Henry	43,619
4	Bolton Wanderers	H	1-1	Toure	59,778
R	Bolton Wanderers	A	3-1	Adebayor 2 Ljungberg	21,088
5	Blackburn Rovers	H	0-0		56,761
R	Blackburn Rovers	A	0-1		18,882

League Cup

3	West Bromwich Albion	A	2-0	Aliadiere 2 (1 pen)	21,566
4	Everton	A	1-0	Adebayor	31,045
5	Liverpool	A	6-3	Baptista 4 Aliadiere Song Billong	42,614
SF 1	Tottenham Hotspur	A	2-2	Baptista 2	35,485
SF 2	Tottenham Hotspur	H	3-1aet	Adebayor Aliadiere himbonda og	55,872
Final	Chelsea	Neutral	1-2	Walcott	70,073

ARSENAL IN EUROPE

1963–64 INTER CITIES FAIRS CUP
Round 1 (1st Leg)
v Staevnet (Denmark) ,Away, 7-1
Scorers: Strong 3, Baker 3, MacLeod
McKechnie; Magill; McCullough; Brown;
Ure; Groves; MacLeod; Strong; Baker;
Eastham; Armstrong

Round 1 (2nd Leg)
v Staevnet (Denmark), Home, 2-3,
(Aggregate 9-4)
Scorers: Skirton, Barnwell,
McKechnie; Magill; McCullough; Brown;
Ure; Groves; Skirton; Strong; Court;
Barnwell; Armstrong

Round 2 (1st Leg)
v Standard Liege (Belgium), Home, 1-1
Scorers: Anderson
R Wilson; Magill; McCullough; Brown;
Ure; Barnwell; MacLeod; Strong; Baker;
Eastham; Anderson

Round 2 (2nd Leg)
v Standard Liege, Away, 1-3,
(Aggregate 2-4)
Scorers: McCullough
Furnell; Magill; McCullough; Barnwell;
Ure; Snedden; MacLeod; Strong; Court;
Eastham; Armstrong

1969–70 INTER CITIES FAIRS CUP
Round 1 (1st Leg)
v Glentoran (Northern Ireland), Home, 3-0
Scorers: Graham 2, Gould
Wilson; Storey; McNab (Nelson);
McLintock; Simpson; Graham; Robertson;
Court (Kelly); Gould; Sammels; Armstrong

Round 1 (2nd Leg)
v Glentoran (Northern Ireland), Away,
0-1, (Aggregate 3-1)
Webster; Rice; McNab; Court; Neill;
Simpson; Robertson; Sammels; Radford
(Kennedy); Gould; George

Round 2 (1st Leg)
v Sporting Lisbon (Portugal),
Away, 0-0
Barnett; Storey; McNab; Court; Neill;
Simpson; Robertson; Sammels; Radford;
Graham; Armstrong

Round 2 (2nd Leg)
v Sporting Lisbon (Portugal), Home, 3-0,
(Aggregate 3-0)
Scorers: Graham 2, Radford
Barnett; Storey; McNab; Court; Neill;
Simpson; Robertson; Sammels; Radford;
Graham; Armstrong

Round 3 (1st Leg)
v Rouen (France), Away, 0-0

Wilson; Storey; McNab; Court; Neill;
Simpson; Robertson; Sammels; Radford;
Graham (Kelly); Armstrong

Round 3 (2nd Leg)
v Rouen (France), Home, 1-0,
(Aggregate 1-0)
Scorers: Sammels
Wilson; Storey; Nelson; Court (Graham);
Neill; Simpson; Marinello; Sammels;
Radford; George; Armstrong

Round 4 (1st Leg)
v Dinamo Bacau (Romania), Away, 2-0
Scorers: Sammels, Radford
Wilson; Storey; McNab; Kelly; McLintock;
Simpson; Marinello; Sammels; Radford;
George; Graham

Round 4 (2nd Leg)
v Dinamo Bacau (Romania), Home, 7-1,
(Aggregate 9-1)
Scorers: Radford 2, George 2, Sammels 2,
Graham
Wilson; Storey; McNab; Kelly; McLintock;
Simpson; Marinello; Sammels; Radford;
George; Graham (Armstrong)

Semi-Final (1st Leg)
v Ajax Amsterdam (Holland), Home, 3-0
Scorers: George 2, Sammels
Wilson; Storey; McNab; Kelly; McLintock;
Simpson; Marinello (Armstrong);
Sammels; Radford;
George; Graham

Semi-Final (2nd Leg)
v Ajax Amsterdam (Holland),
Away, 0-1, (Aggregate 3-1)
Wilson; Storey; McNab; Kelly; McLintock;
Simpson; Armstrong; Sammels; Radford;
George; Graham

Final (1st Leg)
v Anderlecht (Belgium), Away, 1-3
Scorers: Kennedy
Wilson; Storey; McNab; Kelly; McLintock;
Simpson; Armstrong; Sammels; Radford;
George (Kennedy); Graham

Final (2nd Leg)
v Anderlecht (Belgium), Home, 3-0,
(Aggregate 4-3)
Scorers: Kelly, Radford, Sammels
Wilson; Storey; McNab; Kelly; McLintock;
Simpson; Armstrong; Sammels; Radford;
George; Graham

1970–71 INTER CITIES FAIRS CUP
Round 1 (1st Leg)
v Lazio (Italy), Away, 2-2
Scorers: Radford 2
Wilson; Rice; McNab; Kelly; McLintock;
Roberts; Armstrong; Storey; Radford;
Kennedy; Graham

Round 1 (2nd Leg)
v Lazio (Italy), Home, 2-0, (Aggregate 4-2)
Scorers: Radford, Armstrong
Wilson; Rice; McNab; Kelly; McLintock;
Roberts; Armstrong; Storey; Radford;
Kennedy; Graham; (Nelson)

Round 2 (1st Leg)
v Sturm Graz (Austria), Away, 0-1
Wilson; Rice; McNab; Kelly; McLintock;
Roberts; Armstrong; Storey; Radford;
Kennedy; Graham

Round 2 (2nd Leg)
v Sturm Graz (Austria), Home, 2-0,
(Aggregate 2-1)
Scorers: Kennedy, Storey (pen)
Wilson; Rice; McNab; Kelly; McLintock;
Roberts; Armstrong; Storey; Radford;
Kennedy; Graham

Round 3 (1st Leg)
v SK Beveren-Waas (Belgium), Home, 4-0
Scorers: Kennedy 2, Sammels, Graham
Wilson; Rice; McNab; Sammels;
McLintock; Simpson; Armstrong; Storey;
Radford; Kennedy; Graham

Round 3 (2nd Leg)
v SK Beveren-Waas (Belgium), Away,
0-0, (Aggregate 4-0)
Wilson; Rice; McNab; Storey; Roberts;
Simpson; Armstrong (Marinello);

Sammels; Radford (George); Kennedy; Graham

Round 4 (1st Leg)
v FC Koln (West Germany), Home, 2-1
Scorers: McLintock, Storey
Wilson; Rice; McNab; Storey; McLintock; Simpson; Armstrong; Sammels (Graham); Radford; Kennedy; George

Round 4 (2nd Leg)
v FC Koln (West Germany), Away, 0-1, (Aggregate 2-2 lost on away goals rule)
Wilson; Rice; McNab; Storey; McLintock; Simpson; Armstrong; Graham; Radford; Kennedy; George

1971–72 EUROPEAN CUP
Round 1 (1st Leg)
v Stromgodset Drammen (Norway), Away, 3-1
Scorers: Simpson, Marinello, Kelly
Wilson; Rice; Simpson; McLintock; McNab; Roberts; Kelly; Marinello; (Pavis); Graham; Radford; Kennedy

Round 1 (2nd Leg)
v Stromgodset Drammen (Norway), Home, 4-0, (Aggregate 7-1)
Scorers: Radford 2, Kennedy, Armstrong
Wilson; Rice; Nelson; Kelly; Simpson; Roberts; Armstrong; George; Radford; Kennedy; Graham

Round 2 (1st Leg)
v Grasshoppers (Switzerland), Away, 2-0
Scorers: Kennedy, Graham
Wilson; Rice; Nelson; McLintock; Roberts; George; Armstrong; Kelly; Radford; Kennedy; Graham

Round 2 (2nd Leg)
v Grasshoppers (Switzerland), Home, 3-0, (Aggregate 5-0)
Scorers: Kennedy, George, Radford
Wilson; Rice; Nelson; Storey; Roberts (Simpson); McLintock (McNab); Armstrong; George; Radford; Kennedy; Graham

Round 3 (1st Leg)
v Ajax Amsterdam (Holland), Away, 1-2
Scorers: Kennedy
Wilson; Rice; Nelson; Storey; McLintock; Simpson; Armstrong; George; Radford; Kennedy; Graham

Round 3 (2nd Leg)
v Ajax Amsterdam (Holland), Home, 0-1, (Aggregate 1-3)
Wilson; Rice; Nelson (Roberts); Storey; McLintock; Simpson; Armstrong; George; Marinello; Kennedy;Graham

1978–79 UEFA CUP
Round 1 (1st Leg)
v Lokomotiv Leipzig (East Germany), Home, 3-0
Scorers: Stapleton 2, Sunderland
Jennings; Rice; Nelson; Price; Walford; Young; Brady (Gatting); Sunderland; Stapleton; Harvey (Heeley);Rix

Round 1 (2nd Leg)
v Lokomotiv Leipzig (East Germany), Away, 4-1, (Aggregate 7-1)
Scorers: Stapleton 2, Brady, Sunderland
Jennings; Rice; Nelson; Price (Vaessen); O'Leary; Young (Walford); Brady; Sunderland; Stapleton; Devine; Rix

Round 2 (1st Leg)
v Hajduk Split (Yugoslavia), Away, 1-2
Scorers: Brady
Jennings; Rice; Nelson; Price; O'Leary; Young; Brady; Heeley; Stapleton; Kosmina; Rix

Round 2 (2nd Leg)
v Hajduk Split (Yugoslavia), Home, 1-0, (Aggregate 2-2 won on away goals rule)
Scorers: Young
Jennings; Rice; Nelson; Price; O'Leary; Young; Brady; Gatting; Stapleton; Heeley (Kosmina/Vaessen); Rix

Round 3 (1st Leg)
v Red Star Belgrade (Yugoslavia), Away, 0-1
Jennings; Rice; Nelson; Price; O'Leary;

Young; Heeley; Walford; Stapleton;
Sunderland; Rix

Round 3 (2nd Leg)
v Red Star Belgrade (Yugoslavia), Home,
1-1, (Aggregate 1-2)
Scorers: Sunderland
Jennings; Rice; Nelson; Price; O'Leary;
Young; Heeley (Kosmina); Sunderland;
Stapleton; Gatting; Rix (Macdonald)

1979–80 EUROPEAN CUP
WINNERS' CUP
Round 1 (1st Leg)
v Fenerbahce (Turkey), Home, 2-0
Scorers: Sunderland, Young
Jennings; Rice; Nelson; Talbot; O'Leary;
Young; Brady; Sunderland; Stapleton;
Hollins; Rix

Round 1 (2nd Leg)
v Fenerbahce (Turkey), Away, 0-0,
(Aggregate 2-0)
Jennings; Rice; Nelson; Talbot; O'Leary;
Young; Brady; Sunderland; Stapleton;
Hollins; Rix

Round 2 (1st Leg)
v Magdeburg (East Germany), Home, 2-1
Scorers: Young, Sunderland
Jennings; Rice; Nelson; Talbot; O'Leary;
Young; Brady; Sunderland; Stapleton;
Hollins; Rix

Round 2 (2nd Leg)
v Magdeburg (East Germany), Away, 2-2,
(Aggregate 4-3)
Scorers: Price, Brady
Jennings; Devine; Nelson (Walford);
Talbot; O'Leary; Young; Brady; Gatting;
Stapleton; Hollins (Price); Rix

Round 3 (1st Leg)
v IFK Gothenburg (Sweden), Home, 5-1
Scorers: Sunderland 2, Price,
Brady, Young
Jennings; Devine; Nelson; Talbot; O'Leary;
Young; Brady (Hollins); Sunderland
(McDermott); Stapleton; Price; Rix

Round 3 (2nd Leg)
v IFK Gothenburg (Sweden), Away, 0-0,
(Aggregate 5-1)
Jennings; Devine; Nelson; Talbot;
O'Leary; Young; Brady; Vaessen;
Stapleton; Price; Rix

Semi-Final (1st Leg)
v Juventus (Italy), Home, 1-1
Scorers: Bettega og
Jennings; Devine (Vaessen); Walford;
Talbot; O'Leary (Rice); Young; Brady;
Sunderland; Stapleton; Price; Rix

Semi-Final (2nd Leg)
v Juventus (Italy), Away, 1-0,
(Aggregate 2-1)
Scorers: Vaessen
Jennings; Rice; Devine; Talbot (Hollins);
O'Leary; Young; Brady; Sunderland;
Stapleton; Price (Vaessen); Rix

Final
v Valencia (Spain) at Brussels, 0-0,
(Aggregate 4-5 on penalties)
Jennings; Rice; Nelson; Talbot; O'Leary;
Young; Brady; Sunderland; Stapleton;
Price (Hollins); Rix

1981–82 UEFA CUP
Round 1 (1st Leg)
v Panathinaikos (Greece), Away, 2-0
Scorers: McDermott, Meade
Jennings; Hollins; Sansom; Talbot;
O'Leary; Young; Davis; Vaessen (Meade);
McDermott; Nicholas; Rix

Round 1 (2nd Leg)
v Panathinaikos (Greece), Home,
1-0, (Aggregate 3-0)
Scorers: Talbot
Jennings; Devine; Sansom; Talbot; O'Leary
(Whyte); Young; Hollins; Sunderland;
McDermott; Nicholas; Rix

Round 2 (1st Leg)
v Winterslag (Belgium), Away, 0-1
Jennings; Devine; Sansom; Talbot;
O'Leary; Young; Hollins; Sunderland;
Meade (McDermott); Nicholas; Rix

Round 2 (2nd Leg)
v Winterslag (Belgium), Home, 2-1,
(Aggregate 2-2 lost on away goals rule)
Scorers: Hollins, Rix
Jennings; Hollins; Sansom; Talbot;
O'Leary; Whyte; McDermott; Vaessen
(Davis); Meade; Nicholas; Rix

1982–83 UEFA CUP
Round 1 (1st Leg)
v Spartak Moscow (Soviet Union),
Away, 2-3
Scorers: Robson, Chapman
Wood; Hollins; Sansom; Talbot; O'Leary;
Whyte; Davis; Robson; Chapman;
Woodcock; Rix

Round 1 (2nd Leg)
v Spartak Moscow (Soviet Union), Home,
2-5, (Aggregate 4-8)
Scorers: Chapman, Dasaev og
Wood; Hollins (Sunderland); Sansom;
Talbot; O'Leary; Whyte; Davis
(McDermott); Robson; Chapman;
Woodcock; Rix

1991–92 EUROPEAN CUP
Round 1 (1st Leg)
v FK Austria (Austria), Home, 6-1
Scorers: Linighan, Smith 4, Limpar
Seaman; Dixon; Winterburn; Campbell;
Linighan; Adams; Rocastle; Davis; Smith;
Merson; Limpar (Groves)

Round 1 (2nd Leg)
v FK Austria (Austria), Away, 0-1,
(Aggregate 6-2)
Seaman; Dixon; Winterburn; Thomas;
Linighan; Adams; Rocastle; Campbell;
Smith; Merson (Groves); O'Leary

Round 2 (1st Leg)
v Benfica (Portugal), Away, 1-1
Scorers: Campbell
Seaman; Dixon; Winterburn; Davis; Pates;
Adams; Rocastle; Campbell (Groves);
Smith; Merson; Limpar (Thomas)

Round 2 (2nd Leg)
v Benfica (Portugal), Home, 1-3,

(Aggregate 2-4)
Scorers: Pates
Seaman; Dixon; Winterburn; Davis; Pates;
Adams (Bould); Rocastle; Campbell;
Smith; Merson; Limpar (Groves)

1993–94 EUROPEAN CUP
WINNERS' CUP
Round 1 (1st Leg)
v OB Odense (Denmark), Away, 2-1
Scorers: Wright, Merson,
Seaman; McGoldrick; Winterburn; Davis;
Linighan; Keown; Jensen; Wright (Smith);
Campbell; Merson; Selley

Round 1 (2nd Leg)
v OB Odense (Denmark), Home, 1-1
Scorers: Campbell
Seaman; Dixon; Winterburn; Davis;
Keown; Adams; Jensen; Wright (Smith);
Campbell; Merson; McGoldrick

Round 2 (1st Leg)
v Standard Liege (Belgium), Home, 3-0
Scorers: Wright 2, Merson
Seaman; Dixon; Winterburn; Davis; Keown
(Linighan); Adams; Jensen; Wright
(Campbell); Smith; Merson; McGoldrick

Round 2 (2nd Leg)
v Standard Liege (Belgium), Away, 7-0,
(Aggregate 10-0)
Scorers: Smith, Selley, Adams, Campbell
2, Merson, McGoldrick
Seaman; Dixon; Winterburn; Davis; Keown
(Bould); Adams; Jensen; Campbell; Smith
(McGoldrick); Merson; Selley

Quarter-Final (1st Leg)
v Torino (Italy), Away, 0-0
Seaman; Dixon; Winterburn; Davis
(Selley); Bould; Adams; Jensen; Campbell;
Smith; Merson; Hillier

Quarter-Final (2nd Leg)
v Torino (Italy), Home, 1-0, (Aggregate 1-0)
Scorers: Adams
Seaman; Dixon; Winterburn; Davis; Bould;
Adams; Jensen (Keown); Wright; Smith;
Merson; Hillier (Selley)

Semi-Final (1st Leg)
v Paris St Germain (France), Away, 1-1
Scorers: Wright
Seaman; Dixon; Winterburn; Davis
(Keown); Bould; Adams; Jensen; Wright;
Smith, Campbell; Selley

Semi-Final (2nd Leg)
v Paris St Germain (France), Home, 1-0,
(Aggregate 2-1)
Scorers: Campbell
Seaman; Dixon; Winterburn; (Keown);
Davis (Hillier); Bould; Adams; Jensen;
Wright; Smith; Campbell; Selley

Final
v Parma (Italy), in Copenhagen, 1-0
Scorers: Smith
Seaman; Dixon; Winterburn; Davis; Bould;
Adams; Campbell; Morrow; Smith; Merson
(McGoldrick); Selley

1994–95 EUROPEAN SUPER CUP
Final (1st Leg)
v AC Milan (Italy), Home, 0-0
Seaman; Dixon; Winterburn; Schwarz;
Bould; Adams; Jensen (Hillier); Wright;
Hartson; Selley; Campbell (Merson)

Final (2nd Leg)
v AC Milan (Italy), Away, 0-2,
(Aggregate 0-2)
Seaman; Dixon (Keown); Winterburn;
Schwarz; Bould; Adams; Campbell
(Parlour); Wright; Hartson;
Merson; Selley

1994–95 UEFA CUP
Round 1 (1st Leg)
v Omonia Nicosia (Cyprus), Away, 3-1
Scorers: Merson 2, Wright
Seaman; Dixon; Winterburn; Schwarz
(Morrow); Keown; Linighan; Jensen;
Wright; Smith; Merson; Parlour

Round 1 (2nd Leg)
v Omonia Nicosia (Cyprus), Home, 3-0,
(Aggregate 6-1)
Scorers: Wright 2, Schwarz
Seaman; Dixon; Winterburn; Schwarz;

Linighan; Adams; Jensen (Hillier); Wright;
Smith; Merson (Campbell); Parlour

Round 2 (1st Leg)
v Brondby (Denmark), Away, 2-1
Scorers: Wright, Smith
Seaman; Dixon; Winterburn; Schwarz;
Bould; Adams; Jensen; Wright; Smith;
Campbell; Parlour

Round 2 (2nd Leg)
v Brondby (Denmark), Home,
2-2, (Aggregate 4-3)
Scorers: Wright (pen), Selley
Seaman; Dixon (Bould); Winterburn;
Selley; Keown; Adams; Jensen; Wright
(Campbell); Smith; Merson; Parlour

Quarter-Final (1st Leg)
v Auxerre (France), Home, 1-1
Scorers: Wright (pen)
Seaman; Dixon; Winterburn; Schwarz;
Bould; Adams; Jensen; Wright; Kiwomya
(Parlour); Merson; McGoldrick (Hartson)

Quarter-Final (2nd Leg)
**v Auxerre (France), Away, 1-0, (Aggregate
2-1)**
Scorers: Wright
Seaman; Dixon; Winterburn; Schwarz;
Bould; Adams; Keown; Wright; Hartson
(Morrow); Merson; Parlour

Semi-Final (1st Leg)
v Sampdoria (Italy), Home, 3-2
Scorers: Bould 2, Wright
Seaman; Dixon; Winterburn; Schwarz;
Bould; Adams; Hillier; Wright (Kiwomya);
Hartson; Merson (Morrow); Parlour

Semi-Final (2nd Leg)
v Sampdoria (Italy), Away, 2-3,
(Aggregate 5-5), Arsenal won
3-2 on penalties
Scorers: Wright, Schwarz
Seaman; Dixon; Winterburn; Schwarz;
Bould; Adams; Keown; Wright (Kiwomya);
Hartson; Merson; Hillier (McGoldrick)

Final
v Zaragoza (Spain), at Paris, 1-2
Scorers: Hartson
Seaman; Dixon; Winterburn (Morrow);
Schwarz; Linighan; Adams; Keown
(Hillier); Wright; Hartson; Merson; Parlour

1996–97 UEFA CUP
Round 1 (1st Leg)
v Borussia Moenchengladbach
(Germany), Home, 2-3
Scorers: Merson, Wright
Seaman; Dixon; Winterburn; Platt; Keown;
Linighan; Parlour (Bould); Wright; Merson;
Bergkamp (Helder); Hartson

Round 1 (2nd Leg)
v Borussia Moenchengladbach
(Germany), Away, 2-3,
(Aggregate 4-6)
Scorers: Wright, Merson
Seaman; Keown; Winterburn; Linighan
(Parlour); Bould; Adams (Helder); Platt;
Wright; Merson; Hartson; Vieira

1997–98 UEFA CUP
Round 1 (1st Leg)
v PAOK Salonika (Greece),
Away, 0-1
Seaman; Dixon; Winterburn; Vieira; Bould;
Adams; Parlour (Platt); Wright; Petit;
Anelka (Wreh); Overmars (Boa Morte)

Round 1 (2nd Leg)
v PAOK Salonika (Greece), Home, 1-1,
(Aggregate 1-2)
Scorers: Bergkamp
Seaman; Dixon; Winterburn; Vieira; Bould;
Adams; Parlour (Anelka); Wright; Petit;
Bergkamp; Overmars (Platt)

1998–99 UEFA CHAMPIONS LEAGUE
GROUP STAGE
Group E
v Lens (France), Away, 1-1
Scorers: Overmars
Seaman; Dixon; Winterburn; Vieira;
Keown; Adams; Parlour; Anelka; Petit
(Hughes); Bergkamp (Garde); Overmars
v Panathinaikos (Greece), Home, 2-1

Scorers: Adams, Keown
Seaman; Dixon; Winterburn; Vieira;
Keown; Adams; Garde (Vivas); Anelka;
Petit; Bergkamp; Overmars
v Dynamo Kiev (Russia), Home, 1-1
Scorers: Bergkamp
Seaman; Dixon; Winterburn; Garde;
Keown; Adams; Parlour; Anelka (Vivas);
Hughes; Bergkamp; Overmars
v Dynamo Kiev (Russia), Away, 1-3
Scorers: Hughes
Seaman; Dixon; Winterburn; Vieira;
Keown; Bould; Parlour; Vivas (Garde);
Petit (Grimandi); Wreh; Boa Morte
(Hughes)
v Lens (France), Home, 0-1
Seaman; Dixon; Winterburn; Garde
(Vivas); Keown; Adams (Bould); Parlour;
Anelka; Hughes; Wreh (Boa Morte);
Overmars
v Panathinaikos (Greece), Away, 3-1
Scorers: Asanovic og, Anelka, Boa Morte
Seaman; Vivas; Grondin; Grimandi; Bould;
Upson; Vernazza; Mendez (Black); Anelka;
Wreh; Boa Morte

1999–2000 UEFA CHAMPIONS LEAGUE
GROUP STAGE
Group B
v Fiorentina (Italy), Away, 0-0
Manninger; Luzhny; Winterburn; Vieira;
Keown; Adams; Ljungberg; Grimandi;
Suker (Kanu); Bergkamp (Henry);
Overmars
v AIK Stockholm (Sweden), Home, 3-1
Scorers: Ljungberg, Henry, Suker
Manninger; Dixon; Winterburn; Vieira;
Keown; Adams; Ljungberg (Henry);
Grimandi (Silvinho); Suker; Bergkamp;
Overmars (Kanu)
v Barcelona (Spain), Away, 1-1
Scorers: Kanu
Manninger; Dixon; Winterburn; Vieira;
Keown; Adams; Parlour (Henry); Grimandi;
Kanu; Bergkamp (Suker); Overmars
(Ljungberg)
v Barcelona (Spain), Home, 2-4
Scorers: Bergkamp, Overmars
Seaman; Dixon; Winterburn; Vieira;
Keown (Upson); Adams; Parlour;

Ljungberg (Henry); Kanu (Suker);
Bergkamp; Overmars
v Fiorentina (Italy), Home, 0-1
Seaman; Dixon (Suker); Winterburn;
Vieira; Keown; Adams; Parlour
(Ljungberg); Petit (Vivas); Kanu;
Bergkamp; Overmars
**v AIK Stockholm (Sweden),
Away, 3-2**
Scorers: Overmars 2, Suker
Manninger; Dixon; Winterburn; Vieira;
Luzhny (Vivas); Upson; Ljungberg; Petit
(Malz); Suker (Hughes); Kanu; Overmars

**2000–01 UEFA CHAMPIONS LEAGUE
GROUP STAGE
Group B**
**v Sparta Prague (Czechoslovakia),
Away, 1-0**
Scorers: Silvinho
Seaman; Dixon; Silvinho; Vieira; Keown;
Luzhny; Ljungberg (Vivas); Grimandi;
Kanu; Henry (Wiltord); Pires
**v Shakhtjor Donetsk (Ukraine),
Home, 3-2**
Scorers: Wiltord, Keown 2
Seaman; Dixon; Silvinho; Vieira; Keown;
Luzhny; Ljungberg (Bergkamp); Grimandi;
Kanu; Henry; Pires (Wiltord)
v Lazio (Italy), Home, 2-0
Scorers: Ljungberg 2
Seaman; Luzhny; Silvinho; Vieira; Keown;
Adams; Parlour; Kanu; Henry (Wiltord);
Bergkamp (Vivas); Ljungberg
v Lazio (Italy), Away, 1-1
Scorers: Pires
Lukic; Dixon; Vieira; Keown; Luzhny;
Parlour (Pires); Grimandi (Lauren); Kanu;
Henry; Ljungberg (Wiltord)
**v Sparta Prague (Czechoslovakia),
Home, 4-2**
Scorers: Parlour, Lauren, Dixon, Kanu
Seaman; Dixon; Silvinho (Cole); Vieira;
Luzhny; Vivas; Parlour; Lauren; Kanu;
Henry (Wiltord); Pires (Bergkamp)
**v Shakhtjor Donetsk (Ukraine),
Away, 0-3**
Taylor; Dixon; Cole; Vivas; Keown; Upson;
Parlour (Vernazza); Lauren; Kanu; Henry
(Ljungberg); Wiltord

**SECOND STAGE
Group C**
v Spartak Moscow (Russia), Away, 1-4
Scorers: Silvinho
Manninger; Luzhny; Silvinho; Vivas;
Keown; Adams; Parlour; Ljungberg; Kanu
(Wiltord); Henry; Pires (Lauren)
**v Bayern Munich (Germany),
Home, 2-2**
Manninger; Luzhny (Lauren); Cole; Vieira;
Keown; Adams; Ljungberg; Grimandi;
Kanu; Henry; Pires (Wiltord)
v Lyon (France), Away, 1-0
Scorers: Henry
Seaman; Dixon; Cole; Vieira; Grimandi;
Adams; Parlour; Lauren; Kanu (Vivas);
Henry; Pires (Ljungberg)
v Lyon (France), Home, 1-1
Scorers: Bergkamp
Seaman; Dixon; Cole; Vieira; Grimandi;
Luzhny; Parlour; Ljungberg; Henry (Kanu);
Bergkamp (Wiltord); Pires (Lauren)
**v Spartak Moscow (Russia),
Home, 1-0**
Scorers: Henry
Seaman; Dixon; Cole; Vieira; Grimandi;
Adams; Pires (Wiltord); Lauren; Henry
(Vivas); Bergkamp (Kanu); Ljungberg
**v Bayern Munich (Germany),
Away, 0-1**
Seaman; Dixon; Cole; Vieira; Grimandi;
Adams; Pires (Silvinho); Lauren; Kanu
(Wiltord); Henry; Ljungberg (Parlour)

**2001–02 UEFA CHAMPIONS LEAGUE
GROUP STAGE
Group C**
v Mallorca (Spain), Away, 0-1
Seaman; Lauren; Cole; Vieira; Campbell;
Keown; Van Bronckhorst; Ljungberg
(Jeffers); Wiltord (Kanu); Henry; Pires
(Parlour)
v Schalke (Germany), Home, 3-2
Scorers: Ljungberg, Henry 2 (1 pen)
Seaman; Lauren; Van Bronckhorst; Vieira;
Keown; Grimandi; Parlour; Ljungberg;
Wiltord (Bergkamp); Henry (Upson); Pires
(Inamoto)
v Panathinaikos (Greece), Away, 0-1
Seaman; Lauren; Cole; Vieira; Keown;

Upson; Parlour (Van Bronckhorst);
Ljungberg (Kanu); Wiltord (Jeffers); Henry;
Pires
v Panathinaikos (Greece), Home, 2-1
Scorers: Henry 2 (1 pen)
Wright; Lauren; Cole; Vieira; Campbell;
Upson; Van Bronckhorst; Ljungberg;
Wiltord (Bergkamp); Henry (Grimandi);
Pires (Parlour)
v Mallorca (Spain), Home, 3-1
Scorers: Pires, Bergkamp, Henry
Wright; Lauren; Van Bronckhorst; Vieira;
Campbell; Keown; Grimandi (Parlour);
Ljungberg (Kanu); Henry; Bergkamp
(Wiltord); Pires
v Schalke (Germany), Away, 1-3
Scorers: Wiltord
Wright; Luzhny; Cole; Edu; Campbell
(Keown); Upson (Stepanovs); Parlour;
Grimandi; Wiltord; Kanu (Pennant); Pires

SECOND STAGE
Group D
v La Coruna (Spain), Away, 0-2
Wright (Taylor); Lauren; Cole; Vieira;
Campbell; Upson; Van Bronckhorst (Edu);
Ljungberg; Wiltord (Kanu); Henry; Pires
v Juventus (Italy), Home, 3-1
Scorers: Ljungberg 2, Henry
Taylor; Lauren; Cole (Keown); Vieira;
Campbell; Upson; Ljungberg; Parlour;
Kanu (Bergkamp); Henry
(Grimandi); Pires
v Leverkusen (Germany), Away, 1-1
Scorers: Pires
Seaman; Lauren; Van Bronckhorst; Vieira;
Campbell; Stepanovs; Parlour; Wiltord
(Grimandi); Kanu (Edu);
Henry; Pires
v Leverkusen (Germany), Home, 4-1
Scorers: Pires, Henry, Vieira, Bergkamp
Seaman; Dixon; Lauren (Inamoto); Vieira;
Campbell; Stepanovs; Wiltord (Pennant);
Grimandi (Edu); Henry; Bergkamp; Pires
v La Coruna (Spain), Home, 0-2
Seaman; Lauren; Luzhny; Vieira; Campbell;
Stepanovs; Wiltord (Kanu); Grimandi
(Ljungberg); Henry; Bergkamp; Pires
v Juventus (Italy), Away, 0-1
Seaman; Lauren; Luzhny; Vieira; Campbell;

Stepanovs; Wiltord (Kanu); Grimandi
(Ljungberg); Henry; Bergkamp; Pires

2002–03 UEFA CHAMPIONS LEAGUE
GROUP STAGE
Group A
v Borussia Dortmund (Germany),
Home, 2-0
Scorers: Bergkamp, Ljungberg
Seaman; Luzhny (Lauren); Cole; Vieira;
Campbell; Keown; Bergkamp; Silva;
Wiltord (Toure); Henry; Ljungberg (Cygan)
v PSV Eindhoven (Holland), Away, 4-0
Scorers: Silva; Ljungberg; Henry 2
Seaman; Lauren; Cole; Vieira; Campbell;
Keown (Cygan); Wiltord; Silva; Henry;
Bergkamp (Kanu); Ljungberg (Toure)
v Auxerre (France), Away, 1-0
Scorers: Silva
Seaman; Lauren; Cole; Vieira; Campbell;
Cygan; Wiltord (Luzhny); Silva; Kanu;
Henry (Pennant); Toure (Edu)
v Auxerre (France), Home, 1-2
Scorers: Kanu
Seaman; Lauren (Toure); Cole; Vieira;
Campbell; Cygan; Wiltord; Silva (Pires);
Kanu; Henry; Ljungberg
v Borussia Dortmund (Germany),
Away, 1-2
Scorers: Henry
Seaman; Lauren; Cole; Vieira; Campbell;
Cygan; Wiltord (Kanu); Silva (Edu);
Ljungberg; Henry; Pires (Toure)
v PSV Eindhoven (Holland), Home, 0-0
Shaaban; Luzhny; Toure; Vieira (Silva);
Stepanovs; Cygan; Pires; Edu; Henry
(Bergkamp); Jeffers (Wiltord); Van
Bronckhorst

SECOND STAGE
Group B
v Roma (Italy), Away, 3-1
Scorers: Henry 3
Shaaban; Luzhny; Cole; Vieira; Campbell;
Cygan; Ljungberg (Edu); Silva; Wiltord
(Keown); Henry; Pires (Van Bronckhorst)
v Valencia (Spain), Home, 0-0
Seaman; Lauren; Cole; Vieira (Parlour);
Campbell; Cygan; Ljungberg (Wiltord);
Silva; Henry; Bergkamp; Pires (Kanu)

v Ajax (Holland), Home, 1-1
Scorers: Wiltord
Seaman (Taylor); Lauren; Cole; Vieira;
Campbell; Cygan; Wiltord; Silva (Jeffers);
Henry; Bergkamp (Kanu); Pires
v Ajax (Holland), Away, 0-0
Seaman; Lauren; Cole; Vieira; Campbell;
Keown; Wiltord (Parlour); Silva; Henry;
Bergkamp (Jeffers);
Pires (Van Bronckhorst)
v Roma (Italy), Home, 1-1
Scorers: Vieira
Seaman; Lauren (Kanu); Van Bronckhorst;
Vieira; Cygan; Keown; Wiltord (Ljungberg);
Silva; Henry; Bergkamp (Jeffers); Pires
v Valencia (Spain), Away, 1-2
Scorers: Henry
Taylor; Lauren; Toure (Kanu); Vieira;
Campbell; Cygan; Wiltord (Jeffers); Silva;
Henry; Ljungberg; Pires

2003–04 UEFA CHAMPIONS LEAGUE
GROUP STAGE
Group B
v Internazionale (Italy), Home, 0-3
Lehmann; Lauren; Cole; Vieira; Campbell;
Toure; Ljungberg; Silva (Kanu); Wiltord
(Parlour); Henry; Pires (Bergkamp)
v Lokomotiv Moscow (Russia), Away, 0-0
Lehmann; Lauren; Cole; Silva;
Toure; Keown; Parlour; Edu; Wiltord;
Henry; Pires
v Dynamo Kiev (Ukraine), Away, 1-2
Scorers: Henry
Lehmann; Lauren; Cole; Silva; Campbell;
Toure; Parlour (Ljungberg); Edu (Vieira);
Wiltord (Kanu); Henry; Pires
v Dynamo Kiev (Ukraine), Home, 1-0
Scorers: Cole
Lehmann; Lauren; Cole; Silva; Campbell;
Toure; Ljungberg (Wiltord); Parlour (Kanu);
Henry; Bergkamp (Edu); Pires
v Internazionale (Italy), Away, 5-1
Scorers: Henry 2, Ljungberg, Edu, Pires,
Lehmann; Toure; Cole; Edu; Campbell;
Cygan; Ljungberg; Parlour; Kanu (Silva);
Henry (Aliadiere); Pires
v Lokomotiv Moscow (Russia), Home, 2-0
Scorers: Pires, Ljungberg
Lehmann; Toure; Cole; Vieira; Campbell;

Cygan; Ljungberg; Silva; Henry; Bergkamp
(Kanu); Pires

Knock-out Round (1st Leg)
v Celta Vigo (Spain), Away, 3-2
Scorers: Edu 2, Pires
Lehmann; Lauren; Clichy (Cygan); Vieira;
Campbell; Toure; Ljungberg (Bentley); Edu;
Reyes (Kanu); Henry; Pires

Knock-out Round (2nd Leg)
v Celta Vigo (Spain), Home, 2-0
Scorers: Henry 2
Lehmann; Lauren; Cole; Vieira; Campbell;
Toure; Ljungberg; Edu (Silva); Henry;
Bergkamp (Kanu); Pires (Reyes)

Quarter-Final (1st Leg)
v Chelsea (England), Away, 1-1
Scorers: Pires
Lehmann; Lauren; Cole; Vieira; Campbell;
Toure; Ljungberg (Reyes); Edu; Henry;
Bergkamp (Silva); Pires

Quarter-Final (2nd Leg)
v Chelsea (England), Home, 1-2
Scorers: Reyes
Lehmann; Lauren; Cole; Vieira; Campbell;
Toure; Ljungberg; Edu; Reyes; Henry
(Bergkamp); Pires

2004–05 UEFA CHAMPIONS LEAGUE
GROUP STAGE
Group E
v PSV Eindhoven (Holland), Home, 1-0
Scorers: Alex og
Lehmann; Lauren; Cole; Vieira; Toure;
Cygan; Reyes (Edu); Silva; Henry;
Bergkamp; Pires
v Rosenborg (Sweden), Away, 1-1
Scorers: Ljungberg
Lehmann; Lauren; Cole; Vieira; Toure;
Campbell; Ljungberg; Edu; Reyes; Henry;
Pires (Van Persie)
v Panathinaikos (Greece), Away, 2-2
Scorers: Ljungberg, Henry
Lehmann; Lauren; Cole; Edu; Toure;
Campbell; Ljungberg; Fabregas; Reyes;
Henry; Pires
v Panathinaikos (Greece), Home, 1-1

Scorers: Henry (pen)
Lehmann; Lauren; Cole; Vieira; Toure;
Cygan; Ljungberg (Van Persie); Fabregas;
Henry; Bergkamp (Reyes); Pires
v PSV Eindhoven (Holland),
Away, 1-1
Scorers: Henry
Lehmann; Lauren; Cole; Vieira; Toure;
Campbell; Ljungberg; Fabregas; Reyes
(Van Persie) (Flamini); Henry; Pires
(Hoyte)
v Rosenborg (Sweden), Home, 5-1
Scorers: Reyes, Henry, Fabregas, Pires
(pen), Van Persie
Alumnia; Hoyte; Cole (Van Persie); Flamini;
Toure; Campbell; Pires (Owusu-Abeyie);
Fabregas; Henry; Bergkamp (Clichy);
Reyes

Knock-out Round (1st Leg)
v Bayern Munich (Germany),
Away, 1-3
Scorers: Toure
Lehmann; Lauren; Clichy (Cole); Vieira;
Toure; Cygan; Ljungberg (Van Persie); Edu
(Flamini); Reyes; Henry; Pires

Knock-out Round (2nd Leg)
v Bayern Munich (Germany), Home, 1-0
Scorers: Henry
Lehmann; Lauren; Cole; Vieira; Toure;
Senderos; Ljungberg (Van Persie); Flamini
(Fabregas); Henry; Bergkamp; Reyes
(Pires)

2005–06 UEFA CHAMPIONS LEAGUE
GROUP STAGE
Group B
v Thun (Switzerland), Home, 2-1
Scorers: Silva, Bergkamp
Aluminia; Lauren; Cole; Silva; Toure;
Campbell; Ljungberg (Hleb); Fabregas
(Bergkamp); Reyes (Owusu-Abeyie);
Van Persie; Pires
v Ajax (Holland), Away, 2-1
Scorers: Ljungberg; Pires (pen)
Aluminia; Lauren; Cole; Flamini; Toure;
Campbell; Hleb (Cygan); Fabregas; Reyes
(Owusu-Abeyie); Ljungberg; Pires (Clichy)
v Sparta Prague (Czechoslovakia),

Away, 2-0
Scorers: Henry 2
Lehmann; Lauren; Clichy; Silva; Toure;
Cygan; Flamini; Fabregas (Owusu-Abeyie);
Reyes (Henry); Van Persie (Eboue); Pires
v Sparta Prague (Czechoslovakia),
Home, 3-0
Scorers: Henry, Van Persie 2
Aluminia; Lauren; Clichy; Silva; Toure;
Campbell; Reyes (Eboue); Flamini; Henry
(Van Persie); Bergkamp; Pires (Fabregas)
v Thun (Switzerland), Away, 1-0
Scorers: Pires (pen)
Aluminia; Eboue; Cygan (Lauren); Song
Billong (Fabregas); Campbell; Senderos;
Ljungberg; Flamini; Van Persie; Henry
(Pires); Reyes;
v Ajax (Holland), Home, 0-0
Aluminia; Eboue; Lauren (Gilbert); Flamini;
Toure; Senderos; Hleb (Fabregas);
Larsson; Owusu-Abeyie; Henry; Reyes
(Van Persie);

Knock-Out Round (1st Leg)
v Real Madrid (Spain), Away, 1-0
Scorers: Henry
Lehmann; Eboue; Flamini; Silva; Toure;
Senderos; Ljungberg; Fabregas (Song
Billong); Reyes (Diaby); Henry; Hleb
(Pires);

Knock-Out Round (2nd Leg)
v Real Madrid (Spain), Home, 0-0,
(Aggregate 1-0)
Lehmann; Eboue; Flamini; Silva; Toure;
Senderos; Reyes (Pires); Fabregas;
Ljungberg; Henry; Hleb (Bergkamp)

Quarter-Final (1st Leg)
v Juventus (Italy), Home, 2-0
Scorers: Fabregas, Henry
Lehmann; Eboue; Flamini; Silva; Toure;
Senderos; Hleb; Fabregas; Reyes (Van
Persie); Henry; Pires

Quarter-Final (2nd Leg)
v Juventus (Italy), Away, 0-0
Lehmann; Eboue; Flamini; Silva; Toure;
Senderos; Hleb (Diaby); Farbregas; Reyes
(Pires); Henry; Ljungberg

Semi-Final (1st Leg)
v Villareal (Spain), Home, 1-0
Scorers: Toure
Lehmann; Eboue; Flamini; Silva; Toure;
Senderos; Hleb (Bergkamp); Fabregas;
Ljungberg (Van Persie); Henry; Pires

Semi-Final (2nd Leg)
v Villareal (Spain), Away, 0-0
Lehmann; Eboue; Flamini (Clichy); Silva;
Toure; Campbell; Hleb; Fabregas; Reyes
(Pires); Henry; Ljungberg

Final
v Barcelona (Spain), in Paris, 1-2
Scorers: Campbell
Lehmann; Eboue; Cole; Silva; Toure;
Campbell; Hleb (Reyes); Fabregas
(Flamini); Henry; Ljungberg; Pires
(Almunia)

2006-07 UEFA CHAMPIONS LEAGUE
Third Qualifying Round, 1st leg
v Dinamo Zagreb (Away) 3-0
Scorers: Fabregas 2, Van Persie
Almunia; Eboue; Hoyte; Toure; Djourou;
Hleb; Fabregas; Silva; Rosicky (Flamini);
Adebayor (Aliadiere) Van Persie;

Third Qualifying Round, 2nd leg
v Dinamo Zagreb (Home) 2-1
Scorers: Ljungberg; Flamini
Almunia; Eboue; Toure; Djourou; Hoyte;
Hleb (Silva); Fabregas; Flamini; Ljungberg;
Van Persie (Walcott); Adebayor (Henry)

GROUP STAGE
Group G
v Hamburg SV (Away) 2-1
Scorers: Silva (pen); Rosicky
Lehmann; Hleb (Flamini); Silva; Fabregas;
Toure (Hoyte); Djourou; Rosicky;
Adebayor; Eboue; Gallas; Van Persie
(Baptista)
v FC Porto (Home) 2-0
Scorers: Henry; Hleb
Lehmann; Toure; Gallas (Song Billong);
Eboue; Hoyte; Hleb (Walcott); Fabregas;
Rosicky; Silva; Henry; Van Persie
(Ljungberg)

v CSKA Moscow (Away) 0-1
Lehmann; Hoyte; Toure; Djourou (Clichy);
Gallas; Hleb; Silva; Fabregas; Rosicky;
(Walcott); Henry; Van Persie (Adebayor)
v CSKA Moscow (Home) 0-0
Lehmann; Toure; Gallas; Clichy; Hoyte;
Hleb (Walcott); Fabregas (Flamini);
Rosicky; Silva; Henry; Van Persie
(Alaidiere)
v Hamburg SV (Home) 3-1
Scorers: Van Persie; Eboue; Baptista
Lehmann; Toure; Senderos; Clichy; Eboue;
Flamini; Fabregas; Ljungberg (Walcott);
Hleb (Baptista); Van Persie (Adebayor);
Henry
v FC Porto (Away) 0-0
Lehmann; Fabregas; Toure; Ljungberg;
Hleb; Flamini; Silva; Djourou; Clichy;
Adebayor; (Van Persie); Eboue
v PSV Eindhoven (Away) 0-1
Lehmann; Toure; Senderos; Gallas; Clichy;
Fabregas; Rosicky; Hleb (Baptista); Silva;
Henry; Adebayor
v PSV Eindhoven (Home) 1-1
Scorers; Alex og
Lehmann; Toure; Clichy (Walcott); Silva;
Gallas; Hleb; Fabregas; Denilson; Baptista;
(Henry); Adebayor; Ljungberg (Diaby)

STATISTICS

⚽ LEAGUE APPEARANCES ⚽		
/ = substitute appearance		
1	David O'Leary	523/35
2	Tony Adams	500/4
3	George Armstrong	490/10
4	Lee Dixon	439/19
5	Nigel Winterburn	428/8
6	Bob John	421
7	David Seaman	405
8	Pat Rice	391/6
9	Eddie Hapgood	393
10	Peter Storey	387/4
11	John Radford	375/4
12	Peter Simpson	353/17
13	Graham Rix	338/13
14	Paul Davis	331/20
15	Cliff Bastin	350
16	Ray Parlour	282/57
17	Joe Hulme	333
18	Martin Keown	304/28
19=	Jack Kelsey	327
	Percy Sands	327
	Paul Merson	289/38

⚽ FA CUP APPEARANCES ⚽		
1	David O'Leary	66/4
2	Pat Rice	67
3	George Armstrong	58/2
4=	Tony Adams	53/1
	Lee Dixon	52/2
6	Peter Simpson	53
7	Peter Storey	49/2
8=	David Seaman	48
	Patrick Vieira	48
10	Nigel Winterburn	47
11	Bob John	46
12=	John Radford	42/2
	Graham Rix	42/2
14	Ray Parlour	39/4
15	Cliff Bastin	42
16=	Alf Baker	41
	Eddie Hapgood	41
18	Martin Keown	37/3
19=	Joe Hulme	39
	Bob McNab	39

☻ LEAGUE CUP APPEARANCES ☻

1	David O'Leary	68/2
2	Tony Adams	58/1
3	Nigel Winterburn	49/3
4	Paul Davis	46/5
5	Kenny Sansom	48
6	Graham Rix	45/2
7	Lee Dixon	45
8	Paul Merson	38/2
9=	David Seaman	38
	Alan Smith	36/2
11	Peter Storey	36/1
12	Pat Rice	36
13	George Armstrong	35
14=	Frank McLintock	34
	John Radford	34
16=	Steve Bould	33
	David Rocastle	32/1
	Peter Simpson	32/1
19=	Pat Jennings	32
	John Lukic	32

☻ OTHER APPEARANCES ☻

(including European matches)

1	Thierry Henry	76/6
2	David Seaman	73
3	Patrick Vieira	71/1
4	Freddie Ljungberg	62/9
5	Lee Dixon	64/2
6	Robert Pires	56/9
7=	Lauren	50/7
	Ray Parlour	45/12
9	Tony Adams	55
10	Martin Keown	46/8
11	Dennis Bergkamp	42/11
12	Nigel Winterburn	51
13	Ashley Cole	46/3
14	Kolo Toure	36/5

15	Paul Merson	27/2
16	Jens Lehmann	28
17	Pat Rice	26/1
18	George Armstrong	24/2
19	George Graham	23/2
20=	John Radford	24
	Bob Wilson	24
	Steve Bould	18/6

☻ OVERALL APPEARANCES ☻

1	David O'Leary	678/41
2	Tony Adams	666/6
3	Lee Dixon	600/23
4	George Armstrong	607/14
5	Nigel Winterburn	575/15
6	David Seaman	564
7	Pat Rice	520/7
8	Peter Storey	494/7
9	John Radford	475/6
10	Peter Simpson	458/19
11	Bob John	467
12	Ray Parlour	389/76
13	Graham Rix	446/17
14	Martin Keown	408/41
15	Paul Davis	414/31
16	Eddie Hapgood	434
17	Paul Merson	382/45
18	Dennis Bergkamp	344/78
19	Patrick Vieira	396/10
20	Frank McLintock	401/2

☻ LEAGUE GOALSCORERS ☻

1	Thierry Henry	164
2	Cliff Bastin	150
3	Ian Wright	128
4=	Jimmy Brain	125
	Doug Lishman	125
6	Ted Drake	124

7	David Jack	113
8	John Radford	111
9	Joe Hulme	107
10	Reg Lewis	103
11	Jack Lambert	98
12	David Herd	97
13	Joe Baker	93
14	Don Roper	88
15	Dennis Bergkamp	87
16	Alan Smith	86
17	Cliff Holton	83
18	Tim Coleman	79
19	Paul Merson	78
20	Frank Stapleton	75

☺ FA CUP GOALSCORERS ☺

1	Cliff Bastin	26
2	Joe Hulme	17
3	Alan Sunderland	16
4=	John Radford	15
	Frank Stapleton	15
6=	Dennis Bergkamp	14
	Jimmy Brain	14
8	Reg Lewis	13
9=	Ted Drake	12
	Jimmy Henderson	12
	Ian Wright	12
12=	Charlie George	11
	Jack Lambert	11
14=	George Armstrong	10
	David Herd	10
	David Jack	10
	Doug Lishman	10
	Freddie Ljungberg	10
	Malcolm Macdonald	10
	Charlie Nicholas	10
	Robert Pires	10
	Sylvain Wiltord	10

☺ LEAGUE CUP GOALSCORERS ☺

1	Ian Wright	29
2	Alan Smith	16
3	Frank Stapleton	14
4	Alan Sunderland	13
5	John Radford	12
6=	Liam Brady	10
	Paul Merson	10
	Charlie Nicholas	10
9	George Graham	9
10	Dennis Bergkamp	8
11=	Kevin Campbell	6
	Perry Groves	6
	David Rocastle	6
14=	Tony Adams	5
	Martin Hayes	5
	David Jenkins	5
	Malcolm Macdonald	5
	Michael Thomas	5
	Sylvain Wiltord	5
20=	Jeremie Aliadiere	4
	Tommy Baldwin	4
	Paul Davis	4
	Nwankwo Kanu	4
	Ray Kennedy	4
	Frank McLintock	4
	Niall Quinn	4

☺ OTHER GOALSCORERS ☺

(including European matches)

1	Thierry Henry	42
2	Ian Wright	16
3	Freddie Ljungberg	14
4=	Dennis Bergkamp	11
	Robert Pires	11
	John Radford	11
7	Ray Kennedy	8
8=	George Graham	7

	Jon Sammels	7
	Alan Smith	7
	Alan Sunderland	7
12	Paul Merson	6
13=	Kevin Campbell	5
	Charlie George	5
15=	Tony Adams	4
	Liam Brady	4
	Frank Stapleton	4
	Willie Young	4
19=	Joe Baker	3
	Geoff Strong	3
	Sylvain Wiltord	3

⚽ OVERALL GOALSCORERS ⚽

1	Thierry Henry	214
2	Ian Wright	185
3	Cliff Bastin	176

4	John Radford	149
5	Jimmy Brain	139
6	Ted Drake	136
7	Doug Lishman	135
8	Joe Hulme	124
9	David Jack	123
10	Dennis Bergkamp	120
11	Reg Lewis	116
12	Alan Smith	115
13	Jack Lambert	109
14	Frank Stapleton	108
15	David Herd	107
16	Joe Baker	100
17	Paul Merson	98
18	Don Roper	95
19	Alan Sunderland	91
20	Cliff Holton	88